ALL
INDIANS
DO NOT
LIVE IN
TEEPEES

↓

(OR CASINOS)

Catherine C. Robbins

UNIVERSITY OF NEBRASKA PRESS
LINCOLN AND LONDON

☺

Publication of this volume was made
possible in part by the generous support of
the H. Lee and Carol Gendler Charitable Fund.

Library of Congress
Cataloging-in-Publication Data
Robbins, Catherine C.
All Indians do not live in teepees
(or casinos) / Catherine C. Robbins.
p. cm.
Includes bibliographical references
and index.
ISBN 978-0-8032-3973-9
(pbk.: alk. paper)
1. Indians of North America—
Social life and customs. 2. Indians
of North America—Material culture.
I. Title.
E98.S7R64 2011
970.004'97—dc22   2011011320

Designed and set in Chaparral Pro
by Ashley Muehlbauer.

For Carla and Nick—
Remember.

CONTENTS

List of Illustrations	ix
Preface: For the Reader	xi
Introduction: Flying Together	1
1. The Unconquerables	15
2. Thoughts from the Chief	59
3. An Encampment	87
4. The Way We Should	117
5. Where Hatred Was Born	155
6. The Drum	195
7. Buckskin Boxes, Galactic Explosion	235
Disclosures: We Help Each Other	269
Acknowledgments	285
Notes	289
Bibliographic Essay	359
Index	365

ILLUSTRATIONS

Map

People and places in this book   xviii

Figures

The Kumeyaay-Diegueño Nation's flag   7
Jane Dumas   7
Ancient Pecos layout   35
The ancestors come home to Pecos   36
Celebrating Pecos ancestors' homecoming   36
Zonnie Gorman   71
Navajo gang members—a Los Angeles export   72
The Murphy family   101
Gordon Yawakia and Harold Gray   102
Children at the Navajo zoo   135

Growing radishes on the moon   135
John Bennett Herrington   136
Bosque Redondo Memorial   175
Embassy of Tribal Nations   176
Sovereignty in a T-shirt   176
Young women at the Gathering of Nations   213
Veronica Tiller   213
A radio station for Hopi   214
Susan Braine and Harlan McKosato   214
The buckskin box, Santa Fe Indian Market   251
James Luna's *The Chapel of Pablo Tac*   251
Lorenzo Clayton's *Mythistoryquest*
Indigenous: Cosmos   252
Steven Deo's *America's Child*   252
The author at work   275

This book is about contemporary American Indians and how modernity and a restorative vision of the past have generated a new energy among them.

The teepee symbolizes that idea. Zonnie Gorman, a Navajo woman, inadvertently provided most of the title, which reminds us of the diversity in Indian Country. The full title also suggests that a new stereotype has supplanted an old one. Nearly universally, the teepee has been *the* icon representing American Indians and their "primitiveness." But the traditional dwelling of Navajos is the hogan, and the teepee is more common among Plains groups.[1]

The teepee is not an artifact, however—some remnant of the past. It is a superb and efficient technology that is also graceful, even monumental. Because its owner decorated its skin coverings with well-chosen designs, the teepee is also a highly personal dwelling that satisfies an aesthetic yearning. Artist Jaune Quick-to-See Smith tells us that many of her people, the Flathead Salish, still keep a teepee near their homes, and some even sleep in one during a storm. "The ground and the teepee shake, but the stakes are driven into glacial rock, so it holds," she said.[2]

Repatriation is like that teepee. It constitutes a heartfelt desire, a glacial rock that anchors the palpable events and activities—some brutal and others triumphant—that the reader will encounter. The artist Nadia Myre (Anishinaabe) has spent the past decade exploring the ideas of loss, longing, and healing. But however much we might want to reconcile these notions, the longing remains, "a thread that binds us to this world." The strongest longing is "for desire itself to remain."[3]

American Indians have been subjects of much study and preoccupation. European American fiction writers and practitioners of various academic disciplines—especially history, anthropology, and other social sciences—have built careers on Indians. About every decade, trends appear to filter Indian Country through their lenses and to capture the "truth" of Indian life—the civil rights movement, New Age philosophies, diversity goals, and ethnic, cultural, and feminist studies, among others. Indian Country defies such labels, however.

This book began as an unsentimental journey. Journalism was the first driver—three decades of work on many subjects, from arts to government to business. During those years in the Southwest, I ferreted out story ideas, gathered facts, met deadlines, and wrote and filed stories. From that corpus, published pieces about contemporary American Indian life emerged as the platform to which I added more research and interviews.

The book is experiential. My eyes have focused on my subjects and their stories, free of labels and trends. Since these are human and messy stories, readers conventionally need a theme or "arc" to unify them. Some writers describe what has happened among American Indians over the past two decades as a *revival*, but this is a tepid term, given the energy in Indian Country. *Renaissance* is a tempting alternative. But these words and others like them are troublesome. Their Latin roots and the prefix *re-* suggest that the life force has left, been misplaced, or even died—and come back.

Much of what I have seen and heard, however, suggests a *return*, not of something that has disappeared or died but of something that has been there all along and is now stronger and more visible. The return of American Indians to their physical and cultural homes in some way or other has given Native life new energy. This idea applied to Native America is not always acceptable, however. Some smell a cliché, the somewhat romantic notion of Indians as lost, vanishing, or trapped between two worlds (or worse, a sentimental context: click your ruby-red heels three times and repeat, "There's no place like home").

As readers can see, Indians are not lost. They never left, and they are not immigrants or exiles. They have been here for thousands of years, and they have fought for their homelands and their ways of life—forever. Neither are they trapped between two worlds; rather, they live along a continuum, moving with varying degrees of ease. The search for home, however, is an old story. Odysseus was not lost or dead. He was very much alive, he knew exactly where he wanted to go (home), and he was desperate to get there. *The Odyssey*, Homer's story of Odysseus's return, gave Western literature a masterpiece.

Return denotes going back to what was, but Indians are not simply moving backward in time or place. Ojibwe poet and scholar Gerald Vizenor suggests a process called "survivance," a word that combines "survival" and "resistance."[4] In this context, the tribe, nation, and people continue into the future by transforming the past and not simply by remembering its joys or terrors. The return is not a restoration but a *restorative* that gives them the strength for transformation.

This is a personal book. At a talk in Albuquerque, the writer Simon Ortiz (Acoma Pueblo) answered a comment from a white woman in the audience. She apologized for the city government's decision to build a road through an Ancestral Puebloan site, a natural formation covered with petroglyphs, to serve sprawling subdivisions. Ortiz replied, "Instead of apologizing, you should get pissed off. Get angry so that some real change can be acted out."[5]

After years of witnessing the treatment of American Indians, I too was angry. But as I embarked on this project, I had to go beyond indignation for the story I wanted to tell. Over the years, American Indians had enriched me and my family. My children were regulars at Pueblo Indian ceremonials that their East Coast cousins could barely imagine. My grandchildren have heard about Coyote and Raven, two of Native America's more enchanting figures, from marvelously illustrated books. Watching powwow dancers, they have been attentive and full of questions. My five-year-old grandson heard Sherman Alexie (Spokane) speak at a children's book fair. Afterward, when the writer gave him gentle high-fives, the little guy remained awestruck.

The reader should consider this work as journalism—as a group of double-exposure snapshots, showing past and present. Anyone who ventures into Indian Country understands that it is old and vast, even though the number of Native Americans is small—just over four million.[6] Its hundreds of tribes and nations have their own languages, belief systems, and personalities. Of necessity, I have limited my scope to selected areas of history and contemporary life, and readers might find that information is sometimes wanting or insufficient. The notes provide ample sources for further investigation.

Although this book is about Indians, I direct it particularly to non-Indians. Among those who appear in it was a passenger on a train across the Southwest who remarked that Indians today might be living as they did a thousand years ago; she made me wince. Too many Americans know little of Indians beyond casinos, and the history of European Americans and Natives is a blank page or a blur of old movies about the West. Governor Arnold Schwarzenegger and other Californians insisted that casino tribes pay "their fair share" with revenue-sharing agreements—compacts—that would funnel money into the state's coffers.[7] What's fair? How about returning Marin County to the Miwok or San Diego to the Kumeyaay?

I am not an Indian wannabe—neither "going native" nor finding salvation in Indian life.[8] Indians cannot "save" me or anyone else. Even though whites have been trying for five hundred years, the converse is also true. A promotional piece from Lakota Funds, a community development organization, screams "Stop 'saving' Indians!" While I do not expect Indians to save me, I have learned from them that personal, family, and community ties weave the details of daily life into a vessel of caring that dispels or soothes the effects of transience, anomie, and pain.

In the course of my work, many individuals have asked about casinos. I have come to share the sentiment from Alonzo Coby, a Shoshone-Bannock leader, who said, "Gaming is important, but more important is culture and land base; without these we have nothing."[9] In that comment, we learn where Indians came from, where they are, and where they are going. Their destination isn't a casino.

Because of its personal dimension, this book sometimes blurs the conventions of objectivity that constrain journalism. Although the foibles of Indians are evident throughout the narrative, I write in the certain knowledge that, for me at least, the Native people I have met are some of the finest people I have known.

A Note on Usage

Mainly for the sake of rhetorical variety, I alternate terms: "American Indian," "Indian," "Native American," "indigenous people," "Native(s)," and "Native people." In Alaska the term is "Alaska Natives," and the preferred Canadian forms are "First Peoples" and "First Nations." "American Indian" is the designated term in both the *Associated Press* and *New York Times* style manuals. Most people I know refer to themselves simply as "Indians," even though whites invented this word. Many dispense with that term and go directly to their tribal, group, and even clan affiliations—Diné, Tlingit, Ashiwi. Those names reflect the many differences and identities in Indian Country; more important, they resonate with memories of people, places, and stories. Except to discuss it, I avoid the term "Pan-Indian," which suggests some kind of overarching "Indianness." This is primarily a political and academic term, and few Native people I have met use it. Most Indians refer to Americans of other ethnicities, including African American and Mexican or Hispanic, as "whites" or "non-Indians." I generally follow this practice to refer to all non-Native peoples from 1492 to the present. For variety, I also use the terms "European American" and "Anglo," except for discussions of specific ethnic groups. I have chosen "teepees" as the preferred spelling because it seems to be the most common. As for "Indian Country," I mean those Native places that were inhabited by people before Europeans arrived. Thus, "Indian Country" is the United States, although, of course, it is the entire Western Hemisphere.

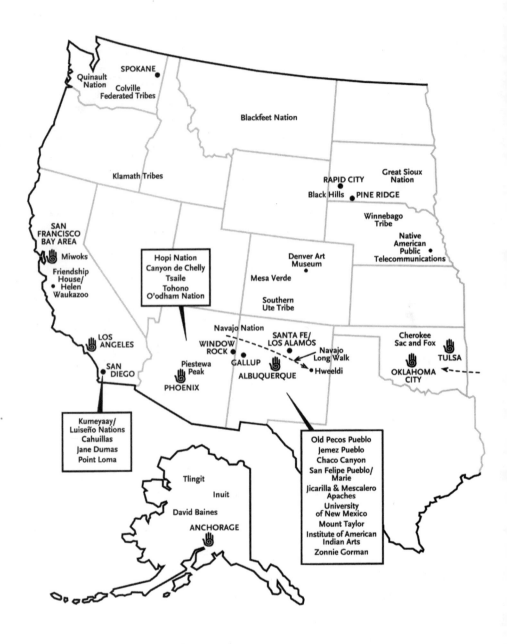

SPOKANE

Quinault
Nation
Colville
Federated Tribes

Blackfeet Nation

Klamath Tribes

RAPID CITY
Black Hills   PINE RIDGE

Great Sioux
Nation

Winnebago
Tribe

SAN
FRANCISCO
BAY AREA
Miwoks

Friendship
House/
Helen
Waukazoo

Hopi Nation
Canyon de Chelly
Tsaile
Tohono
O'odham Nation

Denver Art
Museum

Mesa Verde

Southern
Ute Tribe

Native
American
Public
Telecommunications

LOS
ANGELES

SAN
DIEGO

Piestewa
Peak

PHOENIX

Navajo Nation

WINDOW
ROCK

GALLUP

ALBUQUERQUE

SANTA FE/
LOS ALAMOS

Navajo
Long Walk

Hweeldi

Cherokee
Sac and Fox

TULSA

OKLAHOMA
CITY

Kumeyaay/
Luiseño Nations
Cahuillas
Jane Dumas
Point Loma

Tlingit

Inuit

David Baines

ANCHORAGE

Old Pecos Pueblo
Jemez Pueblo
Chaco Canyon
San Felipe Pueblo/
Marie
Jicarilla & Mescalero
Apaches
University
of New Mexico
Mount Taylor
Institute of American
Indian Arts
Zonnie Gorman

PEOPLE AND PLACES IN THIS BOOK

Mannahatta
Shinnecocks
Lenapes
Mohawk Ironworkers
Heye Center
Museum of Arts & Design
Museum of Modern Art

Peabody Museum, Harvard

Ojibwe Nations

Anishinaabe/ Algonquin Peoples

Haudenosaunee Nation

Mashantucket Pequot Nation

NEW YORK CITY

Eiteljorg Museum

WASHINGTON D C

Cahokia Mounds

National Museum of the American Indian

National Congress of American Indians/ Embassy of Nations

Trail of Tears

VENICE →

 CITIES WITH SIGNIFICANT CONCENTRATIONS OF AMERICAN INDIANS

ALL INDIANS DO NOT LIVE
IN TEEPEES (OR CASINOS)

INTRODUCTION
Flying Together

In 2006 the twelve bands of the Kumeyaay-Diegueño Nation raised a new national flag—their own—at Cabrillo National Monument on San Diego's Point Loma. For the first time, their flag took its place alongside the banners of the nations that had invaded and gained control of their land: Portugal, Spain, Mexico, and the United States. Those had flown regularly for years over historic Point Loma during an annual ceremony marking the European American arrival that had begun five centuries before. Now a Native American nation that has called the area home for millennia hoisted its own standard. The Kumeyaay-Diegueño flag flew firmly in a stiff breeze that day, a signal of the love and sacredness that American Indians attach to an occupied and besieged homeland. It also demonstrated the return of Kumeyaays to a place where historians estimate they had first set foot between eleven thousand and thirty thousand years ago. With energy and dedication plus the inspiration of one of their respected elders, Jane Dumas, they had circled back to a place they had never really left.[1]

This book reveals a similar and broader story unfolding across Indian Country. It begins with the 1999 repatriation of ancestral remains to Jemez/Pecos Pueblo in New Mexico. The return of two thousand bodies was the single largest repatriation to an American Indian group in history under the terms of NAGPRA, the Native American Graves Protection and Repatriation Act.[2] The restoration of remains and cultural artifacts taken from Indian communities during centuries of European American occupation is more than a piece of legislation.

At its most basic, NAGPRA affirms a human right to maintain death rituals. But in its larger meaning, it has become a centripetal cultural force within Native America. Through repatriation, American Indians collect memories ripped out of their communities, bring them into the present, and use them to shape the future. Indians' memories are not stuck in photo albums or digital recordings or on bookshelves. They are alive in still-told stories and the restoration of Native names for people, towns, and geographical landmarks.

As Indians collect ancestors, hope, joy, and savage nightmares into their lives, repatriation has expanded the significance of sovereignty. W. Richard West (Cheyenne), the founding director of the Smithsonian Institution's National Museum of the American Indian (NMAI), asserts that repatriation is the most potent metaphor for cultural revival and political sovereignty.[3] It expresses sovereignty as self-determination, a basic desire to be and to live as one wishes, a longing for a place on the land and in the cosmos.

What happened at Point Loma was a small symbolic flare-up of that yearning, which has never diminished even after centuries of occupation. The reinstatement of Jane Dumas and her people to prominence at Point Loma shows how repatriation drives contemporary American Indian life. The flag she inspired not only affirmed self-determination in the broad sense of the word but also mended a tear in memory's fabric.

João Rodrigues Cabrilho, a Portuguese explorer sailing for Spain, wove the first thread into the modern design of that fabric in 1542, when he became the first European to visit present-day California. After sailing northward along what the Spaniards had already named Baja California, he dropped anchor at the eastern base of sandstone cliffs that curve into the Pacific—a peninsula today known as Point Loma. One account from Cabrilho's voyage called it "an enclosed harbor which is very good," and he claimed it for Spain. Cabrillo—his better-known Spanish name—called it "San Miguel."

The expedition's stay was short. Cabrillo's three ships turned out of the bay after just six days and continued along the California coast, perhaps as far as Monterey. He found much of value on this "savage" continent. At one coastal village, his shipbuilder's eyes noticed finely crafted, ocean-going *tomols* (boats); they were so numerous that he called the place Pueblo de las Canoas, "town of the canoes." In the 1540s an estimated twenty-five thousand Native people were organized into about fifty bands living in what today are Imperial and San Diego Counties across Southern California and the Baja Peninsula of Mexico. Later European visitors described them as skilled agriculturalists who built water systems, conducted controlled woodlands burns, and reaped the harvest that their ecosystem management produced.[4]

Cabrillo's expedition was one of three that set out from New Spain (Mexico) in the early sixteenth century to explore lands to the north. Hernando de Soto sailed from Cuba, landed on the west coast of the Florida peninsula, and during the next three years used the Panhandle as a base to survey the South, from the Carolinas to Texas. Francisco Vásquez de Coronado launched an expedition through southern Arizona, turned into New Mexico, and sent several groups as far as the Texas Panhandle and Kansas. None of these three conquistadores found a passage to the Indies, gold, or fabled cities. All died in the New World, far from home.[5]

The Spanish explorations were extensive. Together they covered the entire southern span of the continent 250 years before the well-known voyage of Meriwether Lewis and William Clark into the northern reaches. The expeditions allowed Spain to claim an expanding empire. Sebastián Vizcaino stopped in Cabrillo's good harbor in 1602 while mapping the Pacific coast and gave San Miguel a new name: San Didacus, familiar today as San Diego. In 1769 Spaniards led by Gaspar de Portolá and the Franciscan Junípero Serra arrived in San Diego. It was the first stop as they began to stake claims along California's coast, ahead of Russian expeditions.

These newcomers stayed and set the disruptive pattern of conquest. The conquerors confiscated Native lands, and the Catholic Church's missionizing tried to deprive Natives of the spiritual succor of their own beliefs. The Europeans' impact on indigenous cultures was especially devastating to their agriculture, which provided not only food but also a natural pharmacopeia. Indians quickly succumbed, Native populations diminished, and their cultures weakened or went underground. Mexico took control of California in 1821 after winning its independence from Spain. The Kumeyaays' lands passed into the hands of the victors, the Americans, in January 1847 during the Mexican-American War. The land grabs and attempts to eliminate the Indians who were in the way of American expansion continued well into the twentieth century.

Today, California sprawl covers Point Loma's fat northern end. A single four-mile, two-lane road leads from residential and commercial areas through Fort Rosecrans Military Reservation.

The U.S. military, San Diego's primary economic engine for most of its history, has been active on Point Loma since 1852. Fort Rosecrans National Cemetery and empty gun emplacements from World War II offer sobering reminders of this role.

Beyond the military installation is the site of the national monument on a spectacular series of cliffs four hundred feet above the sea, where Pacific gray whales migrate. The largest kelp forest on the West Coast thrives just under the water's surface. The military and the Interior Department are restoring the ecological systems. Cold winds and fog frequently sweep across the cliffs. With just the Cabrillo monument, a light station, and walking trails, the peninsula here feels like an island.

Without discussing his action with the Indians, President Woodrow Wilson created the national monument at this remote spot in 1913. But local boosters had been honoring the explorer with a Cabrillo Festival since 1892. Like Los Angeles, San Diego turned its Hispanic heritage into a stimulus for tourism during an economic downturn. Conforming to the national craze for historical pageants at the turn of the century, the festival featured a re-creation of Cabrillo's ship and a reenactment of his landing. Luiseño and Diegueño Indians from nearby missions appeared in the big downtown parade, alongside impersonators of Hernán Cortés, Mexican *rurales*, and American cowboys, and they performed Native dances.

The National Park Service (NPS) participated in the annual Cabrillo Festival after 1935, when the agency assumed responsibility for Point Loma. By then, the festival had evolved into a modest wreath-laying ceremony. The "modern" Cabrillo Festival began in 1964, when the NPS was looking for a way to tie the national monument more closely to community groups, especially Portuguese residents, Cabrillo's "kissing" countrymen who had arrived in the nineteenth century to commandeer the fishing industry. Although the agency planned a nine-day grand celebration, over the years the festival slimmed down. Today San Diego celebrates Cabrillo's visit in a couple of hours. Representatives of the nations associated with the European American presence, usually consular officials from Los Angeles and San Diego, as well as of the federal, state, and city governments participate with speeches. Their national flags are raised together, next to a tall statue of Cabrillo carved by a Portuguese sculptor.

American Indians have been present minimally at these European American celebrations of exploration and conquest.[6] Then at the 2006 festival, on September 29, a fifth flag joined the others. "With the flag it feels like we belong there," explained Jane Dumas, who had inspired the banner and helped to inaugurate it. (Out of affection and deep respect, she is universally known as Aunt Jane.)[7] An eighty-two-year-old Jamulian of the Kumeyaay Nation, she appeared at the ceremony wearing the traditional woven juncus grass hat. (The Kumeyaays commonly carried food and other items in net agave bags that hung from their heads down their backs; the cap cushioned the burden.) A "Native Pride" windbreaker and some shell jewelry, which is as common in Southern California as turquoise and silver in the Southwest, also evoked her Indian origins. Barely five feet tall and using a cane, Aunt Jane joined Miss Kumeyaay Nation and other dancers; they swayed gently to the low voices of bird singers. She braved a brisk wind and stepped to a podium under Cabrillo's statue to recite a Kumeyaay prayer and give a short talk. A part of her life had been missing, but the new flag restored it, Aunt Jane told the crowd: "I feel like I'm a whole person."

Aunt Jane's life, especially her childhood, explains why seeing a piece of cloth fluttering from a pole was so meaningful. Some weeks after the ceremony, over lunch at a favorite restaurant near her neighborhood, she recalled her life and how the flag

Above: The flag of the Kumeyaay-Diegueño Nation flies alongside that of the European American nations. Photo by Zachary Ormsby.

Left: Jane Dumas joins the Bird Dancers for the flag raising. Photo by Zachary Ormsby.

came to be. Aunt Jane is a lineal descendant of Manuel Hatam, the last head of Kumeyaay people inhabiting a large village on the site of San Diego's Balboa Park.[8] While some of her relatives lived on the Jamul Reservation east of San Diego, her parents settled in a nearby Anglo town built on land once the exclusive domain of her people. To make a living, they gathered olives and earned perhaps a dollar a day. They chopped salt out of mines for twenty-five cents a bin the size of the booth table where we sat.

Non-Indians did not like Native people very well and thought of them as savages, Aunt Jane remembered. When she was a child, her white classmates were told, "Don't play with her. She's Indian." Some Natives tried to pass themselves off as Mexicans. Despite this environment, "my parents never told me about the racism or negative energy," she said. People who made racist remarks were simply "in a bad mood." As a young woman, Aunt Jane held many service and menial jobs, such as waitressing.

Most important for Aunt Jane, her mother was a renowned *kuseyaay*—a healer, midwife, and herbalist. In 1981 the knowledge she gained from her mother brought Aunt Jane and her sister to the San Diego Indian Health Center, a private nonprofit provider where she worked for twenty years. Because she was trilingual, she acted as a bridge between conventional and traditional medicine. Aunt Jane would tell Indian people, "The creator gave this person the brains to be a medicine person; you have to trust him." She also taught her people about Western medicines and about taking responsibility for their own health. With some satisfaction, Aunt Jane described how she helped convince Native Americans to have a blood pressure check. Because so many had been diagnosed with hypertension and feared medications, Indian patients frequently avoided screenings. She suggested to the medical staff that they teach young interns how to take blood pressures—and then ask the patients to allow the students to "practice" this new skill on them. The patients were happy to help, and cases of hypertension that might have gone undetected were caught.

Aunt Jane also teaches individuals how to gather herbs and roots with care in order to conserve useful species. Willow is a sacred plant for her because it has been used for clothing, fuel, and shelter and as a medicine as ubiquitous as aspirin.[9] "I try to protect Mother Earth and her garden. We don't own Mother Earth, she owns us, and she can take us any time she wants," she explained.

Eventually, Aunt Jane joined the health center's public outreach to the Cabrillo Festival. She took part in the welcoming ceremony and made fry bread. Kumeyaay bird singers and leaders of some of the tribal groups also came to the event occasionally. Aunt Jane mentioned to another Indian participant that the ceremony had no lasting evidence of the historic and contemporary existence of their people. She also began to arrange sprigs of sage in the four cardinal directions on the ceremony's wreath.

While recovering from cancer that doctors had diagnosed in 2000, Aunt Jane took some time to visit the monument. One evening, she saw a number of hummingbirds. "I'm from the Hummingbird Clan, and I thought, 'These must be people.'" She later discussed her vision with several elders and introduced it to Kumeyaay-Diegueño Unity, an association of the bands' leaders. She proposed that they find a way to "fly up there with them." Somewhere in a series of conversations, someone suggested a flag. Aunt Jane demurred to the notion that she was a Kumeyaay Betsy Ross. "I turned it loose," she said simply.

Louis Guassac, a member of the Mesa Grande band, spent a year working with Kumeyaay elders and leaders who jointly came up with the design—the logos of the twelve Kumeyaay bands on a brown field crisscrossed by the nation's four colors. The Sycuan band paid for its manufacture. Aunt Jane also credited Terry DiMattio, the superintendent of Cabrillo National Monument whom she described as "a very caring person." As the project progressed, he asked her where to place the flag. Her answer was, "We work together. Why can't we fly together?"[10]

For Aunt Jane, the flag is yet another way to promote her culture. One of the last fluent speakers of Kumeyaay, she teaches the language and ethnobotany at Kumeyaay Community College, which the Sycuan band established. Aunt Jane has done presentations for children in schools, and she is a frequent lecturer at California colleges and universities. "We do our best to tell them [non-Kumeyaays] we're still here," she said. Aunt Jane has received honors from San Diego Women's Hall of Fame, the California Daughters of the American Revolution, and the University of California, Berkeley School of Public Health.

Aunt Jane assumes she is cancer-free; "I tire easy, but that's it," she said dismissively. Walking slowly to the restaurant's parking lot (she drives a shiny ivory-colored PT Cruiser, venturing "only a few blocks" from her house, she assured me), Aunt Jane looked out at a sea of cars and a Wal-Mart. She and her mother had collected herbs in the fields that the shopping center has obliterated. Over lunch she had said, "I'm trying to collect history."

The 2006 Cabrillo Festival's flag ceremony was a triumph for the Kumeyaays. It also illustrates the multiplier effect of repatriation beyond the return of remains and artifacts. It provided an opportunity for the bands to collaborate on design, manufacture, and ceremony. But a small drama that played out on the flag raising's periphery told a more complex story. As some Kumeyaays sang and danced in front of the monument's visitors' center, a mixed group of Indians and a few whites watched attentively from one side. However, on the other side, a group of non-Indian officials and VIPs stood in small groups, some with their backs to the dancers, chatting and apparently waiting for the "real" ceremony to begin. Their rudeness disturbed me, but I could not break out of my role as journalist to walk over and ask them for simple courtesy.

DiMattio told me some weeks later that someone else had also noticed and had asked him to quiet the group. By way of explanation, DiMattio said that the dance element was a first for the annual flag raising. The officials did not realize that it was ceremonial and required an etiquette that had not been explained in the program or to them. He said that whites and Indians are still trying "to come to an understanding of how to behave in each other's presence." As Aunt Jane later commented about the incident, "Whites don't accept the fact that we were left out. We were the first nations here. They discovered us but don't recognize us." When DiMattio told me about the details of this incident later, he added that the Kumeyaays, too, had "violated" etiquette. Individuals who were supposed to bless the flag before it was raised arrived an hour late.

Even as repatriation sends a surge of unifying energy through Indian Country, a centrifugal force—physical and cultural *ex*-patriation—spins many Indians away from home. This broader expatriation trails behind repatriation, like the loosely structured cloud of debris following the densely packed material of a comet's nucleus. The twentieth century's Indian migration to cities is a torrent. Parents complain that the attractions of mainstream America—television, video games, computers, fast-food restaurants, convenience stores, schools, music, the mall—draw young people, even those relatively isolated on reservations, away from tribal life. The success some young people experience in the larger society—as entrepreneurs or working in fields as diverse as space exploration, business, law, and medicine—can diminish the power of values like the bond among generations. New configurations of Indian life both in and far from the homelands alter conventional and even Indian images of Indians. At the genetic level, research even raises the question, Who is Indian?

In these circumstances, repatriation reconstitutes missing pieces of time and place. In many American Indian beliefs, time is a process, not a thing to be meted out, sliced into eras, decades, even years. Rather, time is elastic, moving freely among "past," "present," and "future," and it carries people and communities along with it. A popular notion holds that Indians do not think linearly, that is, sequentially and logically. But Indians follow movements of the seasons, attend college classes at particular times, and write monthly rent or mortgage checks. Time carries them forward. Indians also define time in another dimension, through events that are culturally and personally relevant to them—ceremonials, puberty rites, and refreshing their residential and community structures at the appropriate seasons of year.

The term "Indian time" brings smiles to many non-Indians, but many Indians roll their eyes. This can be a pejorative, because it assumes Indians are always late, not reliable. Also, they do not value the idea of clock measure—seconds ticking, hours passing—because they are childlike and might not even wear watches. Mainstream Americans, however, may be the unreliable ones who do not value time as the context for relationships and for the natural world that sustains us. Sherman Alexie's definition of "Indian time" in *The Lone Ranger and Tonto Fistfight in Heaven* is relevant here: "The past, the future, all of it is wrapped up in the now."[11]

Like time, place also is not an abstraction but that which sustains and defines Indians today as it has for thousands of years. For Native Americans, the struggle to reclaim and hold on to their homelands is more than a territorial imperative. Place binds body and soul and cements the universe. Some places are portals to the spirit world of the ancestors and to the Creator. Native American communities often are organized physically around those portals, just as surely as settlements in other cultures are organized around the church or mosque square. Time and place define the individual and the community as well as proximity to the sacred.

White America is more than a backdrop to this story, because we cannot escape from Indians and our history with them. Repatriation compels us to stop and look at the bones, pots, and other cultural patrimony we have snatched from the first peoples of this continent. We can also view repatriation as a receptacle that contains the jumbled history that American Indians and whites have lived together—filled with rancor, love, misplaced good intentions, torture, extermination, theft, religious persecution, and fumbling.

NAGPRA released repatriation's energy. Reclaiming ancestors is not easy and requires money, lobbying, marching, and even litigating. This book is not just about this process, however. Through repatriation American Indians sweep up the times, places, and cultures that the reclaimed ancestors represent and hold them close to the heart. Repatriation impels people to hoist a flag in San Diego; transmit ages-old knowledge to Native American medical students; save the bison across the plains; mount an exhibit of contemporary Indian art; open a clinic in San Francisco's Mission District; and, in an urban Indian center in Albuquerque, provide support for displaced people.

Throughout this book, individuals like Aunt Jane move among their own people and the non-Indian world. They stream their cultures out of the past into today, where they will not be stilled.

If white Americans turn away, we miss the gift of memory and more. Aunt Jane explained, "We're here on earth, we do what we can. I do what I think should be done without thinking. Being Indian was not very easy. Trying to survive was my main goal. Books say, 'Indians used to . . .' What do you mean? We still do it."

1

THE UNCONQUERABLES

"Ted" Kidder had struck pay dirt. Bodies tumbled out of a burial mound at ancient Pecos Pueblo in northeastern New Mexico. So eager was Kidder to find remains of the people who had lived there that he offered a bounty of twenty-five cents to the workmen for each skeleton they found. On the first day, one body appeared; the next day, six. He reduced the reward to ten cents, and fifteen more appeared. Within a week, the dirt ceased to pay (for the workers). Kidder ended the bonus, which threatened to bankrupt his expedition. Pecos turned out to be one of the most important sites in early twentieth-century American archaeology. Dating from around the twelfth century, when Puebloan cultures began to coalesce in New Mexico and Colorado, Pecos did not become dormant until the middle of the nineteenth century. "It was obvious that we were digging in the greatest rubbish heap and cemetery that had ever been found in the Pueblo region," Kidder wrote.[1]

Alfred Vincent Kidder was one of several researchers working in the Southwest during the boom decades for American archaeology. Between 1915 and 1929, Kidder was at Pecos during every field season, except for two years he spent serving in World War I. He and his team unearthed about two thousand bodies and thousands of artifacts. Kidder sent his findings to the Peabody Museum at Phillips Academy in Andover, which had financed the multiyear excavation. The school eventually gave the collection to Harvard's Peabody Museum of Archaeology and Ethnology. In 1999 Harvard returned—repatriated—Kidder's collection to the people of Pecos and their kin at Jemez Pueblo.

The Pueblos had begun their efforts to bring their ancestors home years before Congress enacted and President George H. W. Bush signed the Native American Graves Protection and Repatriation Act (NAGPRA) in 1990. With the legislation American Indians had the tools they needed to retrieve artifacts and remains from museums and other institutions. As the repatriation revealed, Kidder's work in New Mexico had caused pain for the Pecos people that was nearly indescribable, although he had helped define American archaeology in that project. In the long history of the Puebloan people—thousands of years on the continent—a decade was a short span of time. But it was an unimaginably long time to bring two thousand family members home.

In this chapter, repatriation moves out of its legislative cocoon. Starting with a single act of recovery—at Pecos—the story follows a somewhat convoluted line through the development of archaeology and shows repatriation as a logical conclusion, even a cultural vindication that emerged organically and continues. Finally, it avers that repatriation has gone beyond returning remains and artifacts to Indians gaining sovereignty over their stories and their lives.

"Why so many bodies?" Paul Tosa asked seven decades after Kidder had gleefully described his finds.[2] Tosa put the question to no one in particular. A teacher and leader of the Jemez and Pecos people, he ruminated over Kidder's project during a week in May 1999, when his people were preparing to receive and bury their ancestors' remains. Then he answered it quietly and deliberately with a word picture, speaking to anyone who would listen. His alliterative language fell into a cadence so striking that it begged for verse form.

> Dig, find, and find another—
> with no limits.
> It's hard for me to relate in English
> to the person doing the digging,
> the digging part,
> the destruction of the sacred things
> the person went with.
> Indian people are so much with nature
> that to have two thousand removed
> without any, any, any respect whatsoever—
> just keep digging, find some more.
> Is it that people get real greedy?
> That they want more?

Tosa's anguished picture of the archaeologist as grave robber could not be more different from Kidder's delight as skeletons emerged out of Pecos. For the Jemez and Pecos people, Kidder's bone hunt was an abomination. The Pueblos had to draw on the deepest and most sacred of their personal and community resources to recover their ancestors and bring them home; the repatriation united and strengthened them. It was the largest return of Indian remains under NAGPRA. The act requires federal agencies, museums, and other institutions receiving federal funds to return human remains and items to any tribe that formally asks for them and can identify its link to the materials. By 2009 museums and universities had conveyed 38,671 deceased individuals and 1,144,664 objects to tribes.[3]

A few days after Paul Tosa's poetic queries, the quiet power that the repatriation had generated over ten years began to intensify at Jemez Pueblo, a snug village in northern New Mexico. In the chilly predawn hours of a spring morning, one or two vehicles crawled quietly along the narrow dirt lanes of Jemez Pueblo. Soon the sound of shuffling feet whispered along its pathways. As they prepared to welcome their long-lost ancestors, the townspeople were re-creating another journey.

Their forebears had left their homes at Pecos Pueblo in 1838 because it had fallen into economic, cultural, and physical decay and walked westward to refuge at Jemez. Now the Pecos and Jemez walkers headed east on the three-day trek to the old pueblo for a long-delayed family reunion with the ancestors who had been stored on Harvard's shelves for eighty years.[4] The walkers were purposeful. Their mood was serious though lightened a bit by the excited children as they walked toward State Route 4, the main road through the Jemez Valley and their village's eastern edge. At the highway, most of the walkers stopped. About two hundred younger men and women continued across the road and mesas toward the mountains. Food, fresh water, clean clothing, and beds would be waiting for them along the way, and they would spend the next two nights at Cochiti Pueblo and Santa Fe. Across the mountains, more than one thousand family members, kin, and well-wishers waited for the walkers in modern Pecos, a mile from the old pueblo. They, too, would escort the ancestors on the final mile of their journey home. Also waiting was a fifty-three-foot semitruck loaded with the ancestors Kidder had removed. The big white truck that had transported the remains from the Peabody Museum in Cambridge, Massachusetts, was parked at the edge of the meadow. To protect the cargo from potential hijacking, the

National Park Service kept its route secret, and armed federal rangers had accompanied the rig on its three-day trip. Inside the truck the ancestors rested, one body and associated funerary objects per cardboard museum box. A mile away, inside the boundaries of Pecos National Historical Park—the Pecos people's homeland—a communal pit was ready to receive the ancestors.

The crowd was ebullient. They milled about a sun-splattered meadow thick and sweet with grasses and wildflowers, although snow still covered the surrounding Sangre de Cristo peaks. Many Indians wore their jewelry and celebratory dress. The women blazed with color: embroidered dresses, woven belts, and shawls. An elderly man waited in a wheelchair. Mothers pushed baby strollers over the grass. Cyndee, a Pecos descendant and Jemez potter, called it "a happy day and a sad day." She and her brother and sister had walked the entire route from Jemez. Like many Pecos descendants, Cyndee visits the ancient pueblo every year on its feast day, August 1, mainly to honor the ancestors. James, another Pecos descendant, said he had come because "it's important that we acknowledge those people who have been brought home. I'm related to all of them." Joshua Madalena, Jemez's NAGPRA and cultural preservation coordinator, called the day one of "spiritual excitement."

In the middle of this scene, three people embraced. Frail at eighty-seven, Juan Ray Tafoya wept quietly, even though his eyes shone with determination. He was dressed for this occasion in neatly pressed pants and shirt, and he had pulled his gray hair in the traditional *chongo*, or knot, at the back of his neck. His daughter and grandson stood before the old man, quietly pleading with him in their native language. They were trying to convince him to use a van that was shuttling the elderly to the burial site. "He wants to walk the last mile," his grandson explained. "It's spiritual for him." Tafoya finally relented, and his family helped him climb into a van. The Pecos repatriation had reached across three generations, and I wondered how many other families like this one were in the meadow.

The crowd buzzed when the procession's leaders gave the word in Towa that the final mile of the journey was imminent. At the head of the procession, Bennie Shendo, a former governor of Pecos, carried the cane of office given to his people in 1620 by King Philip III of Spain and Portugal's representative to what is today New Mexico. Ruben Sando carried Jemez's cane from Abraham Lincoln, one of several that the president had issued to the pueblos in 1863 to recognize their authority under the U.S. government. Reflecting the strength of their Native religious practices, they prayed briefly in Towa. A young man sprinkled cornmeal over the canes, and others carried small baskets of cornmeal to sprinkle onto the procession route in a blessing. Then the crowd began to move, striding along the two-lane asphalt country road, past green, open meadows. The semi followed with the ancestors. At the monument, the National Park Service barred the press and all other outsiders from going beyond the gate; only Indians, NPS officials, and approved visitors from Harvard and Andover would attend the reburial. Fearing that the mass grave might be looted, officials refused to reveal its location, and the site was camouflaged after interment.[5]

The repatriation ceremony was an overwhelmingly emotional event for Indians as well as those visitors permitted into the burial. Landis Chase, head of Phillips Academy in Andover, apologized to the people. She expressed "sadness and regret for unintentional disrespect given by the expedition that exhumed the ancestors from their ancient burial places." Chase also talked about the repatriation: "It is right, just, and fitting to return with greatest reverence and care the remains of the ancestors and burial and sacred objects into the hands of their descendants." People of all ages wept freely, reported Patricia Capone, the Peabody's associate curator and repatriation coordinator. "The strongest memory of that day is the impromptu receiving line of members of the Jemez community who came forward to connect with the museum people as we stepped up to pay our respects at the grave," she said later. Capone was happy to see Indian young people at the ceremony so that they could connect with their ancestors' grandeur. She added that she felt honored to be present at what she viewed as the historic culmination of NAGPRA's intent. "This is what the law was written for," she said.[6]

The Pecos repatriation touched many—Indian and white—who learned of it. It revealed a people fiercely determined to do right by their ancestors and honor their history. Patience, dogged pursuit of a goal, faith, respect, forgiveness, and graciousness: the Jemez and Pecos people reached deep into their hearts and their community to bring their people home and to include the outside world in their celebration. The process—with the goodwill that it engendered out of personal and community tragedy—continued.

On a personal level, the repatriation shook my professional cool. Covering the event for the *New York Times*'s national desk, I had spent days at Jemez and had joined the procession for the final mile. Thanks to the NPS staff, I was able to file the story from a desk at Pecos National Historical Park's office. My task was to extract some order out of the impressions and interviews I had scrawled into my notebook like so much detritus. The *Times* had published the Boston bureau chief's story from Harvard and had part of my article with the Jemez material that I had already sent. Now with an early deadline forced by the peculiarities of time zones, I quickly had to write the top, paragraphs with the "nut," or main point of the story, and an account of the final day. The article would shift readers' attention away from leafy, green Cambridge to the New Mexico desert, from Harvard to the Pueblo people. Going through the notes, I found the "heart" for the story—Juan Ray. Tafoya and his family. As I dictated the anecdote to a *Times* editor in New York, I stumbled, overcome by the image of the three generations standing in the meadow. "My heart is in my throat," I apologized to the editor. At the other end of the line, she said, "So is mine." That editor's human connection helped me realize that the Pecos repatriation was not about a funeral but about a homecoming that spilled far beyond the Jemez Valley. In retrospect, the Pecos story made me rethink all the stories I had ever written about Indian Country. It gave me this book.

Through the repatriation, time's elasticity had pulled the Pueblos back into their community's history into a decade of negotiations with Harvard and forward into reconciliation. On their pilgrimage, and especially with their reverse walk, the Jemez and Pecos people traversed space and time, a few dozen miles and centuries upon centuries of families, kin, and culture. They returned home as surely as the ancestors; they folded the past into the arms of the present and the future. But the complex journey of the Pecos repatriation had taken much more than three days. The Pecos and Jemez people had needed a decade or, more accurately, nearly a century to achieve their family reunion. Although NAGPRA gave the Pecos descendants the leverage to realize their dream—the return of their ancestors—the process required relentless persistence. After centuries of European American attempts to reduce their number and wipe out their cultures, Native Americans had been recouping some of their losses. The Jemez, like other tribes, were more than ready for NAGPRA.

Soon after the act became law, Pecos's religious leaders directed William Whatley, Jemez's tribal archaeologist and preservation officer, to initiate and complete the return of remains through its provisions. "They're the ones who were pretty adamant about having our ancestors come home," said Whatley, who is white. Time was crucial. In 1992-93 he produced a series of videos, the Pecos Ethnographic Project, for the National Park Service that included interviews with six Pecos elders. By the time the ancestors returned home to Pecos in 1999, three of those elders had died. With each death of an elder, memories slip away and threaten to weaken a tribe's cultural fabric. Although Whatley undertook much of the repatriation work, members of the tribes were actively engaged in negotiations in both New Mexico and Massachusetts. Raymond Gachupin, Jemez's governor in 1999, proudly pointed out that they never used a lawyer to retrieve the ancestors. Emotionally, the effort fell most heavily on those Pueblos actively pursuing the remains and on Whatley. Because funds for the project did not exist, Whatley sometimes worked without pay, and he continually had to take time out to find money.[7]

In 1991, when the formal repatriation process began, the Jemez and Pecos people had no idea of the number of ancestors at Harvard. Randy Padilla was the governor of Jemez in 1996, when he and other tribal leaders went to Cambridge to see the collection and meet with Peabody officials. Although the meetings went well, Padilla said that "the boxes and boxes of human remains was overwhelming." The notion of so many bodies being unearthed was difficult for the Pueblos to grasp, although later they learned why anthropologists took so many bodies. Gachupin defined the Pueblos' "context"—not scholarship but community. "It's hard to imagine having that many bodies. That's 75 percent of the village. It's unimaginable. Just removing one body is mind-boggling." For Whatley, the eight-year process "was nothing for us considering the ancestors had been gone for eighty years." Gachupin took a more critical view: "The fact that it took eight years speaks to why it took so long."

The Jemez and Pecos people carefully planned the actual return. "How do we bring our ancestors home?" was the first question they considered. Gachupin said the Pueblos unsuccessfully appealed to New Mexico's U.S. senators and its governor to obtain military or some other transport.[8] Finally, Regis Pecos, of Cochiti Pueblo, then head of the state's Office of Native American Affairs, connected the Pueblos with Flintco, a large Indian-owned construction firm based in Tulsa. Flintco donated $38,000 in transportation resources, and the National Park Service provided the security escorts.

The Pueblos then faced a vexing spiritual question. At death, a body is laid to rest and presumed to go on to the spirit world. Digging up a body is not even to be imagined. "What do we do about *reburial*? We don't have a reburial ceremony. We've never had to do that. We went back and forth with religious leaders to decide what to do," Padilla said. They settled on a basic ceremony derived from the original burial rites, with one crucial difference. As Padilla put it, the people dedicated this burial "for all first peoples." Because Pecos had been a trading center, a gateway to the plains, Padilla said that Kiowas and Comanches were also probably buried at Pecos, so those tribes as well as all the Pueblos were invited to the ceremony.

Although the loss of ancestral remains was not uppermost in daily conversations, repatriation is not ancient history. As recently as 1900, Pecos people who had migrated from Pecos to Jemez in 1838 were still alive. For all the anecdotes about archaeologists finding bodies tossed into prehistoric middens, or "refuse heaps," the Pecos burials were intentional and attended by ritual.[9] Individuals among the two thousand bodies were known to the tribe by name, and some of the funerary objects bear traces of burial practices that are still extant. Indeed, eighty-seven-year-old Juan Ray Tafoya might have had a grandfather or great-uncle among the people who had left Pecos—or among the dead whose bodies had been excavated.

The stories are alive in families and schools. Religious leaders integrated the story of Pecos and the ancestors into their ceremonies. Like other younger people, Joshua Madalena had learned about what happened at Pecos from his grandmother; she was one of the last Pecos potters. As the day of the ancestors' return approached, the children of Jemez had to be prepared for the upcoming events. In the week before the walk to Pecos, Paul Tosa was teaching history to his sixth graders in the reservation's middle school. Loud, joyful mayhem filled the dirt yard of the rural school under a canopy of trees. Inside, the walls were covered with student art, notices, and other bits of the school's paper trail. Displays around Tosa's classroom—a picture of the Hubble Space Telescope, models of fossils, and an aboriginal chronology poster—prompted me to ask how he reconciles Indian and white ways of looking at phenomena. A scientist, he began, is "the person who is here just to study." But in Towa, the word "scientist" has acquired another connotation that springs out of the people's experience. The scientist also represents "a disturbance," a figure "who has no consideration for a way of life, for tradition." Tosa encourages his students to think like scientists, for instance, to learn about the parts of the skeleton, even though they may fear real skeletal remains.[10] But he draws a distinction between a medical student working with cadavers and archaeologists disturbing a grave site. "The burial part is what you don't mess with," he said. "You don't find many Indian anthropologists digging up bones." As they learned about the original dig and the repatriation, the children came back with the persistent question—"Why so many bodies?"—that Tosa had repeated to me.

Tosa encouraged the children to look everywhere for answers, especially in the history of their people. He could see his students looking exclusively to the outside world—especially to television. I imagined his method was like our conversation. Although I tried to ask questions in logical steps, Tosa led me in and out of crannies he wanted me to see. All the locations he triangulated led to a single message: the Jemez and Pecos people live and learn through their stories.

Tosa had begun recording his grandfather's stories about the two communities when he was still in elementary school. As a high school sophomore, he began to tape other elders in a more extensive project. Through the stories, Tosa said, he can take Pecos history back beyond 1838. That history's continuing vitality added memories of centuries or even millennia to the repatriation. The trail is not easy to follow, but it's there in the language and words that certain elders use to tell their stories.

Tosa personally holds on to the stories in his traditional family because the children dance at ceremonials. Although he faces an uphill battle with his students, who are plugged into the digital world, Tosa begins the study of history in his classroom from the beginning. The Jemez people came not from a place but "from time immemorial," a phrase that is common for Puebloan origin stories. He leads his middle schoolers through Jemez history using poetry, legends, and folk tales as he had heard them from elders. The people of Jemez and Pecos lived peacefully and sustained themselves by living closely with nature. Then other tribes invaded, and problems began. The elders used Towa for words like "raid" and "warfare." They talked about the loss of "harmony" and "peace." Tosa recalls how his grandfather described the Europeans by saying, "It's unbelievable how far they crossed the very big water to travel to our ancestral land. They had to claim it for someone across the ocean. It's unbelievable."

The Europeans intruded into the long histories of Pecos and Jemez, times of great achievements and then tragic loss that illuminate the significance of repatriation. Pecos and Jemez were Towa-speaking communities of the greater Tanoan pueblo culture of the Rio Grande. The two developed contemporaneously, with Pecos to the east of the river and Jemez to the west. Pecos Pueblo had become a trading and agricultural center by 1300, as communities of the Colorado Plateau world consolidated, for instance, at Chaco Canyon, the Galisteo Basin, and other large settlements.[11] Pecos was—is—a place of unsurpassed beauty. Standing at the old pueblo and turning full circle, the visitor can imagine life in the busy community. Located about seven thousand feet above sea level on a rocky ridge, it commands a view of the valley formed by the Pecos River and embraced by stark mesas and the deeply forested Sangre de Cristo Mountains. Hawks follow soaring trajectories in the wide, turquoise-hued, New Mexico sky.

Pecos asserts itself even though the outlines of its walls and rooms are barely visible through a cover of soil and grasses. Layers of debris demarcate where people had lived in large stone apartment houses, some several stories high, with about a thousand rooms. (The ruined Spanish church constitutes the largest remaining structure.) Despite the protective circle of mountains, which make Pecos seem like the most secure place in the world, it was built like a fortress. The doors of most houses faced onto the plaza, and the settlement limited openings toward the valley that might have been vulnerable to intruders. Inhabitants traversed the settlement on interior multilevel walkways, and a defensive wall defined the "city limits." Pecos's wealth lay in storage rooms overflowing with grains produced by its skilled agriculturalists. The pueblo was strategically located for trade between tribes living on the endless plains to the east and surrounding pueblos. Commerce took place on the east side of the ridge, on an expanse as large as two football fields. At Pecos's trading fairs, Pueblos, Kiowas, Apaches, Navajos, Utes, and Comanches spent days bartering with hides, captives, crops, pottery, and rare minerals like turquoise. As many as two thousand people—who called themselves Cicuye—lived in this thriving community.[12]

To the west of the great river, Jemez, known as Walatowa ("this is the place") to its inhabitants, also grew into a powerhouse. According to the pueblo's history, Jemez's ancestors came from a place to the north called Hua-na-tota, then migrated southward in the thirteenth century. Jemez's own historical account describes an ancient world comprising several towns a few miles apart and hundreds of smaller settlements and field houses. For their primary towns, residents built stone fortresses up to four stories high and with as many as three thousand rooms on high mesas and cliffs that were virtually impenetrable barriers. From these strategic locations, the people protected access to springs and religious sites, monitored trail systems, and watched for invading enemies. Other groups often called upon the powerful Walatowa to help settle disputes. Walatowa rivaled Chaco Canyon, the most famous of the Ancestral Puebloan sites.[13] Two centuries after the collapse of the Chacoan culture system, Walatowa had emerged as a major power in the northern Southwest. At its peak in the late sixteenth century, the population exceeded eleven thousand, making it the largest in the region. Some decline had already set in, however, as the rivalries for the plains trade flared into warfare.[14]

The Spaniards stepped into this thriving and complex world in the middle of the sixteenth century. In 1540 Hernando de Alvarado undertook an expedition to Pecos, and his chronicler admiringly described the pueblo's architecture and military strength, including five hundred warriors. The residents boasted that "no one has been able to conquer them and that they conquer whatever village they wish," he wrote.[15] At first the Cicuye welcomed the visitors with flute music and gifts, but then, as Alvarado became more insistent about taking various valuable items, they expelled the Spaniards.

The Spaniards' admiration did not restrain them from ruthless colonization of the Pueblos. The injustices have been well documented: slave labor, rape, murder, economic demands, and religious persecution. Less well known is the structural dissolution of Pueblo life. One scholar has estimated that the number of Pueblo settlements in the Southwest declined by 62 percent between 1602 and 1680.[16] By the late seventeenth century, the conquistadores had gone, leaving the province to settlers and friars.

After decades of persecution and abuse, the Indians drove out the Spaniards in the successful Pueblo Revolt of 1680. The rebellion's immediate spark was the hanging of three men for "sorcery" at three pueblos and the imprisonment or public lashing of forty others. One of those whipped was Popé of San Juan Pueblo, who emerged as the revolt's leader. Jemez and Pecos were among the fiercest rebels. In what is sometimes called "the first American revolution," the Spaniards ran for their lives southward toward El Paso as Pueblos destroyed churches, homes, and other material remains of the Spanish occupiers. Resistance from the Pueblos weakened, however, when the Spaniards returned to northern New Spain for good in 1692.[17]

Subsequently, war and disease nearly destroyed the Pueblos, and within four years they were drastically reduced in numbers. Over the next three centuries of colonization, most of their land was taken from the Towa. By 1750 Pecos had just 449 residents and by 1821 about 50. In 1838, when only a handful remained, the Pecos people left the home they had known for centuries and walked for three days across the Rio Grande and the mountains.[18] They arrived among their kin at Jemez, with whom they shared a culture and the Towa language. The Pecos made a new home at Jemez, intermarrying with its people.

In 1936 the Pecos and Jemez groups merged legally through an act of Congress, although the Pecos people retain their own governor and religious leaders. Pecos Pueblo—the original settlement with its ruined mission church—was declared a national monument in 1965 by President Lyndon Johnson and became part of a 6,700-acre national historical park in 1990. This quiet, secluded park draws only about thirty-eight thousand visitors annually, so it is possible to wander alone through the church's tall, stark skeleton and the partially excavated pueblo.[19]

That the small communities of Jemez and Pecos were able to take on a challenging repatriation project is unsurprising given this history. Their contemporary world continues their story. The three thousand Pecos and Jemez people live for the most part in a single village, which they call by its historical name, Walatowa, along the Jemez River. They occupy eighty-nine thousand acres of their once vast lands.[20] The biggest employer is the tribal government, which provides services such as education funded partially through the federal government as part of treaty obligations. Some Jemez residents describe their pueblo as very "traditional" because its people are committed to preserving their songs, stories, and art. At the same time, they are neither isolated nor insulated in their valley. The people inhabit the cultural continuum from total assimilation to conservative. While some continue traditional farming, others commute daily to jobs in Albuquerque, Los Alamos, or Santa Fe. The Pueblos have historically revered their runners, and those from Jemez are legendary. The late Fred LeBow, the founder of the New York Roadrunners Club, invited Al Waique of Jemez into his group.[21] Today, Jemez men are among the most skilled hot shots—elite firefighters—and they boost their incomes considerably by working in forests throughout the West. The pueblo had rejected gaming until 2004, when it entered into an agreement with a white developer to purchase land and build a casino in southern New Mexico, far from its homeland. But the Bureau of Indian Affairs (BIA) turned down the request because of the agency's rule that casinos must be located within twenty-five miles of a reservation's headquarters.[22]

Tourism also connects the pueblo with the outside world. The federal government declared the twenty-seven-mile Jemez River corridor a national scenic byway in 1998. The corridor snakes along the river and State Route 4, passing the pueblo and the non-Indian village of Jemez Springs (population around four hundred) before turning into the high country. Visitors stream through to fish, hunt, hike, view autumn color, and ski. Nearby, the remnant of a thousand-year-old Puebloan community inside Bandelier National Monument draws an international crowd. Adjacent to Bandelier is Los Alamos National Laboratory (LANL), no longer the remote place where Robert Oppenheimer and his scientists built the world's first nuclear weapon. The 1990s brought new residents and a new sport—real estate—to the Jemez Valley. Nevertheless, Jemez Pueblo protects its privacy. Although the pueblo throws its doors open for feast days, nontribal members cannot wander through the village and must check in at the visitors' center.

Their long history gave Jemez and Pecos a context for repatriation. The outside world had another context. Just as repatriation challenged and unified the Pueblos, it was a seminal event for Harvard's 140-year-old Peabody Museum. Because of NAGPRA, the Peabody became one of the nation's cultural institutions that found itself in new relationships with Indians. Those relationships had previously been framed mostly in glass cases and storage boxes. Now, however, many museum curators regularly meet with living descendants of their skeletal charges.

The Peabody's response was methodical. The museum completed an inventory in 2001 that enumerated more than ten thousand individual Native Americans and nearly sixteen thousand funerary objects. Only the Smithsonian Institution had more remains than the Peabody. Of the 3,136 remains at the Peabody that were eligible for repatriation under NAGPRA, 64 percent were from Pecos. Whatley described the Peabody's Pecos collection as "the largest collection in U.S. history, in terms of material culture and human remains, from a single-site assemblage."[23] During the course of the inventory, Harvard spent $3.6 million on repatriation, adding staff like data verifiers, curatorial assistants, and osteologists. Patricia Capone, who holds a Harvard doctorate in anthropology, worked exclusively on NAGPRA mandates, and most of the museum's staff was involved as needed.

For more than seventy years, the Pecos ancestors and others had been stored in acid-free boxes under careful environmental conditions. Since NAGPRA, the museum had consulted with tribes about the care of remains, and access to the area where they were kept had been strictly limited. With NAGPRA, records of the museum's collection were integrated into the Peabody's overall database, although some information—about sacred objects, for instance—is withheld from public view. Each of the individuals is identified according to age, sex, where he or she was found, cultural affiliation, what bones are actually present, and osteological information, such as the presence of arthritis or infection. Only one individual in the entire collection has a name.[24]

Harvard's task went beyond staff, funding, and an inventory. The Peabody was one of the first museums to undertake repatriation, and legislation had not defined any federally mandated protocols being designed by the NPS. So the staff sometimes improvised. They undertook five thousand consultations with hundreds of federally recognized American Indian tribes and Native Alaska and Hawaiian groups. Sometimes, curators had to deal with unfamiliar and emotionally charged personal issues, said Rubie Watson, the Peabody's director since 1997. For instance, the staff wasn't quite sure what to do when a delegation of Indians arrived at the museum. What about seating arrangements? Was the Peabody to feed and house visiting delegations? Did the Indians know what to ask for? For help, the museum turned to Harvard's Native American Program, which became the cohost for visits of Indian groups.

Mainly out of respect, a certain formality marked consultations. But still sometimes worlds collided. The museum accommodated tribal requests to conduct offering ceremonies on behalf of their ancestors in Harvard's custody. Some of these included burning material or scattering cornmeal, but fire was out of the question, and cornmeal would attract insects. European American conservators focus on preserving objects, and Indians often have a different view of what are the important things. Although museum and Indian cultural concerns frequently seemed incompatible, Watson explained that the Peabody never simply said "no" and worked through conversations to find ways to meet Indian concerns.

The Peabody arranged for the Pecos group to meet with Michelle Morgan, the museum's osteologist, who described how their ancestors had been used for research. The Pueblos responded with such enthusiasm when they learned of their ancestors' contribution to knowledge about human health that Morgan organized a volume for them containing papers on a variety of topics, including nutrition and osteoporosis, resulting from the Pecos research.[25]

Technical issues also arose. The Peabody had already returned individuals to other tribes, usually in a quiet place with a ceremony to mark the transfer. But the Pecos repatriation was on a scale that the museum had never experienced. What was to happen when the semitruck pulled up at the Peabody? The law specifies that the institution moves items to the museum's threshold. From there, the tribe assumes control over the repatriated material. So the Jemez/Pecos group carried each individual with associated funerary objects in its own box from the museum's door to the truck parked outside.

Despite the challenges of repatriation, Harvard gained an important benefit. During consultation visits at the Peabody, the staff and Indian visitors slowly created a partnership. The result has been good for the profession, said Watson, a cultural anthropologist, because it has raised a question about scholarly understanding of the Americas and how to accommodate Native American knowledge of the past. "NAGPRA forced, created these conversations," said Watson.

For American Indians, the conversation about NAGPRA provokes a gamut of emotions. Tosa's uncomfortable question—"Why so many bodies?"—is one starting point for understanding. Author N. Scott Momaday, a Kiowa who has lived in the Jemez Valley since the age of twelve, has other contributions. In his first novel, *A House Made of Dawn*, Momaday had imagined the departure of the broken and "wretched people" from their ancestral city of Bahkyula (Pecos) and their welcome at Walatowa (Jemez) in 1838.[26] The book won the Pulitzer Prize in 1969.

During the week before the Pecos repatriation ceremony, I had found my way to Momaday's simple adobe house in Jemez Village, just up the road from the pueblo. The author was not sure that the repatriation would completely close the chapter of what had happened at Pecos, particularly after the passage

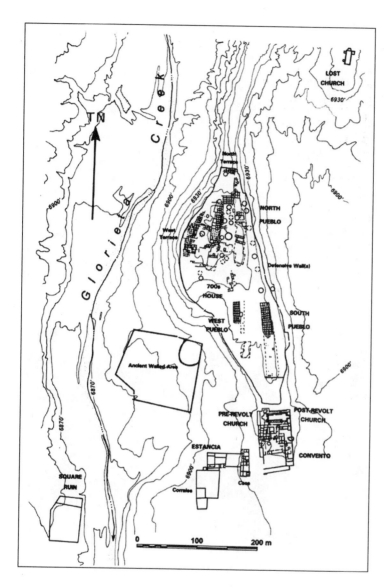

Ancient Pecos was a complex, fortified, and well-organized community, as this layout of the pueblo with associated Spanish structures shows. National Park Service, *From Folsom to Fogelson: The Cultural Resources Inventory Survey of Pecos Historical Park* (2002), app. E, fig. E-2, www.nps.gov /history/history/online_books/pecos/cris/images/fige-2.jpg.

Top: The ancestors come home to Pecos. Photo by Cary Herz.

Bottom: Celebrating a homecoming. Photo by Cary Herz.

of so many generations: "It's so massive—the injustice—that there's not much you can do about it." I told Momaday about the frank yet welcoming attitude of everyone at Jemez whom I had interviewed for the story. I had expected the people to be close-mouthed. Momaday said that the Jemez people are capable of great generosity, even in the context of injustice. "There have been so many things to be angry about. But it does no good to be angry," he said.

For Randy Padilla, the former governor of Jemez, the conversation took a thoughtful turn. Archaeologists were "just trying to help with research on the Pecos people for their benefit, not desecration. They're saying what they believe. They're going to defend their trade," he said during the week before the reburial ceremony. The anthropologists took "so many bodies" because the large cohort provided important information about human history.

With NAGPRA, however, Indians have entered this conversation. The Pecos repatriation forced the Peabody and the Pueblos to talk to each other, and the return finished a decade of work.

Arriving at this hopeful point has taken nearly a century. Like a juggernaut, non-Indians took control of the Indians' story at the end of the nineteenth century. American anthropology developed with a primary focus on Native America, or, as Ben K. Rhodd, a Potawatomi anthropologist put it, "the discipline 'cut its teeth on American Indians,'" and the people were "test subjects for scientific models and theory development."[27] Driven by moralists, gentlemen ethnographers and wealthy collectors, professional interests and other motives, the field of anthropology spawned decades of scholarship and scholars. The results were sometimes good and other times crackpot or highly questionable, and the methods were sometimes haphazard and even less than savory.

On the hunt for the exotic and the "primitive," the collectors rounded up people, living and dead, as well as pots; all were "curiosities" to display in the "civilized" world. As early as the sixteenth century, some Natives were transported to Europe as slaves or as interpreters of language and culture for business enterprises. Later, white conquerors wanted to impress Indians with their power, and European artists found them colorful subjects. Thomas Jefferson excavated a burial mound in Virginia, and Lewis and Clark sent three shipments to Monticello for Jefferson's "Indian Hall," a private museum. "Explorers" who moved into archaeologically sensitive places early in American history were simply collectors rather than scholars. By the early nineteenth century, Henry Rowe Schoolcraft had developed the broad strokes of American anthropology rooted in science and based upon Native Americans as the prime source. The momentum of anthropology was irresistible. Throughout the century, Americans saw increasing evidence that extensive, well-organized societies predated European contact in the eastern woodlands and beyond.[28]

In the Southwest, the focus of this chapter, anthropological traffic picked up as transcontinental railroads opened up the region to mining, tourism, ranching, agriculture, and commerce. Thanks to stories in the pulp press and the ready availability of cheap souvenirs and genuine artifacts, turn-of-the-century Americans became "Indian-crazy." During this time, the entire world seemed to turn into an archaeological site, with digs in Egypt, Troy, and the jungles of Mesoamerica. Why not the United States' own "classical" place?

Americans became obsessed with their own exotica. A parade of American and European explorers arrived to uncover ancient cultures across the Southwest, where Puebloan peoples built thriving cities from about AD 850 to 1250. Financing these expeditions were leading museums, organizations, universities, and individuals. Wealthy Boston philanthropist Mary Hemenway supported the Hemenway Southwestern Archaeological Expedition, the first scientific archaeological exploration of the region. Between 1886 and 1894 explorers such as Adolph Bandelier, Frank Hamilton Cushing, and Jesse Walter Fewkes directed activities in Arizona and New Mexico. The enigmatic Cushing had earlier explored Zuni in western New Mexico and lived among its people for five years. A photo of Cushing in full Zuni dress replicated in a portrait by Thomas Eakins shows how intensely he pursued his objectives.[29] In 1896 Edgar Lee Hewett began exploring at Frijoles Canyon north of Santa Fe.

Americans learned of Chaco Canyon when soldiers moving across the Southwest after the Mexican-American War came across it in 1849; drawings of it were available by 1852.[30] In 1896 New York philanthropists B. Talbot and Frederick Hyde organized the Hyde Exploring Expedition to undertake excavations at Chaco. During the expedition, Richard Wetherill and Harvard's George H. Pepper uncovered two hundred of the eight hundred rooms and kivas in Chaco's gem, Pueblo Bonito, and the American Museum of Natural History in New York accepted the artifacts. Its sponsors also opened their own Navajo rug store in New York.[31]

The discovery and exploration of Mesa Verde, Chaco's sister site in Colorado, however, show that European American myths die hard. According to lore, on a cold December day in 1888, Richard Wetherill and Charlie Mason, a couple of Colorado cowboys on horseback, were looking for stray cattle. They stumbled on magnificent Cliff Palace, the largest and best preserved of Mesa Verde's settlements. Researcher Joseph Weixelman has found another version of this story, however. In tape recordings made by Marietta Wetherill, Richard's wife, we hear that a Ute Indian named Acowitz actually guided the two men to Cliff Palace while he was helping them find their cattle. Weixelman believes that Acowitz has been left out of the discovery story because Indians just don't count. "How many times in the history of North America did Indians guide whites across the continent or give them information?" he asked rhetorically.[32]

In 1891 the Wetherills helped Gustav Nordenskjold pull artifacts out of Cliff Palace and other sites. The twenty-three-year-old Swedish explorer sent his finds back to Stockholm. In Colorado, Americans watched crates filled with archaeological materials for shipment to American and European museums crowd the Durango railroad station. They began to exert pressure for federal protection of their treasures. A group of women in Denver formed the Colorado Cliff-Dwellings Association to have Mesa Verde designated a national park. In 1906 Congress passed and President Theodore Roosevelt signed the Preservation of American Antiquities Act, the nation's first preservation legislation designed specifically for archaeology. Mesa Verde became the first archaeological site designated as a national park.

At that time, Hans Randolph, Mesa Verde's superintendent, described Cliff Palace's dire condition after twenty years of indiscriminate digging and pot hunting. Artifact hunters had cut large openings in the five walls at the front of the landmark building, broken down other walls and floors, and wrecked buried kivas. "Beams were used for firewood to so great an extent that not a single roof now remains," he wrote. For the next twenty years, Jesse Fewkes, the able former director of the Hemenway Expedition, moved from one project to another at Mesa Verde. With other explorers, he helped stabilize the site and initiated new research using scientific methods.[33]

Several institutions and policies shaped American anthropology and archaeology. In 1879 John Wesley Powell, the first white man to traverse the treacherous Colorado River through the Grand Canyon, encouraged Congress to establish the Bureau of (American) Ethnology to move materials related to Native Americans from the Interior Department to the Smithsonian Institution. With Powell directing, the agency also mounted large-scale archaeological projects, including Cushing's excursion to Zuni.[34] Throughout the nineteenth century, researchers raced to conserve what Native peoples had produced in pre-contact days. Between 1879 and 1880, the Bureau of American Ethnology sent more than forty thousand historic Indian items from the greater Southwest to the Smithsonian.[35]

Most Americans had never heard the word "anthropology," already current among scholars, until 1893, when Franz Boas organized an exhibit for the World's Columbian Exposition in Chicago.[36] As researchers toiled in the field, scholars were also busy in universities. At the turn of the twentieth century, Boas, who had moved to America from Germany in 1883, Frederic W. Putnam, and Alfred Kroeber, among others, created programs at Columbia, Harvard, and Berkeley. In the nation's archaeological hot spot, Edgar Lee Hewett established the School of American Research in Santa Fe, became the first director of the Museum of New Mexico, and organized an anthropology department at the state university's flagship campus in Albuquerque.[37] Clark University in Massachusetts conferred the first doctorate in anthropology in 1886. Scholars formed professional associations such as the American Ethnological Society and American Anthropological Association. They defined the discipline and collected, classified, and reconstructed societies according to where they fit into the Western European ideal.[38]

Scholars quickly divided along several lines. Cushing, Lewis Henry Morgan, and others believed cultures evolved in a straight line, through stages from a state of savagery to modern. Using "science" to prove their proposition, some scholars measured masses of skulls to "prove" that the Caucasian race had achieved superiority to all others.[39] Boas rejected their proposition and insisted on cultural relativism, the idea that cultures had to be studied for their own sakes outside the definitions of "civilization." With this broader palette, Boas and others shaped the direction of research and, ultimately, the representation of Native Americans. Among the scholars whom Boas trained at Columbia were Kroeber, Ruth Benedict, and Margaret Mead. The Boasians shaped the field as a combination of humanities and scientific method that eventually dominated anthropology.

A year after Mesa Verde became a national park, Kidder, a restless premed student at Harvard, landed a summer job working for Hewett on a dig there. Reminiscing in 1960, he described how Hewett took him and other young fieldworkers to a high mesa in the early morning hours of July 4, 1907. Kidder, who had never traveled west of Chicago, wrote that the vistas and landscape of cliffs, rock formations, and canyons "dazed" him. Then he recalled what Hewett did next. "He waved his arm, taking in it seemed, about half the world. 'I want you boys to make an archaeological survey of this country. I'll be back in three weeks.'" Romanced by archaeology, the "dazed" Kidder went on to earn a doctorate in 1914. He then picked up an offer from the Phillips Academy in Andover, Massachusetts, to direct a major project of his choice. Kidder selected Pecos.[40]

Pecos Pueblo may have gone dark when its inhabitants left in 1838, but it launched the thirty-year-old Kidder's career. From the bones and sherds he excavated, Kidder developed a structure and methodological principles that he and others used. These embraced systematic excavation, detailed records, and new technologies such as dendochronology (tree-ring dating). Kidder was a synthesist who integrated other disciplines like history into the archaeological enterprise. In 1924 Kidder produced a chronological framework for southwestern research that became a model for scholarship in the field: *An Introduction to the Study of Southwestern Archaeology*.

In the summer of 1927, Kidder also founded what has become a premier event in American archaeology, the Pecos Conference. He invited colleagues working in the Southwest to Pecos at the end of the digging season. About forty-three researchers arrived in late August. They set up camp and described their activities during that summer's field season in brief reports. In those few days, the researchers laid out a fundamental agenda for the future: increase contacts among fieldworkers; uncover fundamental problems of the region's archaeology; pool knowledge; and develop a system of nomenclature for data. Kidder coined the word "Anasazi" to describe some of the ancient cultures that dominated the Southwest for centuries before the arrival of Europeans. The term "Ancestral Puebloan" is replacing "Anasazi" among the Pueblos themselves and scholars, although popular culture continues to use it.[41] The Pecos Conference still meets annually for a long weekend of outdoor camping, with brief field reports from scholars, and camaraderie, including a contest for brewing the archaeologist's libation of choice—beer. It also draws what anthropologists call avocationalists (also known as "amateurs") and cultural tourists.[42]

Whether they were fieldworkers, museum curators, academics, or avid members of local historical and archaeology societies, Americans were looking for answers to questions that reflected their own values. After the first discoveries of Ancestral Puebloan communities, they wondered who had built Mesa Verde and Chaco Canyon. No Native societies—"primitive" as they were—could have built such spectacular structures as Cliff Palace and Pueblo Bonito. One view held that these places were the remains of Egyptian or Phoenician exploration.[43]

Also, the prevailing view in the nineteenth century was that living Indians would soon disappear—"vanish" being the favorite term—in the onslaught from "civilization." "Americans wanted to hear about a vanished race because they believed all Indians were vanishing," says Weixelman, who has worked as a National Park Service interpreter at Mesa Verde.[44] As late as the 1960s, some of Mesa Verde's park rangers told romantic stories of the sites because it was easier to say the people vanished than to say they moved south to the Rio Grande. Weixelman suggests that the myth has had its uses. For one, it provides the justification for cultural appropriation by archaeologists excavating artifacts wholesale as well as for New Age interpretations of the vanished culture. One extreme version holds that the Anasazi disappeared when they were sucked up by a space ship. The manufacture of a vanished people also played into another American expectation. With Indians gone, the continent was empty, and Manifest Destiny—appropriating the land—made sense.

The later twentieth and early twenty-first centuries have brought dramatic change to anthropology, with new technologies, cultural advances, ethical challenges, and the entrance of many more American Indians into the field.[45] Remote sensing devices found hundreds of miles of roads at Chaco Canyon and can even explore underwater sites; lidar maps buried cities in a matter of days rather than decades; paleoethnobotany and DNA analysis follow the movements of ancient peoples.[46] Archaeologists and computer specialists have reconstructed one ancient Puebloan settlement—Long House in northern Arizona—in cyberspace to trace the group's history.[47]

Thanks to additional protective legislation, today any publicly or privately funded projects on public lands must be surveyed for archaeological remains. Most archaeology is "compliance-driven" to insure that public and private projects comply with federal, state, local, and tribal standards. The archaeologist works just ahead of construction teams excavating for a gas line, an optic fiber cable, or a highway.

Compliance-driven archaeology has engendered enormous growth in the private sector. At the first Pecos Conference in 1927, virtually all the attendees were from museums, universities, and the Bureau of Ethnology. By 2002 museums and universities employed only 12 percent of the seven hundred or so professionals in southwestern archaeology. The rest work as contract archaeologists for private companies (more than one hundred are for-profit), national and local governments, and tribes.[48] Compliance-driven archaeology must fit into a construction timetable and not a semester or summer session academic schedule.

In a coincidence of legislation and the region's explosive population growth, the number of archaeological activities increased from five hundred during the 1970s to twelve thousand in the 1990s. The sheer volume of fossil and archaeological records has overtaken the old anthropology. By the end of 2000, contract archaeologists had uncovered so much material in the Southwest that museums and other institutions were running out of storage space. Curators had to make some hard choices: refuse to accept artifacts, dramatically increase the charges for curation, or press for additional facilities to be built. Also, with cultural resource *management* (CRM) rather than collecting, researchers have paused. Linda Cordell, the former director of the University of Colorado Museum, said curators today must try to link information amassed in nearly a century of collecting.[49] In 1927 she said scholars asked, "What is a kiva?" Today they ask, "When is a kiva? Why is a kiva?" One example of this new approach is the Chaco Synthesis Project, in which several institutions collaborated for six years to examine and consolidate evidence about Chaco Canyon.[50]

Anthropologists have also been examining their own behavior. Ethics issues are not new to anthropology. One of the best-known controversies occurred at the University of California, Berkeley. Alfred Kroeber "adopted" a man, apparently the last survivor of the Yahi/Yana people who walked out of the wilderness of northern California in 1911. The scholar took the man into his care, gave him the name "Ishi," and allowed him to live in the Museum of Anthropology. Ishi became a living artifact—or in today's lexicon, "a Native informant." He cheerfully related Yahi stories and songs for the anthropologists and many visitors who flocked to see him. But Ishi never "assimilated" fully into white culture. Later, scholars hotly debated the issue of anthropologists working for intelligence agencies during World War II. New rules of conduct govern the use of anthropologists for military purposes, the disposition of cultural materials, and the researcher's relationship with living subjects of study, especially where the field researcher lives among them.

The anthropologists' very identity—ethnicity, gender, education, and political persuasion—is a criterion for evaluating their work. Women advocated for conservation in Colorado, bankrolled expeditions, and were active in the field from the beginnings.[51] At Harvard, Frederic W. Putnam brought women to work at the Peabody in traditional support roles and in independent research, and he opened anthropology classes to Radcliffe women in 1881.[52] Ruth Benedict and Margaret Mead were among the women pioneers. Today, the Committee on the Status of Women in Anthropology monitors the progress of women in the discipline and in the American Anthropological Association.[53]

This chapter focuses on Indians and "anthros," and in the next section, we turn to how Indians have entered the conversation more forcefully. To ignore how ordinary Americans have responded to the nation's archaeological heritage would be remiss, however. Many European Americans have always known that sizable populations of peoples and their cultures preceded them on this continent. Early explorers like Giovanni da Verrazano reported that the shores of the New World were crowded with people.[54] But for the most part, the newcomers saw North America as a continent of vast, empty spaces, waiting for them to settle and "civilize" it. From the Oklahoma Land Run of 1889, when fifty thousand people raced to occupy "unassigned lands," to contemporary real-estate development, ordinary Americans have mostly ignored the Native past and aggressively pursued the dream of an open frontier, even after that frontier "closed."[55] NAGPRA and other recent legislation have come at a time when Americans migrated in large numbers into the archaeological treasure house of the Southwest.[56]

The result has been mixed. On Albuquerque's west side, for perhaps five thousand years Ancestral Puebloans chipped more than twenty thousand petroglyphs into boulders along a fifteen-mile ridge formed by volcanic eruptions. This massive outdoor gallery constitutes North America's single largest collection of petroglyphs close to an urban area and sits in the path of the city's growth. Until the extent of the collection was understood, the petroglyphs were easy prey. Looters with backhoes carted away glyph-covered boulders for the world's antiquities markets. Local marksmen used them for target practice. Nearby Keresan Pueblo Indians conduct religious ceremonies there, however, mostly in secret for the sake of privacy and safety.

Protecting the petroglyphs sparked public interest. Preservationists pleaded with developers to keep a protective buffer between houses and petroglyphs, but some subdivisions sit right up against the boulders. Beginning in the 1960s, Albuquerque's city government and the state of New Mexico began to acquire portions of the ridge for a park. And then in 1990 the federal government designated 7,239 acres for Petroglyph National Monument. Also, near Petroglyph, the city of Albuquerque acquired the Mann site, an entire one-thousand-room pueblo, one of the largest in the Rio Grande valley.

But politicians and businesspeople brushed aside the religious objections of the Pueblos to build the road through the monument that Simon Ortiz and a white sympathizer had discussed. U.S. Senator Pete Domenici sponsored legislation to remove a slice of the monument from federal authority and protection, and President William J. Clinton signed it. As Judith Cordova, a former superintendent of the monument, once said, "In Albuquerque, developers rule."[57]

Many Americans first learn of NAGPRA and similar laws when a construction crew blading the landscape finds some bones or sherds in their town or neighborhood. All work for a project stops while archaeologists consult with government and tribal representatives to retrieve the materials in the CRM process. In their response to such finds, Americans vacillate. Some are willing to sacrifice the heritage to "progress," while others are eager to support preservation efforts.

Among the nonprofit organizations in which Americans can address the nation's antiquities is the Archaeological Conservancy. The group is in the business, for want of a better handle, of "ancient real estate," acquiring archaeological (and some historic) sites through either purchase or donation. Today, the conservancy has more than 325 sites in 39 states, ranging in size from a few acres to more than a thousand. Some are incorporated into national parks. Others are covered and locked or under guard for later excavation. Technology is changing so rapidly that waiting a generation or more will yield more information than could be achieved today.[58]

This is a very brief summary of the role that the general public plays. While many Americans have been careless or downright venal, others have made serious efforts to protect resources by supporting legislation and nonprofit organizations.

No one can estimate the amount of Indian heritage that quietly fell to bulldozers accommodating growth before federal, state, local, and tribal governments enacted stringent regulations. But in the late twentieth century, Native Americans became significant players in telling their ancient stories. Some have entered the field of anthropology, where their presence has become a force; others have helped build institutions within tribes. The National Historic Preservation Act of 1966 specified that Indians were to be included as partners rather than as objects of study.

The "vanishing people" reappeared with a vengeance. In 1969 Vine Deloria jolted American anthropology with a groundbreaking chapter in *Custer Died for Your Sins*. It opens with a scathing description of how Indians view researchers: "Into each life, it is said, some rain must fall. Some people have bad horoscopes, others take tips on the stock market. . . . Churches possess the real world. But Indians have been cursed above all other people in history. Indians have anthropologists."[59] Deloria later acknowledged reforms like new codes of ethics that sought permission from subjects of study, but he maintained that a colonial mentality persisted in academia. Anthropologists continued on a one-way course, applying "scientific" methods to tribal peoples without respect for Indian perspectives and values, he charged. Because of Deloria, newly mandated Indian rights, and the development of American Indian studies, anthropologists had to look over their shoulders.

NAGPRA came nearly twenty years after Deloria sent his formidable shot over anthropology's bow. Most anthropologists today would agree with Stephen Lekson, the director of the Chaco Synthesis Project, that NAGPRA "is a long-overdue correction of a historical wrong."[60] More important, the legislation has provided another layer that some researchers, such as Fewkes, Kidder, Boas, Benedict, and others, recognized: the living descendants and their culture. While Deloria had acknowledged reforms in the field, he challenged anthropologists to go further, to employ Indian views in their work.[61] Linda Cordell says that southwestern archaeology is a bellwether "collaborative archaeology" because of the number and diversity of vibrant Native American traditions in the region. Indeed, non-Indians increasingly turn to American Indians and their way of knowing to help interpret the past.

Three examples of collaboration come from individuals and organizations. Kurt Anschuetz, a non-Indian archaeologist, works in several hundred square miles of central New Mexico between Albuquerque and Taos. He regularly consults with Tewas, Towas, and Keresans who inhabit this area. "The past is not a pickle," he has concluded, that is, to be preserved in a jar on a shelf.[62]

In the models that non-Indian and Indian researchers have constructed, nothing is static, Anschuetz says. For example, the Tewa physical world is a bowl contained by the mountains, and its parts—the center of the bowl, the village itself, and everything in between—engage in active relationships. The design of Taos Pueblo, for instance, recalls the jagged Sangre de Cristo Mountains around it. Other features are similarly related: water, energy, agricultural fields, and the mountains where the sacred spirits dwell and to which the spirits of the dead return.

With the models, Anschuetz tracks ancient fields and settlements that have been used to the present. In fields near Zia Pueblo, just south of Jemez, Anschuetz has found "phenomenal systems" of ancient agriculture, plotting three thousand acres of rectangular grids, each about the size of a pueblo room.

Ancestral Puebloan engineers managed water in complex and sophisticated ways. The Pueblos rotated their fields and occupied and left settlements near the fields as needed in an ebb and flow that constitutes their "history" and cosmology.

Native cultural memory is as important to the archaeologist as findings from science and technology. Contemporary Pueblos have a dynamic and fluid relationship with the past's physical landmarks and its people. A "landmark" is not merely a place but also a cultural context. Puebloan people have never abandoned what scholars consider to be "ruins"; rather, they remember the old settlements in songs and stories, and they return regularly to the old houses. Some also continue to gather water from springs near Ojo Caliente near Santa Fe, where their ancestors stopped during migrations from Chaco and other towns.

Anschuetz says archaeologists have substituted measurement—years, number of room blocks, and so on—for history. Seeing the Tewa world in the larger context—patterns of stories and landscapes—expands understanding and reveals complexity. The history of humanity is talking about the cosmos. "Folks aren't simple. They're incredibly complicated. And we're surprised," he says.

A second instance illustrates the differences between non-Indian and Native approaches to archaeological finds. At the 2001 Pecos Conference, Bennie E. LeBeau, a Shoshone from Wyoming, and Merry Harrison, a non-Indian clinical herbalist, presented their analyses of the "Patterson bundle," a collection of herbs and other materials in the custody of the Bureau of Land Management. The four-hundred- to six-hundred-year-old bundle consists of a piece of leather wrapped around four plants of medicinal value, a stone blade, some strips of basketry, exquisite necklace material, and some animal parts. After a detailed study, Harrison concluded that the herbs, such as osha, had powerful antiviral properties. The bundle was more than a stash of supplies, and it was unique.

LeBeau, a student at Northern Arizona University, agreed that the bundle was not a haphazard collection. LeBeau explored the area where the bundle had been found and discovered shrines and familiar natural and cultural landmarks. From these he concluded that the Patterson bundle was not unique and was similar to others used by American Indians in vision quests. Researchers simply do not always recognize information, he explained. Further, although removing the bundle from its ledge increased understanding, he said, "the spirit was devastated." LeBeau's ambivalence about modern archaeology was clear. Despite the spiritual dislocation, when science includes people like him, it helps Native Americans "tune back in to learn who we are," he said.

Finally, also from the 2001 Pecos Conference, researchers detailed extensive Indian partnership during a highway survey. Over a period of three years, archaeologists excavated seventeen miles of right-of-way on both sides of U.S. Highway 89 north of Flagstaff. The more than one hundred thousand artifacts at forty sites revealed a thriving agricultural and trading society from about AD 450 to 1500. The contract firm, Desert Archaeology, Inc., of Tucson, employed eight Hopis in fieldwork and turned frequently to some thirty Hopi members to help identify and analyze artifacts. Although the Hopis had no direct cultural memory of the settlements, they did recognize the period as an epic era of events, with migrations of people, volcanic eruptions, earthquakes, and vicious storms. One of the field team members, Micah Lomaomvaya, a University of Arizona graduate in anthropology, said that twenty-six Hopi clans are associated with ancestral villages and religious sites in the area. "Archaeology plays back and serves as a monument to the history of my people," Lomaomvaya said. "We see our footsteps on the lands. These are chapters of our own history that we're writing today."[63]

Mark Elson, the president of Desert Archaeology, described a poignant moment in the archaeologist-Hopi collaboration. Around 1064 as many as three hundred tremors shook the earth during the days preceding an eruption that disrupted the busy settlements.[64] Although ash was plentiful, lava covered a relatively small area, about eight square kilometers. As the lava cooled, ancestral people pressed corncobs into it. They then cut the corncob impressions into blocks, which Elson's archaeologists named "corn rocks." Archaeologists found fifty-five of these unusual specimens strewn on the ground. At least one of the corn rocks was ritually placed into the wall of a structure. Elson said the rocks were "the first indication of ritual behavior related to volcanism in the United States." When the Hopi community team saw the corn rocks, tears came to their eyes, Elson said.[65] The corn rocks testified to a thousand years of cultural continuity. For the Hopis and other Pueblos, corn is not only an agricultural product but also a sacred ceremonial substance. The corn rocks were Hopi "footsteps."

At the same time that they are collaborating with non-Indian researchers, Native Americans have independently reclaimed more of the history that Europeans had captured, despite their best efforts to protect their physical and cultural homes. Tribes like the Navajos (Arizona, New Mexico) and the Colvilles (Washington State) began to develop preservation policies and offices even before NAGPRA.[66] By 1984, a survey of 186 tribes showed that less than half had tribal laws or departments responsible for archaeological and historical resources. Nations and tribes engaged with federal agencies in setting policy for especially sensitive subjects such as sacred and religious areas.[67] Before gaming brought in revenue for cultural ventures, the

Navajo, Hopi, and Akwesasne Mohawk Nations, among others, had established libraries or cultural centers.

The pace has quickened. Today, Indian Country has 125 cultural institutions, of which about 55 are predominantly museums; the rest are libraries or archives.[68] Some are quite modest, and most focus on the story of tribal lifeways rather than "art" in the European American sense. The Mashantucket Pequot Museum has a graceful building with a reconstructed "Native village." In 2006 Acoma Pueblo opened an elegant cultural center and museum with the slogan "a thousand years of living history." The Quinault Tribe's museum in Washington State and the Hupa Tribe's in northern California are in converted retail establishments. Jemez Pueblo has an on-line virtual museum.[69]

The Navajo Nation created its Department of Archaeology in 1978, and today it has a full-time staff of twenty. Robert Begay, the department's first Diné director, said that it operates like any consulting firm, undertaking field surveys for public works projects and data recovery from excavations. Archaeological activities have been occurring on the reservation for more than a century, but the Navajo Nation has changed the course of those activities to benefit the Navajo people. For instance, the nation has developed policies for the care of human remains and ceremonial bundles.[70]

The largest institution for Native cultural expression is the Smithsonian's National Museum of the American Indian (NMAI), which opened on the National Mall in Washington DC on September 21, 2004. At the core of the museum's collections are eight hundred thousand material items and nearly ninety thousand photos and other audiovisual images. Most came from the huge collection of New York philanthropist George Gustav Heye, who had gathered them into the Museum of the American Indian (MAI) in Manhattan in 1916.[71] In 1990

Congress brought the MAI into the Smithsonian with a mission to preserve, study, and exhibit the life, languages, literature, history, and arts of Native Americans. Almost immediately after he took charge as the NMAI's founding director, Richard West began consulting with tribes throughout North America for ideas on how the museum could be, as its organizers say, "a truly Native place."

The museum's designers were Douglas Cardinal (Blackfeet), Johnpaul Jones (Cherokee/Choctaw), Ramona Sakiestewa (Hopi), and Donna House (Navajo/Oneida). The architects included Lou Weller (Caddo) and the Native American Design Collaborative.[72] With its rough-textured stone that resembles Ancient Puebloan work, the building—which cost $219 million—undulates around a small wetland environment and crop area. Directly across the mall, I. M. Pei's modernistic National Gallery is a sharp contrast. The opening day's celebration collected tribes into a new fellowship. In West Falls, Virginia, during the morning rush hour, American Indians in traditional dress and accessories hopped on the Washington metro to get to the National Mall. Commuters threw sidelong glances their way.

At the Smithsonian Castle, a parade of more than twenty-five thousand Indians began to walk at a snail's pace toward the Capitol. Reprising several common traditions, they began the day with a prayer, facing the sun, feasted, and danced. The crowd came from four hundred tribes from North and South America: children in fringed buckskin; men in ribboned shirts or eagle-feather bustles and headdresses; women in ornately decorated beaded or jingle dresses (the dresses literally jingle because of the tiny metal cones sewn onto the fabric or buckskin); the elderly in wheelchairs or golfing carts; entire families and kinship groups; musicians playing Native instruments. Assorted groups with T-shirts or signs that identified their affiliations—Owens Valley Career Development Center and the Intertribal Council of AT&T Employees—also marched. Well-wishers joined the festivities.

To acknowledge the importance of the cardinal directions, four musical groups were positioned at those points that define Indian Country—Halau O Kekuhi from the west (Hawaii), Andes Mante from the south (Peru), Pamyua from the north (Alaska), and Six Nations Women Singers from the east (Canada); the procession paused where they performed. Press and amateur photographers darted around, and onlookers asked Indians in regalia to pose for pictures. Indians complied graciously and seemed to enjoy posing in all their finery. Indians, tourists, and other visitors lined up at food tents and drink kiosks. Navajo, Onondaga, Lumbee, Algonquian, and Inca cooks dispensed thousands of pounds of buffalo burgers, venison stew, fish chowder, blue corn fry bread, wild rice soup, and pumpkin bread. At other booths Native artisans showed off their musical instruments and other wares, told stories, and sold regalia. Dwain Campo, a sixty-seven-year-old Ponca reveler from Oklahoma, surveyed the scene and concluded, "Just gorgeous."

On the stage at the foot of the Capitol, an honor guard of Hopis presented the colors, and Black Eagle, a drum group from Jemez Pueblo, performed a flag song.[73] Resplendent in pale fringed and beaded buckskin and a full Cheyenne chief's war bonnet, Rick West spoke to the crowd. "Native America takes its rightful place on the National Mall in the very shadow of the nation's Capitol itself." The museum, he said, recognizes the first citizens of the Americas with a powerful marker. Through the repatriation process the world would begin to sense that with deaths and disappearances, Indians have suffered at the deepest level of their souls.

The NMAI's opening felt like the Pecos repatriation, a family reunion but on a grander scale. The range of ages, from young adults to elders, many in regalia, reminded me of the gathering in the Pecos meadow. Inevitably, like many family reunions, this one also produced some disaffection, notably from the American Indian Movement (AIM). In an official statement, Dennis Banks, the chairman of AIM's board, congratulated everyone who had brought the museum into being. But he regretted that the museum did not display the history of aggressions against the peoples of the Americas and the toll it has taken. Banks said that NMAI was indeed a "National Holocaust Museum of the American Indian."[74]

The final words at the ceremony belonged to West. His voice is a deep baritone with soft traces of his Oklahoma upbringing and a steady, measured cadence. Without wavering from the reality of his people's suffering, he spoke of triumph. Native Americans must insist, he said, that they remain a part of America's cultural future, as they have always been. To the descendants of those who came to the continent from across the seas, West said, "Welcome to Native America." For those who descend from the Native ancestors, he said, "Welcome home."[75]

2

THOUGHTS FROM THE CHIEF

Welcome home.

The Navajo Nation is a good starting point for understanding how so many American Indians relate to their homelands. The Navajos are one of the best-known groups because of their size, location, and popular recognition. The Cherokees outnumber the Navajos (partly because of a high number of members of mixed descent), but with 175,000 residents, the Navajo Nation has the largest reservation population as well as the largest land mass among the reservations.[1] Sharing a boundary with Grand Canyon National Park, the reservation is accessible and open, a natural stopping point for domestic and international visitors. AMTRAK's Southwest Chief and Interstate 40 both skirt the southern side of the reservation, and some smaller but good roads cut across it. Also, except for a brief but brutal period of exile in the nineteenth century, the Navajos have remained on their homeland. (The Great Sioux Nation, occupying parts of the Dakotas and other north-central states, is similarly well situated.)

Some three hundred thousand travelers annually get their first view of the Navajo Reservation from "The Chief," as it is widely known.[2] Every morning, the train pulls out of Gallup, New Mexico, continuing a forty-eight-hour journey from Los Angeles to Chicago. Along the route between Gallup and Albuquerque, AMTRAK employs Navajo guides to give miniseminars on what passengers see outside the speeding train. The informal talk follows breakfast on the first morning of the journey after an overnight run across California and Arizona. The tutorial ends in Albuquerque right around lunchtime.

On a chilly January day in 1988, Zonnie Gorman stepped up to the public address microphone and invited passengers to the lounge car. Over the next three hours Zonnie told them about the land beyond the train tracks, where Navajo and Pueblo Indians live. I was on the train for a story about the guides, yet as I learned after more experience in Indian Country, Zonnie's life and that of her tribe mirror, although imperfectly, the state of Indians in the late twentieth century.[3] Zonnie's invitation drew a quick response, and she sipped on a soft drink and bantered with the dozen or so passengers as they settled into their seats. Anyone on a first visit through Indian Country surely would find her "exotic." Under a woolen vest woven with an Indian design, a heavy silver *concha* belt encircled the waist of her plain grayish dress. A distinctive beaded bolo tie hung around her neck, and silver bracelets gripped her arms. At the edge of Gallup, the train glided slowly eastward past a group of tall, phony, plywood "teepees" just south of the tracks. The entire ensemble, intended to attract tourists to Indian Country, looked abandoned. As passengers stared at the shambles, Zonnie said tartly, "Contrary to popular belief, all Indians do not live in teepees." Through her dress and demeanor she prompted her passengers to look beyond stereotypes.[4]

East of Gallup the train enters a wide, flat plateau. Tall buttes rise before the endless western horizon. Two buttes, Pyramid Peak and Church Rock, and a refinery sprawling at their base starkly contrast what nature and human beings have wrought on this land. The name of one of the exits from Interstate 40 that parallels the train tracks is simply "Refinery." Most of the time on this leg of the Chief's journey, the landscape outside the train's windows appears barren, brown, and sere, yet it holds promise. The sculpted red sandstone formations change color and shape as the earth rotates and follows its orbit.

Surprisingly intimate before a train car full of strangers, Zonnie told passengers, "My family history follows tribal history." Her first name is derived from the Navajo word *adzaani*, meaning "lady." But "Gorman" is the figment of a nineteenth-century U.S. cavalry officer who was rounding up Indian children for the boarding schools that had been established to "civilize" Indians. The now-defunct policy—"grab 'em and drag 'em to school"— separated children from families in a systematic attempt to remove all traces of their Native identities: language, history, religion, dress—and names. As surely as European Americans took artifacts and remains from the ground, they snatched Indian children away from parents, communities, and culture. When a group of Navajo children stopped at Fort Defiance in Arizona on their way to the Santa Fe Indian School, the American soldiers gave them new names drawn from the post's roster. The soldiers wrote "Nelson Carl Gorman" on a piece of paper and hung it around Zonnie's grandfather's neck. "That's how we received our name—from an army roster," she said matter-of-factly. Throughout the journey, the passengers, who were all non-Indian, listened in silence. At this story, however, one woman muttered wryly, "My God, we were wonderful when we came here."

As the train climbs to the Continental Divide, 7,300 feet above sea level, the landscape changes rapidly to low stands of conifers—the last substantial patch of greenery until Albuquerque. Then the train descends into a dry, flat, wide corridor between buttes, distant hills, and mountains. This is a land dotted with small houses, including hogans, traditional eight-sided Navajo dwellings—not a teepee in sight.[5] As the train nears the halfway point from Gallup to Albuquerque, the land speaks dramatically about the natural forces that have shaped it. Blackened, pockmarked, otherworldly lava beds that Spanish explorers called the *mal pais* (bad country) sprawl along both sides of the tracks. About one hundred thousand acres of these remnants of volcanic eruptions form El Malpais National Monument. Volcanic activity began millions of years ago, and the lava flowed as recently as the eleventh century AD, when this area was well populated.

Zonnie directed passengers to look past the *mal pais* at some small yellow hills north of the tracks, not a creation of nature but of human beings—piles of uranium tailings from the mines where many Native Americans worked in the years following World War II. One of the passengers, an engineer from Washington DC, connected to the scene outside the speeding train. "I once worked in an enrichment plant in Ohio, and I knew about the uranium deposits here," he said quietly. Like other Americans, however, the engineer did not know the history that had affected our national life and that of Indians so deeply. In 1950 Paddy Martinez, a Navajo medicine man, discovered deposits near Grants, New Mexico, at Haystack Mountain, which became the largest uranium-producing area in the United States. By 1979 more than twenty companies were operating or planning about seventy mines in the San Juan Basin.[6] That year, an accident at the Three Mile Island power plant effectively ended the nuclear power industry, which collapsed during the 1980s. New Mexico's uranium mines and mills closed, one after another, creating economic disaster for both white and

Native communities. White mine workers, accustomed to following the vagaries of mineral extraction, moved on to jobs elsewhere, but Natives, tied to their land, stayed and hoped to find other work. Many Navajo miners continue to exhibit ill health resulting from their work.

Standing sentinel over this broad landscape, Mount Taylor punctuates the wide, clear sky and rises to 11,300 feet above sea level. The peak comes clearly into view just past Grants and is visible almost all the way to Albuquerque. Like the Pecos dig, Carl Gorman's new name, and children disappearing into boarding schools, the mountain's history speaks to European American appropriation. Zonnie explained that it is one of the four sacred mountains—one in each of the four cardinal directions across Arizona, Colorado, and New Mexico—that define the Diné homeland. In the Navajo creation story, First Man and First Woman created this mountain, called Tsoodzi or Doot 'izhii Dziil (Turquoise Mountain of Strength). The four mountains shelter the people and help maintain order and balance in the universe.[7] The Spaniards renamed Tsoodzi, the sacred mountain of the south, San Mateo, and to commemorate their conquest of this land, the Americans re-renamed it for Zachary Taylor. The Acoma Pueblos also hold the mountain sacred, and they call it Kaweshtima (Place of Snow); for Laguna, Zuni, and the Hopis, the mountain has cultural significance. Today, Mount Taylor is within the Cibola National Forest, and the American Indians have never abandoned its sanctity. In June 2009 the state of New Mexico's Cultural Properties Review Committee permanently designated Mount Taylor as a traditional cultural property.[8]

How the Gormans got their name and how Mount Taylor got its name helps explain why many American Indians are passionate about restoring Native names for their landmarks or removing them as sports mascots. Otherwise sympathetic non-Indians might bemoan the energy that Indians expend on such efforts. Names are no small matter, in part because they are basic identifiers in any culture. Restoring names is an act of reclamation, a righting of wrongs. European American conquerors frequently deprived Indians of their personal names as well as the names for their places and landmarks and replaced them with English, Spanish, or French ones. The conquerors' names conjure many associations, from violation of sacred places to kidnapping of Native children. On their side, whites debate the use of "American Indian" versus "Native American." That conversation is something of a nonstarter; Indians usually identify themselves by their tribal names and often with their clan lineages or band locations.

Indians are quietly retrieving their own names not only in introductions but also in wider contexts. Some tribes retain or have reinstituted naming ceremonies for infants, sprinkling sacred cornmeal over their newborns and giving them Native names used within the family and tribe along with non-Indian names to use at school. Indians are increasingly and publicly restoring the original names for their tribes. The Navajos call themselves Diné, the People, and the entire Iroquois League is Haudenosaunee, People of the Long House. Turtle Island—a designation for North America—flows easily from many Indian lips; this evocative name derives from a creation story common to several tribes—Seminole and Caddo, for instance—in which the earth was formed on the shell of a giant turtle.[9]

Using Indian names can be controversial. Days after Hopi soldier Lori Piestewa was killed in Iraq in 2003, Arizona governor Janet Napolitano proposed to rename a Phoenix landmark, Squaw Peak, in her honor. Piestewa was the first Native American woman to be killed in combat. To implement the proposal, the state's Board on Geographic and Historic Names would have to set aside a long-held policy of waiting five years before renaming a place after a deceased person. Reaction was swift. The board received more than five hundred communications from both supporters and opponents of setting aside the policy. Despite outright hostility, the state board decided to rename the peak in July 2003. The federal board held to its policy and approved the change in April 2008, five years, nearly to the date, after Napolitano's proposal.[10]

Although Squaw Peak is now Piestewa Peak, Mount Taylor remains Mount Taylor, despite its new cultural protection. Nearing Albuquerque, with the mountain's companionship, the train enters Acoma and Laguna lands. Zonnie directed our sights toward Acoma Pueblo, though it was too far away to see clearly from the train. The pueblos are familiar to visitors to the Southwest, yet their history is not well known. With the exception of the Hopis in Arizona and Isleta del Sur in El Paso, all the Pueblo people today live in New Mexico in communities strung out mostly along the Rio Grande and its tributaries. These people are the descendants of those who built the great cities and towns at Chaco Canyon and other remarkable sites in the Southwest and established compact towns along waterways. The conquistadores dipped into the Catholic litany of saints to rename some of the towns and claim them for the Crown and church.

Acoma was established around AD 900, at about the same time that the great Chacoan culture—eighty-five miles in a straight line due north—was developing. For defense—and perhaps as part of a signaling network that archaeologists now believe covered thousands of square miles across the region— the Acomans built their citadel on a butte rising 357 feet out of a surrounding plain, thus its European American nickname, "Sky City." Having established a civilization long before the Europeans arrived, Acoma had become so desperate for new revenues after the uranium mines closed that it opened a bingo parlor, Zonnie told us. It was New Mexico's first Indian bingo parlor, long before anyone could imagine what was to come; Acoma now has a modern casino.

The Chief continued along a high plateau. Multiple archaic and modern transcontinental pathways intersect this prime piece of multicultural real estate. Indigenous Americans beat footpaths across the plateau for trade and pilgrimages. Spanish and Mexican wagon trains traveled along the Camino Real, or Royal Road, between old Mexico and the northern capital of New Spain at Santa Fe. In the nineteenth century, railroad companies laid track parallel to the east–west trails, and then in the 1930s Route 66, the first paved transcontinental highway, followed alongside the tracks. Interstate 40 displaced Route 66 in the 1960s.

With Tsoodzi/Kaweshtima at our backs, we looked ahead to see the majestic Sandia Mountains, where in 1925 Boy Scouts on a hike found twelve-thousand-year-old remains of human activity in a cave. In winter, light from the setting sun casts a pink hue over the craggy peaks, so the conquistadores named the mountain range Sandia, the Spanish word for "watermelon." (Its Tiwa Pueblo name is Posu Gai Hoo-oo, Where Water Slides down Arroyo.) The eleven-thousand-foot Sandia Peak and its range loom above the Rio Grande valley and Albuquerque. As it descended from the mesas toward this massive landmark, the Chief turned into the gentler environment of the river's floodplain. It crossed the river at Isleta Pueblo and headed north, following the historic route of the Camino Real. As it approached Albuquerque, the train rolled past fields prepared for sowing and then an industrial zone.

Realizing that their time with Zonnie would end shortly, passengers peppered her with questions: Do Indians commute to jobs in Albuquerque? How do they live? Can they live off the land? Zonnie answered all the questions politely. I heard one mythology-besotted traveler suggest to her companion, "They may be living to some extent the way they lived two thousand years ago." I hoped Zonnie was out of earshot. By the time she stepped off the train, some passengers were already hurrying to meet friends and relations or stretching their legs along the platform before getting back on board. A few paused to speak with her, and she graciously accepted thanks and answered more questions.

Zonnie told me that during her years as a guide, the non-Indian passengers she had met held diverse views about Indians. Most have no idea what an Indian is, except what they've seen in popular culture. Among those who live in communities near reservations, some have little knowledge, while others are aware and have questions about current issues, such as reservation politics. A third and rarest group has many misconceptions, for instance, believing that Indians are just sitting around the reservations living off the federal hog, doing nothing.

Conversations about Indians seem split between Indian and non-Indian perspectives. Language reflects this divide, and Zonnie listed the complex and sometimes charged vocabulary for these dialogues that suggest that non-Indians and Indians still dance around our relationship: "white," "Indian," "American," "Native American," "non-Indian," "Anglo," "indigenous," "European," "Amerindian," and so on. Zonnie seemed genuinely gratified by the majority of the people who have traveled the rails with her: "There seems to be a deep, sincere interest in knowing facts. They're sick of the exaggerated stuff from Hollywood." Her attitude displayed compassion and even admiration for some whites and reflected one of the diverse Indian views of non-Indians. Zonnie and I parted at the station. She would spend a few hours in Albuquerque and then return on the westbound train, giving another seminar to its passengers—a shorter one, because at that time of year, night would fall early. Zonnie had a full life to live. At age twenty-four she was a single parent, with three children (including a set of twins), and she attended the University of New Mexico's branch campus in Gallup. I went home to write and file my story.

Circumstances in Indian Country and in Zonnie's life took some significant turns in the nearly fifteen years that passed after that train trip. During those years, my understanding of the complexity of modern Indian life grew as I covered more stories. An element of romanticizing that I had indulged in on the train ride had given way to some harder realities. Landmark legislation was driving revolutionary change. At the same time, the migration to cities had become a torrent, with Indians becoming expats, leaving their reservation homes and families. For some, the move meant new opportunities and success, yet for others, it was a wrenching experience. Still other Indians stayed home, despite difficult living conditions on reservations. As I began planning this book, I recalled Zonnie's comment that her tribe's history and her family's history coincided. I decided that returning to Zonnie could give me a perspective I needed, a broader picture of what had happened in Indian Country over the years: what had changed and what had not.

Locating Zonnie after so many years was a challenge, yet the process also illustrated how small—and how connected— the scattered Indian community is. After a year of searching in telephone directories and on the Internet, I despaired of finding her. I speculated that, like so many young Navajos, she had left the reservation. Then in November 2000 my teenage son and I attended the annual Native American Music Awards ceremony—the Nammys—at the University of New Mexico's Popejoy Hall. An audience of two thousand revelers filled the hall, mostly Indians from across the United States, well dressed in suits and dresses with flourishes like silver and turquoise jewelry, woven belts, and feathered or beaded headbands. The size and energy of the event stunned me. Thinking I might spot Zonnie, I searched the faces furtively, trying not to stare, not to settle my white eyes on any individual for too long. The evening included a special ceremony for two elderly Navajos who had been code talkers during World War II. They were among the four hundred Navajos that the Marine Corps had recruited to operate a complicated code system in the Pacific theater using their native language; the Japanese never cracked the code.[11] As the code talkers were using their language to win a war for America, the U.S. government was trying to kill Indian language and culture on reservations and in boarding schools. Rick West, of the nascent National Museum of the American Indian, and pro golfer Notah Begay (San Felipe Pueblo/Navajo) appeared on the stage to present the awards. The hall's lights dimmed, and a screen descended for a short film about the code talkers. Suddenly, a familiar face appeared on the screen; in a few minutes, her name flashed across the bottom—Zonnie Gorman! I took a sharp breath. The next day, I called the Nammy office in New York and was given the names of a couple of people associated with the film. I lucked out, and in a few days I found Zonnie in Gallup.

During the intervening years, everything—and nothing— had changed. Zonnie earned a degree in history from the University of Arizona, and she and her children were living with her mother, Mary, in Gallup—off the reservation but close to home. In February 2001 I drove out to Gallup for lunch and several hours of talk. New Mexico was emerging from winter, and despite snowfalls, the yard around Mary's middle-class ranch house was a desert place, dry and brown. Inside, the house was impossibly cluttered, the result of merging two households when Zonnie and her three boys moved in. It was first-class clutter, however. Books were everywhere—on shelves, in neatly stacked cartons, or on tables. Sports trophies, framed family photos, clothing, video tapes, and more covered every surface not taken up with books.

Zonnie disappeared for a few moments, leaving me with her mother. At seventy-six, Mary, a non-Indian, was only a bit stooped, and she was decked out in purple knit pants and a T-shirt. Getting Navajo runners to the Queensland games in Australia was on her mind, she told me; Arizona's team was composed mostly of young Indians. A major effort to locate all the Navajo code talkers was also consuming Mary and Zonnie. The film at the Nammys began to make sense; Carl Gorman, Mary's husband, had been one of the founders of the Code Talkers' Association and later its president. Mary and Zonnie were getting ready for a ceremony that would take place in Washington that summer, when President George W. Bush was to give the code talkers congressional medals. The women were helping to coordinate the trip to the award ceremonies for several of the living talkers and family representatives. Most of the men were in their eighties, although Carl had been significantly older than the others when he joined up as one of the first twenty-nine code talkers. "My husband was thirty-five. He lied about his age," Mary explained.

As Zonnie and I headed off to lunch, I tried to look at her unobtrusively; I wanted to examine her face closely, which would have been impolite. She seemed taller, bigger all around than I remembered. Her handsome, oval, tawny-skinned face lacked the sharp, high cheekbones of many full-blooded Navajos. She was wearing a simple, dark-blue outfit, and her dark hair, held in place by a soccer-mom headband, dropped straight to just below her shoulders. Earrings in the shape of turtles dangled from her pierced ears. Like so many Navajo women, Zonnie does not wear much jewelry during the day, saving it for special occasions, when women and men drape themselves with elaborate silver and turquoise necklaces, bracelets, belts, and more.

Zonnie Gorman on AMTRAK's Southwest Chief. Photo by Cary Herz.

Gangs appeared on the Navajo Reservation during the 1980s. Photo by Cary Herz.

As we talked, I learned for the first time about Zonnie's illustrious family of artists and activists. Her family had fought to recover the culture and patrimony that had nearly slipped away only a few decades before. The Gorman name might have come from an army roster, but it is renowned in Indian Country and far beyond. Carl, an artist, became one of the founders of the Native American studies program at the University of California, Davis. In 1973 the university established the C. N. Gorman Art Museum, which features contemporary American Indian works, in his honor; he died in 1998. The Gormans have been noted silversmiths, and Zonnie's half-brother R.C. was a prominent and popular painter who died in November 2005. Zonnie was born in California, and she has spent most of her life on the reservation, with some time in the small and tight Indian community in Davis.

The Gormans witnessed the birth of the modern American Indian rights movement. Zonnie explained that Carl was not a "building burner" type of activist, although many of his Native students participated in the occupation at Alcatraz that energized Indian political life.[12] As Zonnie was growing up, she saw rapid change in Indian Country. The attitude of young people during the 1970s was straightforward. "Finish high school and get the hell off the reservation. Run and don't look back. There was an underlying pride in being Navajo, but it wasn't expressed, it was suppressed," Zonnie said. She explained that this flight was born out of the experience of her parents and grandparents, and its effects reverberate to today.

> There were generations and generations of Indian people raised to build defense mechanisms to avoid being destroyed. When you're in a situation like that, when you are taken to boarding school and you are beaten for speaking your language, and you have children, you don't want your children to go through that. So you speak English and try to give your kids a little better handle on dealing with the situation so they don't have to go through what you went through. You find that in a lot of typical Indian families that went through the experience; they'll try to protect the next generation. Slowly in the process of doing that, you're doing exactly what the government wants you to do. You're slowly giving up something.

Zonnie's family members were among the several generations of young Indians who were placed in boarding schools that the United States operated either directly or through churches. A government report published as early as 1928 described the deadening effect of the institutions and the low level of funding for them.[13] Boarding school alumni revealed grim stories about sometimes brutal treatment: short haircuts that violated traditional practices, mandatory military uniforms, sexual abuse, and beatings when they spoke their native languages. Some Indians now are using class-action suits and other activities to retrieve this chapter of their history with whites and, if possible, the souls they nearly lost. Zonnie's father, Carl, was one of those boarding school students. He was an atypical Indian kid living on the reservation in Arizona with his relatively prosperous and well-educated Christian family. His parents sent Carl to a Christian school near Gallup, but for refusing to respond to a teacher, the twelve-year-old Carl was chained to a wall in a dark basement and fed only bread and water—for a week. He and two relatives ran away from the school and headed home on foot, a three-day trip in bitter cold, snow, and rain. Carl's father refused to return him to the school, and six months later the boy went to Albuquerque for his education.[14]

New thinking about the boarding school experience from both Native and white scholars has produced some reevaluation of them, however. The schools aimed to assimilate Indians into mainstream American life by destroying their culture, but in some cases the children and their families resisted—moved the target, so to speak—and strengthened rather than weakened their cultural identity. In addition, schools did offer "advancement" for Indians, avenues to jobs and to the military, and this book includes some of those "successes." In a small but poignant development, some boarding school alumni founded a marching band for the Navajo Nation after they returned to the reservation during the 1930s. Since then, the fifty-member (men and women) band has played locally and in the Rose Bowl Parade and for U.S. presidential inaugurations. Its uniforms are based on traditional Navajo attire—velveteen shirts, silver and turquoise jewelry, and moccasins. Members in the farthest reaches of the reservation practice on their own and must travel to Window Rock for rehearsals.[15]

Although she was split between the reservation and California, Zonnie considers Gallup her base. Like other Indians, Zonnie fears that her family will lose its Indianness, and sticking close to the reservation can help secure her children's Navajo identity. Ironically, that identity is threatened in part because her children have not had the crushing school experiences that members of her family endured, an endurance and resistance that she believes helped define them. "You worry that if they don't have to go through that, they'll lose the memory of it. And when you lose the memory of it, it is no longer an important part of your life," she said. Clearly, no Indian parents would wish their children to undergo beatings and degradations, but today's young people, even while seeing the residual trauma of those events, miss their cultural impact.

Zonnie believes that the young hear and want more of traditional Navajo life than her generation. When she was growing up, a traditional Navajo teenager who knew about clans and ceremonies and spoke the language was called "John," a derogatory word, although Zonnie did not know its origin. Today, not only do teenagers know their clans, but spoken Navajo is the "in" thing. "I see among the younger generation a strong, renewed pride in who they are," she said. Even more pressing for her children's identity is the shadowy issue of blood quantum, the degree of an individual's separation from Indian forebears.[16] Because her mother and her children's father were not Navajo, Zonnie's sons are only one-quarter Navajo. If they marry outside the tribe, her grandchildren will be denied tribal membership because their blood quantum will be greatly diluted.

Despite the pride among some Navajo youngsters, Zonnie wonders about the direction others take. "I never believed we'd have gang problems," Zonnie said. During the 1980s, Los

Angeles gangs like the Bloods and Crips expanded onto the Navajo Reservation, terrifying residents with their baggy pants, drugs, brawls, and drive-by shootings.[17] By 2009 the number of documented gangs had increased to 225, from 75 in 1997. The nation's small police department was hard-pressed to answer gang-related calls. At first, bewildered parents and elders denied a problem. The ancient kinship system—parents, aunts, uncles, and kin—seemed to be dissolving, however. The gangs had penetrated the Navajo world through a double-whammy: the influence of pop culture through television and the breakdown of cultural and family values. Gang graffiti covering walls in reservation communities "is just not Navajo," Zonnie said.

Other trends reach into the reservation. Economic development and new technologies appear benign, yet they seem to weaken the age-old conduits of language and culture, reducing elders' influence on tribal life. So Zonnie plays a balancing game with Navajo and white worlds by living near the reservation. Although all three of her children were baptized in their father's Catholic faith and commuted daily to Saint Michael, a Catholic school on the reservation, they can choose their own paths to spiritual growth. She hoped that keeping the children near the reservation would strengthen their cultural identity and especially their knowledge of their sacred homeland. Still, the three boys went away to college.

Although she is strong in her Navajo identity, Zonnie has yet to reconcile her love-hate relationship with the Navajo Nation. She said that "exciting things are happening" on the reservation. But as I learned over the years between our meetings, the tribe has been leaping forward and stumbling back. Blessed with a breathtaking landscape, the Navajo Nation is dynamic, with influential traditional peoples and Diné geeks who are wiring the reservation with cutting-edge technologies. The work of its artists can be found from Frankfurt to Los Angeles. Authors carry on the tribe's storytelling traditions, and while writers like Lucy Tapahonso, Laura Tohe, and Irvin Morris are not household names, their books are more widely available.

The Diné are a troubled people, however. Tribal government has roiled for decades, especially beginning in the late 1980s. Four-term tribal chairman Peter MacDonald was convicted in a federal court on charges of kidnapping and conspiracy to commit burglary and sentenced to fourteen years in a federal prison. During the turmoil, two hundred MacDonald supporters stormed the tribal offices, and Navajo police fired on the crowd, killing two of them. A period after MacDonald saw some stability and then a succession of leaders who lasted for about a year, even as the reservation's economy was tanking. In 2003, when the new leaders gave their wives jobs in the tribal offices, the ensuing uproar forced the women to resign.

The Diné stagger from one economic "fix" to another. For instance, energy is still important, and the Navajo Nation has spent decades freeing itself from poorly conceived leases with mineral extraction companies that undervalued its resources. Then in 2007 Navajo officials wanted to enlarge a coal-fired energy plant that would bring $50 million to the treasury annually. Some Navajos joined with environmental organizations in resisting the project because of its carbon dioxide emissions.[18] Similarly, Navajos twice voted against gaming, although the tribal council circumvented the votes. The nation has danced around tourism as a growth option. Although tourism can promote understanding, the industry has disrupted the privacy that traditional Navajos hold dear. Zonnie thinks that the tribe is not exploiting noninvasive tourism like hiking and bed-and-breakfast hogans. Tourists pay up to $300 a night to spend time in an isolated hogan with dirt floors and no running water or electricity—a dream for some white tourists. "They'll pay anything for it," she said with bemusement.

Non-Indians have no such ambivalence about tourism. At the center of non-Indian tourism is the Inter-Tribal Indian Ceremonial, where Zonnie was program director beginning in 1997. The Ceremonial started in 1922, when white businesspeople saw an opportunity to lure tourists to Gallup to see a "dying culture" and buy Indian goods from non-Indian traders. For sympathetic non-Indians, another aim was to save Native arts and traditions. Indians from many tribes came to the Ceremonial and Gallup's numerous trading posts, where they exchanged jewelry, blankets, and sheep for provisions, raw materials for their crafts, and cash. The Ceremonial was also a time to see friends and enjoy the social dances. By the 1970s, Zonnie said, the Ceremonial had grown from a rather informal, low-key event that was essentially a county fair to a highly commercialized one with a "See Live Indians" tone. She had participated in the Ceremonial as a dancer for two decades, and it was part of her life. But in her job as program director she was stunned when old-time Gallupians referred to "our Indians." After three years, she left the job. As Gallup's official visitors' guide shows, the town has locked Indian creativity in a box that appeals primarily to stereotypes and non-Indian attitudes, notwithstanding a nod to contemporary arts.[19]

Gallup is just one of dozens of towns on the borders of reservations that depend on Indians and their world for their economic well-being; health care and mining and mineral extraction, including refining, are big industries. With a population of about twenty thousand nearly evenly divided between white and Indian, Gallup serves as the seat for McKinley County. The county's population is 75 percent Indian, and it ranks third among U.S. counties with the largest number of Indians—fifty-seven thousand—after Los Angeles and Maricopa (Phoenix). Gallupians are in dire straits, with 37 percent living below the poverty level, compared with 19 percent for the state. Nearly

100 percent of the children at one school live below the poverty level, and the school is a source of regular food for them.[20] Located in the Sun Belt, Gallup looks like a Rust Belt town, with decrepit storefronts and barren planters lining some streets. The town has made efforts to turn around, however. The Southwest Indian Foundation has restored the old Santa Fe railroad station as a museum for Indian arts.[21] A downtown mural project recounts both sad and proud moments in Gallup's history. The recently remodeled courthouse has become the center for a revitalized downtown, with nightly Indian dances during the summer months.

Gallup portrays itself as a visitors' gateway to Indian Country. During its heyday, the town thrived with railroad activity and its location on U.S. Route 66. Gallup turned increasingly to tourism beginning in the 1920s and 1930s, especially playing up Route 66 and Indian culture not only in the annual Ceremonial but also in other events that have a heavy overlay of Indian themes. The retail sector boasts more than one hundred trading posts, galleries, and shops that sell goods from fake tomahawks to exquisitely hand-wrought jewelry and pottery; most are owned by non-Indians. For Navajos from the eastern end of the reservation and Zunis, Gallup is a center for shopping, entertainment, and laundromats, which are virtually nonexistent on reservations.[22]

The town is also in the "business" of Indian health care; the Indian Health Service's center is the second largest employer.[23] Health care and alcoholism have a symbiotic relationship. The Navajo Reservation prohibits alcohol consumption, so Indians head to Gallup for drink they purchase at non-Indian-owned stores. Indian alcoholism provides jobs for health care providers who treat Indians with alcohol-related diseases like diabetes. The alcohol wars seesaw regularly. Activists lobby legislators to shut down the liquor industry; liquor lobbyists try to defeat reform measures such as banning drive-up and Sunday sales. Some problem bars have been closed, but the degradation of Indian alcoholics continues. Officials from the Navajo Nation, Gallup, and other border communities in New Mexico and Arizona have signed an agreement to address a common sight—Indians who come to town, drink to the point of collapse, and become victims of assault and other crimes. Despite such efforts, liquor dealers did not agree to limit store hours; they did not muster support for the measure among themselves.[24]

Zonnie has seen slow, positive change. "In the 1970s it was very exploitive in the sense of 'See Live Indians.' In the 1980s Gallup used to call itself the 'Indian capital of the world.' They're slowly moving away from that mentality. They're also taking a renewed interest in historic Gallup. They're doing more outdoor tourism. They're looking more at who they are," she said.

Some non-Indian businesspeople in Gallup acknowledge their debt to the Indian community. Zonnie took me to the Ellis Tanner Trading Company south of town, along the road to Zuni Pueblo. Tanner is a fourth-generation trader; his great-grandfather migrated westward with other Mormons. The trading post's large central room is packed with Indian treasures, cases of jewelry and pots, hundreds of rugs, and a score of saddles. In a far corner, a butcher's case holds cuts of lamb and mutton from the ubiquitous sheep that the Navajos raise for wool and food.

High above the goods is the *Circle of Light*. Using his own money, Tanner commissioned Navajo artist Chester Kahn to paint a mural that covers the store's upper walls. Circling over the customers is a continuous line of fifty-nine portraits of Navajos who had succeeded in their chosen fields or interests. They have balanced being Navajo with the demands of the modern world while contributing to the well-being of the Navajo people. As we walked around, necks craned, Zonnie read off some of the names. Taylor McKenzie was the first Navajo medical doctor, and Beulah Allen was the first Navajo woman physician. Fred Begay, the first Navajo to hold a doctorate in nuclear physics, never finished high school and worked at Los Alamos National Laboratory. Annie Wauneka, the first woman to be elected to the Navajo Tribal Council in 1950, was a tireless advocate for health care; she received the Medal of Freedom from President Lyndon Johnson. Zonnie's father was represented as a code talker, although the mural could not tell his full story. "He grew up listening to opera in the middle of the rez," she said. As we came to the end of the mural, Zonnie pointed to a painting of a blanket hanging from a portal that was inscribed, "Walk in Beauty." The blanket's design includes an opening, a "spirit line," an imperfection in the weave that represents life's imperfections and life's continuity. It allows the weaver's creative spirit to travel to her next creation. "Navajos are amazed at how many successful people we have in all walks of life," Zonnie said.

Tanner also set up the Circle of Light Navajo Educational Project (CLNEP), a nonprofit organization that offers more role models to Navajo young people and assists in educating them and non-Navajos about the tribe's legacy through programs, projects, curriculum development, and research. Plans include an oral history project utilizing the mural. Its ultimate aim is to establish a Navajo history and cultural library and archive facility—not a museum, Zonnie was careful to say. She is the project coordinator for the organization. The job is one of several she has had in education, nonprofit organizations, and tourism, the kinds of jobs she favors, in which she interprets Navajo life for outsiders. "What I do better is to help build a bridge so that non-Indian people can understand," she said.

We stopped by Tanner's office, remarkably sparse compared with the riches piled up out in the store. Tanner told me that he had funded the mural project and the nonprofit organization "because I got tired of having the young people complaining that there was nothing for them. It's all built on trust and friendship. I'm more Navajo than I am white. I've got a white man's skin, a Navajo heart." Despite Tanner's concern, his generosity with the CLNEP, and the assurance from Zonnie and others that Tanner is "one of the good guys," my journalist's skepticism was like a mild toothache that wouldn't go away. Over many generations, Indians could be excellent partners, manipulating a trade to their benefit. But more often they have come out on the short end in deals at trading posts on reservations and in border towns.[25]

Private efforts like the CLNEP can be tools for consolidating culture and identity for young people. Still, how much of an impact they have on keeping young Navajos on the reservation is questionable. In mainstream parlance, "how ya gonna keep 'em down on the farm after they've seen Paree"? What bureaucrats call economic issues translate into severe unemployment, limited educational opportunities, isolation, and lack of infrastructure and modern conveniences for many parts of the reservation. Hopelessness engenders alcoholism and substance abuse—Navajo police saw a 100 percent increase in the use of methamphetamine between 2000 and 2005—as well as physical and sexual abuse of women and children. For those under nineteen, the rate of suicide is double the nation's.[26] Given these conditions, it comes as no surprise that about one hundred thousand Navajos live off the reservation. Raised with pride in their Native origins, an expansion of Navajo culture, and language classes in schools, the young have college degrees in hand, but they cannot live on the economically depressed homeland.

Zonnie understands firsthand what young people face. "Over the years of raising three sons and listening to endless teenage conversations when they have friends over, they talk about coming home after they graduate from college. I have heard these same conversations among many other young people I come across in work," she said. Zonnie believes that the Navajo Nation must shift from what is essentially a government-controlled economy to entrepreneurship, although the mainstream marketplace is unfamiliar to most tribal members. Banks have begun to make home loans to Navajos in recent years, but business loans are virtually impossible because of a lack of collateral. "Sheep? A pickup truck?" she asked archly, recognizing that those might be the only assets of a typical family.

Monumental changes have occurred in Indian Country over the past three decades. Zonnie had witnessed many of them because of her family's history and her broad, somewhat hopeful perspective of life both on and off the reservation. During the 1970s and 1980s Indians took their cue from the civil rights movement and their own "radicals" like the American Indian Movement (AIM), which began its activities in 1968. Some of AIM's activities gained significant media coverage. This was particularly true of its seventy-one-day occupation in 1973 of Oglala Lakota tribal offices in Wounded Knee, South Dakota, on the Pine Ridge Reservation. Bullets flew between the occupiers and a large federal force, but a judge dismissed all charges against the Indians in a subsequent trial. During this time, Zonnie said, Indians began to think: "Wait. Dig in our heels. Stop going down this road. Do something—because we are losing our culture and our language." This personal and community pause led almost imperceptibly into repatriation in its broadest senses—retrieval, rebirth, and recovery.

The energy in Indian Country certainly comes in some measure from the rapid economic and social development that has taken place over the past two decades. No doubt, gaming has contributed to this growth. As Anthony Pico, chairman of the Viejas band of Kumeyaay Indians in Southern California, put it, "Gaming to me is a factory that fashions the bows and arrows that will create a place for our people seven generations from now."[27] But economic progress is occurring among gaming and nongaming tribes alike, according to a study from the Harvard Project on Indian Economic Development at the John F. Kennedy School of Government.[28]

Many tribes now have the financial wherewithal, whether from gaming, natural resources, business development, or other sources, to press claims regarding land, sacred sites, education, governance, sovereignty, and religion—all elements of Indian life that have been under attack for decades. Indian America is stronger today, despite persistent pathologies that result from extreme poverty and spiritual dislocation. Indians are recovering identity and cultures that they nearly lost along with their "artifacts," ancestors, and lands despite centuries of resistance. New resources and strength also support a spirit of collaboration across Indian Country.

The Harvard report also points out that economic success bears a direct relationship to strong and legitimate institutions of self-government.[29] In 1975 Congress passed the Indian Self-Determination and Education Act, and President Richard M. Nixon signed it. Indian Country changed forever. The act asserted that the federal government had failed in its management of tribal affairs and recognized that Indians would never surrender their desire to manage their own lives. The legislation acknowledged Indian sovereignty and turned over more and more responsibility for governance to the tribes. Thus began a chain of events the end of which is still not clear more than three decades later. On many issues—gaming, health care, environmental protection, education, land claims, religious freedom, and adoption—Indians have been using the act to cut a sovereign swath across the United States in a momentous process that has picked up speed in the past decade. The Self-Determination Act, Zonnie said, "was like the screeching halt of the *Titanic*. Now there's this long process of having the ship turn around. It's still not out of danger, but it's a lot less dangerous than twenty years ago."[30] Thirteen years passed between passage of the act, which drives governance in Indian Country, and NAGPRA, which is a cultural and spiritual engine.

Our lunch conversation eventually turned to the day we had met on the Southwest Chief.[31] In all, Zonnie had worked on the train part time for eleven years, and she estimated that she talked with nearly fifty thousand travelers. She sometimes played a game of "chicken" that taught passengers about cultural discomfort. Taking her time, Zonnie would repeatedly tell a group of passengers that for Navajos eye contact is impolite in certain situations. At the same time, she maintained strong eye contact with them. Then in a split second, their eyes would look away from her. Zonnie relished those moments when she could show passengers in a firsthand manner the discomfort of being the cultural "other," the *object* of staring eyes.

Zonnie recalled one of her more memorable moments on the train—one that reflects her ironic yet hopeful approach to the situation of Indians in America. A newly married non-Indian couple showed her their Navajo embossed "storyteller" wedding rings. Zonnie told the newlyweds that the rings portray common sights on the reservation: a hogan, a horse or sheep, a corral, clouds in the sky, and an outhouse. The young man said of the outhouse: "Well, that'll remind us that once in a while you have to put up with a little bit of shit."

Zonnie's and her family's lives and her tribe's history together constitute a metaphor for Indian America. Pushed and pulled against white America, Indians have navigated more than "a little bit of shit." The Indian Self-Determination and Education Act, NAGPRA, language preservation, and gaming are recent developments for peoples who have a complex history on a continent where they have lived for perhaps thirty thousand years; the Diné migrated to the Southwest around 1450, however. DNA evidence links ancient peoples along the entire Pacific region.[32] In that context, the European Americans just arrived.

Navajo Nation president Joe Shirley Jr. has pleaded with tribal members to stick close to their homeland. Shortly after he took office, he spoke with Diné living off the reservation in Utah. He reminded the expatriates that they have an obligation to participate in mutual family support. Shirley acknowledged the difficulties of reservation life, including high unemployment and lack of basic services like running water and electricity. "They say we're 30 years behind the times, and it doesn't appear we'll be catching up any time soon," he said. He urged them to come home at least for a visit and asked those who were financially secure to "share it with the world, share it with your relatives."[33]

Zonnie countered that many Diné remain on the reservation, and even those who leave maintain homes there. Also, expatriates are not far from home, wherever they live. "The strongest reason for remaining on or near the reservation is spiritual. We are part of the land and the land is part of us. For Navajos, home is within the four sacred mountains." Zonnie noted that when a child is born, the detached umbilical cord is buried with prayers in a special place. "This ensures in a spiritual way that the child will always know where home is," she said.[34]

3

AN ENCAMPMENT

After our train ride in 1988, Zonnie returned to Gallup until 2010, when she began doctoral studies at the University of New Mexico in Albuquerque. During those years thousands of Navajos, Lakotas, Potawatomis, Oneidas, and others left their reservations, took the train or the interstate to nearby cities, and stayed there. As recent censuses have shown, most Indians don't live on reservations, much less in teepees, hogans, or longhouses; they have moved to cities and suburbs. If repatriation can pull Indians back into their tribal or group identities, urban migration is a centrifugal counterforce, spinning Indians out of their physical and spiritual homelands. Nevertheless, Indians try to reconcile the demands of their new lives in the city with homes left behind. For many, the city is like "an encampment we have set up out there that extends our territory," according to a commentary on urban Indians in Albuquerque.[1]

Propelled by trade, conflict, or environmental conditions, Natives historically moved freely, sometimes over long distances.

Agricultural peoples rotated among farm and garden plots over hundreds of square miles. Hunters traversed the land to follow bison herds. During the twelfth century, Ancestral Puebloans consumed chocolate stored in cylindrical jars found at Chaco Canyon's Pueblo Bonito. The chocolate could have come only from far-off Mesoamerica, and the vessels' design was distinctly from that region. Economic exchanges were common among the geographically disparate California tribelets, although they lacked the political alliance of the Haudenosaunee (Iroquois) League of the northeastern nations.

Native populations altered settlement patterns for various reasons that included their war and peace relationships with other groups. Ancestral Natives enjoyed urban life in well-designed and engineered centers like Chaco Canyon, Mesa Verde, Pecos, and Cahokia. Those populations moved because of environmental conditions or conquest. Smallpox ravaged the Bayogoulas west of present-day New Orleans in the eighteenth century. They nevertheless welcomed into their community refugees from nearby villages devastated by disease and war.[2] In the nineteenth century, federal policy forced entire peoples out of their traditional lands. After World War II, termination and relocation policies were designed to push Indians off reservations and into jobs in urban areas. Today, American Indians find each other in complex, sometimes disheartening American cities.[3]

Population shifts beg the question of mutual cultural exchange if not assimilation. Scholars have created a long record that tells us something of the historic Indian diaspora both before and after European contact. Academics have also examined contemporary migrations, including trying to define what has been called the "urban Indian identity."[4] While the migration is big news in Indian Country, the rest of America hardly notices. New York and Los Angeles have the largest numbers of Indians, but they are less than 1 percent of the populations of those cities. Smaller numbers of Indians have a proportionately greater visibility in cities like Anchorage, Tulsa, Oklahoma City, and Albuquerque.[5]

Repatriation in its strictest sense has been specific to distinct groups, but a cogent cultural picture for expatriation is unclear. The urban Indian community is as diverse as urban European and Asian groups. Native Americans come to the city from hundreds of tribes. They weave new lives amid brothers and sisters from other tribal groups. They carry different languages, histories, and traditions, and they encounter the most intense form of mainstream culture. Their settlement patterns differ. Like other ethnic groups, they sometimes huddle together in neighborhoods, or they move in stages, one generation, and then another. If urban American Indian culture has any definition, it is akin to one from physics—a critical mass of individuals, shocked by the city into a fluid state of becoming.[6]

Young people have led the most recent two-decade-old migration. What pulls them to cities is the push from desperate conditions on many reservations. Isolated communities sometimes lack even the basics—like water. In 2002 a Navajo town in northwestern New Mexico finally got a spigot that delivered water to their community center so they no longer had to drive twenty-five miles to get it. They threw a party to celebrate, with a medicine man blessing the water station and a feast of mutton stew and fry bread.[7] Education offers little for Pine Ridge's high school, for instance, where only about 40 percent of any incoming freshman class will graduate.[8] Crime and violence in Indian Country is hard evidence of despair, sometimes accompanied by anesthetizing alcoholism and other substance abuses, and it cuts across tribes indiscriminately.[9]

Suicide can roll over a reservation like a series of plagues. Over five months of 2009–10, five residents—including four teenagers—of the Navajo community of Thoreau, New Mexico, population 1,800, were suicides; two others made unsuccessful attempts. Family members and officials offered a number of explanations: the extremely depressed economy, easy access to drugs, boredom, and the failure of school officials and families to follow up with troubled youth. Less than a year earlier, four Mescalero Apaches between the ages of fourteen and twenty-five, near Ruidoso, New Mexico, killed themselves over a three-month period.[10] Here and there, especially among gaming tribes, this bleak picture does have some bright spots.[11]

If the reasons for leaving the reservation are numerous, so are the paths Natives take once they get to the city. Because of the texture of the Indian presence there, Albuquerque is a good model for the looks and sounds of an urban Indian community. The 2000 census counted 22,000 Indians in a population of 450,000. Albuquerque's Indian leaders believe the figure is closer to 30,000, based on the addresses of patients served by the regional Indian Health Service unit; that would make Indians nearly 7 percent rather than 5 percent of the population. An additional 26,000 live on their tribal lands within a fifty-mile radius of Albuquerque.[12] Those who commute into the city for work, school, and shopping enhance the Native presence. Indians have a high profile. They are at the university, workplace, mall, and multiplex; they are college students, doctors, lawyers, teachers, social workers, carpenters, house and office cleaners, hotel room maids, computer consultants, clerks, artists, and business owners. Albuquerqueans also regularly see Indians when they attend Native events in town or at the pueblos and Navajo Reservation for feast days, arts fairs, and casinos.

Although Indians are represented by more than one hundred tribes, Navajos comprise the dominant group in Albuquerque because their reservation lands are nearby.[13] Pueblos from several villages are Albuquerque's neighbors, while people from other groups arrive from homelands that are hundreds of miles away. Success in the city can be elusive, and outright failure is easy to find. The Indian poverty rate in Albuquerque is around 23 percent, double that of the city's overall rate but lower than that on many reservations. Indians comprise about 19 percent of Albuquerque's homeless population, which numbers about thirteen hundred on any given night.[14]

Living in a "transitional" neighborhood in downtown Albuquerque, our family saw the people behind those numbers; Indians occasionally slept in our side yard. In summer's relentless heat and winter's bitter cold, they sought refuge in downtown's alleys and parks or under railroad bridges. Some ventured into wildcat camps in the Bosque, the name of the woodlands flanking the Rio Grande. Lugging backpacks, they were haggard, and sometimes their hands sculpted a brown paper bag into the telltale shape of a beer can or liquor bottle.

Native American families in Albuquerque don't do as well as the general population; in 1990 the city's median income was about $28,000 and that of its urban Indians $20,000.[15] But the Navajo spigot and Pine Ridge's high school remind us that things can be worse. Moving probably means getting a better job than what's available on the reservation. About 64 percent of Indians employed in Albuquerque are in technical, managerial, professional, sales, and administrative support positions, compared with 36 percent having such employment on the reservation.[16]

Some scholars who have analyzed urban Indian migration and its consequences for Native culture portray a cohesive, in particular, a "pan-Indian," urban culture. But individuals in Albuquerque—educators, activists, social workers, counselors, and community planners—see a panoply of urban Indian experiences and offer a narrative that bucks such generalization.[17] They see some who are desperate, line up at church soup kitchens and shelters, or panhandle; the most despairing seek a drink or a fix. They also see parents working to put food on the table, to find a dentist or doctor, and to cope with children and teens who become more distant with every passing day. More than mere witnesses, those who are Indian are also embedded in the narrative of their people.

An important stop for both newcomers and longtime urban Indians is the Albuquerque Indian Center, in the Trumbull neighborhood on the city's east side. Trumbull is home to the largest concentration of the city's Indians—about 20 percent. Some of the poorest families—especially young women and their children—land here. Coming from economically distressed reservations, the women often head into low-paying domestic service with few or no benefits, and some shattered souls turn to prostitution. The children bring low reading, writing, and even speaking abilities from reservation schools.[18] One former counselor, Norman Sitting Up, described some of the most despairing who arrive in the city. Many of the 250 people who take advantage of the mail service that the center provides are hiding from ex-spouses and their own communities. Quietly, almost grimly, he added, "They're hiding from themselves."

Sitting Up grew up in Pine Ridge on the Lakota Sioux Reservation. As Aaron Huey has reported graphically, this is arguably one of the most troubled communities in Indian Country.[19] Suicide, fetal alcohol syndrome, wreckages that serve as shelter, and hopelessness are an end product of massacres, treaty violations, and isolation. Sitting Up saw it all firsthand. Relationships were difficult because of the abuse and fear that underlie life in a chaotic alcoholic family, a subculture from which nondrinkers are barred. The underlying cause of Indian alcoholism, Sitting Up said, is simply "boredom." The word has appeared on a list of reasons for suicides in Thoreau, New Mexico—the boredom, a hellish emptiness of interminable misery.

Next to Huey's and Sitting Up's portrayals of Pine Ridge, a place like Albuquerque is a relief. East Central Avenue, one of Trumbull's boundaries, is a lifeline for migrants. All of Central's fifteen-mile route is a spine that connects the western mesas, the Rio Grande valley, and the mountains to the east before merging with Interstate 40 into the eastern plains. It is one of the last remaining stretches of historic Route 66, once known as America's Main Street and still called the Mother Road.

For Indians who can barely scrape together enough money for a meal, Central's buses are essential to jobs, education, health care, and social services—and the Indian Center. East Central can also be a first home in the city. It evokes none of fabled Route 66's romance, however. Instead, mobile home dealerships, old motels, and fast-food restaurants line the Mother Road. Sometimes an entire family will occupy just one room in one of those motels. When they accumulate enough money, they might move into one of the cheap rentals—quick-buck real estate investments—that fill Trumbull's street grid.

The tattered neighborhood's residents have fought for better police protection and improved schools, demonstrated against drug dealers, crime, and violence, and generated "cleanups." Beginning in 2003, Albuquerque's city government boarded up vacant buildings and approved financing for affordable, single-family housing. Residents have pleaded with the media and others to drop the area's unfortunate nickname, "the war zone." Despite its conditions, Trumbull is a lively place, the point of arrival not only for American Indians but also for immigrants from south of the border and Asia.[20]

Sprawling southward from Trumbull is a stark contrast, the complex of Sandia National Laboratories and Kirtland Air Force Base. They are in the business of cutting-edge weapons, energy development, and arms control.[21] Employees and visitors enter the complex through gates manned by security officers. They are probably more aware of the chaos in physics than that in a squat, ramshackle steel building a few blocks from the labs.

The Albuquerque Indian Center does what others like it have been doing since they first appeared during the 1970s—helping Indians to navigate the city.[22] By 2010, its shabby, cavernous, single room with shaky lighting and drab walls had been subdivided into more workable spaces and a new kitchen. In a large meeting room on earth-colored walls, Duane Scares Hawk (Lakota Sioux) had painted a mural with heroic images: an eagle with wings spread over Native people and the animals sacred to them—bear, horse, and buffalo. With an annual budget of about $900,000 in public grants and contributions, the non-profit center serves about three thousand people a month with fifteen or so full-time and part-time staff and contractors.[23]

Marisa Ramos, the program director of the Albuquerque Indian Center, easily named the top priority for its patrons: "Their first basic need is—they're hungry." Besides food, the center also offers "wraparound" help: diapers, clothing, counseling, job consulting, and education (getting kids into schools and finding supplies for them). Beyond the basics, the organization helps individuals decode city systems through general family assistance, and referrals to other resources in health care, employment, and higher education. The center also puts Indians in touch with home. At gatherings, young people learn Indian stories and crafts. Sweat lodges built by volunteers in the center's backyard were dismantled, however, after widely publicized deaths at a New Age spa in Arizona. Instead, the center refers people to an Albuquerque medicine man.

The center relies on "community capital." A nearby charter school, the Native American Community Academy, helps with food donations and recruits youngsters for youth programs.

From the National Indian Council on Aging (NICOA) older individuals come to do clerical work and provide advice. The LGBTQI coalition helps members of its community who leave the violence directed at them on the reservation and turn to prostitution simply to survive.[24] The center regularly distributes free food that it receives from food banks and at Christmas sponsors a toy giveaway.

One counselor, Harold Gray, helps newcomers prepare for the job hunt. Many of those he advises start from scratch, have no idea what a résumé is, and have never touched a computer. A Navajo, Gray has lived in the city on and off, and he proudly asserts that he has been around the world twice during his service in the military and that he has earned two MA degrees. But Gray returns to the reservation frequently to care for his father, a World War II veteran. Native Americans are "vanishing," he said, although "we have to preserve as much as possible of what we have left." Gray tries to draw out his advisees' Native identities so that they have the strength to work with white managers who do not always recognize that a Native American is as good as any employee. Life is tough and not just in the city, Gray concluded. "The Indian way is harsh. Europeans are harsh. Christianity is harsh." Then, perhaps recalling his Desert Storm service, he added, "Terrorists are harsh."

When substance abuse follows Indians from the reservation to the city, family, medicine man, and health programs are left far behind. The center redirects Indians to help in town, and its own counselors use Native culture to help them.[25] In a smoking prevention program, Gordon Yawakia (Zuni) contrasts the harm in commercial tobacco with its ceremonial use. "Being urban, a lot of these kids don't have access to a medicine man, so I tell about the medicine and the use of our sacred herbs." Each tribe has its own tobacco ceremonies, he explained as he arranged sage and sweet grass on his desk. Between his fingers he held a thin, pale tube—a corn husk rolled around herbs. Some Indians smoke, while others chew or eat the herbs. Indians sometimes use the bare roots of tobacco and herbs for healing. They chew a small bite, then spit it out and rub it on their ears, nose, and mouth to detect bad spirits. Yawakia lives in Albuquerque but returns regularly to the reservation where he grew up. He speaks movingly about the sacred winter Shalako and the summer solstice ceremonies. But he left Zuni because basic services were far from his home. Also, training off the reservation gave him skills for a lifetime in construction, electrical, and refrigeration work.

The Indian Center also has brought in programs like the White Bison Native American Alliance for Wellbriety. Based in Colorado Springs and funded in part with a federal grant, the nonprofit organization is dedicated to what it calls "wellbriety"—combining sobriety with physical, emotional, and spiritual wellness.[26] Wellbriety planned to bring one hundred Indian communities into wellness by 2010 through its annual Sacred Hoop Journey. Although it had previously toured 32 college campuses and 127 smaller Indian communities, in the summer of 2002 the Journey targeted 16 cities in the western United States because that's where most Indians—especially young Indians—are, said its organizer, Don Coyhis, a Wisconsin Mohican. White Bison couples traditions, stories, and healing techniques that are common to many tribes with twelve-step programs like Alcoholics Anonymous. "The culture, keeping the spirituality, is key," said Coyhis during a stop in Albuquerque.[27]

The group's name and logo—a white bison and symbols like the sacred hoop—evoke spiritual associations, especially for the Sioux. The white bison or buffalo is the incarnation of White Buffalo (or Calf) Woman, who appeared about two thousand years ago. She brought the sacred pipe to the Sioux, unified them, and taught them rituals, such as the naming ceremony (in which an individual receives an Indian name) and the vision quest, and how to live a life of balance.[28] When American soldiers slaughtered three hundred Lakota Sioux men, women, and children at Wounded Knee, the hoop broke. Repairing the hoop brings the people together again, heals the nations.[29] White Bison uses a hoop as the symbol of the journey that participants make to wholeness.

At the Journey's opening ceremony in Albuquerque, White Bison's hoop, which has been blessed by elders, was carried around the central meeting room. About 150 mostly Indian people had gathered for the event, which included a meal of sandwiches, chips, and fruit. To begin the day, the Dancing Horse drum group chanted a Lakota sobriety song that one of its members translated:

Grandfather, look upon us and have pity
The people are living day to day with fully conscious minds.
We are living a sober life.
Grandfather, look at us and have pity.

The participants, who sat in rows of metal folding chairs, pulled out the beliefs and songs of their childhoods. Then everyone stated a tribal affiliation. Some—Diné, Pueblos, and Apaches— were from neighboring homelands, but others reflected the Indian diaspora—Lakota Sioux (South Dakota), Potawatomi (Michigan), Penobscot (Maine), and Arapaho (Oklahoma and Wyoming).

Coyhis told the gathering of so many seeming strangers that coming together is a healing time. He noted other signs of healing. Sacred eagle feathers had gone into outer space and back.[30] Also, legend spoke of a spiderweb spun by a woman—an allusion to Spider Woman or Spider Grandmother, a central figure in Native creation myths—that has morphed into today's Internet. Coyhis's life reflected such disparate elements.

While working as a NASA engineer, he went on a vision quest every four years, asking the questions, Who am I? Why am I? Where am I going? During one quest, he had a vision of a white bison, quit his job, and founded the organization he now heads. Coyhis wants to reach urban young people who are particularly susceptible to a string of troubles that can lead to suicide. For instance, White Bison conducts naming ceremonies and puberty rites. "We're bringing that way of looking at childrearing," he said.

Leaders in Albuquerque's Indian community unfailingly mention their young people. Norman Sitting Up pointed out that Native America has a new generation of young people born in the city. His daughter, whose mother is Navajo, grew up in Albuquerque and then moved to the reservation with her mother. There, Native children would not accept her because she was better educated, said Sitting Up. When his daughter returned to a high school in Albuquerque, she rejected her Indian connections and spent most of her time with non-Indian friends. Trying to help young people regain their equilibrium as Indians is not easy. Adults can shuttle back to the reservation easily. "With kids, it's harder once they find the mall," he said.

Indian children cruise the mall effortlessly, but they stumble in school.[31] In moving from reservation to city, they "are coming from a hostile area into an even more hostile area," said Nancy Martine-Alonzo, New Mexico's assistant secretary for Indian education. She also was the director of the Indian education program for the Albuquerque Public Schools (APS) for four years. Daisy Thompson succeeded Martine-Alonzo in the Albuquerque post. Educating Indian children is a special challenge for Albuquerque in part because of their numbers. The district has the fourth largest Native American school population in the country, 5,800 children from 115 tribes (about

3,000 are Navajo). With 80,000 students, the district is the twenty-fifth largest in the nation.

Intractable pathologies follow Native children from reservation to city, where they must also deal with cultural alienation, mistrust, and chronic budget inadequacies in their schools. Nearly 60 percent of the Indian children in the APS system come from families that qualify for federal assistance. Across the district, 80 percent of the students are on academic alert, failing to meet basic minimum requirements. Indian children in APS have the least number of gifted children and the most number of learning disabled. They are the lowest academically achieving group in reading and math, but the city high schoolers outpace their reservation peers on the SAT.[32] The district receives about $1.5 million in mostly federal money—about $300 per child—for Indian students, but it is not nearly enough, said Martine-Alonzo.[33]

Because Indian nations are sovereign, they do not consider themselves as subcultures, subgroups, or minorities. But the most pressing difficulties among Indian children are common to minorities and immigrants: language deficiencies and abysmal dropout rates. They have a more difficult time with assimilation than, say, Asians who have left their countries behind permanently. Indian children operate in two societies all the time, with many returning to the reservation regularly to see kin and participate in ceremonials.

Urban children take off their reservation hat and put on their city hat, Thompson explained. The more complex urban setting intensifies the displacement of tradition with gang and drug cultures across Indian Country. Urban young people can easily adopt the baggy pants, chains, and hip-hop language of Chicano and African American adolescents.[34] To counter the trend, Thompson's division has begun to give Native children an opportunity to reconnect with their roots. In one high school resource room, children start each morning with a Native song they choose. The music prompts them to reconnect, and, over time, behavior changes. "We'll see an impact with academics and self-identity. We're not teaching just to the head but the total child," Thompson said.

Martine-Alonzo cautioned that no magic bullet can address all the needs of these children, but the district uses a number of strategies. For the most part, Indian children are not in separate classes, although they may be tutored individually, and some small groups work on language skills for part of the day. Teachers use basic multisensory exercises, including phonetics, and they often draw on Native American literature. A class at one elementary school looked for topic sentences in a book about Navajo code talkers. "You can't take a canned curriculum to the classroom and expect it to be effective. You need enhancements, Native stories, to stimulate memory and retention," said Martine-Alonzo. Also, Thompson pointed out that the division has shared instructional strategies across the district for teachers. Indigenous teachers train non-Indian colleagues. In another development, students can enter a lottery for admission to the tuition-free Native American Community Academy, a charter school that opened in 2006.

For both women, students are more than test scores and classroom strategies, however. Martine-Alonzo anguished over young Indians crushed by family pressures, and she described one high school senior who fell through the cracks. With a 3.0 average, he was just beginning finals week when his parents threw him out of the house because he had turned eighteen. Homeless, he missed exams, graduation, and the chance to win a scholarship. "How do you begin to help a student in that situation?" she asked in a sad voice.

Getting parents involved is particularly critical for Indian youngsters—and difficult in an atmosphere of mistrust. While

The Murphy family at the mall. "No matter where you are, home is always going to be there," said seventeen-year-old Shaine. Photo by William Rodwell (author's collection).

other minorities had to fight to get into schools, Indians were forced into them, Thompson said. Schools became places of trauma: separation from families and sometimes brutal deculturation. Parents who remember this history are leery of formal education, so while they need to navigate the public system, they stay away from their children's schools. When Thompson encourages parents to become involved, she meets skepticism. Thompson shares their distrust. "I feel it. I'm an educator. I've been in education for thirty-four years."

In this context, one of the most important resources to deal with dropouts and absenteeism are home liaisons, Indian counselors who visit the homes of failing children to improve attendance and expand communication with families. They track parental contact times by phone and with personal visits, and they provide a manual with information about clothing and food banks, legal services and health care. Martine-Alonzo

Counselors Gordon Yawakia and Harold Gray at the Albuquerque Indian Center in front of a mural by Duane Scares Hawk (Lakota Sioux). Photo by William Rodwell (author's collection).

called the liaisons the "bricks" between school and home that support families who have left reservation kin behind. To serve the eighteen hundred Indian school children in crisis, APS has eleven home liaisons. But many Indian parents feel inadequate to advocate for themselves and their children. To encourage them, Martine-Alonzo gave them a lesson about the sovereignty deal: land for Americans, education for Indians.

Like some other Indians who live and work in the city, both Thompson and Martine-Alonzo stick close to home. Both were born and raised on the Navajo reservation. A mother of seven, Martine-Alonzo is from Ramah, New Mexico, where she taught, was a school principal for sixteen years, and served as a tribal official for nine. She still owns a home in Ramah and has also served on its community board, which conducts business in the Diné language. Thompson is from Teesto, Arizona, didn't speak English until she went to school, and now holds two graduate degrees and is working on a doctorate. A grandmother, Thompson calls "home" a house in Gallup, where she attends an all-Indian Christian church during weekend visits to care for her parents, who live in rural Thoreau, New Mexico.

Alonzo and Thompson slide easily between their reservation communities and the city. But not all are so deft. Norman Ration, the director of the National Indian Youth Council, describes the limbo in which urban Indians find themselves because of the trust relationship. American Indian tribes and the United States are partners in this relationship, in which the federal government guarantees health care, education, protection of rights and property, and other benefits. In exchange, Indians turned over millions of acres of their lands. The funding that defines the federal role is grounded in the reservations and tribes. Once individual Indians leave their reservations, that support is not readily available. Also, tribal governments sometimes abandon urban Indians, in effect denying them their guaranteed benefits. Urban Indians vote, they are counted in the census, and their numbers generate money for the tribes. "But the money never gets to the city," Ration said.

Health care, for instance, prompts country mouse–city mouse tension between urban and reservation tribal members.[35] In cities, the Indian Health Service suffers from a triple-whammy: not enough dollars for urban health care, the agency's funding structure, and new tribal sovereignty initiatives.

First, even as the urban Indian population grows, money for urban health care programs has remained static at around 1 percent of the agency's budget nationally.[36] As Ration pointed out, health care dollars that reservation individuals generate through the census or tribal count do not go with them when they move to the city. The allocation for IHS services for the Potawatomi tribal government in Michigan does not cover a Potawatomi who moves to Albuquerque.

Second, IHS units operate under a formula that allocates money according to the tribes the unit serves. For instance, the Albuquerque unit's budget comes from "shares" that the tribes it serves own and control. With that money, the unit operates a twenty-eight-bed hospital and an ambulatory care center in the city as well as field clinics in nearby Navajo, Apache, and Pueblo communities. But many of the 100,000 patients who used the Albuquerque IHS unit in 2000 went to the *city's* facility, not the field clinics. To serve patients in Albuquerque, the IHS has stretched dollars from the tribal allocations to serve its urban patients, including about twenty thousand from other tribes who live in the city.[37]

Third, in a final complication, this arrangement is now shaky. Thanks to self-determination and casino revenues, some tribes have opened their own clinics. In 2002 Jemez and Isleta withdrew their "shares" of the Albuquerque unit's eleven-million-dollar allocation—$2 million and $3 million, respectively—and shifted them to pueblo clinics. The withdrawals amounted to a 30 percent cut in the IHS unit's budget, and that reduced the resources that Albuquerque had stretched for urban Indians. But Cheri Lyon, the Albuquerque IHS chief executive officer, who is part Cherokee, said, "The word 'cut' is not really accurate. We've redistributed it."[38] By 2005, in its "redistribution," the unit ended weekend and evening clinics and eventually closed its urgent care center, which was used by twenty-five thousand patients.

Many Indian leaders watched the reductions in Albuquerque with alarm, fearing that cuts would leave thousands of urban

Indians without health care. Patients do have some alternatives. Urban Indians can return to their tribal communities for care at an IHS unit there, but that can mean days, perhaps weeks, away from jobs and the expense of trips to a far-off reservation. Those whose employers offer health insurance are fortunate. Others can go to contractors such as the nonprofit First Nations Healthsource, which has clinics across the country. Eligible Indians can receive some care, such as diabetes prevention, primary care, and emergency care without charge, although they must pay for other services. In Albuquerque they could turn to the city's only public—and already overburdened—institution, the University of New Mexico Hospital, which has instituted the Center for Native American Health. The center brings together tribes, the IHS, and local and state agencies. The cycle of reservation versus urban Indians care spins on, however.

Ration also focuses on education. He has been with the National Indian Youth Council since it was established in 1961 to improve the political, economic, and social well-being and education of off-reservation people. NIYC's annual budget of about $1.1 million comes from the U.S. Department of Labor and private contributions to serve about three hundred Indians who are mostly Navajo, ages eighteen to thirty-five. They start ahead of the game; they have not surrendered to hopelessness. These young people come to a city with just one purpose—to work. But they often arrive without jobs and are unprepared to look for them. With remedial work, getting a college degree might take eight to ten years. Ration uses every available secondary and higher education resource to improve academic and other skills. No matter the impact of mainstream culture, he insisted, "they're Native, tied to culture, tradition, and language. They have a certain set of beliefs and values. And requirements— dances, spiritual practices. Each tribe is different."

Ration looks beyond support from federal and other public agencies to help his young charges. He tries to draw on two sets of relationships that could be helpful: that between urban Indians and reservation Indians, and a second set between newly arrived young people and urban Indians farther along on their career paths. But these relationships do not uniformly benefit urban Indians.

For those who move to the city, deculturation accelerates, especially in those who leave behind elders and other kin. Traditionally, parents and elders held primary responsibility for teaching young people, first within the extended family and then at the tribal level. Today, with children in schools, away from parents all day, that coherence frays on the reservation and especially in the city. Displacing grandparents—ostensibly honored as keepers and conduits of the family's and the tribe's language, history, and values—is a flashy outside world. Ration's reverence for the older generations was clear. His voice shifted volume and pitch when he spoke about his grandparents' pedagogy. The classroom might be a walk in the mountains, with lessons on the trees and herbs. "They had the gentle power, the power of persuasion. They didn't have to threaten. They just talked with you."

Ration appeals to tribal leaders to help their urban members. He scoffs at the tribal contention that the urban movement is a threat to sovereignty because it weakens the cultural fabric. Crossing the border into the city doesn't make young people less Navajo. Tribal officials do not understand the pressures that students face off the reservation. He tells tribal leaders that "when a Navajo goes to Harvard, they all go into the same class. There are no 'slow' classes."

Ration is equally disappointed, almost enraged, with Indian professionals who could be mentors but will not help young people on the lower rungs of society, the poor and unskilled.

That lack of involvement runs contrary to the common ethic of collaboration and community. Mentors can help prepare young Indians in the city and keep them from becoming dropout statistics.

A "take-charge" attitude could advance the causes of urban Indians. In Albuquerque, an alliance of Indian organizations meets regularly to support each other's efforts to improve conditions for their people. So insistent are Navajos in Albuquerque, Phoenix, and Denver to achieve recognition from the tribe that in the early 2000s some took preliminary steps to establish chapters that would act as the governing bodies for urban Diné and provide representation on the Navajo Nation tribal council.[39] The council, however, has resisted any attempt to establish chapters outside the reservation.

Zooming out from the minutiae of urban Indian life, a picture of a cohesive culture remains elusive. A study of Indians in Albuquerque completed by one of Theodore Jojola's classes at the University of New Mexico (UNM) suggests some broad trends.[40] The experience of urban Indians smudges the line between them and their reservation kin. In addition to a statistical portrait of Albuquerque's Indian community, the study addressed their quality-of-life issues through lengthy questionnaires completed by individuals from forty-five different tribes.

The report found that Albuquerque's community is tribally diverse and scattered across the city, despite the concentration in Trumbull. It has a distinct social structure, with a network of individuals and organizations as well as relationships built on extended families and tribal affiliations. Although poverty is a reality, a small middle class has developed, and while many urban Indians are young, the community is multigenerational. Indians maintain cultural ties that reinforce their sense of place and of home through organizations like the Native

American Students Association at UNM; professional groups such as the American Indian Science and Engineering Society; the Albuquerque Indian Center; and informal occasions like powwows. These mechanisms have evolved over decades of interaction with non-Indians, perhaps even as a reaction to total assimilation, and they seem to work. A large majority said that they follow their own traditions in their homes. Local Indians make newcomers from reservations in other states feel welcome, and they can enjoy traditional cultural activities.[41]

Some of Albuquerque's Indians—newcomers and longtime city dwellers alike—keep home close. With that bit of turquoise on a ring or in a beaded bracelet, an Indian can sense an entire world of souls left behind in time and place. As Norman Ration suggested, urban Indians also have more practical needs. Although benefits of tribal membership weaken with absence from the reservation, successful urban Indians expect the trust relationship to remain in play. They want the federal government to meet its treaty obligations to Indians no matter where they live.

Urban Indian life is as diverse as the tribes that live on Turtle Island, sometimes heroic and mostly merely mundane. The term *pan-Indian* has been used to describe urban Indian culture. On the ground, however, I have rarely heard Indians themselves use the word. Many individuals retain strong tribal identities, and they do not always internalize those of others, even if they might borrow songs and dances from other groups. The urban reservation—or "encampment"—is nascent and growing, although it lacks a clear definition. Searching for an overarching "pan-Indian" urban culture is not a fruitless exercise, however. Indeed, some scholarship illuminates commonalities in the Native American experience. Urban Indian women, for instance, consistently maintain traditional social and family values and cohesion. They keep the "campfires burning."[42]

Jojola said that urban migration is changing the notion of "Indian Country." The idea of tribes as rural and isolated is no longer valid. As Albuquerque has grown to several pueblos' borders, those towns have become bedroom communities, within an hour's drive of jobs and shopping. Moreover, they are behaving like suburbs. At the most basic level, pueblo governments take advantage of their suburban location to benefit their tribal members. Santa Ana and Sandia, for instance, use gaming revenues to send their children to private schools in Albuquerque. Like other suburbs, pueblos use their status as independent government entities to gain concessions from the city. The western face of the Sandia Mountains, which Sandia Pueblo reclaimed, not only constitutes the pueblo's ancestral lands but also uniquely defines Albuquerque's identity.

Suburbanization turns the table on Indian-city relationships. Some merchants routinely complain that casinos draw customers who would otherwise patronize the merchants' stores and entertainment venues. Although pueblo casinos generate fees to the state of New Mexico through state compacts, the loss of retail business to the pueblos reduces gross receipts (sales) tax revenues for cities. Albuquerque does benefit, however. By 2002 Sandia Pueblo had hired the New Mexico Symphony Orchestra to play several concerts at the pueblo's casino complex and became the group's single largest source of income. "For the first time, the surrounding tribes are influencing the pattern of growth in Albuquerque," said Jojola.

Because so many of New Mexico's pueblos are near Albuquerque or sizeable towns like Santa Fe, the situation there is skewed. But in other parts of the United States, tribal entities are using sovereignty combined with new and sometimes outside capital to reach broadly beyond their reservations' boundaries into cities. In Connecticut, the Mashantucket Pequots, who operate the massive Foxwoods casino, were among the leading investors in a project to add 130,000 square feet of office space to downtown Norwich, Connecticut.[43] The Sycuan band of Kumeyaay restored the historic U. S. Grant Hotel in downtown San Diego.

The Interior Department has opposed tribes' efforts to extend their sovereignty far beyond their reservations and especially across state lines, however. In 2008 the department rejected an attempt by tribes from Wisconsin and upstate New York that had tried for five years to acquire what had been their traditional lands in New York communities for casinos.[44] These deals and megadeals are far from the daily lives of most urban Indians, and they distract attention from the effort Indians must make when they leave their reservations. As the Indians living in Albuquerque show, individual lives are just that: individual. Yet they do have special circumstances of history, heritage, and family that shape those individual lives.

Albuquerque is only one town with an urban Indian experience, and across the country, conditions differ. San Francisco does not have a concentration of Indian communities nearby like Albuquerque. Yet Native Americans come together there in a special blend. In the spring of 2005 a group of Chinese American architects joined a crowd of well-wishers in the Mission District for a ribbon cutting at Friendship House, an Indian center. The new eighty-five-bed treatment facility they had designed was a dream come true for the center's longtime director, Helen Waukazoo. The architects had received thickly woven Pendleton blankets as gifts, but they seemed perplexed until someone explained that the blankets were gestures of respect and thanks.[45]

The new Friendship House was more than another urban Indian milestone, however. Rather, it once again illustrated the effective blend of Indian communitarian ethos and individual leadership. A dedicated corps of supporters—board members, tribal members, staff, family, foundations, and federal and city officials—had worked with Waukazoo to make Friendship House the largest facility for American Indian substance abusers in the United States. Its program combines traditional healing methods—including San Francisco's only licensed sweat lodge—with conventional medical consultation. Formerly housed in a ramshackle wooden structure, the new twelve-million-dollar building evokes the colors of Waukazoo's home on the Navajo Reservation—straw yellow and pumpkin walls and terra cotta in the courtyard.

At the opening, warmth bathed the assembled crowd after a San Francisco winter of bone-chilling rains. This Friendship House was yet another stop on a forty-year journey for Waukazoo. After boarding school, she had landed in San Francisco in the early 1960s and worked as a clerk-typist at the Christian Reform Church's Friendship House, a drop-in social service agency where a growing number of relocated—and disoriented—Indians found a haven. She worked her way up to executive director.

In 1973 the American Indian community assumed control of Friendship House, incorporating as a nonprofit. San Francisco gave Friendship House a grant in 1981. Over the next two decades, as the American Indian population of six Bay Area counties increased by 27 percent, Friendship House grew to serve them.[46] A new generation of urban Indians far from home fell into substance abuse and health problems, including HIV-AIDS. Today, Friendship House has a budget of $4 million, mostly from various government sources and private support.[47]

About five hundred people had come to witness Friendship House's new setting. The crowd was as diverse as the city they called home. Former mayor Willie Brown and representatives from Mayor Gavin Newsom's office, the IHS, and other agencies were there. Friendship House's mostly Indian staff of about forty and eight board members mingled with the crowd. Waukazoo's family had driven all the way from Crownpoint, New Mexico, to accommodate a sister who didn't want to fly. The sister sat quietly in full traditional Navajo dress of broomstick skirt, velvet blouse, moccasins, and turquoise jewelry.

The ceremonies were understated and the speeches short, giving little indication of the struggle that had turned "Helen's dream"—as Mayor Brown called it—into a reality. To celebrate, the Indians turned to Friendship House's own drum group, drawn from the staff. Tom Phillips (Kiowa/Creek), the ceremony's emcee, stepped to the microphone and delivered a prayer. Like Waukazoo, he had come to San Francisco during relocation. He teaches sobriety techniques based on the traditional healing practices that Friendship House uses in its therapies. Marveling at relocated Indians, Phillips said, "We're probably the most adaptable people in the country."

With the drum group, the Kiowa prayer, and a number of people in traditional dress, Friendship House once again pulled into its Native past to charge into the future. The understated Waukazoo was on the podium in the center's patio, wearing a basic black dress adorned with a simple necklace and turquoise earrings. She spoke briefly, trying to remain composed. Later, inside the building's large meeting hall, Ron Powell, the president of Friendship House's board, surprised her in a second ceremony. Turning to Helen, he said, "What you do is sacred." Then he announced that the room was being dedicated as the Helen Waukazoo Great Hall. At a loss for words, Helen simply said she was going to call it the Navajo Nation Room. Then she reached a hand to her husband, Marty. A Lakota Sioux, Marty is the CEO for the consortium of Native American Indian health centers in Oakland, Sacramento, San Francisco, and San Jose. He and Helen met when he came to Friendship House for treatment.

Individuals work out their own definition of what it means to be Indian and how to maintain family and culture in a city or within its orb of influence. Keith Franklin, a Sac and Fox raised on the reservation in Oklahoma, is an advocate for Indians in Albuquerque, including his work as a leading figure of the Albuquerque Metro Native American Coalition. He spent nearly forty years as a government employee, first in the air force and then as the director of computer systems for a federal agency.

Franklin and his family live on Albuquerque's east side, in one of dozens of suburban-style subdivisions that consume arid mesas—and water. A small, yapping poodle greets visitors, and a pool sparkles in the backyard. Franklin's daughters were excellent students at one of the city's better high schools. The older girl played tenor saxophone and toured nationally with her school's jazz band, and the younger one was her school's first female tuba player. Franklin raised his pride another notch: "She's the first Indian tuba player they've had!"

Indian Country is not far from this middle-class suburban success story, however. One day, Franklin's older daughter told her dad about her history class's discussion of President Andrew Jackson. Surprised that the lesson had neglected to cover the Cherokee Removal, Franklin told her how Jackson had engineered the effort to drive the Cherokees (and Choctaws and Creeks) from their homelands to Indian territory in faraway Oklahoma. During a torturous march that the Cherokees call the "trail of tears," one-quarter to one-half of their population perished. Some Americans have heard this story; Franklin himself did not hear it until he went to college.[48]

When schools fail to teach the Indian removal lesson, children suffer a loss of knowledge. The omission erodes understanding. White students can comfortably ignore something they were never taught. For young Indians, the omission weakens the bond with tribal history that shaped their grandparents and parents in a shared identity of resistance and strength. As the bond slips away, many Indian teens find new identities in gang attire or at the mall.

The attractions of the mall do not overwhelm all young Indians. On a late winter weekend, most of the Murphys were at Coronado Mall in Albuquerque. In the glitzy Indian-themed food court, the Murphys talked about their lives. They had come to town from their home at Acoma Pueblo to take Mom, Lorissa Garcia, to the airport for a trip to a conference. A full-time student, she is also on the committee of Acoma Language Nest, a program for infants of the tribe. The family is a blend of Laguna, Navajo, Acoma, and Yankton Sioux, with an Irish great-grandfather thrown in. Todd, a former police officer in Gallup, is now a manager for an Albuquerque construction company. His stepdaughters Shaine, eighteen, and Chantel, fourteen, study at the Santa Fe Indian School and commute home on weekends, and two daughters, Erin, four, and Denai, three, attend school at Acoma.

The older girls speak some Keresan, the language of Acoma, and the family participates in ceremonials regularly. Chantel is unsure of college plans but wants to go to law school and work for her community. At the time we met, Shaine was waiting on college acceptances; later, her father e-mailed that the University of Colorado had accepted her. With a major in entrepreneurship, she hopes to open a Native American bakery at Acoma. She'll produce pueblo goodies: blue-corn mush, blue-corn chocolate chip cookies, traditional cookies topped with sugar and cumin, prune and pumpkin pies that resemble turnovers, and hot Indian tea. Shaine already has its name—Dessertopolis—and a business plan she developed in a management class. Although I swooned at the thought of such a shop in the city, Shaine said it would be at Acoma, because rural people don't get to eat traditional foods. Wherever the girls land, however, she said, "No matter where you are, home is always going to be there." Erin sang me a song in Keresan, while shy Denai just grinned.[49]

Finally, during the Sacred Hoop Journey's Wellbriety Day in Albuquerque, another family had no question about their Indian identities. In the Dancing Horse group, Casey Church sang and beat a large drum with one hand and balanced his two-year-old daughter on his knee with the other. Nearby, his wife, Lora, joined in singing the Lakota sobriety song. Casey had once "gone missing" to alcohol, but he overcame the addiction that began when he was a Marine (he proudly displays his Marine Corps pin on his cowboy hat). A Potawatomi from Michigan, Casey works as a supervisor for a building contractor. He has not forgotten the history of his people, and he spoke movingly of his own tribe's "trail of death" during the relocation of the 1830s. Lora, slender, serene, and beautiful, was born on the Navajo Reservation, and she manages a substance-abuse program for teenagers.

The Churches and their four children live in a new subdivision on Albuquerque's west side, and they are Christians. Lora seemed bemused by the question of how they reconcile apparently divergent religious views and cultures. She does not separate Christian and Native beliefs. Being a good Indian parent is not a tough job if parents hold mainstream America's "clutter" at bay. Their family rarely watches television or goes to the mall, and they engage in family activities such as the drum group. "We touch the drum, then touch our hearts to bring the spirit to us," said Casey.

Repatriation, even in the broad sense, is not an issue, because the Churches have not let go of being Indian. As Lora put it, "You do it everywhere you're at. It's not a locality. It's who you are, the essence of who you are."

4

THE WAY WE SHOULD

Spring comes to Diné Bikéyah—the Navajo Nation—with a morning breeze that gathers strength throughout the day. Nearly every day, stiff winds usually sweep out of the northwest to buffet the expansive reservation on even the sunniest afternoon. Gusts laden with sand sting your face, clog your nostrils, thicken your hair, and scrape off your car's paint. If you open your mouth to gasp for air, sand clings to your teeth, your tongue, and the roof of your mouth. The wind follows you everywhere. Even indoors you hear it whistling through cracks in window frames, heralding the fine dust that covers everything. The wind is inescapable, a life force. According to traditional belief, deities send wind into newborns to initiate breathing and life, and a person's fingerprints are the marks of the wind entering the body. The wind stays with you, embedded in you for life.[1]

On a particular spring morning in Window Rock, Arizona, a breeze promised an afternoon of sandy gales. At the small Navajo zoo, Yogi the bear sprawled in the dirt of a fenced enclosure, sedated for his annual checkup from visiting veterinarian Scott Bender. A purple sweatshirt draped over Yogi's face shielded his eyes from the sun. A dozen workers, including Loline Hathaway, the zoo's curator, and visiting reservation children watched intently from outside the fence. To listen to Yogi's heart, the burly Bender used a stethoscope with tubes wrapped in delicate bright blue and white Indian beadwork. As used as I was to seeing silver, turquoise, and beads on just about anything from hat bands to napkin rings, this was the first time I had seen such handiwork on a stethoscope.

This nearly pastoral scene belied the controversy that was swirling around the small zoo. Shortly after the New Year, when time began to slide into a new millennium, the Diné's embrace of their beloved homeland seemed, at least temporarily, less secure. Early in January 2000, as he left office, the tribe's outgoing president, Milton Bluehouse, announced that two Navajo women had reported to him a sighting of Holy People—sacred deities—who had issued a warning. The deities had said that the Diné were not living according to tradition and that they were upsetting the natural order by keeping animals caged in the zoo. So Bluehouse ordered the zoo closed and the animals set free.

The assertion of tradition and the cultural reverence for animals had combined to put in doubt the future of the thirty-six-year-old zoo, which had started many years before as a shelter for abandoned and injured wild animals. The controversy started immediately as some tribal members pressed for the zoo's closure. President Kelsey Begaye took office on January 12, and the letters about the zoo began to arrive—more than on any other issue, according to his press officer. Most were from children wanting it to stay open.

From one end of the twenty-five-thousand-square-mile reservation to another, ordinary residents chattered about the zoo on talk radio in New Mexico and Arizona in both Navajo and English. Medicine men and tribal officials argued, and a few non-Natives also tossed in their views. First local, then regional, and finally national news media picked up the conversation. The dispute brought smiles to the outside world, but, as I found while covering the story, it signaled the stresses among the reservation's 175,000 Navajos.[2] It also revealed how complex Navajo thinking is.

This chapter deals with American Indians and the natural world and science. Outsiders might see Native people torn between the sacred and the secular or the traditional and the modern, but American Indians traverse gradients in time and space. In their day-to-day lives and in diverse fields, they reach back and stretch forward along many points, or, as Philip Deloria asserts, they enter the flow of history.[3] Tribal members debate about the proper proportion of traditional to modern as noisily as classical philosophers in Athens might have argued their own issues. The stakes are no less important, because the outcome can shake the very foundations of a culture's beliefs and worldviews, from which flow ceremonial and healing practices, standards for governing, and values for conducting their lives.

The zoo story was about maintaining the homeland's spiritual integrity as economic, social, and political stresses tore at the Navajo Nation. The conversation was also about the commonplace in the context of cosmic forces. At the same time, it allows us to move on to other stories. In one, American Indians take up Western science and medicine but pack up their Native kits and bags to go along. In another, non-Indians make small, tentative efforts to listen to the Indian "other" about nature, the universe, and alternative paths to knowledge. The "first Indian astronaut," "first Indian nuclear physicist," "first Indian surgeon"—these "firsts" are notches on the diversity-in-science belt, but they represent a one-way street. For the most part, non-Indians have yet to incorporate Indian approaches to learning and managing natural forces. That can help us answer a question that one of the individuals in the zoo story asked: "Are we going the way we should?"

Navajo officials could not have predicted the extraordinary consequences of Bluehouse's order to close the zoo. Other urgent issues crowded his successor's agenda. Political upheavals had left the tribal government in disarray. Begaye was the fourth president to take office during a twelve-month period amid revelations of financial wrongdoing and personal transgressions by his predecessors. He acted quickly to reverse Bluehouse's order temporarily. Throughout the spring, the zoo's eighty animals remained ensconced while the president's office sought other alternatives to shutting the zoo down and releasing the animals. The facility could remain open as a natural resource center, but it would be renamed; the word "zoo" was considered disrespectful to the animals. Alternatively, it would not accept any other animals, and the facility would close after all the current residents died naturally. The Hataalii Advisory Council, the Navajo Nation's religious leaders, then imposed a period of silence on the issue until the first thunderstorms of the spring season. To speak of the animals while they were sleeping or hibernating would be disrespectful, they said.

As the advisory council pondered, I headed for Diné Community College, where Harry Walters, the director of the Center for Diné Studies, traced some of the stress fractures in the Navajo Nation that the zoo controversy exposed. The college's home is on some of the most beautiful land on the reservation, in Tsaile, fifty miles north of Window Rock; the students and most of the faculty are Navajo. Walters hunched over a small table in the snack bar and leaned close to my face so that I could hear his soft voice over the rock music coming from the intercom. The small café looked like most college hangouts—a rack of candy bars on the counter, a fast-food menu, and students studying or playing chess over coffee or soft drinks.

"It's a culture shock that we're experiencing," Walters said. He chose his words carefully. I wasn't surprised at his caution; media characterizations of Indian beliefs occupy a range from inexcusable ignorance to New Age hokiness. He compared the sightings of the Holy People to similar appearances of the Virgin Mary in western Europe—but with a critical difference: "Rather than focus on the sightings to determine if who saw it was nuts or not—that's what a Westerner would do—we look at it as a message: 'Are we going the way we should?'"

It was a dazzling query that illuminates the trail to knowledge. "Going the way we should" means maintaining the natural order, the balance in the cycles of life, Walters elaborated. "The natural order is everything. In Navajo you can't stand alone. The environment is part of you. The space you occupy is part of you." This striving for balance in the natural world is one of the core cultural and religious beliefs that Native Americans share. Within that general belief, tribal traditions strictly govern the treatment of animals. Navajo Nation law, not just custom, Walters emphasized, forbids keeping deer because doing so endangers the animal. The exception: if you kill a doe with a fawn, you can raise the fawn. How to use or dispose of every part of a deer killed in a hunt is also prescribed. Sport hunting has grave consequences because it violates the natural order that ensures rain, bountiful crops, and effective ceremonial life.[4] "When we use these living things, we do it within this order, so we don't upset the balance," Walters explained.

Navajos do keep domestic animals such as horses, sheep, and cattle, but they are always outdoors. Sometimes dogs and cats are allowed into a home, but the Diné language has no word for "pet." Instead, Navajos use a term derived from the word for "horse," which was coined for the animal brought to the New World by Europeans. Walters, who is Navajo, repeated the Diné word several times, but I could not grasp the sounds, so I asked him to transcribe it into the script devised by non-Indian and Navajo scholars to represent Diné words. Walters, a trained anthropologist, confessed that he cannot write Navajo. Then he waved over a student at a nearby table, who wrote it out quickly in my notebook. The student helped us sound it out using the phonetic spelling. The two of them—the middle-aged teacher of Diné culture who can't write Navajo and the younger, modern college student probably raised on computers and television who can—personified the cultural differences among the people. They erased the stereotypical contrast between traditional and modern among generations.

Most Americans think of the Navajo Reservation as dry and lifeless. This image doesn't hold for the landscape at its northern end, between Tsaile, at the northeastern tip of Canyon de Chelly, and Window Rock, the capital of the Navajo Nation. Connecting the communities is Indian Route 12, a two-lane road with arrowhead highway markers that meanders across the New Mexico–Arizona state line. Pine trees embrace verdant meadows, and patches of late winter snow cling to the northern faces of mountains that rise out of a wide, green valley. The blue of Tsaile Lake, which is visible from the campus, merges with that of the wide sky. As Route 12 weaves southward, mobile homes are scattered among cabins, ranch homes, and hogans. Backyard satellite dishes reach to the sky. Then the green of the north gives way to the reservation we know from the postcards—a vast sculpture garden. Gigantic red sandstone land masses formed through eons of erosion change shape at almost every turn. This is also a scruffy, brown, and dusty place where dirt roads bake into solid, rough ribbons during the summer. In winter, humans and beasts are isolated and, during a thaw's muck, trapped; helicopters drop food for them into strategic locations.

But for both versions of the reservation, Window Rock is the capital. Near the Navajo Nation's government headquarters is a tall sandstone formation with a hole in its center—the window in the rock—that gives the town its name. Sheep nibble under the watchful eyes of Navajo herders within sight of the road, and free-ranging cattle take shelter from the wind and sun wherever they can, even under the small pine trees next to the low, stone office buildings.

Inside, cool blue décor in the reception area contrasts with the brown outdoors. An elder, his hair tied in the traditional knot at the nape of his neck, sits before a television set, while the "suits" work in inner offices. Between meetings, President Begaye stopped a moment to talk; the zoo controversy exasperated, even bewildered, him. "To be honest, I knew the zoo was there. I learned later that they were wounded animals. I'm thinking, let these animals live out their lives. By not closing the zoo, we're saying keep it open," he said. He seemed relieved to change the subject to economic conditions on the reservation. "If we can make just four giant steps in the next four years, we'll do a lot," he said. But Begaye declined to state a policy or decision on the zoo as he disappeared into the safety of another meeting.

Begaye had identified why the zoo controversy simmered: the disastrous economic situation among the Diné. At the Navajo Nation's economic development office—a handful of ramshackle, single-story prefabs connected by a crazily tilting hallway—Trib Choudhary, an analyst, quickly handed me a sheaf of economic reports. In a clipped British accent—he is Nepalese—he assured me these were the most up-to-date numbers, which President Begaye had just presented to the tribal council.

Conditions on the reservation were worse than during the Great Depression. Unemployment stood at 46 percent, per capita income was $5,600, and the reservation's poverty rate was 56 percent. Revenue from natural resource development had dropped by 25 percent. The reservation attracted tourists but not tourist dollars because it did not have enough hotels, restaurants, and other amenities where visitors spend money. Without casinos the Navajos could not break the cycle of depression, Choudhary stated flatly. But the Diné had firmly voted against gaming—twice.[5] Relief seemed unattainable.

In the context of such desperation, people look to core beliefs—some might say, family values—for succor. So it's not surprising that the zoo's caged animals came to symbolize a disruption of the natural order in which "respect" for animals is a given. Even one of Begaye's executive staff members had confessed an affection for wild animals that persists into adulthood. "I used to play with bear cubs when I was four or five," he said, smiling.

Back at the seven-acre zoo, wind and sand threatened to reduce sunlight. A squat cement-block building houses offices and small creatures, while outside pens with dirt floors shelter larger animals. (The zoo has no exotic beasts, only species that are known to Navajos.) As Loline Hathaway, a biologist, and zoo workers stood by, Scott Bender used Yogi's checkup as a bear anatomy lesson for a group of reservation kids on a field trip. He gently spread Yogi's claws to explain how they work, checked the animal's teeth, and dispensed a worming potion. Weighing in at 476 pounds, Yogi was healthy, and when the exam was done, zoo workers tucked him in for a long nap.

Bender is part of the Navajo Nation's veterinary service, staffed by Native and white doctors, and he had brought everything he needed in his Veterinary Mobile Clinic, a camper shell on a pickup truck. No debate about the animals existed between him and Hathaway. Bender said his only interest is "medicine and the care of the animals." Hathaway said, "My job is to run the zoo. If they close it, my job is to close it as professionally as possible."

They offered heart-rending scenarios for some of the options circulating among the Diné. Waiting for animals to die before closing the zoo might take years. Simply to release the animals was the worst option. Many were brought to the park because of irreversible injuries. An eagle with an amputated wing cannot fly, much less hunt. Others, like Gummer the toothless resident coyote, are geriatric. They would simply perish: starved, struck by vehicles, killed by hunters or predators. Animals that had lived at the zoo since they were abandoned cubs were used to people. If they had to fend for themselves for the first time, they might attack people or at least enter populated areas. Bender worried that even healthy deer released from the zoo might transmit disease to wildlife. Nevada once had four hundred bighorn sheep, and only one survived after domestic sheep were introduced into their population. The disposition of the eagle is regulated by the Migratory Birds Species Act, and so it cannot be released; similar rules govern the disposition of wolves. In a comment that the Diné would understand in a different context, the frustrated Bender said, "The animals are the heart of the issue."

Later, in her cluttered office, where a computer and a set of antlers shared space on her desk, Hathaway was less guarded. Although she is the only non-Navajo among the zoo's staff, she lives on the reservation and has learned something about the complex and subtle Navajo worldview. Hathaway explained how Coyote tales repeat a basic story from the points of view of different animals. "The culture is not like white Christian religion, where you learn everything by age seven. In Navajo culture, you're always learning. Learning never ends," she said.

Conflicts are shredding the nation's cohesion, however, even as some desperately try to hold on to that culture.

When I asked her how long she had worked at the zoo, she answered wearily, "Sixteen years, two days." Hathaway showed me the zoo's guest register entries; visitors overwhelmingly supported keeping the zoo open. Two animal rights advocates from Boston wanted it closed. "I give a damn," she said quietly.

Anderson Hoskie, a young medicine man, wanted to keep the zoo open. Barely out of his teens, Hoskie had learned about healing ceremonies from his grandfather, also a Hataalii medicine man. At the Na'Nizhoozhi Center in Gallup, a nonprofit organization that addresses alcohol abuse, he uses traditional healing practices that include herbs and ceremonies. We met at the zoo and walked to the Navajo Nation Inn's restaurant for lunch. On the way, we passed the Navajo Museum. Designed like an oversized hogan, it is one of the largest buildings in Window Rock. In the front yard, an older man talked with a group of schoolchildren crowded around a picnic table. Hoskie identified the man as Alfred Yazzie, his grandfather and a member of the Hataalii Advisory Council, which had shut down discussion of the future of the zoo. He did not stop to greet his grandfather. The reason became clear later.

"From my point of view as a medicine man, a lot of the Navajos are overreacting," Hoskie said of the zoo controversy. Like Paul Tosa answering questions about the Pecos repatriation, Hoskie looped in and out of his story in a voice that was almost a whisper. His explanation went something like this: It's important to view the medicine men who want to close the zoo in the context of religious belief and the ordinary Navajo's misunderstanding of that tradition. Belief tells us that the only way a deity can appear is through the important dream world, so the appearance reported by the two women is significant.

But because so few Navajos understand natural law and tradition, they don't know how to react to the appearance of the deities. In the absence of understanding, medicine men can strongly influence behavior, and in this case both the religious leaders and many people have miscalculated. "In a true belief, you have to maintain natural laws, not overreact," he said.

Hoskie and other medicine men have used the zoo's animals for ceremonial purposes that he was reluctant to discuss. When it comes to Indian religion, the reporter in me usually defers, but I pressed him for details that would promote understanding, and he responded cautiously. With the zoo's eagles (he wouldn't be more specific), Hoskie has performed a rare ceremony that is used for cancer, boils, and general health protection. More circumspectly, he said, "Other medicine men have used the spirit of the animals to guide and protect them."

In the highly charged situation on the reservation, politics had pulled the tribe in many directions. The powerful medicine men were using the zoo controversy for political reasons. Hoskie's earlier furtive look toward Grandfather Yazzie now made more sense. Given the honored role of elders among Navajos, generational tension was another layer in the controversy. Hoskie wanted to keep the zoo open for Navajo children. Children learn about the value of animals in their tradition in the reservation's bilingual schools, but a generation of children had no access to wild creatures. "A lot of kids don't know what a cougar or an eagle is," he said.

After lunch, I browsed through the Navajo Museum, especially an exhibit that featured children's art. Brightly painted pictures of animals accompanied by the kids' stories illuminated the centrality of nature to Navajo life, tradition, and cosmology—a lesson Diné children learn early in life. Cathlena Plummer, age eight, painted "Rainbow Men Meet Water Ox." The anchors of a vividly colored, arching rainbow were Holy People, Rainbow

People at one end and Water Ox at the other. In an explanatory note, Cathlena described a threat to nature from human beings; its elegance drew a deep breath from me.

> The men are telling water ox they want water in their land. Water Ox makes it rain and makes the trees grow. He changes color. Water Ox is mad because the men interrupt him. He changed to a dark color. Then Water Ox told them that he could make it rain.

As I left the museum, I noticed small signs posted at some meeting rooms. Tribal managers were attending a seminar on Year 2000 computer issues with specialists from Johns Hopkins University. On the cusp of the millennium, the afternoon had presented another juxtaposition—the young medicine man talked about a healing chant, while other Navajos prepared for Y2K. Although only about 37 percent of Navajo households had telephones, computer use had grown rapidly.[6] The Bill and Melinda Gates Foundation funded and installed 403 computers, peripherals, and software for the 110 Navajo chapter houses and Boys and Girls Clubs in several communities.[7] Although water is not available across much of the reservation, the Navajo Nation has one of the largest digital networks in the world, with international recognition.[8]

As the zoo story had shown, Diné Bikéyah was spinning out from the past—and resisting. But Harry Walters had spoken eloquently about how over the centuries, the Diné, like other indigenous peoples, have successfully absorbed new ways of doing things. He used the well-known example of how Navajos received sheep, a "new technology," from the Spaniards and initially used them for food and wool. Then they developed an art form—the finely woven Navajo blankets that today command prices up to half a million dollars and hang in museums, homes, and corporate offices. But that was in another, more

expansive time. The problem now, he said, is that "we're changing so suddenly that we have these clashes."

With reporter's luck I collected another piece of the zoo story,
this one from a non-Indian who revealed how messy the whole
business had become. In Gallup I tracked down Martin Link, the
founding director of the zoo, living in a railroad-era bungalow
packed with a lifetime's collection of Indian crafts, books, and
"western" furniture. He had worked for the Navajo Nation for
about twenty years as a ranger/archaeologist in Canyon de
Chelly. He became the first director of the first Navajo Museum,
which was then housed in a cabin, and then of the zoo. Link
said the Navajos got a zoo by accident. Fish and game agencies
from Arizona and New Mexico regularly brought animals of
the Southwest to the annual tribal fair and exhibited them in
a tent for Native children. When the fair ended, the animals
returned to their respective states. But in 1963 New Mexico
officials left behind a bear. Link immediately went to the tribal
council, which appropriated money to build an enclosure on
the museum's grounds, and the vice-chairman of the council,
a medicine man, did a ceremony over the animal.

As news of the bear spread quickly, reservation residents
began to bring wild animals to Link: an injured bird, a stray
raccoon, a badger whose foot had gotten caught in a trap. The
"zoo" kept growing, and Link became its de facto director. School
groups started to visit the small collection of animals, and
medicine people began to use them for ceremonial purposes.
The tribal council approved and funded an expansion, and in
1976 the Navajos built the current zoo. When the original
bear died, medicine men collected parts of the body. Over the
years, they asked Link for feathers to use in ceremonials, and he
plucked them out of the birds. "We were more relaxed then," he
said. Only a few weeks before our meeting, the tribe's director
of natural resources had given Link an award for his service to

the tribe as an historian and as the first director of both the museum and the zoo.

Link noted contradictions in Navajos' treatment of animals. He had heard the complaints about coyotes confined in cages at the zoo, but at Fort Defiance in Arizona, Navajos participated in a coyote shoot that dispensed trophies and cash rewards to hunters. "They need a more consistent approach to those animals," Link said.

Like Walters, Link went to the controversy's underlying tensions. Navajos are faced with multiple economic catastrophes complicated by cultural conundrums. Within the tribe, traditional values are not well taught. "As basic culture changes and parts of it start to disintegrate, the things that hold on are the negatives, the thou shalt nots," he said. Link pointed to tourism as an example of drift. Tribal officials recognized that tourism produced a consistent cash flow. They developed parks and rest stops on roads and increased marketing with maps, brochures, and even links to German and Japanese tourist agencies. But all the marketing cannot overcome the fierce Diné desire for privacy, and non-Navajo people are less welcome. "It's a cultural backlash, a response to television and computers," Link said, reprising Walters's comments on the nation's culture shock. He connected the apparitions of holy deities to more universal unrest. "It's almost like the oracle at Delphi. As soon as a problem comes up, there's an apparition—and a ready answer."

In the end, the Navajo Nation kept the zoo open. On its website the tribe trumpets: "We are proud to be the only 'tribal zoo' in America." The name has been expanded to the more elevated Navajo Nation Zoo and Botanical Park, and the site explains that animals in the zoo cannot be returned to the wild because either they are injured or they came as orphans.[9]

In the same year that the Diné's traditional values went head to head with the zoo, the Zunis turned the science of animal husbandry to their own purposes. While both groups share a deep loyalty to the natural world, their approaches to animals illustrate the diversity of thought among American Indians. They also represent the sometimes unspoken conversation across Indian Country about how Native peoples integrate the outside world into their lives. If we listen, we find that Indian ways can provide us with new perspectives.

Just sixty miles from Window Rock, Zuni Pueblo accepted its first eagle into its Eagle Aviary Sanctuary in 1999. The Zunis' sanctuary began when the tribe lost patience with the National Eagle Repository in Colorado. Because possessing or killing eagles is prohibited by law, the agency maintains frozen carcasses of birds that have died from natural causes. The remains are available only to federally recognized Native American tribes for ceremonial purposes, and tribes must apply for them. Because of the length of time from application to receipt of eagle remains, the Zunis met with federal wildlife officials to explore ways of speeding up the process. One of the alternatives was for the Zunis to build and maintain an aviary and keep live birds that are "nonreleasable." A certified veterinarian determines that the birds have some condition or are so sick and injured that they could not survive if they were released into the wild. Many such eagles are destroyed each year because zoos and other institutions cannot take them. The aviary eagles could provide a regular supply of sacred feathers.

The Zunis, a pueblo of more than nine thousand residents in western New Mexico, needed three years to obtain the permissions, raise the money from the BIA and foundations, hire an architect, and build what is essentially a very big bird cage. The complex consists of the main flight way—one hundred feet long, twenty-five feet wide, and eighteen feet high—and three smaller site mews (cages). The average annual eagle population is thirty-two. Staff members gather feathers as the birds molt or pluck them directly from the birds, which are not killed, and distribute them to the Zuni tribal membership for ceremonial purposes.

The aviary is a project that, like some gifts, keeps on giving. It does more than save birds. The sanctuary returns a cherished tradition to the Zunis, even as the people there have returned to their traditional name, Ashiwi. The tribal members were once adept in eagle husbandry, including daily care and taking and keeping eagles for dance regalia and prayer offerings. Federal regulations on endangered species protection interfered with that practice. Now Zuni schoolchildren visit the aviary to learn about bird husbandry from its keepers and elders. Interns from Zuni High School, the University of New Mexico, and New Mexico State University work at the aviary. In one respect, the sanctuary is a partner in the government's endangered species program. "The Zuni solution to the eagle feather shortage is to assist the Fish and Wildlife Service in working with their regulations by providing a facility to place nonreleasable eagles and combining traditional and conventional governance strategies," said Nelson Luna, the director of Zuni's Fish and Wildlife Department and a biologist. Harvard's Kennedy School of Government in 2002 named Zuni one of eight tribes to be awarded "high honors" and granted the pueblo $10,000 for its work on the project. The sanctuary is open for viewing from the exterior, but the public is not allowed in the facility.[10]

The people of Pecos/Jemez, the Diné, and the Zunis: all three groups engaged in a conversation about their values in the modern world. Repatriation took them beyond technical challenges into their community's heart. The Pueblos had to find a new way to rebury their ancestors and to reconcile what they saw as the barbarism of grave robbing with "science"—for themselves and their children. The Navajos had to reconcile beliefs when some felt that a zoo violated the natural order. The Zunis recaptured culture when they found the resources to operate an aviary.

But non-Indians sometimes freeze the meaning of such conversations in a stereotype: the noble savage grappling with modernity. Reality is more complex. The European American conquest tried to strip cultures of their successful millennia-old ways of dealing with the natural world. Indian restoration of that order is not some quaint exercise. Like the Zunis, many Indians combine traditional and conventional strategies and technologies for what we call "science." In health care and natural resources management, the process and result of this synthesis have value.

Traditional medicine, usually in combination with conventional "scientific" medicine, remains a common healing practice for many Indians. By any measure, the health outlook for Native Americans is dreadful due to the combined effects of social, economic, and medical problems. Indians and Alaska Natives can expect to live about three years less than the average American, and their infant mortality rate is 20 percent higher than the nation's. Death rates from various causes are so dramatically higher than those of the general population that they are hard to believe.[11]

Today's crisis in Indian health relates directly to that in the Indian Health Service.[12] Congress established a health service in 1892 in the office of the commissioner of Indian affairs to address the alarming conditions among the Native population. In 1955 the agency became part of the Department of Health and Human Services as a comprehensive health care system for Native Americans to satisfy treaty obligations with tribes.[13] Today, more than half of America's Indians both on rural reservations and in cities rely primarily on the IHS for their medical needs. The term "disinvestment" describes the agency's condition, but it does not reflect the government's century-long neglect of this trust responsibility. In its 2003 study of disparities in Indian health care, the U.S. Commission on Civil Rights called the IHS's budget of $3.6 billion "anorexic." The National Indian Health Board estimated that the federal government would have to triple the IHS's budget just to keep up with current levels of services; for the 2011 fiscal year, President Barack Obama proposed an 8 percent increase over 2010, bringing total appropriations to $4.4 billion.[14] Per capita federal spending for Indians is dead last on the list of other federal expenditures for health, even lower than that for inmates in federal prisons.[15]

Complicating the IHS's budget shortcomings is the splintering of Indian health care. In self-determination contracts with the IHS, tribes now operate more than 440 facilities.[16] As we have seen, health care for urban Indians threatens to implode because of this shift.[17] These disparities fall squarely on patients. One in five receives an incorrect diagnosis, and one-third of the agency's hospitals have been cited as among the worst in the nation.[18] At a hearing of the U.S. Civil Rights Commission, Lyle Jack, a Sioux tribal councilman from Pine Ridge, noted that just two dentists serve forty thousand Oglala Sioux, and at that time the IHS described braces and root canals as "cosmetic," low on the priority list for treatment.[19]

Conflicting attitudes further exacerbate the agency's troubles. Other Americans continue to view Indian health care as "free." With the growth of gaming, some expect tribes to take care of their own, even though most tribes do not have casinos and not all gaming operations produce a profit. Indians expect the U.S. government to honor its trust responsibility. Jack pointed out that health care, like education, was part of the deal when the Oglala Sioux turned over their lands in the treaty of 1868.

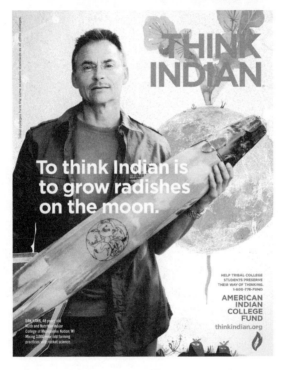

Top: Reservation children learn about animals at the Navajo zoo. Photo by Cary Herz.

Bottom: American Indian science produces results. © American Indian College Fund. All rights reserved.

John Bennett Herrington (Chickasaw), the first American Indian in space. Courtesy of the National Aeronautics and Space Administration.

"It's something we bought and paid for with millions of acres of land. It's not an entitlement," he said.

Jack has seen Indians stay away and risk death before turning to the IHS. They also turn to traditional medicine, an alternative rooted in ceremony and medical knowledge that has survived for millennia. In a survey, 38 percent of patients at an IHS clinic in Milwaukee said they had seen a Native healer, and 86 percent said they would consider seeing one.[20] For many Indians, health care is not an either-or option, either medicine man or non-Native doctor.

Traditional healing practices play an important role, especially in preventing and treating the leading causes of death for American Indians: alcoholism, diabetes, and homicide. For these, the support of family and community is crucial to recovery. Indeed, the Commission on Civil Rights pointed out that tribal management of IHS funds strengthens community-based approaches for chronic conditions that have a behavioral element.[21] But it also leaves the agency short on funds to serve patients directly. As Jon Perez, the director of behavioral health, noted before the commission, "97 per cent of the mental health budget now goes to tribes, not to the IHS."

One physician contends that much of the illness she sees among American Indians is a sickness of the spirit. "Prozac won't fix that," said Tieraona Low Dog.[22] She was talking about patients who are threatened by depression or obesity or are addicted to cigarettes, alcohol, and other substances. "What fixes that is ritual, a return to earth, to spirit, to a quieter way of living." A medical degree gives Low Dog the credentials she needs to practice Western-style medicine, although her starting point has always been what she learned from her grandmother, a Lakota healer. "I grew up never questioning that medicine was anything but spirit. I believed that medicine was that which healed," she said. Low Dog integrates her traditional beliefs and those of modern science rather than choose between them.

As a young woman, Low Dog was a midwife and an herbalist when she realized that her patients' problems exceeded her knowledge. But she hadn't graduated from high school, so she earned her equivalency diploma and then completed her medical training at the University of New Mexico. Low Dog admits that her training was a shock, simultaneously exciting and frightening. She didn't want to touch cadavers and was uncomfortable with jokes about the body. The outspoken Low Dog frankly admits that throughout medical school she had difficulties with people in authority. When a professor told her to get real, "It struck me—I said to him that it was arrogant to say one world was more real than another."

In more than two decades combining tradition and science, Low Dog has reached the top of the alternative-complementary medicine ladder and has taught at the Universities of New Mexico and Arizona and for the Botanical Medicine Course at Columbia University in the Rosenthal Center for Complementary and Alternative Medicine. In 2000 President William J. Clinton appointed her to the White House Commission on Complementary and Alternative Medicine Policy, formed to help the government develop guidelines on these therapies.[23]

The focus of Low Dog's attention is the patient within a circle of healers: surgeon, curandera, nurse, priest, family, and other health workers. Conventional medicine, Low Dog contends, picks symptoms and packages them into a category called "diagnosis." Traditional practitioners don't treat the symptoms or the diagnosis; they treat the person. Low Dog respects science and levels her contempt at its practice and the training of physicians. With other doctors, she alerts both non-Indian and Native medical students to the unique challenge of Indian health care.

Low Dog described taking students to a Navajo community that has a high incidence of diabetes. They met with a diabetic elder who had walked four miles to get to a clinic that is open two days a week. After the students gave the elder a list of proper foods for a diabetic, Low Dog took them to a trading post. They found racks of junk foods and bread beyond its expiration date but nothing fresh or healthful. When the students asked about gardens, she took them to isolated communities with bad roads and no plumbing. Workers at another clinic complained that a patient had missed an appointment, but Low Dog said patients might not be able to walk the distance to the clinic. Clinic physicians and staff and even Indian doctors sometimes do not connect with traditional healers and make no effort to ask how they could help healers serve patients. Low Dog characterized their attitude as arrogant: "'We're the medicine. Come to us, on our schedule. We'll tell you what's good for you.'" Conventional medicine becomes a deterrent to health care. In contrast, traditional medicine's highly personalized approach "can teach us how medicine from this earth—herbs, natural, not processed—can be used."

The students whom Low Dog took to the reservation received a strong dose of Indian reality. Others, especially Indian students, are inoculated with help from the Association of American Indian Physicians (AAIP). The organization's logo consists of the classic medical symbol of the caduceus, a staff entwined with two serpents, and a medicine man's rattle poised above it.[24] At an annual meeting in Santa Fe, New Mexico, about sixty mostly Indian young medical professionals waited for the students' workshop, which the University of Washington sponsors annually. They would first hear from a practicing physician, then analyze a case study, and later meet with traditional healers.

David Ray Baines, MD, a member of Alaska's Tlingit and Tsimshian Tribes, was in a Santa Fe summer uniform: shorts and a T-shirt. His gray-streaked hair was neatly arranged in two long braids, and he had pushed his eyeglasses up onto the top of his head. "Look at what someone is doing wrong, not just what is wrong with someone," he began, using a Sequoia phrase. Baines's path began when he was a teenager in Alaska after a severe work accident. The three-hour trip to a hospital started with forty-five minutes on a stretcher in the back of an old pickup and then a one-hour wait at an abandoned airport on Annette Island. The Coast Guard transported him in a rescue helicopter to the airport near Ketchikan. From there, he had an ambulance ride on a ferry to get to a hospital far from home. He required seventeen surgeries.[25]

From this experience, Baines's lack of interest in school evaporated, replaced with a passion for medicine. After undergraduate work at Arizona State University, he became the first American Indian student at the Mayo Clinic College of Medicine in Rochester, Minnesota. The racism he experienced there often resulted from misunderstanding, even in the smallest details. White people were direct, contrary to his culture, in which a soft handshake was a mark of respect. Like other Indians, he did not have a clock fixation; rather, he was "event-oriented." Even though Baines had cut his hair to fit in, other students felt uncomfortable with him. His education became a game, but he distinguished between the game and the battle. The goal in basketball was "whipping those white boys' asses." In the battle "I was fighting for my people's well-being," he said. Baines's culture was a source of strength and stress. Far from his people, he said the prayers he had learned from elders and sought out other Indians away from the campus. In sweat lodge ceremonies, they prayed for him to finish medical school. Throughout rotations in Chicago and Alaska, he once again found other Indians.

But he had to accommodate his values. His Indian belief system orders society according to tribe first, then family, and finally individual; in the white world, the individual has priority. Baines told the students that the creator in all of us has given us talents as gifts, and we must treat them as such. He faltered only once in his journey. "I almost lost it when I thought His achievements were mine, not the Creator's," he said. In his family practice—"on the rez, this is what you do"—Baines uses a holistic approach based on the idea of health as harmony. "Illness gets us. We don't get the illness," he said. He teaches at the Alaska Family Residency in Anchorage. Despite his individual achievements, Baines acknowledges his teachers, especially Walt Hollow (Sioux and Assiniboine), with whom he worked at the Seattle Indian Health Board. Hollow has mentored many of the American Indian physicians who are practicing today. Baines told the students in the workshop, "We stand on the shoulders of our ancestors."[26]

Then it was the students' turn to play doctor. The "patient" that morning was the fictional Wayne Thunderchild, a middle-aged Blackfeet postal worker. They considered his medical history: obesity with a protuberant abdomen, age, a sedentary lifestyle, a diet of high-fat and high-starch commodity foods, a painful abscess in his groin that would not heal. The students quickly put diabetes at the top of the list of possible diagnoses, which "lab results" confirmed.

In the afternoon, the students turned from this conventional exercise to six traditional healers who offered glimpses of how they work and how they interact with conventional Western medicine either as sole practitioners or in a clinical setting. Carol Locust (Eastern Band of Cherokee) works in the Native Cardiology Program at the Arizona Health Sciences Center in Tucson. She is part of a team of physicians and healers that received a U.S. Department of Health and Human Services Distinguished Service Award for its innovative delivery of cardiac care for Native American peoples.[27] Gerard Kisko (Tohono O'odham) has been a traditional practitioner for thirty years. Rose Auger (Woodland Cree) lives on the Driftpile Reserve in Alberta, Canada, and works anywhere she is called—hospital, jail, home. Lisa Dolchok (Yupik, Aleut, and Filipino) works in Anchorage on the five-member traditional medicine team of the Southcentral Foundation hospital. In a pleasant surprise, Anderson Hoskie, the young medicine man I had met at the zoo, was also on the panel. He had filled out a bit, but his voice was as quiet as ever. Another familiar face was that of Elena Avila, a conventionally trained psychiatric nurse, curandera, and poet with a private practice steeped in Mexican indigenous medicine. She had participated at a conference on traditional medicine I had covered in Albuquerque.[28]

Nature and the power of the mind and spirit are central to the healers' work, but within the group were widely differing methods and beliefs regarding diagnosis, education, and the traditional pharmacopoeia. Avila said, "One of the main principles of curanderismo is that 'heart heals heart.'" Aiming to teach patients about themselves, Avila starts her healing with a plática, a heart-to-heart talk, in which the patients gets to "undrown." This limpia, or spiritual cleansing ceremony, clears the way for healing.

Some of the healers offered more concrete examples of what they do. Dolchok focused on diagnosis. Some Indians might not know how to describe their symptoms because so much pain is emotional and spiritual and often masked by alcohol, drugs, food, and sex (this can also be true for non-Indian patients). She listens to patients' stories—a child with attention deficit disorder, a parent whose son is in prison—in order to elicit information the patient can't see but the doctor needs. Kisko works in the Diabetes Education Program at the Hu Hu Kam Memorial Hospital in Sacaton, near Phoenix. For decades, the program has addressed the high incidence of diabetes among O'odhams living on the Gila River Indian Reservation. Fast food has replaced the traditional diet, which consisted of cholla buds, corn, cactus, squash, pinto beans, and fish from the Gila River.[29] Kisko also tries to help non-Native doctors recognize the value of Native medicine. Before modern pharmacology, Pimas mostly used creosote—"the Indian version of Tylenol"—as an all-purpose treatment for many ailments, Kisko said.[30] Auger reminded the students that Native healing has lasted for thousands of years. Today's healers need to know the waters, trees, and medicines as well as the proper protocol for using them. Hoskie said that he teaches young medicine men ceremonies that rely on the animal kingdom, particularly bears and eagles. "I sound like a zookeeper," he joked. More seriously, Hoskie finds people waiting at his home even after a long day in the clinic. Being a medicine man is a twenty-four-hour job. He is always "on call," but he escapes one harsh reality that the medical students cannot—death. A traditional Navajo healer does not deal with death and doesn't go to funerals.

All the healers talked about their interface with conventional medicine, and the students were ready with questions. They wanted to know how the healers restore themselves when they feel depleted by hospital work. Locust and others answered simply: prayer. Every morning she asks the creator for energy she needs to complete the day; at the end of the day, she asks for energy to get home; and in the evening, she asks for a restful night. One questioner wanted to know if urban Indians are hard to reach. Rose Auger replied, "No, the spirits are everywhere."

The day illuminated how the individual patient occupies center stage for healers and for those who use traditional methods to enrich their conventional training. Human contact—listening as well as touching—are among the healers' instruments. Although Western science continues to debate the power of religion and faith in health, the Native healers felt that prayer is indispensable.[31] The healers encourage patients to unburden themselves, and then changing what the patient does starts the healing process. Nature is the drugstore, clinic, and doctor's office.

Harry Walters's question—"Are we going the way we should?"—puts new generations on the path of traditional healing practices. Because of the emphasis on preparing the body for treatments and nature's role, Low Dog and other traditional healers link health and health care to environmental issues. Low Dog cited the "phenomenal" amounts of pesticides, antibiotics, and other materials in plant and animal husbandry. Incineration of medical wastes harms the environment for miles around the burn site. These pollutants contradict principles of good health. Low Dog said that her grandfather used to tell her, "You always leave footprints, no matter which path you take." Unfortunately, this admirable ethic is not always honored on reservations. Iron Eyes Cody, the stereotypical "crying Indian" weeping over a trash-filled river, could just as well be mourning a roadside or creek in Indian Country littered with beer cans, fast-food containers, and disposable diapers.[32]

The link between health and nature means that the shift from healing to natural resource management is not a great leap. We know that from the Amazon rain forest to the water works at Chaco Canyon, Indians have managed resources since ancient times in technologically advanced though not always beneficial ways.[33] The introduction of European agricultural practices, however, quickly undid generally low-impact Indian cultivation. On Manhattan Island, the Lenapes rotated their fields. When the Dutch moved onto those fields, their intensive farming methods rapidly depleted the land.[34] Ancient peoples did make mistakes. Ancestral Puebloans—at Chaco Canyon, for example—faded in part because they damaged ecosystems.[35]

These examples of mismanagement, however, contrast with European Americans' environmental degradation. The consequences have been catastrophic for Navajo health, for instance. Uranium mines on the Navajo Nation closed after the accident at Three Mile Island, Pennsylvania, in 1979 shut down the nuclear industry, but decades later Indian miners and inhabitants of the area continue to sicken and die from radiation damage. In an incident at Church Rock, New Mexico, thousands of tons of uranium waste burst through a dam and released seven times the legally allowable level of radiation onto the land, worse emissions than those at Three Mile Island. The national press has reported regularly on the condition of miners and other Diné affected by the industry. In 2009 the

Environmental Protection Agency was still tearing down and replacing contaminated houses.[36]

On the path that is the "right way," some Indians are recapturing and passing on their knowledge not only to their own people but also to the wider world. The California Indian Radio Project, which was widely broadcast on public radio, documented resource management among California tribes.[37] Like Natives in the East, California's Indians did not plant neat rows on tilled land, build fences, or domesticate animals. They incorporated the natural topography and learned from the habits of animals. Marion "Kat" Anderson, who coedited a book of essays on environmental management by Native Californians, described their "gardening" techniques. As they sought and gathered tubers, "farmers" popped off cornlets and bulblets that perpetuated the plant populations in the plant's immediate natural environment. The digging process aerated the soil, prepared the seed bed, and thinned the bed so that plants could not overpopulate.[38]

Beyond purely "scientific" practices, Native Americans systematically organized activities in a context that strengthened community bonds. Anthropologist Frank Lobo (Acjachemem) described how women passed on knowledge about harvesting and planting the best seeds to their daughters. Thus, they linked education, environment, sustenance, and social responsibility. "By the time a young girl was fourteen or fifteen, she had a PhD in zoology and botany," Lobo said hyperbolically. Katherine Saubel (Cahuilla) described how she and her mother talked to plants, explaining to the plants why the women were gathering and how they would use specific plants. Saubel and her mother strictly adhered to the rule of always leaving some plants and seeds behind for regermination or for the animals to eat. Even leftovers were husbanded through composting, she said. "When we use these plants, you don't just throw them in the trash can or just throw them out, you burn them or you bury them."

Men and boys had the special duty of harvesting and cooking agave hearts. As the agave roasted, the men used the time to pass on tribal mores to the boys. The Cahuilla people of inland Southern California developed clear and commonly shared principles for hunting, gathering, and ceremonies. "The effect of these rules is management," said Lowell Bean, an anthropologist and professor emeritus from California State University at Hayward. Bean has identified several "rules": don't overuse the environment; plant and hunt at the appropriate times; don't gather or hunt everything; always leave some plants behind for the land and the animals.

Native people hunted or gathered together in structured groups. Their activities would be directed by the religious leaders, who would discuss characteristics of game or land before the tribe initiated a hunt or a seed gathering. "This precluded negative things like overcompetition, overuse of the land, because everything was done in a systematic way," said Bean. Dutch and Spanish newcomers did not recognize Native agricultural practices, which differed radically from their own. The gulf caused irreparable harm to Natives and their food supplies. When Juan Bautista de Anza and his conquistadores arrived in 1774, they allowed their stock to roam freely, and the animals trampled the Natives' prized, genetically manipulated crops and seeds growing in their natural state rather than in neat rows. "They destroyed all the food the Cahuillas had, and they were starving for years before the growth would come back from these animals destroying their food. It was really a sad time," said Saubel.[39]

Across Indian Country, Native Americans draw on nearly forgotten knowledge and methods as a force for renewal. Occasionally, as through the California Indian Radio Project, Native ways can slip into mainstream life, even though scientists continue to discount some of them. Some scientists maintain that Native methods are not "scientifically based"; that is, they do not use the classic steps of the scientific method: hypothesize, test, and replicate. But one scientist insists that Native Americans have always had science, and he uses that science regularly in his work as a restoration ecologist. Thomas Alcoze (of Cherokee heritage) is now a professor in Northern Arizona University's School of Forestry in Flagstaff. But in the early 1970s, when he wanted to study Native American ecology and land-use management, he met a painful response. "I couldn't do that because resource management was a science, and Indians don't have science; therefore, I couldn't study Indian resource management," he said. Alcoze, who earned his doctorate in zoology at Michigan State, set out to prove that this attitude was simply wrong. He first discovered Native science in medicine at a meeting where physicians reported that Native women in South America used a combination of two different plant mixtures for effective birth control. The report, Alcoze said, showed him that Natives had medical science. He inferred that they also probably had ecological science.

Alcoze drew one comparison between Western and Native practices to illustrate the scientific principles in each. Western science might collect data over five years and then analyze them to draw conclusions. Native science collects data and analyzes them over a thousand years and keeps refining them. That Native cultures have survived is further "proof" of the sophistication and complexity of their science. "There's nothing mystical about science. Cultures that survive do so because of their scientific understanding of the natural environment that they must live within," he said.

But some mainstream ecologists still can't believe Indians understand science. "In the West a big issue is fire. Native people managed the Native ecosystem using fire. They knew how to do it. Contemporary fire managers ignore Native ways; they're reinventing the wheel," Alcoze said. In his field, Alcoze draws on conventional and Native methods to address ponderosa pine and other species systems in the West that tend to burn. The restoration ecologist's starting point is the failure of twentieth-century forest management practices. Forest systems have degraded because of excessive resource extraction and overgrazing. The job of the restoration ecologist is to restore health to the ecosystems. "We try to understand what they were doing before they were degraded; they were in pretty good shape in the 1800s. If we return them to health, we can harvest in a sustainable way," he explained. While the field focuses on physical restoration, it gives short shrift to what Alcoze calls the "ethics of land use," the relationship of people to the environment. Without that ethical relationship, people will degrade the environment again. "You get a different result if you view a resource as a commodity or as a gift."

Alcoze does "manipulate the physics," as he put it. But that alone is a linear recipe that dissociates humans from nature: "People have to engage with nature and the environment if they are going to have a sustainable lifestyle in that particular environment." As an example, he compares the high school biology exercise of one hundred children dissecting one hundred frogs to a Navajo woman dissecting a single sheep for a class. The high school frog dissection is abstract, used mainly to identify body parts. The procedure is difficult for Navajo children, for whom the frog is a sacred animal. But the Navajo woman will take each sheep part, identify it, and then describe its use for sustenance. Knowledge goes beyond the abstract. The Navajo "dissection" fits the needs of the Native students, who get cultural and academic understandings of anatomy, both of which include scientific knowledge.[40]

Here and there some resource managers look to Native Americans. California Indians burned the forest with more than one purpose: to make it suitable for reseeding, to keep oaks dominant for a plentiful acorn harvest, and to control pests that might infest plants that were mainstays of their diet. Today, the U.S. Forest Service uses "controlled burns" to prevent catastrophic fires in California and elsewhere. The agency has not always managed them well. In 2000 a burn turned into a disastrous fire in northern New Mexico that destroyed homes and threatened Los Alamos National Laboratories (LANL). Forest Service managers are learning, however. In the Six Rivers National Forest of northwestern California, the Forest Service has been working with healers and basket weavers in the area to manage forests with fire not only to "clean" them but also to encourage better growth of materials for baskets, according to District Ranger John Larson. In his district, the agency began small prescribed burns with guidance from weavers and gatherers. Necessity forced his agency to develop relationships with tribes and other Native groups. "It's helped us to move out in front of other forests that don't quite have the same pressures from the local people to do these sorts of things," he said.[41]

As traditional medicine relies on touch, traditional forestry relies on contact with the natural world. Physicist Stephen Wolfram suggests that conventional science might be ready for similar thinking. In his book *A New Kind of Science*, he narrated his shift away from the accepted path of the past three hundred years, that is, using mathematics to understand nature. Mathematics has worked well for determining the orbit of comets, but it has been less useful for more complicated processes in nature, particularly in biology. "There is in fact no reason to think that systems like those we see in nature should follow only such traditional mathematical rules," he wrote.[42] To delineate a strict correspondence between conventional and Native science is not my purpose here. But respect for perspectives is in order. Wolfram views nature as a computer operating on a few simple rules. Native Americans explored nature's code a long time ago and bent their way of life to it as they planted, built cities in the desert, and explored the stars.

Near the visitors' center at Chaco Canyon, the Albuquerque Astronomical Society has erected a small observatory with sophisticated telescopes and computerized tracking and recording systems. In the clear black sky the stars run riot, and park rangers give talks on what the ancient peoples saw.[43] Chacoans used science, the movements of the sun and moon as well as the constellations, to undertake agricultural and engineering projects. While recording petroglyphs in Chaco Canyon, artist Anna Sofaer discovered a solstice marker atop Fajada Butte. Additional research through the Solstice Project, which she founded in 1978, led her to suggest that a celestial calendar was used to design the complex of great houses in the canyon.[44]

The path from the ancient stargazers to John Herrington (Chickasaw), the first American Indian astronaut, is not as long as one might think. But Native science has not entered the intellectual mainstream, in part because Native and conventional sciences are not particularly accessible to each other. American Indians comprise only 0.2 percent of the nation's 3.2 million scientists and engineers. Native enrollments in college-level science and math programs have increased, but American Indians achieve relatively few graduate degrees. Of the nearly 6,000 doctorates awarded in 2003, Native Americans earned 136—72 in science and engineering.[45]

American Indians not only face financial and educational obstacles but also hesitate to march to the beat of conventional science and technology, given the environmental, cultural, and personal abuse they have endured in the name of science. At the same time, we have seen collaboration in several areas. Even small "nonscientific" steps are noteworthy. Since 1946, scientists at LANL had used the word "kiva" to name fortified, partially buried structures for nuclear experiments. For Pueblo communities around Los Alamos, a kiva is a sacred place, similar to a church, with cultural significance. In December 2000 leaders from Picuris delivered letters to a Los Alamos official, asking that LANL cease using the word "kiva" for these experimental areas. John Browne, the director of LANL, ordered that the word be eliminated from lab buildings immediately.[46]

In another reconnection with their own science, Plains tribes have turned to an old friend, the bison. Mainstream Americans know that people inhabited this land before their own ancestors' arrival. Nearly completely absent from that history, however, are humanity's companions on the continent—up to sixty million bison.[47] In 1500 massive herds of these animals roamed the vast grasslands that covered the interior from New York into the Mountain West and western Canada. The herds of the Texas panhandle were gone by the late 1870s, and their range had shrunk to the eastern plains from Texas to the Dakotas. Bison in North America were nearly extinct in 1884. Over just half a century, Americans had slaughtered them in huge numbers to make room for their cattle, farms, and settlements, and hunters had harvested their hides. The U.S. Army reportedly eliminated herds to stop Indians from roaming off their reservations to hunt and to weaken their resistance to colonization.[48] The slaughter devastated the Indians, not only because their food was gone but also because the animals were family, ancestors, if you will. "In origin stories and creation stories, you'll see buffalo and Indian people are one and the same. They're that closely related," said Fred Dubray, the executive director of the Inter Tribal Bison Cooperative (ITBC).

The cooperative is drawing the animals back into their Native ecosystems. Starting with just seven tribes in 1991, the ITBC had fifty-five tribes caring for about twenty thousand head of bison by 2005. "Caring for" is an inexact description, however.

The organization's larger mission is to restore the animals to the Indian people. In practice, this means that the bison are treated largely as a wildlife resource rather than as an agricultural product; unlike cattle, they are not headed for market. Some tribes do use the meat to feed their own people, especially elders, as part of their efforts to promote traditional nutritional diets. A few tribes also sell some of the wild bison meat to gourmet restaurants, but ITBC animals are not domesticated.

Primarily non-Indian ranchers farm the animals for restaurants and supermarkets. Dubray explained that science has altered those bisons' genes for the ranchers. The result is larger hindquarters—more meat—on the buffalos, but the side effect is to hinder their mobility. Non-Indians also use intensive management practices, such as giving the animals corn on feed lots, so the nutritional benefit of lower-fat meat is lost. The ITBC's tribal bison, however, graze freely on their home grasslands. They eat what they need, including medicinal plants for their health and welfare. People who eat the meat of these wild bison thus benefit from the animals' good health. Although minimal interference with the animals is the rule, conventional science plays a role. The tribes establish relationships with area veterinarians who specialize in bovine science in case animals become ill or are injured. Dubray believes that non-Indian ranchers should have been "disallowed" from raising buffalo because of their methods. "They've pretty well screwed up the process already," he said.[49]

Most of the cooperative's current funding is from a congressional appropriation through the BIA, along with modest membership fees and some private donations. The ITBC obtains bison from the surplus of wild animals on federal lands and distributes them to the tribes; the animals then reproduce on tribal lands. Tribal councils must approve membership in the cooperative and develop a proposal for a bison project, which an ITBC committee reviews before funding. Some tribes want to restore the bison themselves without federal funding. This is a laudable sentiment, Dubray said, "but the federal government is largely responsible for putting us in this situation, and I don't want to let them off the hook. If we do it on our own, that part will be missing, and the healing will be missing."

Dubray said that many tribes link their physical and cultural survival with that of the buffalo. "Over thousands of years, we've formed that kind of relationship, almost a symbiotic relationship," said Dubray. Plains tribes like his own Cheyenne River Sioux derived not just meat and clothing from the bison but also organizational values. A herd might look like a huge, unorganized mass, but it has control mechanisms, leaders, and family structures—even during stampedes. Bison also have a social structure with lead animals and a hierarchy. Activities that disrupt this social organization—killing just one animal, for instance—can lead to chaos; some other animal has to replace the dead one. Seeing the bison's extended family, which is designed to prevent inbreeding, helped the Plains people develop their own extended families and kinship networks. The family structure of the bison is similar to human societies. In times of crisis or for feeding, the animal families came together in herds for mutual support and strength.

The Sioux chose the Black Hills as their homeland because that is where the bison herds came annually in the fall after spending their summers in smaller family units. To prepare for winter, Sioux families gathered berries during the summer months and then met in the Black Hills for the annual Sun Dance and bison hunt. "The Sioux have been organized as long as there have been buffalo on the earth," said Dubray.

Part of Dubray's job is to make the social relationship between bison and Native peoples—which might seem incomprehensible to Americans mostly disconnected from nature—intelligible.

He described a talk he gave at Harvard more than a decade ago. Intimidated by the famed university, he strolled around the campus, trying to decide how to explain the role of bison in Indian societies. Dubray told his audience that a buffalo herd is an institution of knowledge for Indians just like Harvard in mainstream society. If Harvard were to burn down, the institution would recover and rebuild. The bison project is a process of rebuilding a Native institution. "If we can't help the buffalo survive and if they can't survive in this new modern world, we can't either," he said.[50]

As they renew their cultures, Native Americans promote the ways of thinking that have sustained them for millennia. In 2009 the American Indian College Fund launched an ad campaign with the theme "Think Indian." Each ad displays an American Indian student alongside a message about using Native methods to address modern problems. For instance, an individual at the College of Menominee Nation in Wisconsin suggests, "To think Indian is to grow radishes on the moon."

Non-Indians, who take tentative steps into the unfamiliar world of Native thought, might avoid the notion of blending in favor of braiding ideas. As Alcoze put it, braiding combines multiple variables—cultural beliefs, animals, plants, and so on—to understand how a system works while maintaining the distinctiveness of each variable. Kat Anderson also suggests that non-Indians can reach beyond their limited points of view. Setting up a wilderness area doesn't take much knowledge, she said. "What takes knowledge is to meet the dual goals of resource production and the conservation of biological diversity, and this is what Native people in the world have been doing for thousands and thousands of years. This knowledge we can learn from."[51]

5

WHERE HATRED WAS BORN

The women of San Felipe Pueblo had laid out fruit, cheese, and cookies on tables in the lobby of the tribal council's chambers. On this mid-January afternoon, the sun was already warm enough for everyone to shed coats. The leaders of New Mexico's tribal peoples from the nineteen pueblos and the Mescalero Apache, Jicarilla Apache, and Navajo Nations had gathered in the modest office building to meet with two Republican congressmen for a talk about sovereignty. Newt Gingrich, the powerful Speaker of the House of Representatives, was in the state to support the 1998 reelection of Congressman Bill Redmond from northern New Mexico. The day's bright light would illuminate a fundamental gap in understanding about sovereignty between non-Indians and Indians. The history of that divide is complex, yet to grasp even a bit of it allows us to see the link between cultural and political sovereignty that Richard West, the founding director of the NMAI, talked about in the context of repatriation. With their relentless affirmation of sovereignty, American Indians are gathering the tatters of the past and incorporating them in new ways to rebuild their homelands today. Coincidentally, a momentous turn in their history—gaming—simultaneously enhances and threatens sovereignty.

Inside the council chamber, the political leaders crowded around a table. Reporters and hangers-on overflowed past the doorway. Redmond greeted the crowd and briefly described congressional efforts to develop a functional relationship between the U.S. government and tribal governments in New Mexico. Then Albert Hale, the president of the Navajo Nation, stepped forward. "We were here forever, and we will be here forever," Hale said. In just one sentence he had defined sovereignty as Indians see it—elemental and inalienable. Sovereignty is about place, a homeland—"here"—and time—a homeland of "forever." The straight-backed Hale, a lawyer, orated for twenty minutes without notes. The federal government does not give Indians sovereign status; rather, tribal sovereignty is inherent, predating the accidental arrival of Columbus. "We should refer to ourselves as nations. . . . My land is not tribal; it's a nation," Hale continued. Sovereignty means that "we exercise power over anyone who comes into our territorial jurisdiction." When he goes to Washington, he is a head of state and expects the government to treat him as the leader of a nation. Hale said puckishly, "You don't send me to the BIA; you have a state dinner for me."

Before he became president, Hale had served as the Navajo Nation's attorney general, special counsel to the tribal council, and president of the Navajo Nation Bar Association. Nattily dressed, with a short-strand turquoise necklace and a single large turquoise-stone ring, Hale was an elegant foil to Gingrich, who appeared rumpled and frumpy. Addressing the Indian leaders, the Speaker seemed flustered. He asserted that as an easterner, he had difficulty comprehending the difference between a tribe and a nation, the diversity of the groups, and the issue of sovereignty. Because of telecommunications and the tribes' new sources of money, he believed the treaties between the U.S. government and tribes would require revising. Promises were made and not kept, he conceded, and the resulting tension was real. "We need to get ahead of that tension," he said.

Perhaps in the spirit of the Contract for America, which Republicans had unveiled in 1994, Gingrich called for a new partnership based on mutual respect. He said that we need to view "the ancestral right in a unique way that has spiritual meaning." Noting that Indian health care was the principal issue, he called for an allocation of $30 million to fund a diabetes program that could save lives.[1]

Gingrich had missed the point. Like other mainstream politicians, he had fallen back on guilt for broken treaties, paternalism, and a cryptic allusion to spirituality to answer Hale's assertion of sovereignty as self-determination and self-government. I did a double take at Gingrich's professed ignorance of sovereignty. After all, he represented Georgia, a southern, not an eastern, state that successfully initiated the subversion of Indian sovereignty in the 1830s. The federal government subsequently conducted one of the most brutal Native relocations in American history, moving Cherokees and other peoples out of their homelands in the Southeast. Hale and Gingrich were hyperbolic and posturing politicians. By year's end, however, both men had disappeared from high office. A month after the San Felipe meeting, Hale resigned as leader of the Navajo Nation amid charges that he had misused tribal funds.[2] In November 1998 Gingrich had to deal with ethics charges and a GOP rebellion after the party fared poorly in the congressional election. He resigned the Speakership and his House seat. Both remained politically active, Hale as a state legislator and Gingrich as a lobbyist, activist, and writer.

In light of Hale's and Gingrich's exchange, a conclusive meaning of sovereignty remains elusive. At its simplest, sovereignty
signifies the right to be and to rule oneself. The supremacy
of tribal authority on their homelands is the single "right"
that Indians have fought for—forever. That definition rests
unevenly both inside and outside Indian Country, however.
Even at the highest level, Americans remain confused about
Indian sovereignty. At a meeting of journalists of color in 2004,
President George W. Bush said, "Tribal sovereignty means just
that; it's sovereign. You're a—you've been given sovereignty,
and you're viewed as a sovereign entity." Reaction across Indian
Country was swift. W. Ron Allen, the chairman of the Jamestown
S'Klallam Tribe in Washington and a Republican, commented
on Bush's response: "It was clear to us that he didn't know
what he was talking about."[3] The key word in Bush's answer
was "given." As Hale had insisted, sovereignty is inherent, not
"given." A month later President Bush signed a memorandum
on tribal sovereignty and "consultation" to mark the opening
of the NMAI. After a section noting the establishment of tribal
sovereignty in the U.S. Constitution and its acknowledgment
by presidents before him, Bush pledged his commitment to
sovereignty. The document ended with this carefully worded
disclaimer: "This memorandum is intended only to improve
the internal management of the executive branch and is not
intended to, and does not, create any right, benefit, or trust
responsibility, substantive or procedural, enforceable at law
or in equity, by a party against the United States, its agencies,
entities, or instrumentalities, its officers or employees, or any
other person."[4]

Obscuring the basic concept of Indian sovereignty, even for
an American president, is a maze of history, law, and disputa-
tion that has lasted over half a millennium. Most Americans
recognize that something bad happened to Indians, but many

of them do not know the policies that have twisted and turned to reverberate broadly across tribes and deeply into individual lives—to this day. Early Europeans observed and described how Native peoples across the continent built political systems that grew out of trade, territorial claims, war, and social and ceremonial interactions. The founding fathers, including Benjamin Franklin, knew about and even admired the Haudenosaunee League, a "federal" system of governance among northeastern tribes that had been in place for several centuries.

When they were looking for allies in the Revolution, the rebels negotiated the first "American" treaty with the Delawares in 1778. By 1913 the United States had signed nearly four hundred treaties or ratified agreements with tribes.[5] Each treaty was a "nation-to-nation" deal between the United States and a tribal government. The treaties grew out of the exclusive relationship between the United States and Indian nations defined in Articles II and VI of the Constitution. For all practical purposes, however, Indians' ability to sustain and govern themselves diminished as the newcomers spread across and appropriated their lands. Tribes resisted fiercely, most notably in the Indian wars that ranged across the continent on diverse fronts for nearly two centuries. In the treaties, designed to resolve these conflicts, tribes ceded lands in exchange for compensation from the United States, including some portion of their remaining lands as reservations, or confinement areas; annuities; material goods such as tools; health care; protection from American settlers encroaching onto the guaranteed lands; and, later, income from corporate resource development on their lands.

The United States through its Indian agents commonly violated the treaties, for instance, by withholding food and tools. By the early nineteenth century, an agricultural boom combined with the slave trade placed pressure on tribes in the Southeast to sell their fertile lands to tobacco and cotton growers. What followed was a series of policies that facilitated American expansion for the next century and intensified the process of getting Indians out of the way. In one of the early policies, Andrew Jackson, who became president in 1828, encouraged the state of Georgia to take the first steps to remove the Cherokees from their homelands. Congress passed and Jackson signed the Indian Removal Act in 1830, empowering the states to remove tribes from their lands. In a landmark decision, the Supreme Court, led by Justice John Marshall, affirmed Indian sovereignty and the federal-tribe bond. Jackson defied the Court, however, and Georgia triumphed. The forced relocation of Choctaws, Cherokees, and other tribes to "Indian Territory" in Oklahoma began. In their "trail of tears," as many as half of the 16,542 Cherokees enumerated in the 1835 census perished. Over several years, tens of thousands of Indians were forced to leave their homelands with equally devastating population losses.[6]

Another major policy, the Dawes Act of 1887, came with the end of the Indian wars. Also known as the General Allotment Act, the legislation broke up Indian lands and gave the pieces, in 160-acre allotments, to individual members of tribes. The federal government assumed management of Indian lands in trust. It collected royalties from mining and other activities from these "trust lands" and distributed them to the Indian owners. But the numbers of Indians eligible for land could never match, much less exceed, the amount of land available. So the federal government sold the remaining ninety million acres, mostly to American homesteaders. The Dawes Act also defined Native Americans as those living on reservations who could document that one-half of their blood was pure Indian. This notion of Indianness based on "blood quantum" became the controlling principle for tribal membership and property rights.[7] By 1934, when Congress ended the Dawes Act, the Indian homelands of 138 million acres had dwindled from half a continent to a land base about the size of Minnesota.[8]

Sometimes "removals" did not wait for the legislative niceties of "policy" or "regulation." Throughout the colonization process, many European Americans simply pushed Indians out of the way, with devastating results. From the beginning, Natives resisted the destructive impulses of Spanish rule in the Southwest and California, for instance. New Mexico's Pueblo Revolt was not an isolated case. Kumeyaay peoples attacked Junípero Serra's mission San Diego de Alcala in 1775. Later, American settlers and land speculators slowly displaced the fifty or so bands of Kumeyaay-Diegueños from their coastal and inland homelands, which stretched beyond the Mexican border. Delfina Cuero's autobiography graphically describes the hunger and exposure homeless families endured as settlers chased them from one location to another. In the early eighteenth century, Coastal Miwoks forced into mission labor and poor living conditions ran away frequently only to be hunted down, returned, tortured, and imprisoned. They also mounted some organized but relatively feeble resistance. Native Americans lost nearly all their lands, and without land, the tapestry of cultural and political cohesion unraveled. Self-sufficient peoples fell into destitution, and population declined. The Spaniards had estimated the California Indian population at 300,000 in 1769. By 1845 disease, starvation, war, slavery, and murder had wiped out half of them. In just one decade—during the gold rush—the population dropped to 50,000. By 1900 it was only 16,500.[9]

In the twentieth century, the U.S. government moved to mitigate and even reverse the impact of some previous policies, but these efforts sometimes backfired. President Franklin D. Roosevelt implemented the Indian Reorganization Act (IRA) of 1934, a policy designed to restore self-government and self-management of assets to tribes. The IRA has been described as the "New Deal for Indians," but it was loaded with traps. The government encouraged tribes to adopt American-style constitutions with provisions that sometimes ran counter to traditional governance. Indian constitutions validated the blood quantum system established in the Dawes Act. Enrolled tribal members began to carry a "white card"—the Certificate of Degree of Indian Blood (CDIB); they are the only Americans who carry such cards. The BIA uses tribal membership to determine who is eligible for health, education, and other benefits, such as receiving feathers from the National Eagle Repository.

Today, tribes determine membership and voting eligibility—with or without blood quantum.[10] As we have seen, for many Indians, diluting the tribal "blood" by marriage outside the tribe, and especially to non-Indians, endangers sovereignty, their very identities. As sovereignty receded, tribes continued to rely on the federal government and what can loosely be described as "the private sector": churches, corporations, and other organizations.

Some Americans commonly shrug off or ignore policies such as removal, the Dawes Act, and the IRA as something that happened a long time ago, the attitude being, "I'm not responsible, I wasn't there." But one of the most egregious policies—termination and relocation—went into effect in 1953, well within the memory of many Americans.[11] Momentum for such a policy had been building steadily since the 1940s, after a survey found troubling conditions and federal mismanagement on reservations. The policy's strongest proponent was Senator Arthur V. Watkins, a Mormon Republican from Utah and chairman of the subcommittee on Indian affairs, who believed termination would emancipate Indians from the deteriorating reservations. Congress passed 133 separate bills that transferred trust lands from Indian to non-Indian ownership. In 1950 President Harry S. Truman appointed Dillon S. Myer as the commissioner of the Bureau of Indian Affairs. Myer began to oversee the termination policy's implementation. He had no knowledge of Indians, but he had some relevant experience. During World War II he had directed the War Relocation Authority, which managed the relocation of Japanese citizens to internment camps, and later supervised the camps' dismantling. Myer put the policy into place, but he left the BIA in 1953 just as Congress formally adopted the policy.

Designed to force assimilation, termination and relocation had three goals: dissolve certain tribes under federal responsibility; physically relocate Indians to cities and town; and, through Public Law 280, transfer civil jurisdiction in several areas, especially justice, to state governments.[12]

In all, Congress terminated 109 tribes, some large ones, including the resource-rich Klamath and Menominees, and smaller groups, like the various Paiute bands. About twelve thousand individual Indians lost their tribal membership and services protected by treaties and agreements. As the Indians were "emancipated," so were nearly 2.5 million acres of their lands, which lost federal protection. California terminated some forty rancherías (reservations).

By the 1960s the U.S. government realized termination's total failure and abandoned the policy, but restoring the land base has proceeded haltingly. Although Presidents John Kennedy, Lyndon B. Johnson, and Richard M. Nixon repudiated termination, Congress did not repeal it until 1988, thirteen years after the passage of the Indian Self-Determination and Education Act. All tribes resisted termination, and many continue their land claims. A class-action suit settled in 1983 restored recognition to fewer than two dozen of forty terminated rancherías and put others on the road to "untermination." As the government began to distribute repayment checks to Indians, some in California and elsewhere refused even to cash the checks because they could not accept the notion of land—Mother Earth—as a commodity, as real estate.[13] To this day, California's tribes struggle to regain lands and reconstitute their political, social, and cultural systems.

Even as the more brutal actions to shove aside or destroy Indians declined in the twentieth century, the early resistance that the Pueblos and Kumeyaays personified continued. A group of about fifty Native Americans, mostly professionals, gathered in Ohio in 1911 to form the first modern intertribal political organization, the Society of American Indians.[14] In 1919 seventy-five leaders of southern California tribes met to organize the Federation of Mission Indians. The group adopted the slogan "Human Rights and Home Rule." Its membership was almost wholly Indian, although it enjoyed non-Native support and retained non-Indian legal advisors. The federation's members faced arrests and harassment during their fight to secure tribal lands, education, and recognition of Indians as citizens of the United States. Both these groups have disbanded.[15]

After World War II a new brand of activists, including returning veterans, emerged.[16] The campaign for "rights" and "sovereignty" coalesced, prompted by termination and relocation. Fifty tribal leaders met in Denver in 1944 to establish the National Congress of American Indians (NCAI), the oldest surviving national Native organization. Activists used NCAI to respond to termination as a direct threat to treaty rights and sovereign status; theirs was a pan-Indian political action that cut across tribal lines. Today, NCAI has about 250 tribal members. In 2009 the organization opened a new headquarters, which it calls an "embassy of tribal nations," near Dupont Circle in the diplomatic center of Washington DC.

Termination is gone, even as land claims continue, but the mission to protect sovereignty is unchanged. On January 31, 2003, just a few days after the U.S. president's State of the Union message, NCAI president Tex Hall (Mandan, Hidatsa, and Arikara) delivered the first-ever State of the Indian Nations address. Speaking at the National Press Club, Hall framed the discussion in the same stark terms as Albert Hale had: "Tribes are governments, not non-profit organizations, not interest groups, not an ethnic minority. We are one of only three sovereigns listed in the U.S. Constitution, alongside the federal and state governments." Broadcast nationally on C-Span, that first State of the Nations address signaled that things had changed; Indians were flexing more political muscle. NCAI presidents have delivered annual addresses since then.[17]

While the founding of NCAI was a milestone of the postwar period, the American Indian Movement (AIM) came out of the civil rights struggle of the 1960s. AIM gained national visibility in 1969, when it joined a coalition of Indian supporters to take over Alcatraz Island in San Francisco Bay. Before the nineteen-month occupation, Indian activism had been localized in tribes; afterward, that activism coalesced nationally. The action also focused national attention on the condition of Indians, the broken treaties, the disastrous termination policy, and demands for self-determination.[18] In 1973 AIM occupied the community of Wounded Knee for seventy-three days, ostensibly to help tribal members deal with the council's corruption. The occupiers battled two hundred federal agents sent to break up the protest. After two months the siege ended with AIM members in jail, in the courts, or fleeing police, sometimes to Canada. AIM's national influence waned throughout the late 1970s.[19] The issue of American Indian "rights," however, is alive and well. A search on the Internet brings an avalanche of organizations promoting that cause.

Zonnie Gorman said the Self-Determination Act of 1975 stopped the Indian Titanic. It did indeed animate Indian governance with money that started flowing into tribes from two areas, even before Congress enacted self-determination. As federal courts settled major land claims, the tribes gained new resources. Among the tribes that reclaimed lands were Taos Pueblo (New Mexico), the Passamaquoddy Tribe (Maine), and Alaska Natives. Under the Alaska Native Claims Settlement Act, Alaska Natives received forty-five million acres and $1 billion.[20] The total value of the lands far exceeded the cash grant. Also, new money went to tribes from the War on Poverty and Office of Economic Opportunity, while funding for the BIA and the IHS declined as proportions of Indian financial resources.

By 1980 non-BIA/IHS funding for Indians exceeded $400 million, compared to the entire Indian Affairs budget of $345 million in 1960.[21] Using money that federal agencies would have received for programs, tribes took over health, education, and social services. The Navajos, for instance, established their own Office of Navajo Economic Opportunity (ONEO). The agency provided legal services, home improvement training, local community development, alcoholism treatment, clinics, water and road projects, and preschools. The Nation also opened its own school at Rough Rock, New Mexico, and Diné College, the first tribal college.[22]

The Navajos asserted more control over their natural resources. In the 1980s the Navajo Nation filed a suit against Kerr-McGee when the tribe wanted to levy taxes against the company to make up for revenue shortages from mismanaged leases. As the suit proceeded, then–tribal chairman Peterson Zah proposed a deal with Kerr-McGee to establish an escrow account to hold the expected taxes.[23] When the Navajos won the case at the Supreme Court in 1984, the account held $217 million. With it the Navajos established a permanent trust fund that would remain intact until 2005. In 2003 the time approached to unlock the fund. Zah, no longer chairman, and members of a panel appointed by the tribal council toured the reservation to collect Navajo opinion on how to use the money. Despite the tribal leadership's disapproval, the panel also met in several cities with large Navajo populations. "On the reservation, we were always in the dark. For five hundred years, the light never got turned on," Zah told a group in Albuquerque when he explained the open hearings. Urban Diné are still part of the Navajo Nation, and "the trust fund is for all Navajos no matter where they are," he said.[24]

One of the best-known examples of the tribes' new confidence is Cobell v. Norton. In 2010 the complex class-action suit appeared headed for a 3.4-billion-dollar settlement.[25] The case had lasted thirteen years, and it addressed one of the leading causes of the precarious economic condition of tribes and individuals. The system that was supposed to protect Native natural resources and income derived from royalties and leases on mining, timbering, and other development activities on trust lands had broken irreparably. Throughout the twentieth century, congressional commissions had deplored the trust system's continuing mismanagement. The government had done little to address its anarchic operations until 1996, when Elouise Cobell filed a suit on behalf of herself and three hundred thousand other Indians, to force the Department of the Interior to reform the system.

Growing up on Montana's Blackfeet Reservation, Cobell had heard her parents discuss how federal mismanagement had driven their people into dire poverty. By the 1970s Cobell was a banker and the treasurer of the Blackfeet Nation. The trust records she received from the BIA did not square with what she saw on the reservation: poor Blackfeet owned lands that should have brought significant royalty income, but their receipts were puny. Cobell sought a true accounting from Secretary of the Interior Bruce Babbitt and Attorney General Janet Reno. Not satisfied with the government's response, she filed the class-action suit in the U.S. District Court for the District of Columbia in 1996 with the aid of the Native American Rights Fund (NARF) and other attorneys.[26]

During a series of appeals and other actions, the government was unable to meet the court's requirements, and federal district court judge Royce C. Lamberth twice held secretaries of the interior—first Babbitt and then Gale Norton—in contempt. In 2003 Alan Balaran, the investigator Lamberth appointed in 1999, filed several blistering reports on Navajo oil and gas leases. The Navajos received twenty times less for rights-of-way for pipelines across their land than non-Indians and even some other tribes.[27] The total amounts could be staggering because of the number of pipelines crisscrossing Navajo allotment lands. Balaran also found "chaotic document management." He quit the case after 2004, charging that the Interior Department had tried to impede it.[28]

The plaintiffs charged that the government had lost more than $137 billion of funds owed to Indians. In 2004 the fund contained about $3 billion, and Indians received about $500 million in annual payments ranging from a few cents to a few thousand dollars.[29] Finally, in December 2010 the district court granted preliminary approval for a settlement of $3.4 billion, and President Barack Obama signed legislation approving the judgment. As of this writing, the action was pending as members of the suit were notified according to the court's order.

Over the years, the suit became so contentious that in July 2006 a federal court removed Judge Lamberth from presiding over the case. Justice Department lawyers argued that he had lost his objectivity. Such an action is so rare that it has occurred only three times in the nearly one-hundred-year history of the court.[30] In scathing criticism of the government, Judge Lamberth had stated:

> For those harboring hope that the stories of murder, dispossession, forced marches, assimilationist policy programs, and other incidents of cultural genocide against the Indians are merely the echoes of a horrible, bigoted government past that has been sanitized by the good deeds of more recent history, this case serves as an appalling reminder of the evils that result when large numbers of the politically powerless are placed at the mercy of institutions engendered and controlled by a politically powerful few.[31]

While too many Americans view Indian gaming as a bolt from nowhere, it has developed in the context of often disastrous U.S. policies. The Self-Determination Act opened new paths to strength through sovereignty like the Cobell suit and the Navajo trust fund—and gaming. Gaming has also revealed other qualities of contemporary Indian life that are not necessarily new but perhaps more intense. These include heightened entrepreneurship, more aggressive legal activities, and unrelenting protection of sovereignty.

Taking a cue from church bingo halls and the success of state lotteries, tribes entered gaming modestly at first, with bingo in tents and hastily constructed steel buildings. As Indian gaming expanded with the Cabezon and Seminole operations in California and Florida, respectively, those states tried to shut them down. Federal district courts ruled in favor of the tribes, however. Congress passed the Indian Gaming Regulatory Act (IGRA) in 1988, and by 2006, 225 Indian casinos in 28 states (out of 564 federally recognized tribes) generated $30 billion in revenue.[32]

Today, many Americans—11 percent of Californians—live within driving distance of an Indian casino.[33] Repeated visits to the gaming palaces have bruised this reporter's objectivity. From Connecticut to Washington State, the casinos' architecture bows to Las Vegas glitz to intrude on some of the country's most beautiful landscapes. The huge Mashantucket Pequots' Foxwoods, with cavernous gaming rooms, rises insolently out of the gentle Connecticut hills. In California the midsized Barona Ranch Casino (Kumeyaay) in eastern San Diego County and the River Rock Casino (Dry Creek Pomo) in northern California's Alexander Valley ramble over hills and wine country. Smaller than these, the multistory Quinault casino and hotel complex interrupts a broad, windswept, and spare beach on Washington's Olympic peninsula. In a magical valley formed by the Trinity River of northern California, the Hupas' Lucky Bear Casino is in a storefront in a small shopping center.

Gaming rooms are numbingly similar, the atmosphere is honky-tonk, and big-name celebrities have jumped into the lucrative Indian casino circuit. Most casinos display little of Native cultures, although some (like that of the Mashantucket Pequots) display impressive collections of contemporary American Indian art. Indeed, tribal community life takes place far from them. At Oneida's Turning Stone Resort Casino in central New York and others, buses and vans disgorge the elderly, some from nursing homes in wheelchairs or with walkers; they arrive looking as much for social contact as for the doubtful possibility of striking it rich. Asians crowd around baccarat and blackjack tables.[34] Many of the players are low rollers who hunch over the slots or hover at the roulette tables, their cigarettes nervously tapping the ashtrays at their fingertips, their eyes glazed with misplaced hope. One former California official estimated that the state had 250,000 "pathological gamblers."[35] Some tribes have funded addiction programs, and pamphlets exhorting patrons to seek help are part of casino decor.

Americans generally support Indian gaming, with some qualifications. In a survey conducted by the *Los Angeles Times*, the majority of those questioned supported gaming, and nearly half had either visited a casino or knew a family member who had.[36] At the same time, some Americans ask, "Where does the money go?" As Charles Wilkinson has pointed out, the amount of gaming revenue that trickles down to individual tribes varies. After taxes (or revenue sharing), operating costs (including regulatory activities), and debt service to non-Native backers, tribes net about 30 percent of the gross. Leaving aside the twenty highest revenue generating tribes, he calculated that each of the remaining tribes nets $5 to $15 million per year. With this sum tribal governments can initiate modest infrastructure or social programs.

Federal legislation regulates the way tribes can use revenue. It establishes categories of gaming; mandates that the tribes adopt their own gaming ordinances and regulatory agencies; and requires them to establish agreements with states that must be approved by the secretary of the interior. By law, revenues must go for tribal, that is, government, purposes, not for profit. Gaming has bankrolled preschools, water and sewer systems, senior centers, health clinics, housing, museums, scholarships, and environmental protection. Several tribes, such as the Mashantucket Pequots, Sycuan Kumeyaays, and Okay Owingeh Pueblos (San Juan), have diversified gaming revenues with investments, including real estate, resort and convention facilities, manufacturing, construction, and shopping centers. Holdings of the Southern Utes of Colorado cut across twelve states and include oil leases in the Gulf of Mexico, a luxury condominium in Denver, an office building in Kansas City, and more.[37]

Although non-Indian companies have financed and managed Indian gaming, tribes are working to assume greater control over their operations. In California the Sycuans have donated more than $5 million to San Diego State University to establish the Sycuan Band of Kumeyaay Nations Institute on Tribal Gaming; its curriculum covers the broader hospitality industry.[38]

Besides the concerns about gaming revenues and regulation, Americans have other qualms. They object to particular casinos, and they want tribes to share the loot. Gaming has replaced the cigar store wooden Indian stereotype with the "casino Indian": wily, rich, fat, corrupt, ready to ruin neighborhoods. A study by the University of Massachusetts that gauged opposition to projects—the NIMBY (Not in My Back Yard) factor—showed that casinos were second only to landfills as undesirable developments; 80 percent of the respondents would not approve of a casino in their communities.[39]

Some of this opposition is self-serving. When a dispute over a casino on the Jamul Reservation broke out in eastern San Diego County, white neighbors in the town of Jamul organized as Jamulians against Casinos. The residents of the six-acre, postage-stamp-sized reservation had morphed from downtrodden, peaceful Indians to sovereignty-spouting bad neighbors, rapacious casino developers who wanted to despoil the bucolic environs. But "estate houses" sprawl across the Jamul Valley's landscape, and a shopping area squats at an intersection just a few miles from the reservation. The Jamul dispute sounded like a classic NIMBY with one important difference: the Jamuls are a federally recognized tribe, and its relationship to other governments is different from that of a nonprofit organization, a neighborhood association, an environmental group, or a commercial enterprise. By 2008 the much-downscaled casino was still a paper venture, as Jamul, local, and state officials argued about the Indians' jurisdictional rights.[40]

Jobs, state and local revenue sharing, traffic, crime, a shift of consumer spending from towns to casinos, and gaming addiction combine for a heady mix of issues with many casino–state compact negotiations. Public opinion has also questioned "reservation shopping." A tribe buys land away from the reservation near an urban area, gets the land into the trust system, and then uses it for a casino.[41]

Some Americans worry that tribes will use gaming revenues to reclaim their homelands, which disappeared through cessions, fraud, or outright theft, in Georgia, San Diego and Marin Counties in California, and central New York, for instance. Non-Indians fear they will have to surrender their homes and become the dispossessed. Indian efforts to regain their lands have had uneven results, however. Sandia Pueblo obtained its rights over the western face of the Sandia Mountains, but it had to assure nervous homeowners in Albuquerque's foothills that access would remain open. On Long Island, the impoverished eleven-hundred-member Shinnecock Tribe won federal recognition in 2010. On its agenda is not only a casino but also land claims in the fabled Hamptons, including the exclusive Shinnecock Hills Golf Club.[42] The Oneidas of central New York have regained a small portion of their lands. During the American Revolution, they joined the rebel cause in return for protection for their six-million-acre homeland. Both sides ravaged Oneida villages, and the Continental Congress reneged on its promise. With their land base reduced to just thirty-two acres and most of the tribe relocated to Wisconsin, the Oneidas repeatedly pressed their land claims in New York. While they had hoped to regain 250,000 acres of ancestral land, they have received bits and pieces and continue their efforts to assemble the rest. In 2008 the BIA urged the Department of the Interior to put about thirteen thousand acres of land into trust, and a federal judge has ruled for the Oneida Nation on smaller parcels.[43]

For financially stretched towns and states, Indian gaming has been a boon, however. In 1998, five years after the Mashantucket and Mohegan casinos started operating, tiny Connecticut ranked second in the nation in public (government) employment. The eighteen thousand people working for tribes, which are government entities, had inflated the statistic; that number reached twenty thousand in the mid-2000s, then dropped back to eighteen thousand during the recession.[44] "Revenue sharing" has become a mantra for the states. In effect, it is a tax on tribal governments, although in practice governments do not tax each other (individual Indians pay income and other taxes). The Mashantucket Pequots signed the first state compact with Connecticut in 1993, agreeing to a 25 percent revenue-sharing scheme that by 2003 had yielded $400 million for the state.

In 2006 the National Indian Gaming Association reported that casinos generated $2.4 billion to states in revenue sharing, taxes, and other payments. Tribes paid more than $100 million to local governments. California's revenue sharing started with fifty-eight tribes signing a compact in 1999, and the state has regularly asked for more. (California's compacts feature a provision for redistributing a portion of gaming revenues to tribes without casinos.) As the state's budget sank into deficits, Governor Gray Davis asked the tribes in 2003 to pay $1.5 billion into the treasury. The tribes refused, and Indian gaming revenues became a major issue in the gubernatorial election. Candidate Arnold Schwarzenegger pledged to make the Indians "pay their fair share" of their gaming revenues.[45] The newly elected Governor Schwarzenegger successfully opposed gaming measures supported by the tribes, including one that would have imposed a 25 percent rate on all casinos. Schwarzenegger contended that revenue sharing should not be legislated but negotiated—with him. He moved quickly to settle compacts with individual tribes.[46]

The Bosque Redondo Memorial, Bosque Redondo, New Mexico, where hatred was born and sovereignty nearly died more than a century ago. Courtesy of the New Mexico Department of Cultural Affairs and the Museum
of New Mexico.

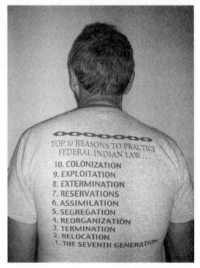

Above: The Embassy of Tribal Nations in Washington DC, where sovereignty lives today. In 2009 the staff of the National Congress of American Indians gathered for the opening of its new headquarters. Courtesy of the National Congress of American Indians.

Right: Sovereignty in a T-shirt from the National Native American Law Students Association. Photo by John Romano (author's collection).

Americans' fears about organized crime moving into Indian gaming seem to have been overtaken by the activities of Jack Abramoff. A lobbyist with strong ties to the Bush administration, he had collected about $80 million in consulting fees from tribes that sought favors with Washington lawmakers. In private messages, Abramoff and an associate referred to their Indian clients as "morons" and "troglodytes." Convicted of fraud, tax evasion, and conspiracy to bribe public officials, Abramoff began serving a seventy-month term in 2006. Tribal leaders worried that gaming opponents would blame Indians for the Abramoff scandal, even though only about a half dozen tribes were involved. David Sickey, the chairman of the Coushatta Tribe of Louisiana, one of Abramoff's clients, quipped, "Indian country is looking forward to the day when Jack Abramoff will become Jack Afterthought." The scandal did prompt John J. Miller of the *Wall Street Journal* to revitalize an old idea—termination. He argued that the United States should dispense with reservations, which he described as "collectivist enclaves" that "have beaten down their inhabitants with brute force rather than lifting them up with opportunity."[47]

Like other Americans, Indians are not single-minded about casinos. Gaming was ubiquitous before contact; peone was and still is a popular game among some California Natives. But various tribes have rejected gambling for several reasons, including tradition, religious belief, and the remote locations of their reservations, where a casino could not succeed. Strongly influencing the Navajos, who rejected gaming twice in the 1990s, is the story of the great gambler, the god Noqoìlpi. He acquired his name—He Who Wins Men—because he took his winnings in slaves. In the story, the Navajos do not participate in gambling; other gods intervene and defeat Noqoìlpi in a series of complicated games.[48] But the tribal government overruled voters' wishes and opened its Fire Rock Casino in 2008 along Interstate 40, eight miles east of Gallup. Despite three consecutive quarters of revenue decline in Arizona gaming, the Navajo Nation has considered expansion with additional casinos there.[49]

Tex Hall reflected ambivalence about gaming when he wrote that the Abramoff situation had diverted attention from a more important scandal—the poverty on reservations. Hall noted that the largest benefits of casinos were limited to only twenty or so tribes.[50] Gaming's benefits are ephemeral, according to a study from the University of California, Riverside, in 2006. Casino tribes saw a reduction in the percentage of families in poverty, from 36 percent in 1990 to 26 percent between 1990 and 2000. But the percentage of Indians living in poverty remained more than double that of the national average for all Americans. Tribal unemployment at 17 percent was still much higher than California's at 7 percent. Even in education, success was not clear. Among gaming tribes, the percentage of those with less than a ninth-grade education was reduced from 11 to 6 percent, but among nongaming tribes, it increased from 12 to 15 percent. Another benefit is that gaming revenues have led to more sophisticated tribal administrations able to capture more federal grants.[51]

By the early 2000s Indian gaming faced several challenges. During the national recession, Indian gaming revenue, which had doubled between 2000 and 2006, slowed to just 7 percent between 2006 and 2008. Some casinos—for instance, the Mashantucket Pequots' Foxwoods and the Mohegans' Mohegan Sun in Connecticut—began to lay off workers and trim plans for expansion; in May 2010 both casinos reported declines in slot machine revenues. In that year, the Mashantucket Pequot Nation had begun talks with lenders on how to restructure a debt that exceeded $2 billion.[52]

Even before the recession, Indian casinos had to deal with regulatory reform. The Internal Revenue Service began to question how tribes spent casino revenues for real estate rather than public works.[53] Also, as gaming has expanded, intergovernmental relationships have become more complex. State and local politics and bureaucracies have increasingly intruded into the long-standing tribal–federal relationship. States demand revenue sharing and require environmental impact assessments, along with local approvals. Knowledge of sovereignty varies enormously among states and localities. Dianne Jacob, a San Diego County supervisor, told a federal commission in 1998 that the tribal–county government relationship was virtually nonexistent, so resolving problems was nearly impossible. By 2005 Ms. Jacob was well versed in sovereignty and led a strong opposition to the Jamuls' plans for a casino in her district.[54]

Native Americans' assertiveness, which is not merely a result of gaming, reflects their self-confidence. Tribes continue to feel besieged by threats to sovereignty from governments and from internal conflicts, however. Shooting has stopped, but the Indian wars have some new weapons. As one Indian leader has put it, "When the war chiefs used to go to Washington, they took peace pipes and war bonnets. When I go to Washington now, I take a briefcase and a couple of lawyers."[55]

The community of Indian lawyers is minuscule. Of the four hundred thousand lawyers in the American Bar Association, about five thousand are American Indians; just over half of those are women. This number has grown over three decades, however, from just twenty-five lawyers and fifteen students.[56] To increase the number of Indian lawyers and students across the country, the University of New Mexico Law School established a summer scholarship program in 1966 for twenty to thirty Indian college graduates headed to law schools. UNM also introduced a comprehensive certificate program in Indian law open to all law students. Since then, more than two hundred

Native students have graduated from UNM Law School, more than from any other law school. While some graduates of law schools around the country have joined mainstream firms, others are in tribal or other government service.[57] The National American Indian Court Judges Association was established in 1969 to strengthen tribal justice systems to better serve sovereignty and self-government. In 2000 the National Tribal Justice Resource Center began tracking the nearly five hundred judicial systems that tribes have established.[58]

Sovereignty is on Indian Country's docket, not just on its mind. In 2002 the Indian law division of the Federal Bar Association devoted its entire annual meeting to this theme. Several hundred non-Indian and Indian lawyers considered the impact of court decisions, the status of tribal jurisdiction, and the protection of tribal sovereignty.[59] At the conference only a silver and turquoise accessory or occasional braid broke through the suits. At a long table, members of the National Native American Law Students Association (NNALSA) hawked T-shirts emblazoned with this call to arms:

TOP TEN REASONS TO PRACTICE
FEDERAL INDIAN LAW . . .

10. Colonization
9. Exploitation
8. Extermination
7. Reservations
6. Assimilation
5. Segregation
4. Reorganization
3. Termination
2. Relocation
1. The Seventh Generation

In the keynote speech, Frank LaMere (Winnebago) used the word "assault" to describe what has been happening to sovereignty in the legal arena.[60] The issues haven't changed much over five centuries. David Getches of the University of Colorado reported that in the first fifteen years after William Rehnquist became chief justice, tribal interests lost 77 percent of their cases, compared with 42 percent of their cases when Warren Burger presided over the Supreme Court.

During Rehnquist's tenure, the Court ruled against tribes, usually in favor of state interests, in all cases relating to jurisdiction over nonmember conduct or property within a reservation. Getches noted that the Rehnquist Court's decisions reflected its decisions generally: the promotion of states' rights, mainstream values, and "color-blind justice," which does not consider the special status of Indians. But, he said, such decisions reverse congressional intent, which favors self-determination and economic self-sufficiency. A warning from the distinguished judge William C. Canby Jr. to the assembled jurists made sense: "Try not to let your cases go to the Supreme Court."[61]

The impact of the Court's decisions has been widespread. One ruling divided zoning authority over nonmembers' land inside a reservation between the tribe and the local county government and undermined land-use planning. The result has been a confusing and hostile atmosphere that discourages investors, increases tensions between non-Indians and Indians, and complicates the work of tribal, state, and local governments. More seriously, tribal governments could not try and punish non-Indian defendants for crimes they committed on reservations. N. Bruce Duthu (Houma) has written eloquently on the impact of these rulings on the prosecution of rapes that occur on reservations. American Indian women overwhelmingly identify non-Indians as their assailants, but tribal law enforcement and judicial organizations have been powerless to prosecute.

In 2010, however, tribes could look forward to expanded jurisdictional and judicial authority, when President Barack Obama signed the landmark Tribal Law and Order Act (TLOA). Generally, tribal and federal officials expect that the new law will give police, prosecutors, and courts more and better tools to deal with the high levels of violence on reservations. It gives tribes more authority for sentencing, according to John Dossett, the general counsel for NCAI. The act also increases funding for additional tribal police officers and reverses what he called "a lack of nuts and bolts of law enforcement."[62] Because tribal systems are so understaffed, criminal elements believe they can escape arrest and punishment.

Finally, the new law will end past practices when the Department of Justice did not aggressively prosecute crimes on tribal lands, an acute problem in cases of sexual and domestic assault. Dossett explained that in nonreservation communities, local government authorities handle such crimes. In Indian Country, federal prosecutors are responsible for prosecuting these cases, but the Justice Department had failed to pursue two-thirds of them. The TLOA provides new tools for federal and tribal police officers to improve coordination among tribes, the Department of Justice, and the Indian Health Service and to develop standardized sexual assault policies and protocols. Now that the department is accountable for prosecutions, it must keep records of its activities and share those records with Congress. The act also supports prevention of violence against women and girls with additional programs for alcohol and substance abuse for men and boys. "In the short term, we need to set a new tone for law enforcement," Dossett said. In the long term, tribes want to build alternatives to incarceration and focus on rehabilitation, especially for juvenile offenders.

The new law had a long gestation period. Dossett pointed out that the issues it addresses have circulated in Indian Country for decades. Its evolution illustrates how Indian leaders have become more assertive in recent years. Dossett said that efforts to deal with law enforcement on reservations had begun during the early years of the George W. Bush administration. At that time, a special committee, including tribal representatives and a number of U.S. attorneys, began work. But in December 2006, when Attorney General Alberto Gonzales fired a large group of U.S. attorneys, some members of the committee, including its chairman, Tom Hefflefinger, the U.S. attorney for Minnesota, were caught up in the sweep.

During their midyear conference in 2007, NCAI's leaders realized that the time for theoretical arguments about jurisdiction had passed, and they had to appeal directly to Congress. They turned to Senator Byron L. Dorgan (D-ND), chairman of the Senate Indian Affairs Committee, who held hearings. "We put 150 solutions in front of Congress to see what would stick," Dossett said. Dorgan and Representative Stephanie Sandlin (D-ND) introduced the bill creating the TLOA, which passed with bipartisan support.

Indian expectations for the power of sovereignty are high, perhaps too high. "We want this pure, unadulterated, untouched sovereignty—sovereignty that we did not enjoy even in our best days generations ago. People want the storybook version of sovereignty," LaMere had said at the 2002 Federal Bar meeting. Indians need to earn the fruits of sovereignty through a full engagement, even in the mainstream political process.[63] Like LaMere, Philip "Sam" Deloria (Standing Rock Sioux) noted that every sovereign state on earth has limits. He heads the American Indian Law Center (AILC), which UNM created in 1967 to help tribes with governance. Sovereignty is no more and no less than the power to govern, and the true test of sovereignty is the quality of tribal governments, how well they serve their people. In that context, Deloria said that "sovereignty" is a meaningless buzzword. "It answers nothing on government and intergovernmental relations and how Indian reservations are governed," he said. Deloria estimated that tribes don't use even half their sovereign powers to govern because they have not addressed large areas of community life that governmental entities across the United States commonly attend to, such as domestic violence and senior services. Such omissions by tribal governments become relevant, he said, "when you hear them bitching about how their sovereignty is so constrained."

Also, Indians and government officials too often dig into stereotypes. In chronic disputes between tribal and fish and game authorities, regulators see themselves as pure scientists with Indians as wild cards, screwing up the system, using spotlights and power guns in hunting. Indians fancy themselves as James Fenimore Cooper characters in the woods, taking game only for subsistence. Animals don't know where jurisdictional lines are, however. Both sides must shed their stereotypes to manage wildlife properly.

Gaming has distorted governance, Deloria said. Tribes must waive bits of sovereignty when they negotiate compacts. As they borrow to start casinos, they subject themselves to mainstream lending practices. A lender can sue in case of default, and those suits must be in U.S. courts. "Tell a lender he can sue in tribal court, and he's gone," Deloria said. Over the next twenty-five years, he continued, tribal governments must enter mainstream political and economic systems in ways they never have before. Their governments are a blend of European American and traditional forms. "So's a slot machine, and if I had to choose the greater threat to the Indian way of life, it would be the slot machine every time," he said.[64]

Deloria's comments became particularly relevant when we consider the example of the Mashantucket Pequots' effort to restructure their debt with Bank of America during 2010. Tribal sovereignty made it difficult to gain information about the situation, except for some details like the 713-million-dollar payment due in July 2010. Also, Moody's stopped rating the Pequots. In another complication, because of sovereignty, tribes cannot file for bankruptcy and lenders cannot foreclose on assets.[65]

The concept of sovereignty is like a continuo in music. It's the perpetual bass line anchoring Native America. In the framework of repatriation, cultural sovereignty and political sovereignty are identical in their essence: the right to be and rule oneself over time, forever. In Indian Country, however, sovereignty sometimes becomes a shell game: now you see it, now you don't. Tribal leaders work to strengthen sovereignty and governance through NCAI, tribal courts, and other mechanisms, but, as Deloria suggested, they are inconsistent; some use or set aside their sovereign status to pursue other goals. Sovereignty can strike at Americans' favored stereotypes, for instance, their view of Indians as the supreme tree-huggers. In Arizona the Hualapai Nation of the Grand Canyon opened Skywalk at Grand Canyon West, a tourist attraction they had established in 1988. Skywalk, a glass-bottomed walkway, extends seventy feet from the walls of the canyon over the Colorado River. It has provoked outrage among many non-Indians. How could Indians do this to the Grand Canyon? Not sounding much like a "natural man" or "noble savage," Hualapai chairman Charlie Vaughn said that the tribe can do anything it wants, no matter how "offensive" the result might be. "We're the ones who are going to have to live with this; we're the ones who are going to be here forever. We have to be able to chart our own destiny."[66]

Sovereignty can also fray tribal cohesion. Because of the Dawes Act, race and genetics continue to influence the question of tribal membership. The issue of who is Indian can take an ugly turn. In 2007 the Cherokees voted overwhelmingly to amend their constitution and end citizenship for freedmen, the descendants of black slaves owned by the Cherokees, freed blacks married to Cherokees, and their mixed-race children, all of whom had been removed with the tribe to Oklahoma. Following the Civil War, the federal government convinced the Cherokee Nation to grant citizenship for the freedmen, despite the tribe's long-standing resistance. The Cherokees' latest assertion is yet another chapter in this long and tortured history.[67]

In 2009, after some freedmen sued the tribe, John T. Cripps of the Cherokee District Court ruled for the tribe's right to determine its membership and that the Cherokee Nation has no treaty-based right to citizenship. If the Cherokee action holds, nearly three thousand enrolled black Cherokees will lose their BIA benefits. Susan Watson, an African American congresswoman from Los Angeles, quickly introduced a bill that would sever the federal relationship with the Cherokee Nation. The tribe would lose its benefits—about 75 percent of its annual budget of $300 million per year—and its gaming rights until it restored the freedmen's membership. The tribe scrambled to block the legislation; by 2009 the conflict was winding through federal courts.[68]

Governance sits unevenly on the tribes in part because of the shifting sands of federal policies and actions. Even strong traditional systems have weakened or disappeared. Tribal governments "modernize" in fits and starts. Taking up a thoroughly contemporary debate, the Navajos passed a measure to prohibit gay marriage. President Joe Shirley vetoed it, but the council overrode the veto.[69]

Since the 1980s women have entered leadership positions, reconnecting to the significant roles they had in traditional governance.[70] In 1987 Wilma Mankiller became the first woman elected to head a major Indian group, the Cherokees. Claudeen Bates Arthur, the first Navajo woman licensed lawyer, became the Navajo Nation's first woman attorney general in 1983 and in 2003 was confirmed as the chief justice of the Navajo Nation Supreme Court, the largest tribal judicial system in the United States. But the way has not been smooth. After Cecelia Fire Thunder's election in 2004 as the first woman to lead the Oglala Sioux, tribal government officials suspended her, although a series of charges brought against her was dismissed. A few months later, after the South Dakota legislature voted for a near-total ban on abortions, Fire Thunder, a former nurse, proposed opening a clinic on the reservation where women could have abortions in case of rape and incest. The tribal council successfully impeached her, and she never regained her position.[71]

Connie Reitman witnesses the ambiguity of sovereignty and governance from the grass roots. A Pomo, she is the executive director of California's Inter Tribal Council. What happened when the council organized a conference for California's one-hundred-plus tribal leaders spoke volumes about the priorities in governance. The planners had announced that the conference in Sacramento in 2005 would address issues "beyond gaming," especially sovereignty and training a new generation of leaders. But most of the tribal leaders sent lower-level officials and went instead to a gaming conference elsewhere. Matt Franklin, the chairman of the Ione band of Miwok, told the conferees that leaders had similarly skipped a conference on education in favor of a gaming meeting. When Franklin asked some why they had neglected the education conference, they answered that they were tending to economic development. "But tribal leaders have to cover all the bases," Franklin said.

Reitman agreed that tribes must directly address domestic issues—health, education, and homeland security—and external relations with state and local governments. She described past leadership strategies that reveal a gap between the governors and the governed in Indian Country today. When California's tribal leaders went to Washington in 1969 to lobby for projects, they were so strapped for cash that they carried bologna sandwiches to eat, she said. The leaders came back with funding for health, education, and housing. "That's the legacy of some of our elders. At a time when our people had nothing, they were able to create viable programs and services."[72]

The feeling that gaming has corroded Indian governance has some currency. In an interview, a distinguished Sycuan elder named one thing she would do differently: "I would have never agreed to build the bingo hall in the first place. These days, it's all about power, money and greed. Those three together will destroy even the strongest nation."[73] The mainstream press has published stories about abuses in gaming and regulation.[74] Powerful gaming tribes try to block other, smaller tribes from opening rival casinos.[75]

The casinos also have other side effects. San Pasqual Kumeyaays dynamited a mountainside to expand their casino in San Diego County. Indians use nature, and, at times, they use it up. Indians slashing the earth have the same effect on the environment as cutting mountains for coal or for monuments like Mount Rushmore or depleting rivers and watersheds for swimming pools and for subdivisions in Arizona.

Some communities where residents oppose gaming mistakenly believe that tribes want sovereignty for ulterior motives. The thinking is that tribes like the Mashantucket Pequots have pursued federal recognition of their legitimate tribal status in order to use sovereignty for business reasons, primarily, to build the giant Foxwoods Casino.[76] Americans should not be surprised at this motive, yet the reverse is also true. As one scholar has put it, "The more people understand how dire things are in many parts of Indian Country, the more they'll realize how casinos have been a brilliant vehicle for the exercise of sovereignty."[77] Outsiders and some Indians cringe at developments like these. But a popular T-shirt offers a vivid context. Under a photo of an aging Geronimo and three other determined warriors gripping their rifles, this legend plays: "Homeland Security: Fighting Terrorism Since 1492." The shirt provokes smiles that camouflage memories of disease, murder, and resistance. Gaming has happened in that context; it is not a deus ex machina, a sudden and unexpected divine intervention.[78]

Smiles were scarce in June 2005, when the state of New Mexico commemorated the Navajo Long Walk by dedicating Fort Sumner State Monument, a division of the Museum of New Mexico. In this series of events between 1864 and 1868, the U.S. Army removed the Diné from their homelands to Bosque Redondo in eastern New Mexico. It could have happened yesterday, given the somber mood of the five hundred people who gathered for the dedication on a breezy and blazing sunny day. Thousands of Diné lived and died in that dusty, hot place as they tried to make a new home far from their own. On this day, the complexity of Indian life was in the details: an elder wore a baseball cap with a legend that seemed oblivious to the Indian mascots controversy: "Redskins XXII Super Bowl Champions."

Lawrence Morgan, the speaker of the Navajo Nation tribal council, told the audience that, traditionally, the Diné do not commemorate the dead. But this, he said, "is a visit to a slaughterhouse." Joe Shirley commented that the monument attests to the resilience of his people. But the darkness was never far away. Whole families died as their ancestors fought simply for "the right to be," he told the audience. "This place can never be celebrated. Hatred was born here." Prominent white politicians—the governor, lieutenant governor, and U.S. senators—also spoke about this bitter chapter in our history and our "selective amnesia."

The Navajo people have emerged from the horror of Bosque Redondo to tell the Long Walk's story with a renewed strength,

Morgan said. In the summer of 1863, as the Civil War raged, Brig. Gen. James T. Carleton, the territorial governor of New Mexico, proceeded in a war against the rebellious Navajos. He recruited Christopher "Kit" Carson to organize the round-up of more than eight thousand Diné. Carson knew that Canyon de Chelly was the heart of Diné Bikéyah. Ancestral Puebloans had a long history in the deeply cut sandstone canyon, one of the more spectacular places on the continent. The canyon had become a Diné population center by 1700. Carson had to strike the canyon decisively in order to overcome fierce resistance. He was efficient. U.S. soldiers and their Ute allies swooped through Canyon de Chelly methodically, destroying crops, chopping down every peach tree (more than four thousand by one estimate), and killing every head of livestock they could find. Some Navajos sought refuge in the canyon's deep crevices. Others escaped to the Grand Canyon and to the western parts of their homeland with their sheep.

Soldiers forced the Diné to walk the 250 miles to Bosque Redondo—a circular grove—at Fort Sumner in eastern New Mexico, one of a string of outposts in the western territories. There the government established what was supposed to be a Navajo reservation, a new home. But thousands died on the forced march, and Bosque Redondo was a concentration camp not only for Navajos but also for Mescalero Apaches. This remote, bleak spot became known as Hweeldi, "a place of suffering." The Americans gave the Diné tools to turn them into farmers and blacksmiths, but drought and unfamiliarity with the land guaranteed failure. Diseases swept through the encampment; syphilis spread when desperate Navajo women turned to prostitution to supply their families with food.

By 1868 the federal government realized that the situation was catastrophic and that the Diné would have to be moved. Gen. William Tecumseh Sherman arrived in the spring of that year to negotiate with Barboncito, a medicine man and head chief. The general tried to convince Barboncito to lead his people to "Indian Territory" (Oklahoma). But Barboncito and other leaders refused. In the Treaty of 1868 that the two men drafted, the Diné Bikéyah became the official Navajo Reservation, and the people went home. In Canyon de Chelly, where their herds had been destroyed and croplands ruined, they rebuilt their lives.[79]

The Diné don't need a ceremony to remember this story. After the speeches, people gathered for a savory picnic barbecue, sitting at long tables under a large tent. A middle-aged woman said she had learned of the Long Walk from her grandfather, who had heard it from his father and grandfather, and she had passed on the story to her children. The Diné will never forget.[80] But for a long time, Hweeldi was officially brushed aside. New Mexico had declared the site a state monument in 1968, but realizing a permanent monument took another thirty-five years. Designed by Navajo architect David N. Sloan, the new visitors' center is a hexagonal cross between the Diné hogan and the Mescalero Apache wickiup. A new circular grove of young cottonwood trees cloned from those planted by Navajos during their exile greets visitors. The exhibits liberally use first-person narratives to describe what had happened here.

The Americas became a killing ground for Native peoples. For many of the conquerors—corporations, individuals, government, institutions—extermination, literally and figuratively, was the agenda. They separated Indians from their lands, their children, their identities. Not even the dead were spared. In 1865 Struck By The Ree, then principal chief of the Yankton Sioux, testified to a government commission about the mistreatment of corpses. The Sioux put their dead on scaffolds, but soldiers cut down the scaffolds, pulled out the teeth, and cut off the hair and sometimes the heads of the dead. "I think the way the white men treated us is worse than what the wolves do," he said.[81]

The memory of infectious disease is still very much alive in Indian Country, and it has gripped mainstream America's imagination because of threats from HIV, influenza, smallpox, and bioterrorism. In 2002 Gregg Bourland, then chairman of the Cheyenne River Sioux, described how smallpox was a living bitter memory for his people. "The rest of the world just might get a taste of what Native Americans went through when conquistadors planted their feet on our soil," he wrote.[82]

The new energy in Indian Country is not simply, as some non-Indians maintain, a direct result of resources gaming has brought to tribes.[83] Today, the challenge for Indians is to forge effective cultural and political sovereignty as they recover ancestors, artifacts, stories, homelands—heartlands—and even the memories of where "hatred was born." The challenge for the rest of America is to let this history transform us. Such a transformation will clarify our attitudes about sovereignty and its issues, including gaming. But amnesia continues. Bosque Redondo monument sits on Billy the Kid Road, named for the famous young outlaw—a psychopath, some say—who was killed in the nearby town of Fort Sumner. On the Chamber of Commerce's website, the renegade's grave is the number one tourist attraction. Hweeldi, where so many died, is second, described simply as "the army's ill-fated experiment."[84]

Navajos still live in Canyon de Chelly, despite a lack of electricity and running water. Canyon de Chelly National Monument was established in 1931 from Navajo trust lands that the tribe owns and manages jointly with the National Park Service.[85] Tourists can traverse the canyon's 131 square miles with Navajo guides. In August 2009 the *New York Times* published a travel story on the growing sophistication and sensitivity of Native tourism operators. The chosen locale was

Canyon de Chelly, and the reporter vividly described three days of touring with a Navajo guide through the gorgeous landscape. Not a single sentence, not a word, however, spoke to what had happened to the Diné of Canyon de Chelly 145 years before.[86]

6

THE DRUM

The Albuquerque city bus was rattling so hard that I had to grip a music score that I was reading. To write a story about an upcoming performance of Bach's Sonatas and Partitas by the British violinist Rachel Podger, I had checked out the music from the library. This was to be no ordinary bus trip home, however. It would be a music lesson.

From across the aisle, over my shoulder, I heard a voice: "You play an instrument, lady?" I turned to find a face leaning toward me, the kind of face I saw often on the buses and streets of downtown Albuquerque where I lived: Indian, friendly, and sometimes deeply lined from age, the elements, or a hard life. This older gentleman was going about his business: to home, a job, or the IHS clinic. "Yes, the piano," I answered. "My piano is in a drum—in a Navajo drum," he said firmly. With a satisfied look on his face, the man relaxed back into his seat.

Unsettled, I closed the score and looked out at the passing scene. The bus's rumbling made talking at anything less than a shout difficult, but we could have had quite a conversation. I have heard the drum, I wanted to tell him. Indeed, many Indians—like Lora Church at the Albuquerque Indian Center—speak not of a drum or drums but *the drum*, with equal emphasis on each word, each word a singularity that unifies the spirit and the physical being. The term goes beyond the instrument and includes the singers.

The drum is inseparable from the entire community; it contains everyone. In some groups, other instruments produce the rhythmic underpinning: clappers in northern California, gourd rattles in southern California. Wherever Indians need a connection to home, the drum is there. Bird singers with their rattles prefaced the Kumeyaay Nation's flag raising at San Diego's Cabrillo National Monument. After a teenager at the Red Lake Chippewa Reservation went on a killing rampage in 2005, men from the town gathered around a large drum within hours, singing for the community. The drum is also a highly personal expression. Although Keith Franklin of Albuquerque has lived in cities since 1957, he returns to Oklahoma every year to join three hundred other tribal members for an annual powwow. Anytime he hears a drum, he says, "I long to go home."

The drum is an energizing and organizing force, whether overtly expressed or as an undertone: in a sacred ceremonial with perhaps a single instrument and a handful of dancers and singers; at a tribal social gathering with dozens or hundreds of participants; at a business meeting; at a powwow at Stanford University, on Brooklyn's historic Floyd Bennett Field, or on a reservation baseball diamond; at graduation ceremonies; and at many other events. Indians turn to the drum for comfort and strength. The drum is where the heart, the heartbeat, resides. Many Indians carry a figurative drum inside them, even as they go about lives as diverse as law, journalism, medicine, software engineering, and ranching. As Lora Casey put it, they touch the drum and then their hearts to bring the spirit to them.

Ritual heals, and the ceremonial drum is at the center of ritual. Ceremonials are not entertainments, and few are as close to the heart, to the soul, as those of New Mexico's Pueblo Indians.[1] On feast days San Felipe's plaza becomes a sacred place like a cathedral, synagogue, or mosque. Communities such as San Felipe, a village between Albuquerque and Santa Fe, turn themselves inside out to pray, dance, feast, and share. San Felipe's 3,185 inhabitants plan and prepare for these events throughout the year.[2] The ceremonials mark the seasons. In summer's relentless sun and winter's snow, hundreds of dancers, singers, and religious and ordinary people gather for events that have sustained them for centuries. For the sacred feast days—the Buffalo Dance in February, the May Corn Dances, and the Winter Dances—the Keres-speaking tribe closes its casino.

Each pueblo's ceremonials reflect an amalgam of Christian beliefs and the traditional practices specific to that pueblo, even though they share some commonalities. Thus, San Felipe's winter dances coincide with Christmas and the solstice and the spring planting dances with the feast day of the pueblo's own patron saint, Philip. In the sixteenth century, Spanish missionaries set aside the pueblo's name, Katishtka, in favor of San Felipe, a Jesuit who had been martyred in Japan.[3] On May 1, to celebrate his feast day, villagers build a three-sided pavilion on the edge of the plaza to anchor the drama. Colorful textiles drape the makeshift sanctuary, which shelters a statue of Philip. Large preserved deer, antelope, and buffalo heads hang on the canopy's structure and along the roof lines of an adjoining two-story house. Elaborate turquoise necklaces and silver belts adorn their necks. Rather than being mismatched, however, the juxtaposition of jewelry and animals reflects an enduring Pueblo value, the union of the natural, the sacred, and the man-made.

Writers, photographers, and anthropologists have produced thousands of words and images to describe Pueblo ceremonials and dances. Yet thirty years of watching them have not dulled my layman's attention. Bits of knowledge accrete, and under-standing expands. Each ceremonial is different. For the epical Corn Dance, the usually quiet pueblo swells with celebrants and visitors. The event in the village plaza occupies much of a day and gathers up to a thousand dancers and singers. As with all pueblos, at the core of San Felipe's social organization are moieties—two groups of related kin—known as turquoise people and squash people or winter people and summer people. At a Corn Dance, each moiety alternates for four rounds with hundreds of dancers and choruses of five to seven dozen men and boys.

Ceremonials are communitarian, gathering the people in ritual and in time. The drums sound from outside the plaza, and dancers and the chorus stream out of the kivas, sacred places that are partly underground and strictly off-limits to outsiders. Participants stroll into the plaza and line its perimeter, with the chorus and drum to the side. Hundreds of dancers become one, intent and intense, as they circle the plaza several times. Directed by cues from the singers and drums, they sometimes break into patterns. The square's dirt floor is depressed about three feet below the buildings around its edge, the result, say the residents, of so many dancers' feet pounding it.

Children enter the ceremonial life of the pueblo at an early age as both dancers and singers. They dance with older family members or at the end of the line of adults. Some of the children are barely old enough to walk, and they sway valiantly under the weight of the elaborate Native dress sized for them. A child who tires may leave the dance at any time and find herself in the comforting arm of a family member. No matter. They still receive the community's spiritual and cultural memes.

Departing from the perception of Indian life as strictly communitarian, dances also invite individual effort. The celebrants' elaborate attire reflect this dual purpose.[4] Men paint their bodies and wear white kilts cinched with embroidered belts, pin feathers to their heads, and carry ceremonial rattles. The women fasten their traditional one-shouldered black dresses—called *mantas*—with silver pins at the shoulder and with elaborately woven belts. *Tablitas*—thin decorated head boards—hold the women's hair in place. All carry an evergreen branch. Despite their similar design and colors, the articles of clothing are highly personal; dancers often make their own. Participants bring out their finest jewelry, some of which has passed through generations. The monetary value of the jewelry at a ceremonial—in the hundreds of thousands of dollars—is breathtaking, although for the dancers, the value has nothing to do with dollars.

The music is irresistible, insinuating, and organized in a complex aesthetic. Nearly invisible among the singers and dancers is the drum itself. Whether a single drum or seven or eight, however, its insistent beat overrides everything else. The dancers' rattles and jingle anklets made from small bells and shells serve as a delicate counterpoint to the drum's pounding. The prayers sung by the chorus provide the textual framework for the dancers' movements. These multiple sounds at different pitches rebound off a nearby rocky mesa to produce an orchestral texture, rich with overtones.

Maria Williams, a Tlingit ethnomusicologist, said that Pueblo music is unique, "the only place in the world where you have these metric shifts, out of the blue." The shifts indicate that something is happening in the text, so they are also cultural shifts. Thus, choreography, poetic text, instruments, and music emerge from the life of the people. The aesthetic is not taught, practiced, or memorized. "This isn't music. It's a prayer," said

Williams, a classically trained string player.[5] In this prayer, the *cacique*—head religious official—and his aides drawn from the two moieties maintain the village's spiritual balance and manage the dances. Dressed in their own attire, the aides are dance directors, keeping things on track. One at the head of the line carries a flexible flagpole that towers nearly two stories over the plaza. Its banner displays brightly embroidered corn stalks, and feathers flutter from the top.

Despite—or because of—their religious roots, the ceremonials reconcile life's contradictory values—profane and sacred, traditional and modern. Thus, much as humor appears in the darkest of Shakespeare's plays, the *koshari*, the ritual clowns of the Pueblo world, are part of the ceremonial's serious purpose. Their dress varies from ceremony to ceremony. At the May Corn Dances, the *koshari* might be transformed into corncobs. Their bodies and hair are painted yellow, their heads are topped with yellow caps, and their hair is plastered and pulled up to look like corn silk. During the lunch break they cruise the arts and crafts market set up outside the plaza. Like kings of the hill, they collect booty and good-naturedly harass the vendors.[6]

Clowning even appears at the low-key Buffalo Dance, a subdued winter ceremonial that dramatizes the hunt. A young woman dancer wearing a small animal headdress leads about a dozen male dancers, with antler headdresses, and several others dressed as hunters, with bows and arrows. Waving a sprig of evergreen, she initiates the action. Although the chorus is often large, with seventy-five singers, their voices and the drum seem muted. At one point in the dance, one of the animals breaks away, running across the plaza, as hunters and some male onlookers give chase. Encouraged by spectators, men in street dress carrying bows and arrows will attack the line of "deer" and carry off one or two of them. The men then take the "deer" back to the dance area, holding them by all fours—both arms and both legs. Between rounds, *koshari* stroll around the plaza. Cross-dressed as Navajo women in broomstick skirts and velvet or satin blouses, they tell jokes in Keresan. Using falsetto voices, they are clearly delivering parody of the highest order, and onlookers laugh knowingly.

In some respects, the ceremonials are timeless—they recapitulate the people's unchanging beliefs—but they are not static. Year to year, the basic story remains, but the chorus might introduce new songs, a few dance steps might change, and for some feast days, dancers might don totally different outfits. The Buffalo Dance can expand to two women and more men.

Some ceremonials in New Mexico have gained in stature among the Pueblos themselves as well as visitors who flock to see them. For the most important feast days, Pueblos dress up, the women with flowered shawls or Pendleton blankets around their shoulders. During the dancing, they are respectful and speak in low voices. An attentive visitor will see Pueblo onlookers sprinkle a blessing of sacred cornmeal onto the ground at appropriate moments, reminding us that this is a religious occasion. Although most visitors have learned not to applaud the dances, those who violate the prohibition on cameras seem surprised or even hostile if a tribal official confiscates them. In summer, insensitive visitors show up in scanty attire they would not consider wearing in a house of worship.

San Felipe's ceremonial occasions are also a time for sharing. In May people carry bowls and platters of chile stew, breads, fruit, and Native baked goods to the shrine. The Pueblos generously invite visitors to share in the bounty spread out on blankets in front of the pavilion. They will sometimes buttonhole visitors and take them home for lunch. Business is part of most ceremonial days. While the casino closes, vendors set up booths and tables to sell food, jewelry, pottery, and items strictly for Indians such as animal skins, *mantas*, and pieces of regalia.

Not every Indian group is as fortunate as the San Felipe people, who retain robust ceremonies. In California, centuries of war, disease, murder, and, more recently, termination shattered communities, families, and culture. California's tribes have spent the past three decades rebuilding. But, like civic life, ceremonial tradition is sometimes frail. Although cultures did not become extinct, "the lineal passing of tradition took a hit," explained O'Jay Vanegas, the director of education for the cultural museum established in Palm Springs by the Cahuilla tribe's Agua Caliente band. The most dangerous time was the period during and after World War II, when termination, boarding schools, public schools, and the departure of many Cahuillas to the armed forces weakened language and culture.

The tribe's bird song tradition continues, however, at celebrations, either in family settings—weddings, birthdays, or funerals—or at "fiestas," larger gatherings where dancing happens on reservation dirt. The Agua Caliente band of Cahuilla Indians organized its first Bird Song and Dance Festival at the museum in December 2005 to celebrate a tradition that derives from their creation story.[7] But this festival was not primarily for Native people. The museum designed the event for the local non-Indian population, and organizers correctly anticipated a large turnout of both whites and Natives. One purpose was to dispel the notion that powwows represent Indian culture. "That's not culture for the local Indian people, the Cahuilla, Luiseño, Kumeyaay people," Vanegas said. For the Agua Caliente festival, the choice of venue—a meeting room set up theater style—was largely a matter of accommodating non-Indian townspeople with facilities and restaurants. Participants also needed dressing rooms. Besides, Indians are contemporary people, said Vanegas, who is Navajo, Mexican, and California

Indian. Why shouldn't they have a party indoors in a hall, even one with a disco light? Indians are always on the lookout for something better, adapting quickly to new technologies and cultures, he added. The Cahuilla were living in *ramadas*—simple shade structures. But when they saw the European-style houses, they expanded the *ramadas*, adding sides, permanent roofs, multiple rooms, and window openings.

On a small stage, a group of younger male singers with rattles led the participants as they swayed to the gentle rhythms. They shake gourd rattles rather than beat a drum, although turtle and deer hoof rattles have also been used in the past. One of the Cahuilla singers, thirty-year-old Michael Mirelez, has been learning the bird songs for about fourteen years. The traditions skipped a couple of generations in his family. "The first time I heard them, I was hooked," he said. Absent was the elaborate ceremonial attire seen at the pueblos. Although some of the Indian women in the audience wrapped shawls around their shoulders, the singers wore baseball caps and baggy pants. But that didn't seem to bother a Cahuilla elder. "I feel good about it," he said.

The Pueblos' ceremonials show an organizational ability born out of cultural strength. The Cahuillas' bird song festival leads non-Indians into a more authentic accommodation of tradition and contemporary life. The powwow shifts the drum into a hybrid of art form, sporting event, family reunion, and country fair.

About a thousand powwows happen annually, usually on weekends, in almost every state, in a variety of locations.[8] Although many Indians avoid powwows as "non-Indian," their roots predate European contact. The word probably derives from the Eastern Algonquin "pahwayaw," which originally referred to a religious ceremonial associated with healing, family, and the relationship to nature.[9] Ceremonies went underground when the newcomers suppressed religious life or disappeared as communities perished. Powwows also evolve from social gatherings. The modern powwow has its own protocols, related to but separate from the ancestral dances. It includes prayers (Indian), but religion is not its focus. Powwows also make time to honor veterans. The powwow "circuit," a string of intertribal competitions for relatively modest purses (a few hundred up to perhaps two thousand dollars), adds a monetary incentive. But "powwow" is a time to eat, socialize, trade, and, most of all, dance. At events in rural and semirural areas, families camp in pickups and tent villages around the powwow grounds.

Intertribal powwows collect the Indian diaspora—dancers, drum groups, Indian families—and crowds of non-Indian visitors.[10] A family of Hopis and Mojaves drove from Arizona to spend a weekend at the Sycuan Reservation east of San Diego, watching the dances and mingling with other Indians. A small army of student volunteers has made the Stanford Pow Wow happen every Mother's Day for more than thirty-five years. At the De Anza College powwow, near Jose, a young Cherokee family therapist came from Marin County to meet other Indians. "I see my relations," he said, spreading an arm out to the mostly Indian crowd. Surprises abound. At Sycuan I spotted an older dancer as we trolled the food booths together, by happenstance. The man seemed familiar, and I thought perhaps I had seen him at another powwow. I was right. He did indeed dance regularly. "It keeps me in shape," he said. I learned from him that he was seventy years old and an actor—Saginaw Grant. He is a legend on the powwow circuit and a member of the Sac and Fox and Otoe-Missouria Nations. Then I recalled Grant's appearance in a PBS television adaptation of Tony Hillerman's *Skinwalkers*; he played Wilson Sam, the medicine man who is Officer Jim Chee's teacher. Grant's own website lists him first as a traditional dancer, then as an actor.

The Barona powwow, which the tribe has hosted annually for nearly two decades, is a template. On a warm August weekend, at the tiny reservation just twenty-five miles from downtown San Diego, the sprawling casino was busy.[11] Barona's heart, where the five-hundred-plus members of this Kumeyaay band live, is a few miles away at the community center, tennis courts, and museum built with gaming revenues. Powwows take place at the baseball field. On this particular weekend, about five hundred dancers performed in the dance circle (the diamond) well into a starlit night. Around the circle, canopies shielded the seating area, where officials, drum groups, dancers, and their families took refuge from the blazing sun. Some of the non-Indian onlookers were veterans, attentive and serious. Others, with awestruck faces, seemed to be newcomers. At food and craft booths, dancers mingled with visitors, and some non-Indians asked dancers to pose for a photo. One could find splendid items: stethoscopes like the one that Scott Bender used at the Navajo zoo, hand-carved flutes, fine jewelry, and embroidered and beaded clothing and moccasins. The kitsch—cheap plastic dolls made in Asia and dressed up in "Indian" clothing—was there too. At the largest powwows, colleges, businesses, and government agencies set up booths to market their education and diversity programs. Powwow food clogs arteries and is hard to resist, although the health-conscious can sometimes find roasted corn, menudo (tripe stewed with hominy in chile), mutton and vegetable stew, and fresh fruit. Here as elsewhere, lines formed for "Navajo shortcake," a California specialty: a small round of fry bread heaped with strawberries and your choice of whipped cream or confectioners' sugar.

Trading and eating are peripheral to the real action: dancing. With deep, strong voices, the emcees and announcers preside over the powwow's own rituals. They narrate the grand entry, when all the dancers file into the circle led by the eagle staff—the "national flag" of Indian Country—as well as the American, state, and tribal flags. The emcees introduce the dance competitions; direct the onlookers on etiquette, moments of prayer, and patriotic speeches; and deliver a steady stream of praise and humor. Protocol arranges dance rounds according to style, age, and gender. Some of the moves in the men's dances relate to traditional pursuits such as the hunt and battle. The flamboyantly athletic fancy dance, a young man's form, produces swirls of feathers brightly colored with commercial dyes. Women's dances have their own aesthetic. For the traditional dances, women bounce and bow at the drum cues, and the long tassels of their shawls sway gently. The fancy shawl dancers, on the other hand, seem to fly across the dance circle. With dazzling footwork, the jingle dancers animate tin cones and ribbons on their dresses. The noncompetitive Gourd Dance honors warriors and veterans. They wear their modern campaign ribbons and medals over the red and blue blankets that symbolize their ancestors' battles against the European American armies.

Accomplished men and women called head dancers judge the dancers' regalia, self-assurance, and skill in executing a particular style and following the drum group's cues. The most experienced dancers stop on a dime, at the same moment as the drum. Like ceremonial dancers, powwow performers often make their own regalia or wear those handed down among the generations. The elaborate outfits take on a sensual, almost erotic quality. Dresses and shirts (some cloth, others buckskin), breastplates, moccasins with exquisite beadwork, fur headdresses, leather and feather armbands, and designs painted on faces and limbs: all beg to be admired and touched. Etiquette prohibits touching.

Like the dancers, the drums compete. Judges look for a group's respect for a particular song's tradition and their skill in guiding the dancers' movements. The judges are role models for young dancers. Teenagers are passionate and train like athletes. Beulah Sunrise, who is associated with the Gathering of Nations powwow, said that as a teenager, she ran daily to prepare for dancing. Sunrise said, "We start as babies. As soon as we walk, we dance." In the tots' "competition" (everybody wins), children teeter under their regalia, and mothers will sometimes simply carry babies through a round, bonding them through rhythm, sounds, and colors.

The annual Gathering of Nations in Albuquerque is the Super Bowl of powwows, the largest in the country.[12] The three-day event draws more than two thousand dancers, and patrons fill the eighteen thousand seats in the University of New Mexico's arena ("the Pit"). For the unforgettable grand entry, a dozen drum groups around the sidelines of the basketball court pound out the beat and sing. The inverted conical shape that gives the Pit its name produces gut-wrenching sonic effects that roll up over spectators. Dancers from dozens of tribes file down the steep aisles and coil around those who carry the eagle staff and flags to center court. By the time they all reach the floor—after more than a half hour—they are so jammed together that the best they can do is shuffle in place. The flaming colors of regalia and the percussive fireworks invade the senses. Clyde Hubbard, a non-Indian marketing consultant for the Gathering, said, "I sit there at grand entry and bawl like a baby."

Although it started in 1983 as a reunion of friends, the Gathering has grown into the largest springtime domestic and international tourism event in Albuquerque. The dancers are among the best; they have honed their skills and built their reputations on the powwow circuit. In recent years, Wal-Mart has become a sponsor, and the archbishop of Santa Fe has participated in the welcoming ceremony. Many contestants in the Gathering's Miss Indian World Contest are college students.

Criteria for the competition include personal interviews, accomplishments, knowledge of tribal history and customs, dancing skill, the regalia she has made herself, and a written essay. With her regalia and modest demeanor, Miss Indian World is a far cry from mainstream beauty queens and a model for young Indian women. The organization has also established a scholarship program for Indian students at UNM. The Gathering has a commercial side, with a busy website that promotes an online shop and a daily, twenty-four-hour, Internet radio service that streams Native music. Its officials say the event's market generates about $2 million in sales for about four hundred vendors, and its traveling show has toured to New York, London, and Singapore.[13]

A ceremonial or a powwow is a fundamental cultural expression for Native Americans. Pueblo ceremonials are religious services and decidedly not powwows. But both connect to the homeland. Knowledge and art have passed from one generation to another, even in times of persecution, cultural dilution, and possible death. In the powwow, dance forms that have evolved over the centuries have been modified. To answer critics who say that the powwows are inauthentic nostalgic remnants of the past, Choctaw musicologist Tara Browner has argued that the powwow is not a reenactment. Rather, the participants draw on historical tradition to dance and sing in the present, to serve their needs and purposes. Attracting hundreds who sometimes travel long distances, a powwow, she said, "is a living event."[14]

The powwow has provided raw material for Mohican composer Brent Michael Davids, who wrote the *Powwow Symphony*. The New Mexico Symphony Orchestra and Chorus premiered the work in 1999 before two thousand patrons. Davids, performing as soloist on a quartz crystal flute, took his place in front of the first violins and David Lockington, the symphony's music director and conductor. Davids talked about his composition during rehearsals before the premiere. Using concert dress as an illustration, the classically trained composer defined the differences between the symphony and powwow experiences. An orchestra's black formal dress minimizes the human presence. "At Lincoln Center, the socializing is understated, the focus is on sound. In Native life, things are more holistic. The sounds, dances, music, food, ceremonies are interconnected, not separated. In Western art music, a song is not a dance is not a symphony is not a sculpture. All are separated into their own spheres," he explained. Davids dedicated the symphony to the two worlds that he inherited: "my very old English and Mohican relatives, the Pilgrim who Mayflowered the ocean to land on native soil, and the native who was there to meet him."

In the *Powwow Symphony*, Davids brings together his ancestors' two musical worlds. Rather than the typical four movements of a symphony, fifteen movements flow into each other and take their names from dances in a daylong powwow. "There's no pause for the audience to rustle," he said. European form pushes Native, too. A percussive powerhouse—three full sets plus timpani—replaces the single drum that opens a powwow. Davids draws on the powwow's incessant heartbeat and on symphonic rhythms that change, sometimes frequently. The result, said Davids, is "layers of rhythms and melodies." He leaves nothing to chance in the *Powwow Symphony*, while some events in a powwow are spontaneous. The powwow emcee was on stage too. Sammy Tone-Kei White, a member of the Kiowa Nation and a familiar face and voice on the circuit, read Davids's script, which included some of White's one-liners. Finally, small groups of dancers in regalia performed in the aisles.

The symphony integrates choreography, text, regalia, instruments, music, and humor. Conductor Lockington noted that although Davids uses Native elements in the symphony, he is a *contemporary* composer. He avoids Native traditional melodies and patterns, and the work has an arrhythmic feel even though the dancing is consistently rhythmic. The piece is complex, Lockington said, yet Davids created a combination of tensions and extraordinary fun.

The *Powwow Symphony* received mixed reviews and some notice in *Symphony Magazine*, the publication of the League of American Orchestras. It is, however, absent from the repertory of other orchestras. Lockington ventured that the symphony is challenging and expensive. It requires a large orchestra, chorus, dancers, and special rehearsals. Also, it is region-specific, and it has not been subjected to a test of separating the music from the spectacle. One of the *Powwow Symphony*'s strengths is its breadth of feeling. But, Lockington said, it has "a slightly over-sophisticated quality that prevents people from getting into the music."[15]

Davids is one of a small group of American Indian composers of fine art music. He is no stranger to mainstream concert halls. Davids grew up in Chicago and earned degrees in music composition at Northern Illinois and Arizona State. The Kronos Quartet, the Joffrey Ballet, and Chanticleer have performed his works, which draw on the Indian "pulse." Jerod Impichchaachaaha' Tate (Chickasaw) orchestrates works based on tribal themes. *Oktibihah*, a twenty-minute piece, is based on a Snake Dance song and the story of the creation of Lake Oktibihah in the old Chickasaw Nation, Mississippi. The piano plays a four-note melody in variations over hushed strings, and the timpani responds with a rumble. In *Tripartita*, cellist and composer Dawn Kawenno:ta'as Avery (Mohawk) matches a cello and voice to perform a duet that uses sounds and text of different fundamental stories from the Quechua language of the Incas and their descendants. The cello begins with a brief, brisk, classically influenced passage. Then the voice slides in with a contrasting Native style. Without percussion, a pulse underscores the whole. Raven Chacon (Navajo) has composed a work that translates as *Lightning*. Written for flutes and other winds, the abstract work is moody, experimental, and inspired by visual Native art. Chacon is not sure in which genre to place the piece. "I hope what we're doing is creating a new style of music, not always associated with the classical genre. We're using these tools, drawing from our musical experiences, seeing what we come up with."[16]

From the small ceremonial event, to the world's largest pow-wow, to the concert hall, the drum asserts its power. Quietly, daily, out of sight, and certainly out of mind, today's Indians also draw the drum into themselves. The internal drum pulses figuratively in their individual lives. Sometimes it beats literally in a number of organizations. They resemble those of mainstream American groups, with an alphabet soup of acronyms and corporate appendages—boards of directors, CEOs, COOs, CFOs, regulatory systems, and so on. Many bend their historic skills to Native purposes, to solve problems *and* to maintain traditional values. Indians are also organized in cyberspace, with thousands of websites dedicated to their tribal governments, social, professional, and cultural organizations, media, and casinos.

Anyone—even a mainstream corporate manager—can feel the pulse's energy and draw on those features that sometimes seem contradictory: sustained core values and flexibility, teamwork and individual initiative, firm focus on broad goals and important details, decorum and spontaneity, seriousness and humor. F. Scott Fitzgerald wrote that maintaining such contradictions in balance is the sign of a first-rate intelligence.[17] It is not easy. Other features, like generosity, are singular. One is difficult to deconstruct: make spirituality, community, art, and history an important part of daily life and business. Finally, stay in touch with nature: keep a plant on your desk, walk around the block daily. Non-Indians often cite the interminable "bickering"—or worse—that often occurs within and among tribes in controversies like the Navajo zoo, yet conversations and debate are commonplace democratic qualities. From the individual businessperson to large groups, Native Americans carry a figurative drum through which they integrate the values of their heartlands and those of the larger society. Innovation and leadership emerge naturally from such dynamics.

In August 2005 Washington State tribes met to consider how they could transform their casino and other revenues into economic and business opportunities. Federal and state agency personnel, corporate representatives, and tribal officials gathered at the Quinault Casino and Resort on the Olympic Peninsula.[18] Over three days, the participants discussed ways that they could enter the larger economy: leverage tribal buying power, attract private investment, develop tourism, control costs, and increase educational offerings. Throughout the conference, which was cosponsored by the Quinault Nation and the Confederated Tribes of the Colville Federation, a core group also brainstormed a first-ever statewide Native American Chamber of Commerce.

But while the other conferees talked business, one tried to propel them beyond it, to follow a path she had been on for decades. Wrapped in a Hard Rock Café jacket her daughter had bought for her, Veronica Velarde Tiller (Jicarilla Apache) walked into a cold, stiff wind on a beach.[19] Behind her, the multistory Quinault Casino rose brashly above the dunes and a scattering of modest houses. Tiller was far from home. She lives in Albuquerque, not far from the reservation in northern

Top: The powwow. Young women prepare to dance at the Gathering of Nations in Albuquerque. Photo by William Rodwell (author's collection).

Bottom: The inner powwow. Veronica Tiller. Photo by William Rodwell (author's collection).

Top: The powwow goes electronic. A radio station for Hopi. Photo by Cary Herz.

Bottom: A coast-to-coast powwow. Talk radio with *Native America Calling*. Susan Braine and Harlan McKosato. Photo by William Rodwell (author's collection).

New Mexico where she grew up. Eight years earlier, Tiller had completed the first study of how Washington's tribes contributed to the state's economy. Commissioned by the governor, the report had opened eyes. Now she was back to deliver the keynote address for the economic development meeting and to market the latest edition of her massive *Tiller's Guide to Indian Country*. The book has become an indispensable reference tool because it covers every federally recognized tribe by state, with information about population, economic development, history, religion, geography, and governmental and social organization.[20]

Tiller's passion is knowledge, and she shared that passion with her audience. Information is the key to economic development, she told conferees, but the information gap in Indian Country is profound. Tribes rely on the U.S. Census for data, but many don't know the basic facts that every government typically has, such as workforce, unemployment rates, crime rate. "We are sovereign, we are great. If you're really sovereign, don't you need to take control of tribal records?" Tiller singled out the Navajo Nation as a model. The tribe employs a statistician who has researched the status of every inch of land on the reservation—how much is allotted, how much the Bureau of Reclamation uses, and so on. "This is a real sign of sovereignty," she said.

Tiller turned her personal history—her drum—into a knowledge business. After attending boarding school on the Jicarilla Reservation, she majored in political science at the University of New Mexico. Forgoing law school, Tiller pursued graduate work in American history and was the only Native doctoral student in the history department. Maintaining a grade point average of 3.8, she became the first Jicarilla to obtain a doctorate. Her dissertation—a history of the Jicarilla Apaches—was published by the University of Nebraska Press and became the tribe's official history. She spent four years teaching American Indian history at the University of Utah, her job complicated by the fact that, at the time, the field had neither textbooks nor curricula—the standards of "knowledge."

Tiller then moved to Washington DC to work on an Indian energy project and decided that she preferred research to teaching. "I jumped off the deep end," she said and launched a business, Tiller's Research, in the nation's capital. Within a year, the company had large contracts for research on water rights from law firms and tribes. When she found herself commuting to the Southwest for work, she moved her company to Albuquerque. Attorney David Harrison, her husband, went with her. Tiller temporarily suspended her business to join him for a year at the nonprofit Council of Energy Resource Tribes (CERT) in Denver, which was founded in the 1970s to help tribes gain control over their resources. CERT asked Tiller to start a publications division, in which she produced a guide designed for tourists visiting reservations. Among Tiller's sources was the Department of Commerce's *American Indian Reservations and Indian Trust Areas*, profiles of the economies of every reservation. When she returned to Albuquerque, Tiller received a grant from Commerce to revise it, but before the project was complete, she ran out of funding, in part because of her policy on travel. She had learned from experience that the worst way to get in touch with tribes is by phone or mail, but Commerce did not want her to travel. Tiller negotiated a deal: she would finish the project for Commerce at her own expense, and she could publish a version for the public—as *Tiller's Guide*.

On a shoestring budget, the project became a family affair. One daughter who was back east in school collected information from tribes in that part of the country. Tiller drove to nearby reservations; Oklahoma groups refused to participate until she showed up. Retaining the copyright, she delivered *Tiller's Guide to Indian Country*, a seven-hundred-page volume. For the first edition, published by her own BowArrow Publishing Company, five thousand hardcover copies went to the Department of Commerce and eight thousand to Tiller Research. Nearly every copy sold, thanks to aggressive marketing to press organizations and direct mailings to government agencies and tribes. The cost of manufacturing the guide was nearly prohibitive, and she was not able to publish a second edition until 2005. The hardcover edition has more than 1,100 pages, 470 photos, maps, and a bibliography; it is also available as a CD-ROM. For the new edition, her teams fanned out to tribes across the United States to gather data. The University of New Mexico Press distributes the work, which has a hefty price of $199.00, to bookstores, libraries, and wholesalers. The guide has given Tiller a unique perspective on Indian Country and especially its economic development. Gaming tribes are in a "new rich" phase, she said, loaded with capital that has never been available to them before. "Once they get over it, they'll look at how to invest" and ask questions like, How do I pay for my child's college education? She believes that diversification is the next phase of economic development, with tribes and individual entrepreneurs engaged in enterprises on and off the reservation.

In the narrow academic sense, Indians are just another civilization, with crime, vices, and bad and good leaders, Tiller said. Early Indian leaders, for instance, made a massive mistake in assessing the European threat. They saw the handful of white-skinned foreigners as their inferiors, slimy and riddled with scurvy. "One of the reasons that Indians were conquered was that they had a life, their own agenda," she said. Also, because Indians outnumbered the newcomers, they were unprepared for the devastation of disease, and Native populations and culture suffered tremendous losses. When the Europeans came in full force, conquest was inevitable. For Tiller, what happened on the American continent was a convergence of historical forces.

Her guide is Tiller's bread and butter, but she has other, less prosaic books in her head. The most intriguing project came out of a family meeting. They have decided to record—in the Jicarilla Apache tongue—their thoughts on the philosophy and meaning of language. Then they will translate religious concepts from Jicarilla Apache to English in a believable way rather than as fables. "White people put Indian concepts in such simple language, and Indians come across as simpletons," Tiller said. As an example, she cited her sister's discussion of "monster slayer," a figure that is portrayed as struggling with an animal. "Monster slayer" is really "killer of fear," not an animal but a concept like Franklin Delano Roosevelt's statement, "We have nothing to fear but fear itself." "Monster slayer" addresses the fear of the unknown, making the world safe from fear. "We are governed by our minds" is the message, said Tiller. The family project brings Tiller back to her Jicarilla values. She recalled that she went to college with two dresses and two pairs of shoes and watched her roommate wash her face with a cleanser while she used soap and water. Commitment, hard work, honesty, and responsibility are values from her family and her own culture that some members of the mainstream society seem to devalue. "We were raised with the idea that we were smart, intelligent people and could do anything," she said. A PhD, a think tank, and a publishing business have strengthened her ties to her Jicarilla Apache culture. She can and does say to white America, "Hell, no. I don't want to be like you."

A few weeks before Tiller pushed Washington tribes along the information superhighway, the Native American Journalists Association (NAJA) convened in Lincoln, Nebraska, for its annual meeting.[21] In the convention hotel lobby, newspapers covered long tables: the *Sho-Ban News* from the Shoshone-Bannock Tribes in Idaho; the *Pequot Times*, Mashantucket Pequots, Connecticut; *Smoke Signals*, Grande Ronde Tribes, Oregon; *Potawatomi Traveling Times*, Forest County Potawatomi Nation, Wisconsin; *Navajo Times*, Arizona; and *Indian Country Today*, a national newspaper based in Canastota, New York. These were just a handful of the six hundred or so newspapers and magazines published in Indian Country. Few Americans ever see them.

In these titles, the drum goes into print. The name of the conference was "A Free Press; a Free People," a stirring phrase that reflected some of the most urgent and intractable issues among Native journalists and their communities. A free press that Americans take for granted is a less secure concept in Indian Country because most of its newspapers are owned by tribes, which are governmental entities. (The Oneida Nation owns *Indian Country Today*.) Editors and reporters daily must reconcile their professional and ethical values with those of a tribe, and their jobs are always on the line. In 1997 then–principal Cherokee chief Joe Byrd fired Dan Agent, the editor of the *Cherokee Phoenix*, and his five-person news staff because of the paper's coverage of the political turmoil in the chief's administration. With support from new principal chief Chadwick Smith, the tribal council passed the Cherokee Free and Independent Press Act in 2001. The act severed the *Phoenix*'s editorial operations from tribal authority, a milestone in its history. Agent, reinstated to his post as editor, distributed copies of the act at the NAJA conference.[22] The *Navajo Times'* longtime editor Tom Arviso weathered many storms, such as stories about alleged improprieties by then–tribal chairman Albert Hale that led to Hale's resignation. Afterward, the tribe cut its financial relationship with the *Times*, and the newspaper became a private enterprise.

The *Phoenix* and the *Times* represent two crises and two approaches to a free press. "There is a way to make it work for each tribe," said Dan Lewerenz, then president of the NAJA board, during a break in the conference. Lewerenz, who was then managing the Associated Press's bureau in Cheyenne, Wyoming, believes that any staff covering its community can reconcile cultural sensitivity and journalistic practices and ethics. In a broad sense, tribal checks on the press do not differ from those of mainstream private ownership. Press freedom in the United States is constitutionally defined as freedom from government, though not from corporate, constraints. As A. J. Liebling, one of America's greatest reporters and editors, once wrote in an oft-repeated comment, "Freedom of the press is limited to those who own one."

Frank King, a Rosebud Sioux publisher, does not base his work on the constitutional notion of a free press; instead, he models it on an *eyapaha*, the Lakota speaker, messenger, or town crier. The community expected the crier to deliver his messages accurately and without bias, whether they were about a battle or a miscreant. "It was important that we had a truth teller," said King, who was raised in a traditional family where he learned the tribal stories and songs. Based in Rapid City, South Dakota, King's *Native Voice* is a privately owned newspaper with a national circulation of about fifteen thousand. King said that in suppressing journalists on their reservation, the Lakota have forgotten about the importance of the *eyapaha*. The messenger prepared for his work with a ceremony that included sacred food, water, and the sweat lodge. He sang to the four directions, praying for everyone and asking the spirits to have compassion for him.

"That's what we do as journalists. Whether it's good or bad news, we have to tell it," King said. In the context of traditional governance, a free press defines a free people. When planning a hunt or a raid, a tribe arrived at a decision not by decree but through discussion that allowed a free interplay of ideas and dissent while seeking solutions. The *eyapaha* provided the correct environment for that discussion. Just as the *eyapaha* was crucial to the consensus form of traditional governance, a free press—the people's right to know—is key to the functioning of modern tribal governments and communities.

The gap between white and Indian America reveals itself most starkly in the distrust and scorn that tribal officials reserve for mainstream press organizations. In its *Reading Red Report*, NAJA analyzed coverage of American Indians in the nation's largest newspapers.[23] The report documented how, with a few exceptions, the press perpetuates misinformation and stereotypes and tramples on Native sensibilities. The best stories reflected fair-minded reporting and good writing that treated American Indians as people, not merely historical figures. The stories explained the status of tribes as sovereign entities, and they portrayed the depth and diversity of Indian communities. But many stories reinforced stereotypes "about barren landscapes, family feuds and poor yet mystical people, the kind you might see in an old episode of *Northern Exposure*." Reporters blithely drop phrases like "trail of tears" and "circling the wagons" and "off the rez" to reinforce stereotypes without understanding their sometimes painful connotations.

An Ojibwe scholar told NAJA conferees that she inadvertently discovered a significant new characteristic of mainstream reporting. Patricia Loew, an associate professor of life sciences communication at the University of Wisconsin–Madison, was researching stories on American Indians and the environment in Madison's two newspapers. She used a database that spanned about a decade in the 1990s. What she found dismayed her: 74 percent of the stories were completely about gaming, and 91 percent had at least a mention of gaming.

"Nothing else was going on in Indian Country except casinos," she said.[24]

Tribal leaders at the NAJA conference also criticized non-Indian reporters for violating the privacy of Indian communities. Floyd Jourdain, the chairman of the Red Lake Chippewa community in Minnesota, described what happened when an army of reporters with television trucks descended on his small community of 9,400 after a teenager shot nine people and then himself.[25] Reporters were looking for grief and pain, he said in a voice laced with disdain. Holly Cook, a Red Lake member and attorney working in Washington DC, went home to help the tribe deal with what she called a "media onslaught." Reporters went through the community, knocking on doors, ignoring common courtesy at a time of grieving. Responding to distraught residents, officials ultimately restricted the press to the parking lot of the tribe's criminal justice offices.

Covering Indian Country challenges Indians as much as non-Indians, especially for issues that are close to the bone, so to speak. In 2005 about twenty tribes disenrolled descendants of families enrolled for decades, even generations, on grounds ranging from blood quantum to violent activities. Harlan McKosato, a Sac and Fox and high-profile national journalist, criticized the tribes. "For a native American, your tribe is your heritage, your culture, your identity, and often provides the foundation for your political and religious beliefs," he said on National Public Radio. Thus, disenrollment is equivalent to exile, a devastating action for a tribe to take against a member. McKosato asserted that the people were disenrolled because gaming tribes want to reduce tribal numbers in order to boost revenues for the remaining members. The new wealth was pitting Indians against each other. Despite its benefits, gaming is "not worth the price of discarding your relatives," McKosato concluded.[26]

With its annual meeting, media awards, and skills workshops, NAJA resembles mainstream organizations like the Society of Professional Journalists. But Indian journalists have unique traditions—like the *eyapaha*—from which they can derive strength they need in a mainstream newsroom, which can be a lonely place for a young Native journalist. In a survey, the American Society of Newspaper Editors counted about 24,740 reporters, of whom about 3,757 are minorities and 143 are American Indian. Adding other newsroom staff, about 300 American Indians work in journalism.[27] Native journalists live with a central tension, making choices and decisions that serve several masters: homeland and tribal values, family, and their profession's standards. Lewerenz, who is part Ioway, said the overriding story in Indian Country today is sovereignty, which was the "free people" end of the conference's theme. In this context, he said, "journalism is another pillar in sovereignty."

The drum goes electronic when the *eyapaha* finds mass expression on the radio. The Hopi Nation built a radio station, and in their remarkable effort, the people overcame a perceived threat to their culture to gather up the threads of their communities.[28] KUYI (88.1 FM) began broadcasting from the Hopi Nation on a winter day when the sun blasted the cold canyons and mesas of the Hopi villages in Arizona. Dating from AD 500, these are the oldest continuously occupied communities in the United States. Their inhabitants are descendants of the Ancestral Puebloans, whom they call Hisatsinom (People of Long Ago). With millennia of teamwork, consensus, persistence, and innovation behind them, the Hopis plugged in. Promptly at 10:00 a.m. on December 20, 2000, KUYI went on the air. In a brief ceremony outside the station's minimalist building, Doran Dalton, the chairman of the Hopi Foundation, announced into a microphone, "You're listening to KUYI." Jimmy Lucero, one the criers that each village has, shouted the same message in Hopi, and Harlan Mahle, an elder and religious leader, gave a blessing. Susan Braine, the station's manager, said firmly, "The voices you heard are all Hopi." Then she declared, "We're on the air!"

That moment was but gossamer wafting over hundreds of hours of work. Well before airtime, dozens of Indian and other well-wishers had gathered at the tiny station. Hopi women filled tables with refreshments, and a few of the elderly, in neat dresses with their hair in the traditional *chonga* (knot), sat quietly against a wall, watching. Teenagers from Hopi High School wandered around. On a wall, a blown-up copy of a five-thousand-dollar contribution check from the high school told only part of their story; young people had volunteered many hours to the station. Photos on a bulletin board illustrated KUYI's physical gestation from a patch of dirt to a prefabricated building the size of a double-wide trailer up on its wheels receiving equipment. Several signs with the station's logo—a cartoon of a striped *koshare* with a wide-mouthed grin seated before a microphone—dotted the building.

In the wider world of bandwidths, American Indian radio occupies a nanohertz. KUYI was the thirtieth Indian station to go on the air, among thirteen thousand stations across the country, and it was a triumph for the Hopis. KUYI's signal reaches only one hundred square miles, just beyond the Hopi Reservation's boundaries. Yet, it is another home run for Indian telecommunications. Reservations are wired, tribes have built their own phone systems, computers have entered Indian homes, and young people are plugged into iPods. Radio and television programming and videos designed for and produced by Indians are either in place or on the drawing boards for broadcast to tribes and to larger audiences through satellite and public broadcasting services. Some traditional Indians fear cultural dislocations from these technologies—and resist. Still, the Hopis have gathered generations and clans to make technology work for their community. "We can give news to elderly Hopi that can't speak English," Mahle said on opening day.

The idea of a radio station for the Hopi Reservation had been circulating for about thirty years. Then, sometime in the 1990s, Dennis Murphy, a Los Angeles filmmaker working with the students of Gerry Gordon, a reservation teacher, picked up the idea. While Murphy was helping during calving season, he noticed that Hopi ranchers were listening to KTNN (660 AM), the commercial Navajo station from Window Rock. They tuned in because it was the only station with Indian-language programming—even though they did not understand Navajo. Murphy and Gordon, both non-Native, submitted a proposal for a planning grant to the Hopi Foundation, an independent nonprofit organization on the reservation. The foundation, which now owns KUYI, jumped in with $100,000, and the largest chunk by far—$400,000—came from the Lannan Foundation of Santa Fe. From 1995, when the Hopis first applied to the Federal Communications Commission (FCC) for a permit to operate, the station's organizers had five years to get it on the air or lose their permit. KUYI began broadcasting with just fifteen hours to spare, a feat that took "hard work, tenacity, and sheer determination," said Loris Taylor, then the associate director of the Hopi Foundation.

The Hopis doggedly took on both cultural and technical challenges. On the cultural side were the eleven Hopi villages. Each is staunchly independent and has its own political structure, authority over its lands, and rules. For instance, the people of Orayvi (the Hopi spelling of Oraibi), established around AD 1100, have chosen to live without electricity and running water. (Taylor said her mother, who lives at Orayvi, hears KUYI on a solar-powered radio.) The three villages on First Mesa achieved consensus to allow the station to locate there, and the Water Corn Clan gave permission for KUYI to be built on its land.

On the technical side, the station's engineer, Burt McKerchie (Chippewa and Ottawa), set up the transmitter and studio, with its salmon-colored announcer's booth, turquoise production studio, and makeshift phone system, with a hybrid of new and old technologies. As equipment was installed just before the first broadcast, McKerchie faced a one-two punch of the mesa's formidable topography and delayed deliveries. The Hopi villages are built on tall mesas separated by deep, twisting canyons. The broadcast studio is in Keams Canyon, and the signal tower is on Antelope Mesa, 6,500 feet high and two miles away as the crow flies, at the end of fifteen miles of twisting road, five of which are dirt. The laser equipment needed to align the studio and the broadcast antenna failed to arrive. Without being aligned, the antenna could not pick up the station's signal. McKerchie's eighteen-year-old son, Marshall, fell back on a far less sophisticated but effective solution. Flashing the sun's rays off mirrors, the men aligned the two points. Human ingenuity had trumped the newest technology; Burt McKerchie noted that the sun is highly significant in Hopi culture.

Susan Braine (Assiniboine and Hunkpapa Sioux) attributed the persistence of the Hopis in their quest for their own radio station to what she said is "a very apparent realization at how fast the language is being lost and how fast the culture is changing with every generation." KUYI was yet another notch in Braine's belt. Once the Hopi Foundation decided to establish the station, the organization hired her, and she mobilized community, professional, and funding resources. Braine is an Indian radio pioneer who has spent more than thirty years managing or starting up stations, including KUYI. By 2009 she had become the chief operating officer for Koahnic Broadcasting

Corporation (KBC). The nonprofit, Native-governed media center in Anchorage, Alaska, generates programs such as *Native America Calling* (NAC), *National Native News* (NNN), and *Earthsongs* for distribution to public radio networks and the Internet. Braine seemed to have boundless energy as KUYI continued its first broadcast day. Finally, she dropped into a chair and said, "Traveling around and living in Indian Country, I'm home wherever I am. Indian people are so accepting."

At 11:00 a.m. NAC devoted its hour-long broadcast to KUYI's opening in a live hookup. Hopi guests sat in Keams Canyon, and NAC's host, Harlan McKosato, was in the program's studio at public radio's KUNM (89.9 FM) in Albuquerque. Listeners across the country learned that a community advisory board would ensure cultural sensitivity in KUYI's bilingual programming. Some traditional Hopis had worried that energy emitted from the antenna and power transformers might affect prayers traveling to the cosmos. Dalton explained that the station would broadcast only general knowledge; sacred knowledge, such as certain stories and prayers, would not be discussed on the air. Throughout the program, which was also streaming on the Internet, congratulations poured in. A Hopi caller wanted to know if the station would broadcast the high school basketball games. Another living off the reservation wanted live broadcasts of the tribal council's meetings. From California, a former resident of Hopi shouted, "Mazel tov!"

Broadcasting KUYI's debut was a classic event for NAC. The live national call-in program has been on the air each weekday since 1995. It reaches about five hundred thousand listeners on fifty-two stations and an undetermined number on the web, where it enjoys an international audience. In 2010 NAC began streaming live video through the Internet. On its fifth birthday, the show, which has been called an "electronic talking circle," merited coverage on the Cable News Network (CNN).[29]

National Public Radio turned to the program for an Indian perspective during the Red Lake tragedy in 2005. McKosato, NAC's founding host and producer, drives it with a tiny staff and budget. In his small office at KUNM, McKosato, a journalism graduate of the University of Oklahoma, glanced at a white board above his desk, where he had inked future shows on a grid. "I have to come up with a magic question every day," he said. McKosato doesn't retreat from controversy and presents many voices. A baseball cap with the logo of the liberal magazine the *Nation* on his head betrays his sympathies. But on a show about homosexuality, he challenged the notion that homosexuals played an important role as healers in traditional culture. An appearance by the Navajo gay men's organization provoked no controversy. McKosato said he wanted opponents on issues because "we need someone we can Custerize on the air."

McKosato arrived at NAC with fire in his heart. "This is what Native America needs, a unifying voice, a way to articulate our anger, our pain, our grievances," he said. But he also wanted the show to reflect Indian Country's successes. Echoing Gerald Vizenor, he insisted that only by eradicating "victim" attitudes will Native people reach their full potential.[30] McKosato rejected the notion that Indian thought is only "holistic" and not "linear." "I also don't think that a long time ago Indians had it good, and today Indians have it bad," he said.

NAC is a reliable tool for journalists, scholars, and anyone wanting to listen in on Indian Country.[31] The show's hottest topics haven't changed much since its inception. Indian identity—blood quantum—is at the top of the list. Generally, listeners want to hear "any program that deals with pain in our communities," McKosato said. While most programs focus on issues important to Indians, from sexual abuse to wiring the reservations, others, like credit counseling, family, and war in the Middle East, have a broader interest. But the starting point is the Indian perspective. Guests include tribal and white government officials, Indian activists and advocates. NAC also has regular features with Native guests: *Book-of-the-Month Club* (interviews with authors); *Music Maker Edition* (Brent Michael Davids wrote the show's theme music); *Native in the Spotlight*; and *Current Events*, a national bulletin board for Indian Country, with callers announcing everything from bake sales to community and organizational meetings.

The parent and support system for many American Indian media initiatives such as Koahnic Broadcasting, KUYI, and *Native America Calling* has been Native American Public Telecommunications (NAPT).[32] Frank Blythe, the executive director of NAPT, recalled that in the early days of Native radio in the 1970s, he was distributing programs to public television station libraries, and "tapes were shipped around by Greyhound bus." The long-term dream for NAPT's board is to increase the capacity of all its services and to diversify its funding sources, said Blythe (Eastern Cherokee and Dakota Sioux). Primary support for NAPT is from the Corporation for Public Broadcasting (CPB). But that funding is specifically designated for generating programs for *public* television, so NAPT cannot pursue advertising as a revenue source. Blythe has sought support from gaming tribes, and because he grew up with the chairmen of three casino tribes, his entrée to that world is personal. "I get criticized for that, but if you get the money, you get the money," he quipped. Fund-raising is difficult in Indian Country. Shirley K. Sneve (Rosebud Sioux), NAPT's director of radio and television, explained that tribes seeking telecommunications opportunities diversify their portfolios with investments in mainstream commercial stations. Tribes don't connect a national public television show with promotional value of media generally.[33] "They don't see what we do as directly benefiting them," she said.[34]

Growth is also slow because federal funding sources for start-up stations are not available. In 2000 the FCC established a tribal initiative after the agency acknowledged that Indian reservations had little or no broadcast service.[35] The initiative explores strategies for issues such as locating broadcast towers near sacred and environmentally and culturally sensitive sites and providing low-income reservation Indians with hookups for receivers in their homes. It does not, however, address some of the most important challenges for Native media such as developing staff in new technologies and producing and distributing Indian-created television programming and films. NAPT collaborates with private and public producers to distribute television programs such as *We Shall Remain*, a five-part series that PBS aired in 2009. Through its VisionMaker Video service, NAPT distributes home and education videos in a broad range of subjects, such as *Dancing with Photons*, about Navajo physicist Fred Begay. NAPT also helps Native filmmakers with small grants for professional development and provides a bulletin board for mainstream events like the Sundance Film Festival.

The technical, policy, and funding concerns that Blythe and Sneve deal with in their offices in Lincoln, Nebraska, seem disconnected from a program like *Native America Calling*, which is so close to the heart of Indian people. But the electronic drum is never far away. Blythe talked about KILI (90.1 FM), the Pine Ridge Reservation station in Porcupine, South Dakota, which broadcasts winter weather alerts and helps to locate cattle and people lost in storms. Sneve wants to produce good stories not told before, contemporary stories that bust stereotypes, success stories, and different perspectives on Native societies and cultures. "Indians are the minority of the minorities; we're not on people's radar screens," she said. "Native Americans are still around, struggling like other Americans to revitalize cultures and heritages but not wallowing in the past, trying to transform cultures and keep them alive for our children."

Connecting these disparate activities—an individual's intellectual quest, a ceremonial, a powwow, the information highway, journalism, broadcasting, and the digital revolution—through the drum may seem a fanciful conceit, and it's a mistake to take it too far. But these activities are of a piece. They transform the traditional pulse of Indian Country to drive it into the future. Although Indian competence and motivation are uneven, Native peoples are not naïfs operating in a zone of pure spirit. Indians know what they're doing, and some of their knowledge is ancient. Charles Mann's *1491* described the complex societies of precontact times. Natives conducted their business of agriculture, commerce, war, architecture, engineering, artistic pursuits, and trade over long distances. Political and diplomatic relations varied in sophistication but served the people who needed them.

Some nineteenth-century Americans might have considered Native peoples ignorant and dirty savages who deserved to be discarded or even eradicated. But early explorers had a different impression. Giovanni da Verrazano, the first European to enter what would be New York harbor in 1524, described the numerous Natives as handsome and healthy, living in well-constructed houses. They generously provided gifts of food and other goods, although the Native New Yorkers were cautious about the Europeans' access to their women. More than a dozen men could sit comfortably in a skillfully made canoe carved out of a single tree; they regularly crisscrossed the great harbor. Verrazano described two of the "kings" who "were as beautiful of stature and build as I can describe."[36]

Linda Cordell of the University of Colorado commented that some European Americans continually underestimated the ability of Ancestral Puebloans to organize their agriculture and their societies in a place like Chaco Canyon without modern technology. But, she said, "that corn didn't just walk there all by itself. People brought it there. That means they were organized on a regional scale that hasn't been seen in the San Juan Basin for hundreds and hundreds of years."[37]

By 1831 European American colonization had broken the strength that had evolved over millennia. In a letter to his mother on Christmas Day in 1831, Alexis de Tocqueville, traveling in the South, described "the expulsion, one might say the dissolution, of the remnants of one of the most celebrated and oldest American nations." He was writing about the Choctaws, who were displaced from Georgia and Alabama in the fall of 1831, even before the Cherokees. Young and old were on the march to destinations in Oklahoma. He graphically described a scrawny, half-naked centenarian traveling with her grandchildren. "What an abomination," he wrote of her plight. "This whole spectacle had an air of ruin and destruction; it spoke of final farewells and of no turning back."[38] As removals occurred during the remainder of the century, this scene would become a familiar one. As we have seen, Native Americans did not always go quietly. From the beginning in so many ways, from New England to southern California, they resisted and protected the integrity of their lands and cultures. Pueblo ceremonials and the modern powwow are microcosmic representations of skill that Europeans found throughout the hemisphere. The Pecos/Jemez people's long repatriation process and the Hopis' tenacity in getting a radio station reflect the power of culture to punch through the pain of loss.

The drum's ancient heartbeat comes alive in *Tesuque Buffalo Dancer* by the noted photographer David Michael Kennedy.[39] The black-and-white photograph evokes the spirit that activates the dancer. He tilts his head, encased by a large buffalo headdress, forward, and his kilt, belt, and feathers flare out behind him. Grasses and snow shroud the dancer's feet, and he seems to emerge from the earth. Kennedy, who is not Indian, does not imprison the dancer, even though the photo "captures" him. Rather, Kennedy keeps him always on the move. Knees and arms slightly bent and clutching a bow and arrow, the dancer moves rhythmically through his regalia. In the dance and on the job, perhaps at nearby Los Alamos National Laboratories or on a construction site, the drum liberates him and calls him home.

7

BUCKSKIN BOXES,
GALACTIC EXPLOSION

Wearing only a loincloth, James Luna lay on a bed of sand in a large, open display case at San Diego's Museum of Man. In an exhibit titled *The Artifact Piece*, Luna (La Jolla Luiseño) turned himself into a live anthropological specimen. Around him, labels identified his tribal affiliations and the scars on his body, and other cases displayed his college diploma, divorce papers, and other personal minutiae. Museum patrons leaned over this "artifact" and sometimes prodded it. They quickly discovered the specimen was alive, listening to and watching them. *The Artifact Piece* by the relatively unknown artist was a brilliant parody.[1]

Visitors to NMAI's Heye Center in New York saw *The Artifact Piece* when Erica Lord reprised it more than twenty years later, in 2008. The particulars on the new specimen's labels were different: her cultural pedigree (Athabaskan/Dena) and her pedicure, for instance. Luna cooperated with the revival, which coincided with the museum's exhibit of his more recent work,

Emendatio. This installation and performance piece was NMAI's contribution to the Venice Biennale in 2005; by then, Luna was no longer "relatively unknown." Not too far from the Heye Center, Jesse Cooday (Tlingit) riffed at his "easel," a computer, at the American Indian Community House gallery in New York. He imagined his digital art one hundred years into the future. Holographic projections high above the earth and as tall as the glittering billboards in Times Square would compete for the attention of interplanetary commuters. "A Tlingit in space!" Cooday said gleefully.[2]

Norman Feder would not have recognized Luna's, Lord's, or Cooday's art. He was one of the nation's leading curators of indigenous art and a cultural tastemaker. For Feder, an authentic Native work was "a traditional item made in the traditional manner by an Indian trained in the tradition."[3] He had developed this principle as a graduate student, and it anchored a lifetime of work, including his *American Indian Art.* The lavishly illustrated oversized book, produced in 1965 by the prominent art publisher Harry N. Abrams, shows page after page of luscious jewelry, masks, baskets, pots, rugs, and other "traditional" and familiar works. The photos testify to the genius of the makers, who remain mostly anonymous to us but were undoubtedly well known in their communities.

Feder noted a new interest in Native creative expression. He attributed this interest to two factors. One was heightened appreciation of "primitive" arts globally.[4] The other was dire. Because of termination and relocation, which Feder could witness firsthand, Indians would finally vanish, and acculturation would be complete. The result would be "the complete disappearance of the native arts," he wrote. At that time, Feder, the curator of American Indian art for the Denver Art Museum, conceded that in the course of blending cultures, something new would probably emerge from Native artists, given their ability to adapt new ideas and technologies. And while traditional art would disappear, "Indian art treasures will always be on display in American museums."[5]

Feder's contributions to our knowledge about American Indian art are indisputable. He dedicated his life to advocating for the value of native materials. But his concept of American Indian art continues well into our time. Artists call it the "buckskin ceiling." Richard Hill (Tuscarora) described it as a multi-million-dollar global "Indian art" market that packages familiar images for its mostly white buyers and sellers. As Susan Shown Harjo (Cheyenne and Muskogee) put it, "The buckskin ceiling is that beyond which native people cannot rise in the art world." The ceiling is more like a buckskin box that encases both artists and consumers in lovely but (borrowing from Kurt Anschuetz) "pickled" images. Buyers expect certain forms, and money flows to producers who satisfy that expectation.[6]

The buckskin box is irresistible. A finely crafted Pueblo pot, Navajo concha belt, or Haida bentwood box draws the viewer almost viscerally. For the artist, who can anticipate a ready market for traditional articles, the buckskin box is comfortable. But it is yet another way mainstream America has bridled Indians. Reservations, missions, boarding schools, museums, and their "ossuaries": these are some of the containers in which European Americans could gain dominance over the highest expression of subdued peoples and their cultures. But just as restraints have weakened elsewhere, the buckskin box has begun to collapse, slowly but unmistakably. The payoff for all Americans is particularly momentous. Thanks to vibrant Indian arts, our spirits may soar.

Feder's attitude was understandable in the context of his times. After all, termination was in effect and had the same impact as outright war. It dispersed whole tribes and shattered cultural foundations. Moreover, many of the founding figures in contemporary art—Fritz Scholder (Luiseño), T. C. Cannon (Caddo/Kiowa), Jimmie Durham (Cherokee), Jaune Quick-to-See Smith (Flathead Salish), George Morrison (Chippewa), and Allan Houser (Warm Springs Chiricahua Apache)—had barely begun to work in the 1960s.[7] Also, by the time Feder proffered his definition, several exhibits in the United States had already called for a fresh, nonethnographic view of Indian art, and he himself had a hand in this turn. But he could not have recognized their work as the kind of creative endeavor he collected and wrote about, explained Joyce Szabo, an art historian.[8]

The full story of the development of American Indian art is complex, and several books (in particular, scholarly analyses) cover it. For the general public, the story of American Indian creativity is either locked into tradition or unknown, however. This chapter is a stroll through that story along a delimited path. "Buckskin" continues to be an overriding theme in the perception of Native art. The other is a recent ferment in contemporary Indian creativity. Richard West connects this activity to sovereignty through NAGPRA. With that legislation, the relationship between tribes and museums has been reconfigured; for the first time, Native peoples have gained some ability to decide what goes into museums. Native peoples today, he said, have "control over the past, living involvement in the future, and the right to call for some kind of ongoing cultural future for native communities." NAGPRA was landmark legislation, yet compared with the force it unleashed, it was "a legislative aside."[9]

Over time, the marketplace—a broad term including a complex set of relationships among consumers, galleries, and other non-Indian and tribal commercial ventures, museums, and educational institutions—and the artists themselves have built the buckskin box and the contemporary escape from it.[10] Creating the box took more than a century, and it occurred in stages. We have seen how almost from the beginning of European American contact, collecting and displaying archaeological and ethnographic materials became a national mania, filled museum display cases, and fired the imagination. European Americans struck out on western rail adventures. An extensive collaboration between the Fred Harvey Company and the Atchison, Topeka and Santa Fe Railroad (ATSF) across the Southwest thrived for decades. In its hotels the Harvey Company swaddled travelers in "Indianness." Architect Mary Coulter, who designed or decorated the Harvey hotels, invented what became known as "Santa Fe style." The Harvey Indian Tour, also known as the Indian Detour, took travelers off the train and put them on buses for side trips to reservations.

American—and European—artists disseminated romantic images of the western landscape and its exotic peoples through paintings and posters that hung in waiting rooms, offices, and international art shows. The romantic stereotype was a useful marketing tool. The ATSF's widely distributed annual calendar featured paintings of Rio Grande Pueblo peoples. *Sunset* magazine employed Maynard Dixon to provide a cover, titled *Blanket-Wrapped Navajo*, a stylized blue-and-red portrait of a mysterious Native. Travelers would follow his intriguing trail and shop at trading posts and hotels along rail lines.

Americans didn't even have to go west, however; by 1900 the Navajo Indian League of Boston had its own shop. Erika Bsumek records how commercial interests, traders, museum curators, anthropologists, consumers, and the Federal Trade Commission "froze" Navajo arts and culture in the first part of the twentieth century. The marketplace conditioned Americans to accept and expect the Indian cornucopia that Feder's book and other similar works cataloged. It connected consumers to goods that embodied the image of the "vanishing" Indian and homogenized artists on one side as "primitive" and consumers on the other as "modern." The result was the racially charged construct Bsumek calls "the Navaho."

Marketing did more than promote tourism; it also helped determine prices for Indian goods, promote exhibits and fairs, furnish houses, and stock department store shelves. On their end, artists were sometimes victims, their labor undervalued and exploited even as they depended increasingly on their skills; in 1930 crafts (weaving and silversmithing) generated one-third of Navajo household income. But frequently, artists rode the choppy waves of their own and wider economic exigencies. Many Navajos could bargain with the best of traders and participate in the marketplace while retaining their cultural integrity.[11]

As the twentieth century opened, galleries, museums, fairs, expositions, railroad shops, and "Indian markets" in places like Gallup and Santa Fe, Eureka, California, and New York strengthened the buckskin box; individuals, too, had enormous influence. During the heyday of world's fairs and international expositions, organizers included displays of American Indian lifestyles and "arts and crafts" that contrasted with the "progress" that the fair celebrated. Matthew Bokovoy has described how world's fairs in San Diego's Balboa Park helped to shape images of Southern California and the Southwest. At the 1915–16 Panama-California Exposition, a Pueblo village, cliff dwellings, and a Navajo "encampment" comprised the *Painted Desert* exhibit. "Real Indians" "lived" in the reconstructed villages. They sang, danced, chatted with fairgoers about their lives, and produced and sold traditional wares. The exhibit's name, taken from the Arizona badlands, was particularly apt. Fossilized images of Indians fabricated by non-Indians have been embedded in *both* white and Native imaginations. As Bokovoy pointed out, even though non-Indians conjured up the *Painted Desert*, the Indians in the exhibit took control of the images presented to the public. Thus, they protected their privacy and controlled the salability of their wares during the fair and in the future. "Through their actions, gestures and words, Indians at the San Diego fair conceived themselves and the European American people they met on their own terms. Indians bent such opportunities to their own advantage and interest," he wrote.[12]

They still do, at the site of the fair and beyond. Many of the buildings from the exposition have survived and make up Balboa Park's impressive cultural complex. A photo in Bokovoy's book taken in 1915 shows a group of Hopi singers and dancers posed on a stage in front of a building with an arched portal. In 2006, on a stage in front of an arched portal at the Museum of Man (the exposition's California Building), hoop dancers performed for the annual Indian Fair, and Irene Bedard and the band Deni played Native pop/New Age music. About fifty artists sold mostly traditional wares that fairgoers in 1915 would have found familiar. Across Indian Country, in reservation shops, tribes sell familiar and traditional items that tourists scoop up. Often the items are not even produced by a tribe's own people; for instance, visitors can buy Navajo and Pueblo jewelry in a Kumeyaay casino shop.[13]

Santa Fe's Indian Market has been the polestar for dozens of "Indian markets" that take place across the country.[14] It sets the sales and, ultimately, the aesthetic agenda across the United States and beyond. Anthropologist Edgar Lee Hewett started the event in 1922. He had founded the Museum of New Mexico in 1909 and was the leading organizer of the anthropological exhibits at the San Diego exposition. The market was designed to rescue Indian items from eternal consignment to the curio shop in order to help Native artists make money from their work. Indian Market (originally known as Indian Fair) brought artists into direct contact with buyers. It grew rapidly as Santa Fe exploited a carefully cultivated "multicultural" tourism image.

The town and the market were steeped in Feder's traditionalist definition of Native arts. Non-Indian paternalistic patrons, especially Santa Fe's doyennes, controlled Indian Market for decades. During the 1950s, however, Native artists began to serve on the board of the Southwest Association of American Indian Arts (SWAIA), the event's managing organization. As Santa Fe style morphed into a global industry and investment strategy for collectors, it affected fashion and home décor, and Indian Market grew dramatically. After 1970 the number of artists increased from two hundred to twelve hundred; the income for SWAIA rose from less than $3,000 to more than $1 million by 1996. In 1970 Santa Fe Indian Market had $1,835 in prize money, but by 2002 it had more than $65,000. The nearly eighty thousand people who flock to the event in downtown Santa Fe every August generate $100 million in revenues to the state. Traditional arts dominate, although in recent years the market has made room for innovators.[15] The carnival atmosphere and skyrocketing prices have led some to dub the event "Indian Markup." Indian and non-Indian artists who constitute the board have developed the judging standards. In the perennial tension between traditionalists and modernists, SWAIA seems to be in constant turmoil, turning over eight executive directors between 1998 and 2008.[16]

Markets and expositions reinforced the ethnographic frame that academe and museums had constructed for Indian arts. With Indian Market, Santa Fe also offers the collections of the School for Advanced Research, the Museum of New Mexico, and the Wheelwright Museum.[17] As early as the 1920s, however, some museums began to ask patrons to rethink the traditional and to consider the new. The Denver Museum, where Feder worked, was one of the first to show Indian materials as art—in 1925. In New York the monthlong Exposition of Indian Tribal Arts of 1931 ran in Grand Central Station's art gallery. Mrs. John D. Rockefeller and artist John Sloan were among the luminaries who supported the show that greeted commuters. The city's press was not quite ready for this new view of Native arts. *Time* magazine described reporters covering the exhibit as "greeting each other with soft cries of 'Ugh! Ugh!' and 'How.'"[18]

In 1941 New York's Museum of Modern Art (MoMA) devoted its entire space to an exhibit titled simply *Indian Art of the United States*.[19] It was a bold move, because the twelve-year-old museum was a fledgling institution. Frederic H. Douglas of the Denver Art Museum and René d'Harnoncourt, in his role as the general manager of the Department of the Interior's Indian Arts and Crafts Board (IACB), organized the exhibit.[20] In the show's catalog, they asserted that American Indian art was both American and art. The curators chose pieces that were "very contemporary and Fifth Avenue" and arranged the displays "'for dramatic and organic unity.'"[21] Blazing theater lights illuminated Northwest Coast masks. Like Hewett in Santa Fe, Harnoncourt brought Navajos to New York to demonstrate their arts. Well before the show, Harnoncourt had imagined the expansion of Native creativity. "I sincerely believe that Indian art, if it is not smothered in its cradle, may become a powerful fresh factor in American art," he said in 1938.[22] With termination and relocation far in the future, he could place the American Indian "in the middle of his greatest struggle to find his place in a civilization." The MoMA show was a huge hit.

Jesse Cooday said in another bit of hyperbole, "When you Google 'Indian,' you get Curtis." As much as and perhaps even more than trading posts and museums, photographer Edward Curtis is an institution that has powerfully reinforced the image of American Indian art and created the buckskin box. Curtis entered Indian arts in the late twentieth century—and posthumously. He completed his monumental work, *The North American Indian*, between 1900 and 1930. But it disappeared until the 1970s. Like others, Curtis wanted to capture "vanishing" Indians. He hauled equipment into remote areas to visit eighty tribes, snap forty thousand pictures, and produce more than twenty-two hundred plates. From these he culled photos and text for his twenty-volume set. Sales never covered the cost of publishing a limited edition of three hundred, and galleries and museums ignored his work. Curtis himself died impecunious—"vanished"—in Los Angeles in 1953, the year that the termination began.

After the plates were discovered at a Boston rare book shop in the 1970s, first the Morgan Library and then the Witkin Gallery in New York displayed the photos. Curtis's work hadn't changed, but the context had; shows at more major museums had again sparked interest in things Indian.[23] The hold of Curtis's images has never abated. They have been reproduced on coffee mugs, prints, postcards, and posters. The *New York Times* shop sells a large print of his famous *Canyon de Chelly* for $1,795 and men's wooden accessories boxes with a Curtis image in ceramic tile on top for $65. As for the original twenty-volume sets, a complete one can fetch more than $1 million.[24]

Curtis's artistic achievement is undeniable, but his legacy is troubling. In luminous and exquisite portraits and landscapes, he used light and shadow to create moods and capture personalities, and his compositional sense was unerring. His photos today belong to fine art photography, not to ethnography. But scholar Ross Frank points out that Curtis collected Indian images like artifacts: dwellings, people, and material culture (baskets, clothing, and cradleboards).[25] He posed Indians in the fashion of his time in sometimes fanciful contexts; his

Hopi women ground corn in ceremonial dress. Because Curtis believed that Indians had no present and certainly no future, he set them in the past. His photo of the Hopi Snake Dance showed only Indians watching, while another contemporary photo showed that non-Indians also attended regularly.[26] Stereotypes crept into the captions he wrote for his portraits. In the text for *A Hopi Man*, he described "the dominant traits of Hopi character": wary, distrustful eyes and a stubbornly set mouth. "Yet somewhere in this face lurks an expression of masked warmheartedness and humanity," he concluded.

Some of Curtis's "vanishing" Indians—alive and well today—admire his portraits. He posed his Native subjects like the society clients he had photographed in his successful business in Seattle. These almost regal depictions dispel the stereotype of the dirty, lazy, and drunken Indian. In her foreword to *Edward S. Curtis: The Women*, author Louise Erdrich (Ojibwe) wrote that he made his subjects "so dimensional, so present, so complete that it is to me as though I was looking at the women through a window, as though they are really there in the print and in the paper, looking back at me." Curtis prompted filmmaker George Birdeau (Piegan Blackfeet) to visit his ancestral homeland on the Montana plains for the first time; tribal members welcomed him. "It's that sense of community that stunned me. Curtis understood the power of that cultural spirit," Birdeau said.[27]

During the twentieth century, museums continued to push Indian arts beyond ethnographic document. At the turn of the millennium, the NMAI's Heye Center in New York City presented shows that celebrated traditionalism while challenging its relentless hold: *Who Stole the Teepee?*, *First American Art*, and *New Tribe New York*.[28] Heye's shows are small, narrowly focused, and sometimes tied to the life of the city.

The first exhibit took its title from *Who stole the tee pee?*, a series of six arresting portraits of Indian families by George Littlechild (Plains Cree).²⁹ The families pose stiffly in the style of nineteenth-century formal photos. Behind the exhibit's title lay other provocative questions: Did Indians aid and abet the European American governments, settlers, traders, anthropologists, missionaries, and educators who appropriated their culture? How much help did Curtis have from his subjects? Drawing from NMAI's historical collection and contemporary artists, the show looked back on Indians' catastrophic history as well as their struggle to maintain their identities. It showed how ordinary people regularly expressed sometimes brutal life experiences in art, said its cocurator Joanna Bigfeather (Cherokee/Mescalero).³⁰ A Lakota family on the Rosebud Reservation—known only as Family No. 205—depended on a ration card for government supplies, the family's basic life support. But they kept the card in an ornately beaded case that bespoke cultural wealth. "They made it beautiful," said Bigfeather. Because modern people are too busy to personalize our precious things, the personal and intimate nature of many Native items is seductive. The beaded stethoscope that veterinarian Scott Bender wore around his neck wrapped him in beauty and science.

First American Art exhibited more than two hundred nineteenth-century works from prominent New York collectors who followed in the footsteps of George Gustav Heye.³¹ The works were historical and traditional, although the exhibit's context was modern. Rather than ethnographic categories, regions, or types (such as pots, jewelry, baskets, etc.), curators arranged the pieces according to seven principles that comprise a visitor's aesthetic experience: integrity, emotion, movement, idea, composition, intimacy, and vocabulary. These principles can overlap in any single work. For instance, Indians made things to *use*, a quality that lends them intimacy. "Use" is a tricky value, however; it can categorize an object as popular art—folk art or craft—or for its ethnographic significance, as opposed to a "pure" or "fine" art. But wrapping our hand around a Zuni fetish expands its aesthetic reach through touch. In *First American Art*, intimacy and movement combine in a Wasco tanned hide dress splashed with a bold black-and-white design in glass beads across the bodice and shoulders. The dress is a testament to grace, as we imagine the woman wearing it, walking, striding, or dancing. The interplay among the principles extends beyond individuals to family and community. A pair of Lakota child's moccasins made of tanned deer hide and beaded all around, even on the soles, speaks to the dedication of their maker and to the love between parents and child. An Acoma artist has covered a sand-colored clay pot with realistic and abstract designs of squash, corn, and flowers. The *olla* tells us about the cosmology of Acoma agricultural life.[32]

Finally, just across a hall from *First American Art*, *New Tribe New York* was decidedly about today. The show's subtitle was *The Urban Vision Quest*, and it included works from four artists who live in the New York area. They seek their vision in the city and recollections of the tribal home. They too grab and twist apart the sinews of stereotype that grip Native peoples and cultures. Mario Martinez (Yoeme) paints color-drenched abstractions with allusions to New York City and his home in Arizona and northern Mexico. Spiderwoman Theater is the creation of Lisa Mayo, Gloria Miguel, and Muriel Miguel, who grew up in Brooklyn listening to stories from their Panama Kuna father and Rappahannock mother. They tour the country with feminist adaptations of Native tales. Painter Alan Michelson was born a Buffalo Mohawk and grew up adopted in a Jewish family in western Massachusetts. His moody paintings and constructions reflect his continuing explorations of a nearly lost heritage. As we shall see, Lorenzo Clayton (Navajo) has constructed mythic metaphors of a vision quest.[33]

In a remarkable commitment, the Museum of Arts and Design (MAD) in New York pushed further into the twenty-first century. Curators devoted its entire space to *Changing Hands: Art without Reservation*, three exhilarating shows with hundreds of works by contemporary Native artists spaced over a decade between 2002 and 2011. Given the scope and diversity of the project, curators reverted to an old standby, regionalism, and split the shows among the Southwest, the Pacific regions, and areas east of the Mississippi (the latter two included Canada). For the viewer, the effect was sometimes overwhelming, even though curators had suggested themes emerging from the art: sometimes savage political commentary and humor, sheer brilliance of artistic execution, explorations of human destiny, and ironic statements about Indian life and American culture in general. In strikingly different voices, the artists draw the viewer into new Indian perspectives. Especially important for both the neophyte and the experienced, the fat catalogs were packed with information on modern Native art. MAD's shows are "phenomenal in importance," said Joyce Szabo. "To give that much coverage rather than just one 'let's-cram-it-together' is great. It allows the audience to see so much more."[34]

Finally, the Denver Art Museum, Feder's professional home, reflects the changes in attitudes about Indian art since his tenure. In 2011, when the museum opened an exhibit in its newly renovated Indian art galleries, organizers identified the individual creators of dozens of "anonymous" works that had been treated as ethnography, identified only with tribal names. Nancy Blomberg, the museum's curator of Native arts, said her work on the show had a special purpose: "I want to signal that there are *artists* on this floor." The movement toward identifying artists has accelerated in the past decade as curators and scholars rethink and recognize individual creativity and not just tribal affiliations in Native art. Past practice "perpetuates a set of ideas, values and historical practices laden with racism, ethnocentrism and tragic and destructive government policies," according to Dan L. Monroe, executive director of the Peabody Essex Museum in Salem, Massachusetts.[35]

Nowhere is the recent growth in Indian arts more visible than in New Mexico, which rides the wave of an earlier incarnation. Between 1970 and 1992, the number of galleries in Santa Fe increased from 26 to 231 and of curio/Indian shops from 15 to 64.[36] These numbers indicate the *amount* of interest. Another source points to more complex and subtle changes. In the mid-1980s, Don and Pamela Michaelis, a young couple in Albuquerque, began publishing the *Wingspread Collector's Guide*, a magazine and catalog of galleries in Santa Fe, Taos, and Albuquerque. From its initial seventy-two pages, the guide has grown to nearly four hundred pages of ads and stories; nearly a quarter million copies are distributed across the United States and abroad. In addition, the website (http://www.collectorsguide.com) records between six thousand and eight thousand page views, or one million "hits," *daily*.

As for the kind of art the guide describes, the Michaelises deliberately narrow their coverage to about three hundred galleries that feature handmade, one-of-a-kind items; 70 percent of the galleries are in Santa Fe, which Pamela Michaelis described as the "engine of the New Mexico art market." About 10 percent of these galleries describe themselves as mostly "Indian"; in Albuquerque the figure is 25 percent. *Collector's Guide* in hand, consumers troll streets lined with purveyors of "Southwest Regionalism"—western-art galleries and "trading posts." Among the "Indian" galleries, some specialize in older masterpieces, such as a Zia pot priced at $9,000. Others occupy a gray area between "traditional" and "contemporary." A handful specializes in contemporary arts. More diversified Albuquerque also attracts contemporary artists (especially sculptors) who need low-rent studio and living space, which is in short supply in pricey Santa Fe. Artists, institutions, and galleries increasingly represent the contemporary market. "Because there is an impressive rise in the number of very talented contemporary Native American artists, many of the top contemporary galleries have at least one major or soon-to-be major or emerging native artist," said Pamela Michaelis.[37]

The Collector's Guide reveals trends in galleries that extend well beyond the hot center of Indian arts in New Mexico. Well-heeled collectors have pushed the envelope in the world's auction houses—though not exclusively for contemporary arts. Sotheby's virtually created an auction market for American Indian items in the 1970s; Christie's followed suit. Sotheby's auction in October 2006 netted $7 million, including $1.7 million for a Tsimshian mask from the Pacific Northwest—a world's record for a Native American piece. The annual auction's revenues dropped to $2.6 million in 2009, a recession year. Since the 1970s, the prices for contemporary ceramics from the Southwest went well beyond prevailing retail levels. David M. Roche, the director of the house's Indian art department, said that subsequently a "frenzy" gripped galleries in the 1980s for both traditional and contemporary articles.[38]

The fine art marketplace—museums, markets, fairs, auction houses, and galleries—has helped both to build the buckskin box and to pry open an escape. Educational institutions have prepared young artists for both. One of the most important— the Institute for American Indian Arts (IAIA)—is in Santa Fe. Dorothy Dunn had established the Studio at the Santa Fe Indian School in 1932, when the town was crackling with cultural revival (with help from federal Depression programs). She recruited students from several tribes and encouraged them to

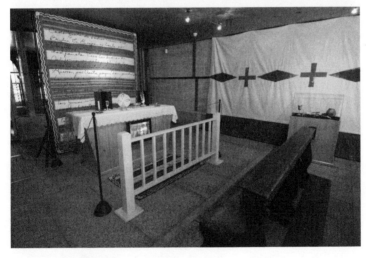

Top: The buckskin box, Santa Fe Indian Market. Photo by Cary Herz.

Bottom: James Luna, *The Chapel of Pablo Tac* at the Venice Biennale, *Emendatio* installation, 2005. Courtesy of the National Museum of the American Indian, Smithsonian Institution (KF05ItalyC238, KF05ItalyG132). Photo by Katherine Fogden.

Top: Lorenzo Clayton, *Mythistoryquest Indigenous: Cosmos*. Courtesy of the artist.

Bottom: Steven Deo, *America's Child*. Courtesy of the artist.

transform what they knew into art while retaining their tribal identities through traditional forms. Partially as a response to Dunn's emphatic traditionalism, IAIA opened as an alternative high school in 1962. With support from the BIA, it was the first and only school devoted entirely to the study and practice of artistic and cultural traditions of Native Americans. Lloyd Kiva New (Cherokee), an art educator at the University of Arizona, helped to establish IAIA because he felt that young Indian artists could use tradition as a springboard to modern creative work. New was also a fashion designer who participated in the wearable art movement with a shop of his own in Scottsdale, Arizona.[39]

IAIA flourished in the 1960s, a time that Joanna Bigfeather called "a golden day we all talk about." At the end of that fruitful decade, the IAIA Museum opened in downtown Santa Fe, and she was its first director. The school also helped nudge the Santa Fe Indian Market into modernity. Although some members of the market's board wanted it reserved for traditional arts, IAIA faculty members also became judges, but relations between the market and the school sometimes frayed. In 1971 Bob Haozous was the first of the new generation of Indian artists to win a prize at the market, and during that decade, nontraditional art began to appear at the event. On two occasions in the 1970s, Fritz Scholder, an early IAIA instructor who had developed an international reputation, offered to fund a new contemporary painting award for Indian Market—with him as the sole judge. With some members insisting on the "traditional" roots for the market, the board refused. Then in 1980 contemporary painter Harry Fonseca (Nisenan/Maidu/Hawaiian/Portuguese) won the award for best painting, signaling a loosening of the market's "constraints." IAIA received a federal charter and funding in 1986, but it nearly failed during the 1990s after a series of financial and personnel crises.

With recovery in the early 2000s, IAIA moved onto a new campus with two- and four-year programs. The school is not without its critics, even among alumni. In a wide-ranging interview, sculptor Robert Haozous (Apache/Navajo) said IAIA is generally ill equipped to develop a language and concepts to address serious issues of identity and culture facing American Indians today. IAIA focused on what he called "the old VoTech concept." Students achieved technical proficiency and made pretty things for sale, so that artists could make money that would trickle down to tribes and encourage economic growth. Haozous, the son of Allan Houser, was the first of the "new generation" of artists to win an award at Indian Market. His multimedia sculptures startle the viewer with their beauty and irreverence. In the same year as the interview, he helped put together an IAIA show centered around a stereotype-cracking theme of Indians trashing nature.[40]

This chapter has briefly reviewed how the "marketplace," especially institutions, has created both traditional and more adventurous contexts for American Indian art. Now we can turn to the artists themselves; they define their art for themselves even though they are an integral part of the marketplace. Samuel Johnson's saying about writers—"No man but a blockhead ever wrote, except for money"—is no less true for artists, including American Indian artists. Here, I borrow loosely from Modest Mussorgsky's piano work *Pictures at an Exhibition*. The composer took listeners through the various moods and images of paintings in a gallery. Mine is a select view of artists I have met or whose work I have seen. Also, I set aside the complexity of these works to examine some general trends in contemporary art. As we have seen, Richard West has drawn a connection between NAGPRA and Indian art in museum environments.[41]

For contemporary artists, repatriation is more like a taking than a "return," however. Whether on canvas or off, in a performance work or in front of a computer, Native artists today "demand to be seen as contemporary people," said Joanna Bigfeather, curator of *Who Stole the Teepee?*. In revolutionary visions, contemporary creators have ignited what one Hopi artist called a "Big Bang." "The expansion of media and visual vocabularies is contributing to the galactic explosion of Native American artists as individual artists. Indian people are no longer tied to form, function and tribal affiliation as the exclusive definition of what art is," said Ramona Sakiestewa, a Hopi innovator in fiber.[42] But even as they eschew "traditional" media and designs—or particular tribal identities—some artists who work on the cutting edge reach back as they generate the future.

The teepee symbolizes how Indians are refashioning their past for today. The teepee is also quintessentially American. The narrative of *Who Stole the Teepee?* states that its portability also speaks to everyone about freedom, the open highway, "an illusion cherished by all Americans." Jaune Quick-to-See Smith remarks that the teepee was never really stolen, at least for her people, the Flathead Salish.[43] Indian artists suggest that we can restore the figurative teepee and combine it with mainstream supports to counter the anger and sorrow that are debilitating by-products of their five-century struggle. Today, all of us, Indian and non-Indian, pick our ways uneasily through the world. Families scatter, mobility is a way of life, and loneliness is endemic. As communities fray, their centers can hold if we anchor them, like teepees, in glacial rock—and make them personal. Today's Native American artists are like the teepee. They hold fast, even in a gale.

Jaune Quick-to-See Smith is one of the artists who had barely begun her work right about the time that Norman Feder was relegating Native arts to museums as remnants of the past. She elicits awe among scholars, critics, and younger artists. Quick-to-See Smith has won acclaim from leading arts institutions, with eighty solo shows over the past thirty years in the United States and abroad. The Whitney Museum of American Art and the Museum of Modern Art in New York, the Museum of Mankind in Vienna, the Smithsonian Institution in Washington DC, and others hold her work in their collections. Yet, she refers to herself simply as "a cultural worker."

Quick-to-See Smith is something of a grandmother to today's younger artists. She is one tough granny, born in 1940 on the Flathead Reservation in western Montana. Belgian Jesuits established a mission there in 1845 for its one thousand or so Indians. The Jesuits provided supplies and health care, helped develop a sawmill, and operated a boarding school. An Italian brother who was the mission's cook splashed the walls of the church with florid frescoes of aliens in an alien land: larger-than-life biblical figures and saints.[44] Quick-to-See Smith's family stayed away from the church. Yet she brings visitors to the frescoes as well as to the bison range and the tribal college founded by her cousin; all are landmarks of the Flathead world. Before she could pursue a life in art, Quick-to-See Smith earned a living as a farm laborer, waitress, Head Start teacher, factory worker, and domestic. She completed her undergraduate education at Framingham State College in Massachusetts and obtained a master's in fine arts from the University of New Mexico in 1980.

Quick-to-See Smith and her husband, Andy Ambrose, live just outside Albuquerque.[45] Dirt lanes connect their house, a studio, and outbuildings, and wild and barnyard critters scurry across the yard. Quick-to-See Smith's pastoral life belies the bold satirical work that is her hallmark. Her solo show *Made in America*—thirty-six paintings from 1992 to 2002—is a primer on how contemporary Indian artists fuse individual visions, cultural experiences, and the contemporary world.[46] The qualities that curators identified for *First American Art* characterize her work. Familiarity, intimacy, and humor appear in *Fry Bread* (1998). Quick-to-See Smith piles the images of six large rounds of fry bread for a mixed-media painting that is nearly six feet tall. Marketing slogans change these mundane images into icons, Native "brands": "6 million now served" and "Love at first bite." But the painting's idea is serious. "If you're expecting more in times like this, you'd better wake up" is the other message, from Native women who turned to fry bread out of hardship and necessity.[47]

To convey ideas, Quick-to-See Smith sometimes inserts verbal messages into her collages—pieces of newspaper headlines, photos, and cartoons—among her brush strokes and drippings. She has found *New York Times* headlines full of irony, although after the World Trade Center tragedy in 2001, they took a serious turn. By 2005 she felt that the paper's headline writers had found their voice again. Her giant *Tribal Map 2001 #2* bears a striking resemblance to Jasper Johns's *Map*. Quick-to-See Smith's mixed-media and oil diptych of the United States measures ten feet wide and nearly seven feet high. Outlined in black, the states resemble a child's puzzle, colored in a few hues—red, brown, lilac, and yellow. Johns uses broad, sometimes slashing brush strokes, but Quick-to-See Smith's technique is relatively orderly, with only an occasional paint drip. Johns names the states; Quick-to-See Smith designates tribal territorial areas. Also, while Johns keeps the states' names within their boundaries, Quick-to-See Smith puts tribal names across the ironclad lines and grids that European Americans laid over the land, as if to gain control over an unruly place and people.

Quick-to-See Smith said that tribal Europeans were disconnected from nature and each other when they moved into cities.

In modern times, many Europeans and Indians have suffered a disconnection from place and time—either from migration or from forced relocations—but with an important distinction. Migrants are from somewhere else, so they have only "threads." "We've never left home. All of our stories, myths, folkways, and taboos come out of this land," she said.

Even in her modernity, Quick-to-See Smith sees traditional art as art moving through time. "Mine's just doing the same thing," she said. She welcomes new technologies and materials into her work. Quick-to-See Smith and her son Neal Ambrose Smith collaborated for *Warrior for the 21st Century*. From a ceiling they suspended a skeletal figure with body parts such as sage for smudging, a piece of fry bread, a T-shirt from the Salish Kootenai College, echinacea, Native music CDs, and a condom. The head of this figure is a photo of an Indian toddler's face.[48] The work offers a remedy for the massive pain of Indian life: stitch the tatters of the past into a new warshirt for the future.

Quick-to-See Smith goosed the European American establishment at the Venice Biennale in 1999. In the style of ancient petroglyphs, a line of silhouetted jackrabbits, their ears straight up, march steadfastly in perspective toward the viewer out of a six-foot by four-foot collagraph (collage print). The painting's title and gnarly message—*Celebrate 40,000 Years of American Art*—leap off the canvas in big letters.[49]

By the time he arrived at the Biennale in 2005, James Luna, creator of *The Artifact Piece*, had built a reputation as a performance and installation artist.[50] Luna, a decade younger than Quick-to-See Smith, works and lives on the La Jolla reservation in northern San Diego County. Surrounded by California sprawl, the gentle wooded hills are home to the Palomar Observatory. After NMAI invited him to appear at the Biennale, Luna had one year to prepare what he calls "the show of my life." Initially panic-stricken, he created *Emendatio*, installations and performances that stretched across centuries, geography, and peoples. The title is from the Latin root for "emendation," an alteration to improve and correct the original. Luna presented a course correction in place and time.

Emendatio took up an entire floor of gallery space and culminated in a solo theater piece.[51] For the focus of the multipart, multimedia installations, Luna lighted upon the story of Pablo Tac, a Luiseño Indian born in 1822 at the Mission San Luis Rey de Francia. At the age of ten, he traveled to Rome to prepare for the priesthood and missionary work. During his studies, Tac produced the only account of a California mission from a Native perspective—a 150-page history—with notes on Luiseño grammar and a partial dictionary. He identified with his people, whom he called Quechanjuis. Tac related their struggle to maintain their cultural and religious identity, and he often used the word "cry" to describe their suffering. Although he achieved his priestly vows, Tac never returned home and died in Rome at the age of nineteen. But he became a hero on a journey of discovery.

Luna's aim was to honor Tac, expose his world, and draw the past and present together. To that end, *Emendatio* is full of things, places, people, and emotions—anger, sadness, love, and humor—across time. "You lead people because they want to be led. The idea was to move them in a circular way through this space, building up anticipation, leaving them curious as to what was next," Luna said. The central installation is *The Chapel of Pablo Tac*, a twenty-five-foot by forty-foot room dedicated to the teenager and California mission Indians. Luna furnished the chapel with Native and Catholic motifs: lace-draped altar, cross with a four-feather design, chalice, small leather medicine bag. A large tapestry with Tac's writings woven into it served as an altarpiece. To suggest the cool relief of a mission church on a hot day, Luna replicated the thick, often whitewashed walls using sheets of white fabric decorated with a horizontal strip of blue crosses alternating with red diamonds. Luna said that the room was a "façade" designed to create a mission "feel." Participating in the art, people quietly slipped into the chapel's pews throughout the Biennale. In *The Artifact Piece* Luna pulled the white man's chain. In the chapel he elicited reverence.

For the performance part of *Emendatio*, Luna again used materials from nature and cultures to navigate through space and time. An inventory he arranged at the four cardinal points of a dance circle included essentials of Native life: acorns, the ubiquitous food for Southern California Native peoples; a can of Spam, a ration staple that he calls "a warm kind of comfort food"; and dried beans. Syringes, medicine vials, sugar, and Sweet 'n Low packets exposed Indians' (and Luna's) diabetes affliction. To original music, Luna performed a series of vignettes in the circle over four continuous days. He appeared as multiple personae, some in semitraditional attire: kilt, breechcloth, buckskin shirt, and beaded moccasins. He described another character in more modern dress as a "biker/metalhead/motorcyclerebel Indian." His alter ego, "the lounge Luna," also appeared. Decked out in a shiny purple-brown tux trimmed in black satin, a multistring beaded necklace, a red fedora with a feather, and sunglasses, Luna carried a rattle made of a metal pepper shaker and a beaded stick with leather tassels. As a gondolier he wore a striped shirt and boat hat, and an assistant served him an espresso in the circle. In this persona, Luna collapsed the time between the 1830s and 2005 and the distance between the Old and New Worlds.

Cocurator Paul Chaat Smith (Comanche) wrote that *Emendatio* "claims Venice as part of Indian history and in so doing demonstrates a belief that every place is a Native place." By repeating his performances, Luna iterated permanence and endurance, the values needed for survival. He became a Southwest warrior in front of an audience. "Before entering the space, I made sure there were no snipers on the third floor. I reminded them that there are still people fighting for their homeland," he said.

Emendatio engages and perhaps enrages. At the same time, Luna added, "You gotta have fun. You're in fucking Venice." Luna said the performance arena allows him to bring together elements others might consider too diverse or even divisive. He achieves the union in a kind of ritual movement that allows him to address contemporary issues. "But going back to the beginning here makes it a necessity to present this and present it in a way that my audience will understand (most of them)," he said. For all its punch, Luna's work is gentle, as if he cannot bear to inflict even more pain on his primary audience, his own people.

If Luna thinks locally and acts globally, Lorenzo Clayton takes the local to the cosmic. Clayton was born in To'hajiilee, a Navajo village in west-central New Mexico, in 1951 and grew up in Albuquerque and Santa Fe. He left New Mexico to attend the Cooper Union in New York, where he teaches today, commuting from New Jersey.[52] In *New Tribe New York*, Clayton seems to pour and then reorder the chaos of the transmigration from reservation to city. In *Mythistoryquest*, a large and complex series of multimedia constructions, Clayton explores the world's great religions and systems of thought: Christianity, indigenous spirituality, Eastern faiths, and atheism. Using different media, he creates a unified vision of the quest out of myth, materials from daily life, his own experience in New Mexico, and mainstream America.

In *Mythistoryquest Christianity: Crucifixion* Clayton records a central myth of the Christian world. On and around a large wooden screen he arranges elements from the story of Christ's life and death. In one assemblage a nail attaches a sculpted hand to an arm of a large wooden cross and a three-dimensional metal human heart. A small bistro table neatly set for one with bread and wine waits. The allusions are multiple: the miracles of loaves and fishes and changing water into wine as well as the body and blood of Christ. Clayton also turned to Native systems in *Mythistoryquest Indigenous: Cosmos*. His "canvas" is a huge printed silkscreen image of a galaxy on a buffalo hide. Before this stellar real estate are Native baskets and bowls with offerings of seeds and herbs. The quest is eternal. Native peoples have been reaching for the stars forever. The Chacoans tracked the cosmos, and a petroglyph in Arizona was probably the only record in the Western Hemisphere of a supernova in 1006.[53]

Quick-to-See Smith, Luna, and Clayton work across large intellectual and artistic canvasses. Most of the works in MAD's *Changing Hands* exhibits were in smaller formats. In *Cloud Image* (1996), Dan Namingha (Tewa-Hopi) splits up a traditional kachina into its parts and creates a three-dimensional sculpture with acrylic collages on wood. Namingha says that his kachinas are metaphors for the changes inflicted on Indian culture and across the world by colonizing influences and by time: "We receive only glimpses into one another's culture."[54] Despite this theme of fragmentation, *Cloud Images* remains unified by color, construction, and form.

Sculptor Roxanne Swentzell (Santa Clara Pueblo) responded to the terrorist attacks in 2001 with a gray-tan earthenware piece, *Vulnerable* (2002). A naked, red-haired man sits with his legs straight before him and his arms curled with his fists against his sides. Tied across his eyes is a slash of color—an American flag bandana. In a traditional form, the sculpture delivers a quiet modern shock.

Steven Deo (Creek/Euchee) achieves a similar result in *America's Child* (2004), a piece with no obvious allusions to

Indian life. Deo gives us what seems at first a charming sculpture of a toddler sitting with arms extended. A closer inspection, however, shows that the toddler is made of tiny, military-green, plastic toy soldiers stuck together; next to the figure are its "toys," a small plastic tank and a tiny red, white, and blue American flag in a stand. The foot-high sculpture threatens to shatter under the weight of the implications that fly out. Deo said that identity is a constant issue for him. Values that were once based on the relationship to the environment have slipped away as nature has receded before concrete and steel. "We have been relocated, dislocated, grouped and regrouped, numbered and scattered. The one commonality we have left is an extended family called 'Indian,'" he said. More specifically, the work is about children and how we shape their identities. "*America's Child* is about calling attention to the indoctrination of children through manufactured toys, and also to bring attention to the history of America."[55]

Susan Point (First Nations Salish) and Preston Singletary (Tlingit) applied Northwest and Pacific Coast symbols to glass, a relatively new material for Native American artists. Her grandmother's weaving tools inspired Point to construct *Return*. On a glass spindle nearly three feet in diameter, Point etched Native images. The huge spindle balances on a slender stainless steel shaft mounted on a red cedar stand. In *Oystercatcher Rattle* Singletary turned a shaman's ceremonial rattle into a sandblasted glass bird of uncommon delicacy, incorporating traditional colors and symbols.

Many of today's younger artists studied with teachers who broke out of the market-imposed straightjacket of tradition over the past thirty years. Splashed with color, their finely wrought paintings and sculptures drip with irony and imagination. In his lifetime, sculptor Allan Houser produced more than a thousand works that ranged from the stylized *Comrade in Mourning* to the abstract *Dawn* and *Reflections*; in 1992 he received the National Medal of Art. Fritz Scholder (Luiseño) stepped boldly into the art world with brassy paintings like *The American Indian* (1970). This is no cigar-store Indian; rather, the artist wraps him in a full-length American flag, tucks a feather in his hair, slaps a breastplate across his chest, and puts a tomahawk in his hand. T. C. Cannon, who grew up in Oklahoma's Kiowa region, was an early IAIA graduate and then a teacher until his untimely death at the age of thirty-one in an automobile accident. In *Osage with van Gogh* (ca. 1980), he poses an elegant Indian in splendid Native dress in a wicker chair. Hanging on the wall behind him is a small painting of wheat fields by Vincent van Gogh. Charlene Teters (Spokane) is a working artist/activist and faculty member at IAIA. With precisely designed and drawn images on canvases, photography, installations, and performances, she twists the persistent stereotypes that portray Indians as playthings and objects into edgy political works. One of her best known is *Route 66 Revisited: It Was Only an Indian* (1993), an installation that documented the environment for Indians in places like Albuquerque and Gallup.

Finally, to return to Jesse Cooday, he is not quite the Tlingit in space—yet. Like other Native artists, however, he turns the pickled images—"vanishing," drunken, or casino Indians—upside down. In his series of digital "paintings" entitled *Wannabe Nation*, Cooday satirizes consumer hunger for Indian "stuff." *Wannabe Romance* neatly balances equal-sized images of a sleek bottle of perfume and Curtis's *Waiting in the Forest—Cheyenne*. Curtis's dreamy photo shows a young Cheyenne man who, except for his eyes, is completely wrapped in a white blanket and standing in a dark forest, apparently waiting for a romantic rendezvous.[56] In a real ad for the Heard Museum in *American Indian Art Magazine*, a beautiful Native-looking woman with long black hair wearing a heavy silver and turquoise necklace beckons to readers: "Be stunning this summer."[57] Reality continues to dull the cutting edge.

"Indian stuff" still stands between artists and consumers, especially for those who seek innovation and originality and find only "authenticity." Chaat Smith opens his *Emendatio* essay with a quote from African American scholar Henry Louis Gates Jr.: "'Authenticity' is among the founding lies of the modern age."[58] Even with its diversity and with growing exposure, contemporary Native art runs risks beyond simply being "new." In museums and galleries, it still inhabits the "ethnicity" ghetto, along with African American, Latino American, and Asian American arts. As Chaat Smith puts it, "Even the most adventurous contemporary American Indian artist faces the prospect of Indian-only shows."[59]

New York Times critic Holland Cotter suggested that categorization can kill. Reviewing a show by Inuit artist Annie Pootoogook at the Heye Center, Cotter said the expectation that American Indian art must have certain traditional characteristics, including spirituality and nature, persists. Any artist venturing into a more modern representation of such characteristics—for instance, Inuit soapstone carvings of whales or prints of shamanistic figures—could be accused of producing kitsch. "By such perversely exacting standards the possibilities for a genuine, living Inuit art to exist at all are slim," Cotter wrote.[60]

Sometimes an artist will break through. In 2008 curators at the Museum of Arts and Design included Steven Deo's *Perpetual Stream* for *Second Lives*, an exhibit that inaugurated its new building. The sculpture was one of two that visitors first encountered as they stepped off the elevator. Deo was not immediately identified as American Indian in a show that drew on fifty established and emerging artists from five continents.

The curator's description of the piece, however, explained that the figures in the sculpture represent him and his Creek and Yuchi people.

Kathleen Ash-Milby (Diné), a curator at the Heye Center, chronicled Native artists' invisibility in the nonmuseum marketplace even before the downturn of 2008. The only nonprofit gallery in New York devoted exclusively to showing contemporary Indian art—the American Indian Community House—has never been able to attract more than three thousand patrons each year. Private galleries have closed or have been unstable. Even shows at the Heye Center do not always receive significant reviews.[61]

James Luna said that the only limit for artists today is *business*: produce work that will sell, build a résumé, and systematically market the work. Luna engages in the business, but he draws a line. "I can't change the system, but the system can't change me," he added.[62] Luna sometimes refers to himself as "one of America's oldest emerging artists" because his work attracts few buyers. But prices for his pieces rose after 2005, what he called "the badge of the Venice Biennale."

Through art, the spirit soars. As the curators for *First American Art* suggest, creative energy in Native work does not center around the artist or some abstract notion of "art." This is not to devalue abstract art but to acknowledge that the connection between maker, material, and viewer/user has value. Bob Haozous described a discussion among contemporary artists at New York University where he was the only American Indian panelist. His colleagues delineated their "community" as other artists. "I was the only one who said my community is an actual people," he said.[63] By considering art in the context of community and history as well as coming from the hands of a solitary creator, we can see it anew, freshly.

American Indian content goes beyond the self-conscious artist in contrast to, perhaps as a relief from, much European American modernism, postmodernism, or pop. This approach does not ignore the worth of a more formal consideration of art. When planning a major exhibit on Russian art at New York's Guggenheim Museum in 2005, director Thomas Krens wanted it to establish centuries of connections. He arranged the works to show that Russia's artistic "genes" followed a trajectory from the medieval icon to a twentieth-century Suprematist artist like Kasimir Malevich.[64]

The "genes" of American Indian art are present in a dry southwestern gully filled with shattered pieces of hundreds if not thousands of pots, petroglyphs scratched on boulders across the continent, and the monumental carvings of the Pacific Northwest. Their communities probably knew the makers, even though the works are unsigned in the conventional sense. Contemporary American Indian artists, whose work goes across the world, sign their pieces as individuals, although community is ever present.

This connection between life and art in American Indian art generates the passion that drives its creators and informs their works. A documentary that has daily screenings at NMAI gives voice to the spirit that draws us like moths to their light: "Indian country is really all of us. Wherever we are in this world, we're traveling together on this journey down a thousand roads, all leading home."[65]

DISCLOSURES
We Help Each Other

For me, Jane Dumas and the Kumeyaay flag clinched the idea
of repatriation as a physical, cultural, and spiritual movement.
Another woman had unknowingly seeded that movement many
years before in a setting that allowed for its slow germination
until it took root at the time of the Pecos repatriation. Marie
of San Felipe Pueblo slowly unfurled to our family the folds of
her ordinary life and that of her people. From a small beginning I absorbed the messages from Indian Country almost
imperceptibly, year by year, layer after layer. The assumptions
that underlie this book—and the decision to write it—grew
out of a personal peregrination that paralleled my work as a
journalist.

Indians came into my life after we moved from New York
City to Albuquerque in 1969. I had a new MA in English from
New York University, and my husband, fresh out of a doctoral
program at Columbia University, had taken his first teaching
job at the University of New Mexico. I had spent time abroad,
picking up a couple of languages, but I stepped into the heart

of Indian Country as *Boobus americanus*. I was suddenly living with a new (to me) group—American Indians. Born in Brooklyn into a family that had slipped out of Italy just before World War II, I was a typical New Yorker. Indians were out west—out there somewhere, far west of the Hudson River.

I had had some dim encounters with Indians. Rockland County, just northwest of the city where my war-weary parents moved, retained tribal place-names—Monsey, Nyack, Nanuet, Ramapo. In civics classes I heard others—Seneca, Oneida, and Mohawk—but always in the context of conflict. Saturday matinees often included cowboys versus Indians—and you know who won. Some students in my high school were kids with mixed ancestry: Ramapough Lenape and European—Dutch, Hessian, and English—who had arrived in the area in the 1700s. We called them "Jackson Whites," but the Ramapoughs reject the term as derogatory. They had names like DeFreese, DeGroat, and VanDunk, olive to dark skins, kinky hair, and blue-green eyes. In March 2010 Ben McGrath, writing in the *New Yorker*, traced the history, myths, and recent events among the so-called Jackson Whites. Intrusions and violence against them seem to have accelerated. The Indian wars are still raging in the New York suburbs.[1] In college the only Indians I ran across were those of James Fenimore Cooper and René Chateaubriand.

As newlyweds, my husband and I lived on Manhattan's far upper west side, and Sunday walks sometimes took us to the original Museum of the American Indian. From another apartment at the very northern tip of the island we could look out our living room window to Inwood Hill Park. This was the site of a mythic New York event—the Big Apple's first big real estate deal, in 1626, when Peter Minuit "bought" Manhattan from the Lenapes for twenty-four dollars' worth of knickknacks. I never met a full-blooded Indian, although I knew about the fearless Mohawk steelworkers who perch high above Manhattan, raising the superstructure of skyscrapers. That happened east of the Hudson, of course.[2]

New Mexico's Indians were both present and *visible*. Numerous Pueblos, Navajos, and Apaches live in and around Albuquerque. We settled in the downtown, an older urban neighborhood in a small city that has been Californicating since after World War II. The nearly abandoned downtown was tattered but lively, diverse, and favored by folks who came to shop from the nearby reservations. In the supermarket, Navajo women pushed their carts down the aisles alongside me. Older women invariably dressed up for the trip to town in ankle-length broomstick skirts, velvet shirts with silver buttons, moccasins, and perhaps a necklace of turquoise and silver. Although I was coming from the ethnic cauldron of Manhattan, where skin color and different dress and languages are simply part of the landscape, I noticed. I found another connection in Guido's Palms, a neighborhood food store that coincidentally bore my father's name. An Italian family that had bypassed seaboard cities and headed west had started Guido's early in the twentieth century. It was the only place in town that sold certain familiar Italian staples. Palms was also an urban trading post, where Indians bartered jewelry and other items for sacks of flour and other provisions. Later, the family closed the grocery store and used the "pawn" stashed in their vault to start a successful Indian shop at the same location.

Marie's family and her village helped fill the nearly blank slate that I brought from New York to New Mexico. While today I think of Marie as a friend, our relationship is complex. She has worked for us as a weekly housekeeper for nearly forty years. We hired her about two years after we arrived in Albuquerque, during my first pregnancy, and she was in our home on the day I went into labor. While working in our home was just a job for Marie, initially it was an uncomfortable experience for me. Although my husband's mother had domestic help, the women in my immigrant family—our "village"—relied on each other in raising children, illness, and death. So at first I resisted hiring anyone, even though, far from family support, I needed some help. Our small house seemed formidable after one-bedroom Manhattan apartments, and a baby was on the way. I was new at being a boss, and from the start I considered Marie an employee, not a maid. I worried about behaviors and attitudes that might hint of subservience on her part or gross insensitivities on mine. Liberal guilt? Not quite. My family was working class, and no job was too humble. To earn money for college I had pushed bedpans in a hospital, clerked in a bank, and shelved books in Columbia's library. In the early years of our acquaintance, I remained distant, mostly out of insecurity, shyness, and respect for her privacy. Then, slowly, aside from our employer-employee relationship, Marie and I developed other ties.

Marie's world and that of her family is San Felipe Pueblo, midway between Albuquerque and Santa Fe. For our many trips to the village, we leave behind Albuquerque's malls and subdivisions. Speeding along Interstate 25, we pass a long strip of corporate office parks, flimsy warehouses, chain restaurants, and parking lagoons splayed across rolling mesas. Thirty minutes later, a relatively new, oversized, blinking neon sign for San Felipe's Hollywood Casino greets us at the exit ramp; the visual noise of the city has reached the pueblo. At the end of the ramp, the road splits. To the right it leads to the reservation gas station and the casino. The left turn heads to the village. This road used to bisect a grassy expanse where horses grazed. Now, new ranch houses on suburban-style lots and resembling modern subdivisions have been built on the south meadow; the north side will probably fill in. Farther along, mobile homes are scattered around the landscape, as are modest "ranch" houses built by the Department of Housing and Urban Affairs. One residence has several wings built around its trailer core. The road proceeds across the Rio Grande on a narrow bridge to the T. Make a right turn for the unpaved back road to Santo Domingo Pueblo; to the left a bladed hard dirt road leads to the village itself, the heart of the forty-nine-thousand-acre reservation.

San Felipe is situated in a place of uncommon beauty along the Rio Grande, where tall cottonwoods that turn golden in fall flank the river. An upriver dam regulates the Rio Grande's water level for the valley's irrigation. San Felipe children spend hours bicycling and playing on the river's levees. No urban planner could place the village better. In its core, attached houses congregate around the plaza and outward along dirt lanes. Made of stone, adobe, or more recent frame construction and covered in varying shades of adobe or paint, they seem to emerge from the earth. A number of houses have grown organically and systematically, room by room. Here and there small wooden barns, tool sheds, fences, and corrals attest to San Felipe's agriculture. Cars and pickup trucks are parked haphazardly in driveways or along the road. The ubiquitous "rez dogs" of wildly indeterminate pedigrees lounge in the dirt yards against sun-drenched adobe walls.[3] Only occasional litter mars the village's rusticity.

The plaza is San Felipe's physical, social, and ceremonial center. Nearby but outside the plaza proper are nondescript tribal government buildings and the historic mission of San Felipe; the present church dates from 1706 and replaced the original built in 1605, which was destroyed during the Pueblo Revolt. At the plaza I first saw a ceremonial dance and afterward shared a meal at Marie's home. On feast days her house is headquarters for a stream of family, friends, and other visitors, including strangers encountered on the plaza during dances and invited in for lunch. Before his death, her father, with his gray hair pulled into a traditional *chonga* (knot) at the nape of his neck, was ubiquitous. He didn't just watch the participants at the ceremonial dances; rather, he fixated on them. Even as a nonagenarian he enjoyed visits to San Felipe's Hollywood Casino on Seniors Day, ate the free lunch, but never used the five dollars that the elders receive for gaming. At family gatherings he sometimes napped in a recliner chair as his large family swirled around him.

Cooking for the four days of Christmas dancing takes the better part of a week. The women bake dozens of loaves of crusty bread at a time in *hornos*, outdoor beehive-shaped ovens made of mud bricks and plaster. They keep the kitchen table permanently set with bowls of pinto beans and venison, mutton, beef, and hominy stews swimming in red or green chile. The feast, simmering in large pots, calls to us with a sweet and pungent scent that fills the small and neatly appointed house. Vegetable salads, rounds of fry bread a foot in diameter, thick slices of baked bread, and pitchers of punch or juice join the hearty dishes on the table. Family members, some in their ceremonial dress, mingle with guests.

We eat in the kitchen, which has a view of the river and the Sandia Mountains from the window over the sink. The table can seat ten to twelve, and dozens of people squeeze around the table in shifts. Guests are first, then dancers. The women shoo away anyone who wants to help with cleanup. I once told Marie I admired how she and the other women are able to organize a continual feast during these celebrations. "As long as we help each other, it's okay," she answered. I recall her comment frequently. "As long as we help each other" defines the strength of San Felipe life, even in the face of difficult circumstances.

Marie and I often exchanged "resources"—her Indian bread and chile, my garden tomatoes and herbs. Through her I sent

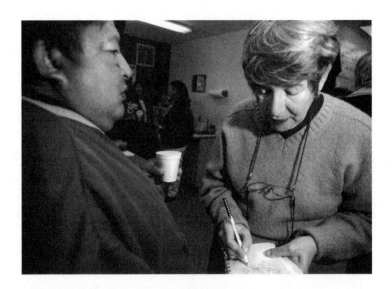

The author at the inauguration of Hopi radio station KUYI. Photo by Cary Herz.

the clothing my children outgrew to San Felipe children, and I recycled our *National Geographic*, *Smithsonian*, and *Newsweek* subscriptions to her father. When the children were small and I was working from home, she occasionally kept an eye on them if I had to run an errand. She sometimes brought along a niece, nephew, or grandchild who played with our children. We have shared our losses—siblings who died in the prime of life and departed parents and grandparents—and happy milestones like births of children and grandchildren, weddings, graduations, and baptisms.

Born just a year apart, we have battled the aches and bulges of aging at the same time. Age has been kind to Marie's wide face, which seems forever firm with few lines, prominent cheekbones, and dark eyes. She dyes her long silky hair pitch black and fastens it into a ponytail or bun; her makeup is understated, always perfect. When she smiles or laughs, the cheekbones get even sharper, and her lips part to show straight white teeth. At times of sadness she furrows her brow and in disappointment or anger purses her lips. None of my languages includes a Native one, and when I hear her and other family members speak in Keresan, I try to guess the subject matter from their intonation. When they talk to children in both English and Keresan, their voices are usually soft and full of affection, even when admonishing.

I have never formed a clear picture of the religious life of Marie and her family. Although the Pueblos accommodated Christianity centuries ago, weekly masses in the mission church are not well attended, she tells me. At San Felipe, Christian and Native traditions blend, although traditional religion seems to have the upper hand. At Christmas, after midnight mass ends, the Catholic priest leaves the church, and the Native dancers enter to begin four days of spectacular traditional dancing that continue in the plaza. The ceremonials dominate the holiday and seem to relegate the Catholic service to a minor status. For group baptisms, a Catholic friar blesses each baby and then leaves the baptistery. The Native religious leader then enters and blesses each baby in Keresan with sacred cornmeal. At a home reception afterward, elders formally address the parents in Keresan, reminding them of their responsibilities and of the community's readiness to help.

Over the years, Marie has politely turned away my questions about the pueblo's ceremonial and religious life. Pueblos have learned from long experience not to share their community's secrets with any outsiders. I don't press. In that same spirit, I gave Marie and another member of her family an early draft of this chapter to read. At her request, I am not using her real name and have omitted details that might reveal the family's identity.

The family's happy times—a wedding, birth, graduation, even a win at the casino—and its difficulties—sometimes fatal substance abuse, teens in trouble, illness, financial crises, and occasional violent deaths—punctuate the rhythm of daily life. Like people from nearby pueblos such as Laguna, Sandia, and Isleta, those at San Felipe commute to school and work in Albuquerque or Santa Fe. The men find jobs in construction (often after a hitch in the military) or computer companies, the women as secretaries, beauticians, and other service jobs as well as teaching or other professional positions. Younger children go to San Felipe Elementary School, teens to a public high school in a nearby Anglo town or to the Indian boarding school in Santa Fe. Older students attend community college or the University of New Mexico.

Despite its hardships, Marie's family is close and supportive. Sometimes I realize that Marie and her family might have disappeared in the conflagration of colonization, like those of other pueblos, including Pecos.[4] Although they bear the marks of their history, they also remain strong mainly because they have sustained the mental—and spiritual—strength of individuals, families, and communities.

So I have also written this book for Marie and her family, to remember and honor all I have learned from them and kept with me. Indians have responded to their existential condition sometimes with despair and anger, always with tenacity, and more often than might at first be expected with generosity and humor. As I now recognize, the term "the Native American experience" misrepresents the complexity of Indian life. The American Indian archipelago constitutes different languages, cultural traditions, and histories, even though tribes share some common beliefs and experiences.

Aside from casinos, many Americans remain largely detached from Indians and their histories, partly because reservations are (or seem) far away. Also, I continue to wonder how many Americans still surround Indians with flimsy fantasies, stereotypes, and mythology that are sometimes hilarious. A slick ad that the Albuquerque Convention and Visitors Bureau placed in an airline magazine in 2004 showed four Indians in traditional dress, their backs to us, with a beautiful traditional pueblo pot on each of their heads. The ad copy read: "In any other city, this pottery would be found in a trendy gallery." The not too thinly veiled stab at Santa Fe tourist chic continues: "Around here, it's still used to haul water."[5]

Click! Most modern Pueblos draw their water from faucets at the kitchen sink or bathtub. Also, like Santa Fe, Albuquerque relies on tourism, with numerous galleries and trading posts filled with Indian pots, jewelry, rugs, and plenty of kitsch. In Europe the romantic West is immortal. Karl May's century-old portrayal of Native Americans still fuels Germans who flock to festivals of weekend reenactments of cowboys versus Indians (the Indians win). The "Tex" comic books, following the western adventures of Tex Willer, his son, Tiger Jack, a Navajo warrior, and Kit Carson, have been published continuously in Italy since 1948.[6] As an antidote, the American Indian College Fund ran a series of ads with photos of Indian professionals, such as Lori Arviso Alvord, MD, a Navajo surgeon, and William Thorne (Pomo), a judge on the Utah Court of Appeals who also served as president of the National Indian Justice Center. The ads' headline asks all of us: "Have you ever seen a real Indian?"[7]

The ordnance of colonization can explode unexpectedly, like road mines that still "live" long after a war has ended. Scars are fresh and easily reopened. For Americans, words like "assimilation" and "termination" seem less damning than contemporary terms like "ethnic cleansing," "final solution," "genocide," or even "injustice" or "colonization." But strategies used with American

Indians have parallels in the horrors that we ascribe to others in Nazi Germany, the Balkans, Darfur, or Stalinist Russia. In a slim volume, the novelist Larry McMurtry described six massacres in the West between 1846, when gold fever swept across the country, and 1890, the end of the Indian wars. The body count, as he said, was small, but the killings reverberate to the present. Indians remember, and so do some whites.[8]

As an Italian American I often witness the crossfire between Italians and Indians; in some cities Italians no longer can have a Columbus Day parade. Columbus was a courageous explorer, say the Italians. Columbus unleashed a holocaust, say the Indians. What a crazy debate. They're both right. Because of his voyages the European footprint was set firmly in a new world and changed human history forever. Columbus's avarice and the forces his "discovery" unleashed also led to the destruction of whole peoples. Both are historical verities.

Searching for an effective metaphor to communicate the indigenous-newcomer encounter in the Americas to young people, I have drawn on the Prime Directive in *Star Trek*, the popular television series.[9] When the starship *Enterprise* found a new civilization, especially one at a lesser technological level, its captains frequently invoked the Prime Directive of the United Federation of Planets, which forbade contact until a full assessment could be made of impacts on a people and their culture. To explain the directive, the show sometimes alluded to the American Indian experience. Columbus did not have the Prime Directive; neither did anyone else. To the contrary, the European crowns, the church, and the companies all primed and paid explorers to contact, convert, conquer, and capitalize. Finding North America extended an age of European global exploration and trade. That included the slave trade, not a new phenomenon in the Americas; Columbus noted the practice of slavery among the Native peoples he encountered on San

Salvador.[10] Indigenous peoples were caught up in these conflicts as bystanders, allies, enemies—and obstacles.[11]

Also, conquest is the oldest story in human history. Lust for land and resources undergirds any ideology that drives conquerors: the British "civilizing" India; the Romans doing the same for their known world; Mongols and their push to unite all the nomadic peoples of the steppe from Mongolia to eastern Europe; Germans and *Lebensraum* in central Europe; and the Incas and Aztecs creating empires in the Americas are but a few examples. Manifest Destiny is not exceptional or even particularly American. Arguably, the Europeans and then the Americans who penetrated the western continent were risk-takers. But explorers and settlers often had help from generous Native people. Also, European and European American governments subsidized colonization with trading contracts, soldiers, forts (or *presidios*), and railroad rights-of-way; they actively worked to push Indians aside.

White Americans can neither ignore nor simply wring their hands or "apologize" for the past. Rather, we can and must remember. Not everyone has been fortunate to have a Marie in their lives to show them a new way, how to do this with respect. As we have seen, Indians *are* our neighbors.[12] They are not invisible. The reality of contemporary American Indian life enriches us far more than the fantasy. To enter it, non-Indians must be prepared to accept the fact that they can never be completely inside. But Indians welcome outsiders who understand that courtesy goes a long way. Reservation homes are private places, yet tourists regularly knock on doors of Indian families just to "see." Obey rules posted at the entrances of many reservations. Dress appropriately for ceremonials.

Besides being courteous neighbors, we can adjust our "sights" in schools. Illuminating the epochal encounter between Europe and the Americas—not just in the dim past but in our own lifetimes—could halt the misconceptions that tear open old scars and inflict new ones. Non-Indians continue to say that Indians get "free" health care and education, but as a woman in Albuquerque put it, "It's not free. My ancestors paid for it with blood and land."[13]

The land shapes Indians' identity, the context for family and entire civilizations. During their relocation to Bosque Redondo, the Diné suffered as much from heartbreak—the loss of the land that defined their community memory and identity— as from the appalling conditions of their prison camp.[14] But admiration for Indians' grit and enthusiasm for their cultures can lead to as much trouble and misunderstanding as keeping them in the usual boxes. As a number of people in this book show, Indians are subject to the same foibles—envy, jealousy, and greed—as the rest of us.

This is not the first book that aims to recharge Americans' memories. Contemporary Indian authors and artists give us powerful expositions of their people's histories and present-day lives. Some non-Indians, too, have created ways to counter the historical and contemporary distortions that many of their fellows continue to hold. In my own profession of journalism, old habits are difficult to break.

Indians have bent into modernity's winds for centuries. Today, hurricane-force winds are buffeting all of us. First from Marie and her family and later from others I learned that the physical and social minutiae of Indian daily life are super-strong strands that ensure "survivance": family, community, ceremony, values like generosity and reciprocity, and cooperation. Indian modernity is a useful model for all Americans because it emphasizes human connection. Archaeology stripped ancient Pecos Pueblo of its humanity literally by removing the remains and figuratively by treating the remains as inanimate, unconnected to people.

Repatriation restored the ancestors in time and place—and it brought humanity back to science. Non-Indian Americans, with families split up and scattered across the continent and even the world to follow jobs or dreams, can learn from that experience and other circumstances of today's Indians.

The joy and power that an event like the Pecos repatriation has released into Indian Country is palpable. Repatriation resonates—booms—through Indian Country because it reunites people with a past that is not an abstraction but alive in stories sung in families and communities. I understood this dynamic again in 2009, with *The Mannahatta Project* and exhibit. The project was central to the celebration of Henry Hudson's entry into what would become New York harbor. Scientists worked for a decade to uncover the ecology of Manhattan Island in 1609, the year of Hudson's voyage. They revealed Manhattan as a place of bountiful flora and fauna—and humans, the Lenape Indians. These Algonquian-speaking peoples inhabited the island and much of present-day New Jersey and the lower Hudson Valley. European Americans dramatically altered Mannahatta—"land of many hills" to the Lenapes. At the exhibition I saw a digital re-creation of the Inwood section of Manhattan in 1609. On a computer keyboard, viewers could type in a contemporary address and see a picture of how it might have looked four hundred years before. I entered one on the street where we last lived before we moved to New Mexico. In the resulting image, a small, rounded Lenape wigwam made of tree bark next to a stand of corn stood where, centuries later, we would step into our building. At that moment, I connected to my hometown, New York, not just to a street but to lifetimes of people and sensations; longing shot through me.[15]

I open and close this book with stories about two women that provoke the concept of "rematriation." While "repatriation" derives from the Latin root for "father," "rematriation" comes from the root for "mother." Repatriation refers first and foremost to the return of prisoners of war or refugees to their native country. Rematriation, however, acknowledges the homeland as sacred mother. Steven Newcomb (Shawnee/ Lenape) has suggested that rematriation might more accurately describe a fully charged meaning of the return or reclamation. Rematriation is a potent form of self-determination beyond legalisms and politics; it restores a culture to its rightful place on Mother Earth. By extension, it means "to restore a people to a spiritual way of life, in sacred relationship with their ancestral lands, without external interference."[16]

This book is an incomplete picture in the manner of the Navajo weaver's "spirit line." Life is incomplete, and to "finish" or hope to finish is a form of excess and imbalance. Non-Indians have a place in this contemporary weave because of our own presence here for more than five hundred years. Now more than ever, Indians are the weavers of their destiny, and the fabric of their lives is far more interesting than any we could make—or make up—for them.

ACKNOWLEDGMENTS

Although writing is solitary work, the luckiest writer works in a supportive community. These acknowledgments suggest how many colleagues and friends have been part of my community. Over the years, as I worked on stories that became this book, many others extended their advice and affection. I am generally indebted to the Native people who trusted me enough to welcome me into their lives and talk with me, sometimes at length. For those who chose not to answer calls or to talk, I understand, even if that made my job harder.

Specific thanks are also numerous, and I beg forgiveness from those I have inadvertently omitted. Throughout this endeavor, my husband, Richard Robbins, took time to read chapters, answer questions about European history, and reassure me, even as he was working on his books and teaching at the University of New Mexico; his income helped me complete this book. Family members who also read portions include my son, Nick Robbins, my daughter, Carla Robbins Silver, her husband, Mark Silver, and his mother, Holly, and father, David.

Cary Herz was the photographer for many *New York Times* stories. She did more than take pictures; she was always at the ready with insights, and I treasured her generosity. Cary's death in 2008 was a loss for photojournalism. Photographers and artists lent a hand, sometimes gratis. Zac Ormsby, a student at the University of San Diego, took the photos of Jane Dumas and the Kumeyaay flag raising, and his youthful enthusiasm fired my spirit. Amy Conover prepared digital versions of photos for publication. John Romano prepared the final photo package and took my picture for the book jacket. Jennifer Pierce (Ioway) helped me sort out endnotes and text when Microsoft Word tangled them during chapter mergers.

In the notes I have cited the many academics who enriched my understanding. I single out Margaret Connell-Szasz, professor of history at the University of New Mexico. After reading an early draft of a portion of this book, she encouraged me to move ahead with the project and continued throughout the process offering knowledge and a ready ear. Others—scholars and nonacademics—who read substantial portions of the book and provided useful insights and encouragement were Joyce Szabo and Sam Deloria (both at the University of New Mexico), Mary Beth Acuff, Zonnie Gorman, Theresa Johnson, James Luna, Anne Manning, Ellen Tufts, Laure Brost Halliday, and Barbara "Alex" Szerlip. Rose Marie Cleese gave me a copy of Norman Feder's book that she had found at a flea market. Members of San Diego Independent Scholars and the Institute for Historical Study (based in Berkeley, California)—affiliates of the National Coalition of Independent Scholars—read drafts of chapters. Steve Lawrence read early chapters and published versions of sections of the book adapted for *Crosswinds Weekly*, his fine New Mexico newspaper, which unfortunately closed in 2005. Scott Lewis, the associate editor of VoiceofSanDiego.org, one of the nation's first nonprofit web news operations, also published portions adapted for the site.

Matthew Bokovoy at the University of Nebraska Press is a no-nonsense yet generous and patient editor, prized qualities for a first-time book writer. Before he became my editor, I had already read and cited his fine book on San Diego's world's fairs.

Two agents helped bring this book to market. Irene Moore, formerly of Frederick Hill Associates, read and reread drafts, encouraging me to continue, but she left the book business during her service to me. Katherine Boyle of Veritas Literary Agency read the manuscript and helped me prepare a saleable package, steered me through the contract process, and was always at the other end of my phone calls.

Libraries are the great repositories of our cultures. I relied especially on the Albuquerque, San Diego, San Jose, and San Francisco Public Libraries, the Suffern Free Library, and those at the Universities of New Mexico, California, Berkeley, and San Diego and at Stanford University. Similarly, information specialists at museums, tribal governments, and national parks and other institutions were invariably generous. Heidi Wigler at the San Diego Public Library and Kathleen Ash-Milby at the Heye Center in New York were especially helpful. Patricia Capone at Harvard's Peabody Museum took much time with me and was patient with my numerous basic questions.

A general thank-you goes to editors and reporters at the *New York Times*. Over many years, editors, especially those on the national desk, were receptive, reporters were collegial to a mere stringer, and copy editors were usually careful wordsmiths.

NOTES

Preface

1. See chapter 2, note 4.
2. See chapter 7, note 42.
3. Nadia Myre, quoted in *Hide: Skin as Material and Metaphor* (Washington DC: Smithsonian Institution Press, 2010), 110, the catalog for an exhibit of the same name at the George Gustav Heye Center, National Museum of the American Indian, New York, November 4, 2009–July 7, 2011 (viewed by the author on May 5, 2010).
4. Vizenor discusses this concept in many of his works. See his essay "Aesthetics of Survivance," in *Survivance*, ed. Gerald Vizenor (Lincoln: University of Nebraska Press, 2008), 31–34. Also in the same collection, see Karl Kroeber, "Why It's a Good Thing Gerald Vizenor Is Not an Indian," 25–38.
5. Simon Ortiz, untitled talk, University of New Mexico, Albuquerque, July 2003 (author's notes).
6. Between 1980 and 2000 the population of American Indians, Eskimos, and Aleuts nearly tripled, growing from 1.4 million to 4.1 million. The most populous groups are Cherokee, Navajo, Choctaw, Sioux, Chippewa, Apache, Blackfeet, Iroquois, and Pueblo (note that Pueblo, Navajo, and Iroquois, e.g., include separate groups within

the general designation). All population figures are from the U.S. Census, unless otherwise noted, and all the figures I use include those who identify themselves as Indians alone or in combination with other ethnic groups (about 60 percent of the total are Indians alone). Between 1990 and 2000 the rate of increase in this population was 110 percent. A change in how the census defined "race" accounts for some of this increase. Individuals who identified themselves as "American Indian" plus "Black," "White," or "Asian" were all counted in the "American Indian in combination" category. U.S. Census Bureau, *The American Indian and Alaska Native Population: 2000, Census 2000 Brief*, issued February 2002, accessed September 25, 2006, http://www.census.gov/prod/2002pubs/c2kbr01-15.pdf.

7. "Their casinos make billions, yet they pay no taxes and virtually nothing to the state. Other states require revenue from Indian gaming, but not us. It's time for them to pay their fair share. All the other major candidates take their money and pander to them. I don't play that game." Script of a thirty-second campaign commercial by Californians for Schwarzenegger, his gubernatorial campaign committee, in September 2003. For a copy of the text, see http://www.bluecorncomics.com/stype39j, accessed August 25, 2006.

8. The appropriation of Indian identity can have disastrous consequences. In 2009 three people died while experiencing a sweat lodge in a New Age spa in Arizona. John Dogherty, "Deaths at Sweat Lodge Bring Soul-Searching," *New York Times*, October 11, 2009, http://www.nytimes.com. One of the best antidotes to Indian wannabes is Philip Deloria, *Playing Indian* (New Haven CT: Yale University Press, 1998). From Campfire Girls to New Age communes, white Americans try to become Indian. Ironically, as they appropriate Indianness, Americans may grow closer to Indians, but they also dilute Indian identity. See also Philip Jenkins, *Dream Catcher* (New York: Oxford University Press, 2004).

9. Alonzo Coby, Fort Hall Business Council District, Shoshone-Bannock Tribes (Idaho), radio interview, *Native America Calling*, February 16, 2008; Catherine C. Robbins, "Selling the White Man His Vice," December 9, 2005, accessed October 16, 2006, http://www.voiceofsandiego.org.

Introduction

1. The population of North America before contact is one of the most hotly debated subjects among historians and demographers. For an excellent review of this debate, see Charles C. Mann, "1491," *Atlantic Monthly*, March 2002, 41. Estimates range from 1.8 million to 18 million and as high as 25 million. By 1900 the U.S. Census found just 237,196 American Indians in its count. Whatever the number, disease and conflict destroyed as much as 70 percent of the Native population in North America after the Europeans arrived. Nancy Shoemaker, *American Indian Population Recovery in the Twentieth Century* (Albuquerque: University of New Mexico Press, 1999), 2, 4. Among recent works that have reviewed the presence and numbers of people in pre-European times are Charles C. Mann, *1491* (New York: Alfred A. Knopf, 2005); Brian M. Fagan, *Ancient North America* (New York: Thames and Hudson, 1991); and Jake Page, *In the Hands of the Great Spirit* (New York: Free Press, 2003). By way of comparison, the population of what we call "Europe" today was about 56 million in the seventeenth century. Eugen Weber, *A Modern History of Europe* (New York: W. W. Norton, 1971), 187–88. A similar debate continues concerning the date of the appearance of people on the North American continent. Nicholas Wade and John Noble Wilford, "New World Ancestors Lose 12,000 Years," *New York Times*, July 25, 2003, http://www.nytimes.com.
2. The NAGPRA legislation is available at http://www.cr.nps.gov/nagpra.
3. David Hurst Thomas, *Skull Wars: Kennewick Man, Archaeology, and the Battle for Native American Identity* (New York: Basic Books, 2000), 225.
4. For information on Cabrillo and his voyage, I relied on a collection of essays in Cabrillo National Monument Foundation, *An Account of the Voyage of Juan Rodriguez Cabrillo* (San Diego: Cabrillo National Monument Foundation, 1999). See also "Native American Watercraft—Chumash and Tongva Plank Canoes," Minerals Management Service, Department of the Interior, accessed November 4, 2006, http://www.mms.gov/omm/pacific/kids/Cabrillo.
5. For Soto, see Herbert E. Bolton, *The Spanish Borderlands* (Albuquerque: University of New Mexico Press, 1996), 70–73; for Cabrillo, see

Cabrillo National Monument Foundation, *An Account*, 78; for Coronado, see Herbert E. Bolton, *Coronado: Knight of Pueblos and Plains* (Albuquerque: University of New Mexico Press, 1949), 405.

6. For a detailed description of the three-day 1892 Cabrillo Festival, see William E. Smythe, *History of San Diego, 1542–1908*, pt. 5, chap. 1, San Diego Historical Society online edition, http://sandiegohistory .org/books. More recently, see Gregg R. Hennessey, "Creating a Monument, Re-creating History: Junípero Serra Museum and Presidio Park," *Journal of San Diego History* 45, no. 3 (1999). See also Dennis G. Sharp, "Reconstructed Adobe: The Spanish Past in the Architectural Records of the San Diego Historical Society, 1907–1929," *Journal of San Diego History* 49, nos. 3–4 (2003): 113–33. Both are available online at http://www.sandiegohistory .org/journal. See also Susan Collins Lehmann, *An Embarrassment of Riches: The Administrative History of Cabrillo National Monument* (Cabrillo Historical Association, 1987), online edition, http://www .nps.gov/history/history/online_books/cabr2. Chapter 8 covers the modern period. David Glassberg has written about historical pageants in *American Historical Pageantry: The Uses of Tradition in the Early Twentieth Century* (Chapel Hill: University of North Carolina Press, 1990), 4. Pageants—historical reenactments, parades, and other events—were a form of popular entertainment that satisfied the urge for boosterism and patriotic moralizing. They also often looked forward in an optimistic view of the future. On a poster for the Indiana Centennial Celebration of 1916, an Indian knelt on a knoll and peered far into the distance to a silhouette of the capital and smokestacks. The image suggested that Indiana, as the "Gateway to the Glorious West," could bring that underdeveloped region (represented by the Indian) into modernity (144).

7. Material for this section came from Jane Dumas, Jamul elder, conversation and comments at the Cabrillo Festival ceremony, September 29, 2006, and an interview with the author, November 13, 2006, and the following interviews with the author: Terry DiMattio, superintendent, Cabrillo National Monument, November 20, 2006; Louis Guassac, Mesa Grande band of the Kumeyaay Nation, executive director, Kumeyaay-Diegueño Unity, November 28, 2006.

8. Roy Cook, "A History of Manuel Hatam and the Kumeyaay People in the San Diego Area," *American Indian Source*, 2001, accessed Novem-

ber 29, 2006, http://www.americanindiansource.com.

9. White willow bark contains salicin, which was used to develop aspirin in the nineteenth century. For more information about its uses since the fourth century BCE, see http://www.umm.edu/altmed/articles/willow-bark, December 4, 2007.

10. The flags of all the nations fly at Cabrillo only during the annual festival. Many federally recognized Native American groups have flags. Donald T. Healy completed an exhaustive survey of tribes with flags and collected his research and illustrations in *Flags of the Native People of the United States, Raven*, the journal of the North American Vexillological Association, vols. 3–4 (1996–97).

11. "Hell, Indians never need to wear a watch because your skeletons will always remind you about the time. See, it is always now. That's what Indian time is. The past, the future, all of it is wrapped up in the now. That's how it is. *We are trapped in the now.*" Sherman Alexie, *The Lone Ranger and Tonto Fistfight in Heaven* (New York: HarperCollins, 1994), 22. Recent studies suggest that the brain registers time according to memory of events. See Benedict Carey, "Where Did the Time Go? Do Not Ask the Brain," *New York Times*, January 4, 2010, http://www.nytimes.com.

1. The Unconquerables

1. Alfred Vincent Kidder, *An Introduction to the Study of Southwestern Archaeology* (1924; New Haven CT: Yale University Press, 2000), 94.

2. In reporting the actual Pecos repatriation, the author conducted interviews with Jemez and Pecos leaders, including Paul Tosa, Randy Padilla, Raymond Gapuchin, and William Whatley, Jemez's tribal archaeologist and preservation officer, and N. Scott Momaday during the week of May 17–20, 1999. Additional interviews took place during the repatriation procession on May 22, 1999.

3. In addition, 4,303 sacred objects, 948 objects of cultural patrimony, and 822 objects that are both sacred and patrimonial. These are items that institutions have listed in notices in the *Federal Register* announcing that the items are eligible for repatriation. The government does not require museums to report actual repatriations; see http://www.nps.gov/history/nagpra/FAQ/INDEX, accessed May 18, 2010.

4. I strolled along Jemez's paths along with the walkers while on assignment for the *New York Times*. In what seemed to me extraordinary coverage, the *Times* devoted two stories to the Pecos repatriation. The Boston bureau chief covered the departure of the remains from the Peabody and wrote a general story. Three days later, the *Times* ran my story about events at Jemez and Pecos. The *Times* stories are as follows: Carey Goldberg, "Harvard Is Returning Bones, and a Pueblo Awaits Its Past," May 20, 1999, and Catherine C. Robbins, "Pueblo Indians Receive Remains of Ancestors," May 23, 1999, both on http://www.nytimes.com.

5. Nevertheless, a story on the repatriation with photos of the burial site appeared in the November 2000 issue of *National Geographic*: Cliff Tarpy, "Pueblo Ancestors Return Home," *National Geographic*, November 2000, 118–25.

6. Patricia Capone, associate curator and repatriation coordinator, Peabody Museum, Harvard University, interview with the author, August 27, 2002; Landis Chase cited in Douglas W. Schwartz, introductory essay to Kidder, *An Introduction*, 54.

7. The Department of the Interior gives grants to groups for the actual repatriation but not for the application process; see http://www.nps.gov/history/nagpra/FAQ, accessed May 18, 2010.

8. The officials were Senators Jeff Bingaman (D), Pete Domenici (R), and Governor Gary Johnson (R).

9. The term *midden* means "trash heap" or "dump," but middens are far from trash; rather, they hold tribal memories. For archaeologists, they are the mother lode of cultural information.

10. Touching or even speaking of dead bodies is taboo in several Native cultures.

11. Organized human habitation in the area dates from 12,000 BCE, based on artifacts from Clovis, New Mexico, 160 miles southeast of Pecos. Among the sources for this section are John Kessell's exhaustive *Kiva, Cross and Crown* (Washington DC: U.S. Department of the Interior, National Park Service, 1979; Southwest Parks and Monuments Association, 2nd ed., 1995, originally published by the University of New Mexico Press, 1987, also available online at http://www.nps.gov/history/history/online_books, accessed September 5, 2007); Kidder, *An Introduction*, 61–139; David Grant Noble, *Ancient Ruins of the Southwest* (Flagstaff: Northland Press, 1981), 135–38;

and Robert H. Lister and Florence C. Lister, *Those Who Came Before* (1983; Tucson: Southwest Parks and Monuments Association, 1993), 184–93. Information also came from the Pecos National Historical Park Visitors' Center and visits by the author to Pecos.

12. Captives, taken during wars, were not slaves like those in Rome or in the Americas; they were not even indentured servants. Rather, when they were sold to a pueblo, they were expected to take their place as members of the tribe. So although they had responsibilities, they also had "citizenship." Judy Reed, cultural resources manager, Pecos National Historical Park, interview with the author, August 16, 2002.

13. Chaco Canyon's population estimates refuse to stand still. Stephen H. Lekson estimates the population at between two thousand and five thousand ("Ancient Chaco's New History," *Archaeology Southwest* [Center for Desert Archaeology] 14, no. 1 [2000]: 1–12, 3).

14. Pueblo of Jemez, http://www.jemezpueblo.org/history, accessed August 25, 2006. David Wilcox has been assembling maps of precontact Jemez in his research on populations and settlements of ancient peoples in New Mexico and Arizona from 1200 to 1599. I viewed early versions of maps at the Pecos Conference, Pecos, New Mexico, August 10, 2002, Pecos National Historical Park; also David Wilcox, phone interview with the author, July 16, 2007. At the time, Wilcox was the senior curator of anthropology at the Museum of Northern Arizona and the head of the Department of Anthropology at Northern Arizona University. His work has since been published in David A. Gregory and David R. Wilcox, eds., *Zuni Origins: Toward a New Synthesis of Southwest Archaeology* (Tucson: University of Arizona Press, 2007); David R. Wilcox, David A. Gregory, J. Brett Hill, and Gary Funkhouser, "The Changing Contexts of Warfare in the North American Southwest, AD 1200–1700," in *Southwestern Interludes: Papers in Honor of Charlotte J. and Theodore Frisbie*, ed. Regge N. Wiseman, Thomas C. O'Laughlin, and Cordelia T. Snow, Archaeological Society of New Mexico, no. 32 (Albuquerque: University of New Mexico Press, 2006), 203–5.

15. G. P. Winship, *The Coronado Expedition, 1540–42* (1896), quoted in Kidder, *An Introduction*, 67. The Spaniards called the Native villages "pueblos," the Spanish word for "towns" and "people."

16. Elinore Barrett, *Conquest and Catastrophe* (Albuquerque: University

of New Mexico Press, 2002), 53–80. In part 2 of her book, Barrett says that a Spanish map of 1602 indicates that up to eighty-one pueblos were present in the Rio Grande Valley in 1598. By the time of the Pueblo Revolt in 1680, that number had been reduced to thirty-one, and Pueblo occupancy disappeared from entire areas, including parts of the Albuquerque-Belen Basin. She listed several contributors to this decline, including the tribute that the Spanish Crown extracted from the Indians; tribute labor, which forced the people to work for little or nothing; the reduced ability of the Pueblos to feed themselves after Spanish settlers appropriated their lands; Spanish interference with the brisk regional trade that had supplemented agriculture and brought other goods into the area; raids by the Pueblos' enemies, the Apaches, who considered the Pueblos "collaborators" in the Spanish subjugation of their lands; drought and subsequent famine that struck periodically; and, finally, epidemics. All these factors combined to cause the abandonment of pueblos, especially during the late 1630s and early 1640s. See D. Hull, "Castano de Sosa's Expedition to New Mexico in 1590," *Old Santa Fe Magazine*, 1916, quoted in Kidder, *An Introduction*, 80.

17. Spain claimed the Indian lands as northern New Spain in all of what is today Arizona, New Mexico, much of Colorado, and the western states to the Canadian border. This claim was maintained until Mexican independence in 1821. The United States gained control of these lands in 1848, after the Mexican-American War. For a concise collection of readings about the Pueblo Revolt, see David J. Weber, ed., *What Caused the Pueblo Revolt of 1680?* (Boston: Bedford/St. Martin's, 1999).

18. Robert H. Lister and Florence C. Lister, *Those Who Came Before* (Tucson: Southwest Parks and Monuments Association, 1993), 186–87.

19. Act of June 19, 1936, 49 Stat. 1528, in Joe Sando, *Pueblo Nations: Eight Centuries of Pueblo Indian History* (Santa Fe: Clear Light, 1998), 40.

20. Jemez's ancestral pueblo constitutes a major archaeological resource and is under federal jurisdiction, outside contemporary Jemez lands.

21. Pueblo runners have inspired many authors, including D. H. Lawrence, Frank Waters, and N. Scott Momaday. See Peter Nabokov, *Indian Running* (Santa Fe: Ancient City Press, 1981), 43–46.

22. Associated Press, "BIA Says Casinos Must Be within 25 Miles of Res-

ervation HQs," July 18, 2008, http://www.abqjournal.com. This is still a live issue across Indian Country.

23. Whatley quoted in Goldberg, "Harvard Is Returning Bones."

24. The exact numbers in the Peabody's inventory were as follows: 10,059 Native American human remains, 15,700 associated funerary objects, and 5,010 other funerary objects. Of these, 3,136 individual human remains and 9,354 funerary objects were subject to physical repatriation under NAGPRA's regulations. As of August 2002 the Peabody had repatriated 2,113 individual remains, 184 funerary objects, 55 objects of cultural patrimony, and 18 objects that are both sacred and objects of cultural patrimony. Unpublished data prepared for the author by the Peabody Museum of Archaeology and Ethnology, Harvard University, in August 2002. See also the Capone interview.

25. Rubie Watson, director, Peabody Museum, Harvard University, interview with the author, August 27, 2002. Two examples of the research are Christopher Ruff, *Aging and Osteoporosis in Native Americans from Pecos Pueblo, New Mexico* (New York: Garland Publishing, 1991), originally a doctoral dissertation for the University of Pennsylvania, 1981. See also Katherine A. Spielmann, Margaret J. Schoeninger, and Katherine Moore, "Plains-Pueblo Interdependence and Human Diet at Pecos Pueblo, New Mexico," *American Antiquity* 55, no. 4 (1990): 745–65.

26. "These immigrants . . . had endured every kind of persecution until one day they could stand no more and their spirit broke. . . . They were struck down by so deadly a disease that when the epidemic abated, there were fewer than twenty survivors in all. . . . The Bahkyush had brought with them little more than the clothes on their backs, but even in this moment of deep hurt and humiliation they thought of themselves as a people." N. Scott Momaday, *The House Made of Dawn* (New York: Harper & Row, 1968), 15–16.

27. Ben K. Rhodd, "Reburial in South Dakota: Two Perspectives," in *Preservation on the Reservation*, ed. Anthony L. Klesert and Alan S. Downer, Navajo Nation Papers in Anthropology, no. 26 (Window Rock AZ, 1990), 370. This volume is a compendium of papers presented at a two-day conference on cultural resource management on Indian lands, April 7–8, 1988, Heard Museum, Phoenix. Participants included Native and non-Native professionals from around the country.

28. Alden T. Vaughan, "Sir Walter Ralegh's [*sic*] Indian Interpreters, 1584–1618," *William and Mary Quarterly* 52, no. 9, (2002), http://www.historycooperative.org. In "Trustees of Georgia," the Dutch artist William Verelst painted a record of Indians from Georgia tribes in Native dress meeting a large delegation of British officials at Westminster—in *their* Native dress of powdered wigs—in 1734. The two haughty groups stare each other down. The painting is in the Winterthur Museum, Delaware, and can be viewed at http://www.uwf.edu/english/Panther-Yates/indians.htm, accessed July 20, 2007. See also Anthony F. C. Wallace, *Jefferson and the Indians* (Cambridge MA: Harvard University Press, 1999), 104; and Brian M. Fagan, *Ancient North America* (New York: Thames & Hudson, 2005), 30–33. Schoolcraft was a noted ethnologist who helped shaped the new Smithsonian Institution. See Curtis M. Hinsley Jr., *Savages and Scientists* (Washington DC: Smithsonian Institution Press, 1981), 20.

29. Also on the expedition were Frederick Hodge, Cushing's personal assistant; Cushing's wife, Emily, who kept track of his daily notes; and Margaret Magill, the project's artist. The basic guide to the project is available online from the Cornell University Library. It includes a brief description of the project, its personnel, and a listing of the papers in the library: http://rmc.library.cornell.edu/EAD/htmldocs/RMM09186.html#s1. Among the sponsoring organizations were the National Geographic Society; Peabody Museums at Harvard, Andover, and Yale; the American Museum of Natural History; the Bureau of American Ethnography, later merged with the Smithsonian Institution; and the Universities of Utah, Colorado, New Mexico, Arizona, and Pennsylvania. The Eakins painting of Cushing is in the collection of the Gilcrease Museum, Tulsa, Oklahoma. For more about Cushing, see http://www.pbs.org/weta/thewest/people, accessed August 30, 2006.

30. Sources for this historical section include an excellent commentary, *The Antiquities Act of 1906*, by Ronald F. Lee (National Park Service), 2001 electronic ed., accessed August 30, 2006, http://www.cr.nps.gov/aad/PUBS/LEE/Index. Originally published by the National Park Service in 1970, Lee's work came back into print thanks to Raymond Harris Thompson and the *Journal of the Southwest* 42, no. 2 (2000). See also Don D. Fowler, *A Laboratory for Anthropology: Science and Romanticism in the American Southwest, 1846–1930* (Albuquer-

que: University of New Mexico Press, 2000); and *American Anthropologist* 104, no. 2 (2002), a special centennial edition that covers the field through the twentieth century.

31. Erika Marie Bsumek, *Indian-Made: Navajo Culture in the Marketplace, 1868–1940* (Lawrence: University Press of Kansas, 2008), 2.

32. Joseph Weixelman, "Hidden Heritage: The Myth of the 'Vanishing Anasazi,'" Pecos Conference, Pecos, New Mexico, August 10, 2002; interview with the author, May 6, 2003. Mr. Weixelman was a doctoral student in history at the University of New Mexico. I wish to thank him for generously sharing his research findings while writing his doctoral dissertation, "Hidden Heritage: Pueblos, National Parks and Vanishing Anasazi."

33. Casa Grande in Arizona was named as the first formal federal archaeological reservation in 1889, and critical lands in Chaco Canyon came under federal oversight in 1905 (http://www.nps.gov/cagr/historyculture). For the significant role women have played in southwestern anthropology, archaeology, and linguistics, see the collection of articles in Nancy J. Parezo, ed., *Hidden Scholars* (Albuquerque: University of New Mexico Press, 1993). Hans Randolph quoted in Ronald Lee, http://www.cr.nps.gov/aad/PUBS/LEE/LEE_CH4.HTM, accessed January 6, 2010. For a full history of the establishment of Mesa Verde National Park, including Jesse Fewkes's work there, see Duane A. Smith, *Mesa Verde National Park: Shadows of the Centuries* (Boulder: University Press of Colorado, 2002), accessed May 20, 2010, http://www.nps.gov/history/history/online_books/smith.

34. Fagan, *Ancient North America*, 32.

35. Nancy J. Parezo, "The Formation of Ethnographic Collections: The Smithsonian Institution in the American Southwest," *Advances in Archaeological Method and Theory* 10 (1987): 1–47, 11.

36. For a highly readable story about Franz Boas and the development of American anthropology, see Claudia Roth Pierpont, "The Measure of America," *New Yorker*, March 8, 2004, 48, http://www.newyorker.com/archive.

37. Today, the School of American Research is known as the School for Advanced Research.

38. Ward H. Goodenough, "Anthropology in the 20th Century and Beyond," *American Anthropologist*, June 2002, 423–35, 423.

39. Both Stephen Jay Gould and David Hurst Thomas have narrated the

pursuit of crania in detail, Gould in the second chapter of *The Mis-measure of Man* (New York: W. W. Norton, 1981) and Thomas in the fourth chapter of *Skull Wars*.

40. Alfred V. Kidder, "Reminiscences in Southwest Archaeology," *Kiva* 25, no. 4 (1960): 1–32, 12. For the section on Alfred V. Kidder and the history of the Pecos Conference, I am grateful for the work of Richard B. Woodbury, who chronicled the conference's history in *60 Years of Southwestern Archaeology: A History of the Pecos Conference* (Albuquerque: University of New Mexico Press, 1993); Richard B. Woodbury, *Alfred V. Kidder* (New York: Columbia University Press, 1973); Douglas R. Givens, *Alfred Vincent Kidder and the Development of Americanist Archaeology* (Albuquerque: University of New Mexico Press, 1992); and Schwartz, introductory essay for Kidder, *An Introduction*, 1–55.

41. The word "Anasazi" comes from a Navajo term meaning ancient "alien" or "enemy." The Indian Pueblo Cultural Center in Albuquerque has eliminated "Anasazi" and other terms from the signs and the interpretive script used by guides.

42. For the insight into archaeologists' drinking habits, I am indebted to Nancy Parezo, professor of anthropology at the University of Arizona. Among the travel articles on the Pecos Conference are Grace Lichtenstein, "Archaeology Jamboree," *New York Times*, July 29, 2005, http://travel.nytimes.com; and Téresa Mendez, "Indiana Jones (for a Weekend)," *Christian Science Monitor*, August 25, 2006, http://www.csmonitor.com.

43. John Hancock, an architecture professor at the University of Cincinnati, makes the same point about the earthworks built by the Hopewell, Adena, and Fort Ancient cultures of Ohio as early as 600 BC up to AD 400. Hancock's three-dimensional digital reconstructions of the earthworks were placed in a permanent exhibit at the Cincinnati Museum Center on June 21, 2003. See Anne Eisenberg, "Ancient Architecture in Ohio Has a 3-D Rebirth," *New York Times*, May 1, 2003, http://tech2.nytimes.com/mem/technology.

44. Joseph Weixelman, interview with the author, May 6, 2003.

45. Two works are useful to tracking changes in the anthropology profession. The first is David J. Meltzer, Don D. Fowler, and Jeremy A. Sabloff, *American Archaeology Past and Future* (Washington DC: Smithsonian Institution Press for the Society of American Archaeol-

ogy, 1986). The second is the entire special centennial issue of *American Anthropologist*, June 2002: see David L. Browman, "The Peabody Museum, Frederic W. Putnam and the Rise of U.S. Anthropology, 1866–1903," 514; James P. Boggs, "Anthropological Knowledge and Native American Cultural Practice in the Liberal Polity," 601; and Goodenough, "Anthropology," 435. Jared Diamond's books are *Guns, Germs and Steel: the Fates of Human Societies* (New York: W. W. Norton, 1997) and *Collapse: How Societies Choose to Fail or Succeed* (New York: Viking, 2005).

46. Tim Flannery, "Who Came First?" *New York Review of Books*, June 12, 2003, 52, http://www.nybooks.com/articles; John Noble Wilford, "Mapping Ancient Civilization, in a Matter of Days," *New York Times*, May 11, 2010, http://www.nytimes.com; Julian Smith, "Extremely Remote Sensing," *American Archaeology* 14, no. 1 (2010): 32–37.

47. Joshua Epstein, a researcher at the Brookings Institution, created an ancient Puebloan cybersociety with George Gumerman and Jeffrey Dean, both archaeologists at the University of Arizona. Jonathan Rauch has described the project in an article, "Seeing around Corners," *Atlantic Monthly*, April 2002, 35 ff.

48. Linda Cordell (University of Colorado), paper presented at the Pecos Conference, Pecos, New Mexico, August 8, 2002; David Philips Jr. and William H. Doelle, "From Salvage to CRM and Beyond: A History of Compliance-Driven Archaeology in the Southwest," paper presented at the Pecos Conference, Pecos, New Mexico, August 9, 2002. The first private company, Archaeological Research Service, was founded in 1974.

49. Anthropologists and curators Linda Cordell, Bruce Huckell (University of New Mexico), and George Gumerman (Arizona State University) discussed this issue at the Pecos Conference, Flagstaff, Arizona, August 11, 2001. See Catherine C. Robbins, "No Room for Riches of the Indian Past," *New York Times*, November 24, 2001, http://www.nytimes.com. (By May 2010 Linda Cordell was associated with the School for Advanced Research.)

50. Lekson, "Ancient Chaco's New History," 2–3. The Chaco Synthesis Project was between 2000 and 2006. Its goals included summarizing the work of the Chaco Center between 1971 and 1982. The project held seven conferences that consolidated archaeological information. Western National Parks Association has produced a brief his-

tory of the national park: http://www.wnpa.org/freepubs/CHCU/ Chaco_History.pdf.

51. See Parezo, *Hidden Scholars*. Parezo titles her opening essay for the book "Anthropology: The Welcoming Science," based on a passage from Margaret Mead (3).

52. Browman, "The Peabody Museum," 508–19.

53. COSWA, the Committee on the Status of Women in Anthropology, is online at http://www.aaanet.org/committees/coswa; the Association for Feminist Anthropology is at http://www.aaanet.org/sections/afa/index.html, accessed May 24, 2010.

54. Evan T. Pritchard, *Native New Yorkers: The Legacy of the Algonquin People of New York* (San Francisco: Council Oak Books, 2002), 122–24. Verrazano's letter to King Francis I of France in 1524 is in appendix 3 (394–404).

55. John Fetto, "Wide Open Spaces: Rural America Awaits a Surge of Retirees," *American Demographics*, October 1999, http://findarticles .com/p/articles/mi_m4021/is_ISSN_0163-4089/ai_57483861.

56. The Four Corners states—Arizona, Colorado, New Mexico, and Utah—where many of the ancient Puebloan sites are found registered an average increase in population of 30 percent in the 2000 census. Three Colorado counties southwest of Denver experienced an average population increase of 133 percent.

57. Catherine C. Robbins, "Monumental Chaos," *High Country News*, October 25, 1999, http://www.hcn.org. See also Catherine C. Robbins, "Archaeologists and Indians against Bulldozers," *New York Times*, February 11, 1986, A14 (not online). Between 1980 and 1990, half of all permits for new housing were on the city's west side.

58. Tour of the Mann site with archaeologists Kurt Anschuetz and Matthew Schmader, May 3, 2003. Also Jim Walker, Archaeological Conservancy, report on the year's activities, Pecos Conference, Pecos, New Mexico, August 10, 2002. Established in 1980, the Archaeological Conservancy is based in Albuquerque. For information about the organization, see http://www.americanarchaeology.com/about, accessed May 25, 2010.

59. Vine Deloria Jr., *Custer Died for Your Sins* (New York: Avon Books, 1969), 83. In the years after Deloria's chapter, anthropologists debated his assessment. For a sampling of this debate, a collection of essays with an afterword by Deloria, see Thomas Biolsi and Larry J.

Zimmerman, *Indians and Anthropologists* (Tucson: University of Arizona Press, 1997).

60. Lekson, "Ancient Chaco's New History," 15. A number of commentaries marked NAGPRA's twentieth anniversary in 2010. One of the more interesting compared Canada's and the United States' handling of this issue. Michelle A. Hamilton, "Native American Repatriation at 20," History News Network, January 3, 2011, accessed January 3, 2011, http://www.hnn.us/articles/134757.html.

61. The best of the professionals had done this in their work. Frederic Putnam had worked with American Indian students at Harvard (see Browman, "The Peabody Museum").

62. This section is based on several sources: Kurt Anschuetz, lectures, January 24, 2002, Maxwell Museum of Anthropology, University of New Mexico, and May 3, 2003, Petroglyph National Monument; "The Past Is Not a Pickle," paper presented for the American Anthropological Association symposium "A Committed Archaeology: Integrating Science, Our Topics, and Public Participation," San Francisco, November 16, 2000; Louie Hena and Kurt F. Anschuetz, "Living on the Edge: Combining Traditional Pueblo Knowledge, Permaculture and Archaeology," *CRM Online* (National Park Service) 23, no. 9 (2000). Also, historian Peter Nabokov says that for Native Americans, former times "usually constitute familiar, contiguous and ever-present terrain, whose deceased occupants may even put in their two cents' worth" (*A Forest of Time: American Indian Ways of History* [Cambridge: Cambridge University Press, 2002], 232–40).

63. Merry Harrison, talk, Pecos Conference, Flagstaff, Arizona, August 10, 2001; "The Patterson Bundle: An Herbalist's Discoveries in a 500-Year-Old Native American Bundle," *Herbal Gram: The Journal of the American Botanical Council*, no. 55 (2002): 34–41; Bennie LeBeau, talk, Pecos Conference, Flagstaff, Arizona, August 10, 2001; Bennie LeBeau, interview with the author, October 9, 2002; Micah Lomaomvaya, talk, Pecos Conference, August 10, 2001.

64. The volcano is part of Sunset Crater Volcano National Monument, fourteen miles northeast of Flagstaff.

65. Mark Elson, talk, Pecos Conference, Flagstaff, Arizona, August 10, 2001; Mark Elson, telephone interview with the author, August 2001.

66. The Colville Cultural Resources Protection Act was adopted in 1980; the Navajo Nation Cultural Resources Protection Act was adopted in

the 1980s. For the Colville document, see http://codeamend
.colvilletribes.com (follow the links to Title 4, Cultural Protection),
accessed January 6, 2010. The Navajo Tribal Council amended its
code in 2005 and is available at http://www.navajocourts.org/
Resolutions/CAP-18-05.pdf, accessed November 5, 2009.

67. Anthony L. Klesert and Barry Holt, *Preservation on the Reserva-
tion*, Navajo Nation Papers in Anthropology, no. 26 (Navajo Nation
Archaeology Department and Navajo Nation Historic Preservation
Department), 247–67.

68. *National Directory of Tribal Archives, Libraries and Museums*, March
2005, American Indians Programs Office, Arizona State Museum,
University of Arizona, Tucson. This directory is available online at
http://www.statemuseum.arizona.edu/aip/leadershipgrant/
irectory, accessed September 27, 2007.

69. Enter Jemez's virtual museum at http://www.niti.org/
virtualmuseum.

70. Robert Begay, tribal archaeologist and director of the Department of
Archaeology, Navajo Nation, telephone interview with the author,
July 23, 2007.

71. Heye began collecting while working as an engineer in Arizona,
living in a rough campsite, far from his accustomed New York af-
fluence. One evening, he saw an Indian woman chewing on her
husband's deerskin shirt to kill the lice on it. Heye bought the shirt
on the spot and became "a great vacuum cleaner of a collector" (Lawrence Small, "A Passionate Collector," *Smithsonian*, November 2000).
In 1916 Heye established the Museum of the American Indian (MAI)
in upper Manhattan to house the "artifacts." Although the new NMAI
absorbed his collection and moved it to Washington DC, it maintains
a presence with the Heye Center, which opened in 1994. The Heye
Center is in the Alexander Hamilton Old Customs House, a splendid
Beaux-Arts structure in lower Manhattan at the foot of Broadway.

72. The construction team included Table Mountain Rancheria's
Rancheria Enterprises, http://news.nationalgeographic.com/
news/2004/09/0914_040913_indian_museum_information
.html, accessed May 25, 2010. For an article on the museum's Native
design, see http://news.nationalgeographic.com/news/2004/
09/0914_040913_american_indian_museum_2.html, accessed May
25, 2010.

73. Formed in 1989, Black Eagle received the Grammy for Best Native American Music Album in 2004.
74. See Dennis Banks's comments at http://www.aimovement.org/ moipr, November 11, 2004, accessed November 9, 2006.
75. Most of the description and quotes in this section are based on notes taken by the author, who was present at the opening day of NMAI, September 21, 2004. See also Hank Stuever, *Washington Post*, September 22, 2004, http://www.washingtonpost.com.

2. *Thoughts from the Chief*

1. U.S. Census Bureau, *Statistical Abstract of the United States, 2004–2005* (Washington DC: U.S. Department of Commerce, 2005), 35. The Cherokees number 730,000; the Navajos 298,000. Reservation populations are 104,000 and 175,000, respectively. See http://www .census.gov/statab/www/sa04aian.pdf, tables 35 and 36, accessed May 25, 2010. The Navajo Reservation covers about 16 million acres in Arizona, New Mexico, and Utah. The Cherokees do not live on a reservation but on trust lands that amount to about 124,000 acres in Oklahoma. See Veronica E. Velarde Tiller, *Tiller's Guide to Indian Country* (Albuquerque: BowArrow Publishing Company, 1996), 214, 502.
2. The Southwest Chief's average annual ridership between 2007 and 2009 was about 322,000 passengers. See *Trains Magazine*, November 20, 2009, http://www.trains.com.
3. Catherine C. Robbins, "For Train Passengers, a Seminar on Indians," *New York Times*, March 2, 1988. The section on the train ride is from the author's notes.
4. In addition to interviewing Zonnie during the ride on the Southwest Chief, I also interviewed her in Gallup on February 20, 2001, and May 3, 2006. We have also stayed in touch. By 2010 she had moved to Albuquerque and enrolled in the doctoral program in history at the University of New Mexico's main campus, where she planned to write a biography of her father. She had spent two decades raising three children, caring for aging parents, teaching, and lecturing. Zonnie was continuing her work with the Circle of Light.
5. The original hogan was five-sided, and the "modern" hogan is eight-sided.
6. The San Juan Basin is a thirty-eight-thousand-square-mile area in

the Four Corners region, most of it in northwestern New Mexico.
See San Juan Basin Regional Uranium Study, U.S. Department of the
Interior, *Uranium Development in the San Juan Basin*, I-22.

7. Office of Navajo Government Development, *Navajo Nation Government*, 4th ed. (1998), 6. This is a publication of the Navajo Nation.

8. Taylor had led three thousand soldiers into the Southwest in 1846
as the Mexican-American War began. The year before, James K. Polk
had swept into the presidency by promising a major westward expansion of the United States into Indian Country on lands that had
already been promised for Natives. When the war ended in 1848,
New Mexico was part of the vast area that the United States claimed.
When the Americans renamed Tsoodzi, they took ownership of it
not only physically but also culturally. The mountain is also sacred
to surrounding Pueblo people. In 2009 the National Trust for Historic Preservation named Mount Taylor, which is part of the Cibola
National Forest, as its eleventh most endangered historic place. The
state's designation requires a review of any development that could
be harmful to the mountain. See http://blogs.nationaltrust.org, accessed June 26, 2010.

9. For discussions of the uses of Diné and Navajo names, see Peter
Iverson, *Diné: A History of the Navajos* (Albuquerque: University of
New Mexico Press, 2002), 4–16; and Clyde Kluckhohn and Dorothea
Leighton's classic, *The Navaho* (1946; New York: Anchor/Doubleday, 1962), 116, 207–8. The Iroquois Confederacy's Indian name is
Haudenosaunee, "people of the long house." For the names of the
original five nations in the confederacy, go to the league's website:
http://www.haudenosauneeconfederacy.ca/index, accessed November 9, 2009. Seminole and Caddo are examples of tribes with the
Turtle Island myth. A useful reference for New Mexico place-names
is T. M. Pearce, *New Mexico Place Names: A Geographical Dictionary*
(Albuquerque: University of New Mexico Press, 1965).

10. The Arizona legislature created the Board on Geographic and Historic Names in 1982 to determine place-names in the state. But long
before that the state's policy was to retain the historic names of geographical features in order to protect the integrity of Arizona's historical records. In 1990 the legislature gave the board the additional
responsibility for appropriate names for geographic features. Arizona's board follows the policies and principles of the U.S. Board on

Geographic Names, which will not consider a commemorative proposal unless a person has been deceased for five years. For information on the board's mandate and the official record on the Piestewa Peak proposal, see the board's 2003 annual report at http://www.lib.az.us/about/pdf/annual2003b.pdf. Newspaper articles provide a taste of the controversy.

11. The code used about 450 Navajo words for objects that did not exist in Navajo culture, such as "iron fist" for "submarine." Although Navajo has no word for "enemy," the code talkers substituted "Utes," a tribe that was the Navajos' historic rival.

12. "Alcatraz was the catalyst for this new activism as it became more organized and more 'pan-Indian.' Many of the approximately seventy-four occupations of federal facilities and private lands that followed Alcatraz were either planned by or included people who had been involved in the occupation of the island" (Troy Johnson, "The American Indian Occupation of Alcatraz Island, 1969–1971," http://www.csulb.edu/~gcampus/libarts/am-indian/alcatraz, accessed September 13, 2006). This is a collection of photos with an introduction.

13. Lewis Meriam, technical director, "The Problem of Indian Administration" (widely known as the Meriam Report), Institute for Government Research for the Department of the Interior, February 21, 1928. This report is available online at http://www.alaskool.org/native_ed/research_reports/IndianAdmin/Indian_Admin_Problms.html, accessed October 3, 2007. One view of the Meriam Report suggests that it represented a shift in policy from assimilation of Indians into the mainstream to greater accommodation of those who want to maintain a traditional way of life. See Malia Villegas, review of K. Tsianina Lomawaima and Teresa L. McCarty, *To Remain an Indian: Lessons in Democracy from a Century of Native American Education* (New York: Teachers College Press, 2006), in *Harvard Educational Review*, Fall 2007, http://www.hepg.org/her/booknote/324; Tom Giago, "Whether Sexual Abuse Happened or Not Is a Matter of Opinion" (Notes from Indian Country), *Lakota Journal*, June 27–July 4, 2003, online edition, http://www.lakotajournal.com/notes. In April 2003 a group of former Indian students of Catholic boarding schools in South Dakota filed a twenty-five-billion-dollar class-action suit against the federal government. See Sharon Waxman, "Abuse Charg-

es Hit Reservation," *Washington Post*, June 2, 2003, http://www
.washingtonpost.com.

14. Iverson, *Diné*, 119; Zonnie Gorman, interview with the author, February 20, 2001.

15. For a review of some new scholarship on boarding schools, see Julie Davis, "American Indian Boarding School Experiences: Recent Studies from Native Perspectives," *Magazine of History* (Organization of American Historians) 15, no. 2 (2001): 20–22 (August 17, 2007); David Wallace Adams, "Beyond Bleakness," in *Boarding School Blues* (Lincoln: University of Nebraska Press, 2006), 35–96; Natasha Kaye Johnson, "Navajo Band Marches On," *Gallup Independent*, September 2, 2006, http://www.gallupindependent.com.

16. The Dawes Act of 1887, which determined the allotment of tribal land among individuals, used blood quantum to determine identity. Indians who could prove their racial identity (by "blood") received 160 acres and were placed on an allotment list. The lists constituted the basic tribal rolls, and tribes used the rolls to define membership. Today, tribal enrollment is one of the most controversial issues in Indian Country. Some Indians refuse to participate in the process defined by the Dawes Act because it is a white invention, and only Indians should define Indian "citizenship." Also, enrolling is difficult because it requires extensive genealogical research. Anxious to hold on to their identities and cohesion, some tribes demand that individuals prove at least 50 percent "pure" Indian blood in order to be included on the membership roll. The tribal membership census determines federal funding for a collection of programs and allocations, including health care and education (see also chap. 5).

17. Seth Mydans, "New Frontier for Gangs: Indian Reservations," *New York Times*, March 18, 1995, http://www.nytimes.com. For reviews of gang problems across Indian Country, see these two articles in *High Country News*: Stephanie Paige Ogburn, "Tribes Tackle Taggers," August 21, 2006, and Arla Shephard, "A Culture of Violence," August 12, 2009, http://www.hcn.org.

18. Felicity Barringer, "Navajos and Environmentalists Split on Power Plant," *New York Times*, July 27, 2007, http://www.nytimes.com. For a report on the divisions within the Navajo Nation between tribal officials and Navajo environmentalists, see Jonathan Thompson, "In-

dians vs. Greens?" *High Country News*, October 26, 2009, 3, http://www.hcn.org.

19. *Gallup Visitor's Guide*, 2006.

20. David Oliver Relin, "Won't You Help Feed Them?" *Parade*, April 4, 2004, http://www.parade.com.

21. The foundation was established in 1968 and provides aid to Navajo and Pueblo people in the Southwest in areas including housing, education, emergency supplies, domestic violence, and others. Among its sources of funding are cultural tours to nearby reservations and a hefty catalog of Indian goods. See http://www.southwestindian.com, accessed September 13, 2006.

22. For Navajos in other areas of the reservation, Flagstaff, Arizona, and Shiprock and Farmington, New Mexico, are also destinations.

23. City of Gallup, Economic Development Center, http://www.gallupnm.org/business/major_employers.cfm, accessed September 1, 2006.

24. Throughout several legislative sessions, lobbyists opposed measures to close drive-up windows at liquor stores. A comprehensive liquor law reform in 1993 closed the windows, but as late as 2006 activists were trying to ban Sunday liquor sales. In 2003 Harvard's Project on American Indian Economic Development presented an award to Na'Nizhoozhi Center, Inc., for its programs for Indian alcoholics. The text of the award provides a brief if incomplete history of those efforts: see http://www.ksg.harvard.edu/hpaied, accessed September 13, 2006. See also Leslie Linthicum, "Four Corners Towns Tackle Alcoholism," *Albuquerque Journal*, January 9, 2003, http://www.abqjournal.com; Associated Press, "Gallup's Alcoholism Proposal Defeated," *Albuquerque Journal*, January 15, 2004, http://www.abqjournal.com.

25. Iverson reports a 27 percent decline in the number of trading posts on the reservation as well as the fact that some have been taken over by Navajos. In addition, by the early 1970s, hearings by the Federal Trade Commission and various exposés about credit abuses led to reforms in the practices of trading posts (Iverson, *Diné*, 259–60). For an extensive history of the relationship between traders and Indians, see Erika Marie Bsumek, *Indian-Made: Navajo Culture in the Marketplace, 1868–1940* (Lawrence: University Press of Kansas, 2008), chap. 2.

26. Joseph J. Kolb, "Growing Meth Use on Navajo Land Brings Call for Tribal Action," *New York Times*, February 5, 2005, http://www.nytimes.com; Centers for Disease Control, "Executive Summary: Atlas of Injury Mortality among American Indian and Alaska Native Children and Youth, 1989–1998," http://www.cdc.gov/ncipc/pub-res/atlas-summary/suicide, accessed September 14, 2006.

27. Ninth annual Western Indian Gaming Conference, Palm Springs; "Tribal Leaders Share Views on Sovereignty," Indianz.com, January 20, 2004, accessed October 30, 2006, http://indianz.com/News/archive/001187.asp.

28. Joseph P. Kalt and Jonathan B. Taylor, *American Indians on Reservations: A Databook of Socioeconomic Change between the 1990 and 2000 Censuses*, Harvard Project on Indian Economic Development, John F. Kennedy School of Government, Harvard University, January 2005. The report is available at http://www.ksg.harvard.edu/hpaied/pubs/pub_151.htm, accessed October 30, 2006.

29. Kalt and Taylor, *American Indians*, overview, http://www.ksg.harvard.edu/hpaied/overview.htm, accessed October 30, 2006.

30. See the Indian Self-Determination and Education Act, Public Law 93-638, at http://www.oiep.bia.edu, accessed October 16, 2006.

31. AMTRAK's Indian guides program continues. The Gallup station is a restored landmark containing a small museum of Native American art, railroad and local history, a café, and the waiting room for trains and buses.

32. Steve Chawkins, "DNA Ties Together Scattered Peoples," *Los Angeles Times*, September 11, 2006, http://www.latimes.com.

33. Leo Dyson Dirr, "Navajos Urged to Keep Closer Ties with Home Reservation," *Salt Lake Tribune*, March 15, 2003, http://www.sltrib.com.

34. Zonnie Gorman, e-mail message to author, August 31, 2006.

3. An Encampment

1. Quoted in Theodore Jojola, *Urban Indians in Albuquerque, New Mexico: A Study, Community and Regional Planning Program*, University of New Mexico and the City of Albuquerque, 1999, 47. Dr. Jojola, a member of Isleta Pueblo, is a professor in the Community and Regional Planning Program in the School of Architecture at the University of New Mexico.

2. Patricia Crown and W. Jeffrey Hurst, "Evidence of Cacao Use in the Prehispanic American Southwest," *Proceedings of the National Academy of Sciences*, early ed., February 2, 2009, http://www.pnas.org. Chaco also had other trade items, including macaw feathers and cloisonné. See Ramon A. Gutierrez and Richard J. Orsi, *Contested Eden: California before the Gold Rush* (Berkeley: University of California Press, 1998), 60; Daniel H. Usner, *Indians, Settlers and Slaves in a Frontier Exchange Economy: The Lower Mississippi Valley before 1783* (Chapel Hill: University of North Carolina Press, 1992), 21–22.

3. Because of the Termination and Relocation Program and simply because they were looking for a better life, by 1960 40 percent of Native Americans lived in cities (see chap. 5).

4. Certainly, one of the most important scholars of this subject is historian Donald Fixico of Arizona State University and a Shawnee, Sac and Fox, Muscogee Creek, and Seminole from Oklahoma. See Donald Lee Fixico, *The Urban Indian Experience in America* (Albuquerque: University of New Mexico Press, 2000). An older work is instructive as a comparison: Jack O. Waddell and O. Michael Watson, eds., *The American Indian in Urban Society* (Boston: Little, Brown, 1971). See also Catherine Robbins, "Urban Indians: New Life, New Culture, Old Struggles," *Crosswinds Weekly*, August 8–15, 2002 (not online; ceased publication in 2005).

5. New York has 87,000 and Los Angeles 53,000. These figures include those who describe themselves solely as Indian or as Alaska Native or in combination with another ethnic group. Other populations as percentages of the total urban area: Anchorage (10 percent), Tulsa (7.7 percent), Oklahoma City (5.7 percent), and Albuquerque (4.9 percent), http://www.census.gov/prod/2002pubs/c2kbro1-15.pdf, accessed August 13, 2007. In the Bay Area, a much larger metropolitan area than Albuquerque, with a total population of 6.9 million, one estimate puts the Indian population as high as 85,000 rather than the official count of 39,000. Helen Waukazoo, executive director, Friendship House, interview with the author, November 14, 2002.

6. Jojola said that urban Indians are identifiable by "their own sense of place, whether you're talking about their commuting back and forth or staying here. It's solidly infused in their mind that what they do here is temporary" (interview with the author, July 15, 2002).

In 2005 physicist Heinrich Jaeger described a fluid-like state of matter that "seems to exist in this combination of gas—air in this case—and a dense arrangement of particles" (University of Chicago news release, December 5, 2005, http://www-news.uchicago.edu/releases).

7. Leslie Linthicum, "Navajo Community Grateful for a Spigot," *Albuquerque Journal*, November 12, 2002, http://www.abqjournal.com.

8. Jonathan Eig, "A Principal Battles Legacy of Failure at Indian School," *Wall Street Journal*, December 26, 2002, http://www.wsj.com.

9. The rate of victimization among American Indians and Alaska Natives is more than twice the national average, with the highest rates for those between the ages of twelve and twenty-four. More than half the Indian victims described their offenders as non-Indian. One glimmer of hope in these dismal numbers was the 45 percent decline in the murder rate among Indians during the last decade of the twentieth century. See U.S. Department of Justice, Steven W. Perry, "American Indians and Crime," December 2004 (NCJ 203097), http://www.ojp.usdoj.gov/bjs/abstract/aic02.

10. Olivier Uyttebrouck, "Navajo Town Reels over Teen Suicides," *Albuquerque Journal*, May 23, 2010, http://www.abqjournal.com. Indians feel that mainstream Americans view violence—murder, suicide, physical abuse, rape—as part of the wallpaper of Native life. After the Red Lake massacre in 2005, during which reservation teenagers opened fire in their school, killing seven people, Indians asked why the event received less coverage than a similar event at Columbine High School in Colorado in 1999 when thirteen died. Was it because Red Lake was just a bunch of Indians? But Indian Country is not passive in the face of violence. Several organizations have operated shelters and promoted prevention and intervention services for women in the Oglala Nation. "Violence against Oglala Women Is Not Lakota Tradition" is a message that screams off the cover page of a handbook produced by Cangleska, Inc. See South Dakota Coalition against Domestic Violence and Sexual Assault, accessed August 25, 2006, http://www.southdakotacoalition.org/history; Marlin Mousseau and Karen Artichoker, "Violence against Oglala Women Is Not Lakota Tradition," 2.

11. In Nebraska the Winnebagos have used resources from their rela-

tively small casino to establish Ho-Chunk, Inc., the umbrella for several tribal enterprises. Nonetheless, the unemployment rate among
the twenty-six hundred reservation Winnebagos was 20 percent in
the early 2000s, higher than that in the general population, although
during the 2007–10 recession, some mainstream groups and regions
experienced rates equal to or higher than that among the Winnebagos in 2004. See http://www.winnebagotribe.com, October 4, 2004.
See also Bradford McKee, "A New Indian Town Rises from the Dust,"
New York Times, September 30, 2004, http://www.nytimes.com.

12. U.S. Department of Commerce, Economics and Statistics Administration, U.S. Census Bureau, *The American Indian and Alaska Native
Population: 2000*, 8, accessed November 12, 2009, http://www
.census.gov/prod/2002pubs/c2kbr01-15.pdf. See also Jojola, *Urban
Indians in Albuquerque*, 5–25.

13. The school population reflects this dominance. About 47 percent of
Indian school-age children are Navajo; the rest come from more than
one hundred other tribes. See Albuquerque Public Schools, *Native
American Education Crisis*, prepared by the Albuquerque Metro Native American Coalition, April 17, 2002.

14. "Five Year Consolidated Plan and Workforce House Plan,"
City of Albuquerque, Department of Family and Community
Services, January 2, 2008–December 30, 2012, accessed
January 15, 2011, http://www.cabq.gov/family/pdf/
Consolidated-Workforce-Housing-Plan-2008-2012-final.pdf, 30–31.

15. On nearby reservations, median income ranges from $7,600 to
$19,700. See Jojola, *Urban Indians in Albuquerque*, 16. Other groups
whose household income was under 50 percent of the median family
income: 32 percent of Hispanic households, 32 percent of African
American households, and 27 percent of Asian households. See City
of Albuquerque, "Consolidated Plan for Housing" (updated, September 18, 1997).

16. Jojola, *Urban Indians in Albuquerque*, 16.

17. During 2002 I conducted the following interviews: Norman Sitting
Up (July 1); Nancy Martine-Alonzo (July 3); Keith Franklin (May
28); Norm Ration (June 30); Theodore Jojola (July 15); then director
of the center David Cade (July 2). During 2002 I attended several
meetings of the Albuquerque Metro Indian Coalition. In 2009 I interviewed Daisy Thompson (May 27); in 2010 I interviewed Marisa

Ramos, program director, and counselors Gordon Yawakia and Harold Gray (March 5).

18. For a chart and map showing the distribution of the American Indian population in Albuquerque, see Jojola, *Urban Indians in Albuquerque*, 12–13. The 2000 census showed that 17.4 percent of American Indian households headed by couples were made up of unmarried couples, compared with 9.1 percent overall; 16.9 percent of African American households headed by couples were unmarried, and the group identified as being of two or more races had 13.7 percent unmarried. See Christopher Marquis, "Total of Unmarried Couples Surged in 2000 U.S. Census," *New York Times*, March 13, 2003, http://www.nytimes.com.

19. Aaron Huey, *Pine Ridge Reservation*, TedxDU, May 13, 2010. In this moving video, Huey talks about the history and dire conditions at Pine Ridge and shows his disturbing though outstanding photographs. See http://www.du.edu/tedxdu/video/huey.html, accessed July 12, 2010. See also Aaron Huey and Matthew Power, "Ghosts of Wounded Knee," *Harper's*, December 2009, 63–73.

20. Jim Ludwick, "City Boards up Vacant Property," *Albuquerque Journal*, September 27, 2003, http://www.abqjournal.com. The nickname persists. In 2009 a *New York Times* story referred to the "War Zone, a neighborhood of housing projects, heroin and sex shops near the University of New Mexico" (capitalization is in the story). The report was about nearly a dozen female murder victims found in graves on the city's outskirts, some of whom had been prostitutes operating on East Central. See Dan Frosch, "Bodies Found but Mystery Lingers for Kin of Missing Women," *New York Times*, March 23, 2009, http://www.nytimes.com.

21. Sandia's budget is about $2 billion, and it employs eight thousand scientists, engineers, and support personnel. Sandia National Laboratories does operate the Dreamcatcher science program for Native American students in grades 6–12. The program is free of charge and includes courses in engineering, health sciences, and economics. See http://dreamcatchers.sandia.gov, accessed March 24, 2009.

22. Fixico, *Urban Indian Experience*, 129–39. With funding from federal as well as private sources, the centers have helped Indians adjust to cities. In addition, they have also driven Pan-Indianism, the unified effort of tribes for political ends.

23. Return of Organization Exempt from Income (Form 990), 2007, accessed March 30, 2010, http://www.guidestar.org.

24. The acronym LGBTQI stands for Lesbian, Gay, Bisexual, Transgender, Questioning, and Intersexual.

25. In Albuquerque several programs address Indian alcoholism, including the IHS and CASAA, the Center on Alcoholism, Substance Abuse, and Addictions, at the University of New Mexico. Fixico states that city life is so overwhelming that urban Indians experience a kind of schizophrenia (*Urban Indian Experience*, 178–79). Boredom is not a pathology only of Sitting Up's reservation. It underlies the alcohol abuse that occurs across large swaths of the United States that are isolated and rural, according to a story by Timothy Egan in the *New York Times*. Egan reported on a survey by the Substance Abuse and Mental Health Services Administration (SAMHSA) in 2006 that showed a high incidence of binge drinking concentrated in North Dakota, South Dakota, Montana, and Wyoming. While the report did not ascribe this phenomenon to boredom, Egan interviewed local officials who made the connection. See Timothy Egan, "Boredom in the West Fuels Binge Drinking," *New York Times*, September 2, 2006, http://www.nytimes.com; *National Survey on Drug Use and Health*, Substance Abuse and Mental Health Services Administration, Office of Applied Studies, issue 25, 2006, http://www.oas.samhsa.gov/2k6/subStateAlc.

26. The grant is from the Substance Abuse and Mental Health Services Administration of the U.S. Department of Health and Human Services, accessed November 16, 2009, http://rcsp.samhsa.gov/about/grantees.

27. Don Coyhis, president, White Bison, interview with the author, July 5, 2002. Also see http://www.whitebison.org, accessed September 25, 2006.

28. White Buffalo Woman told them she would return as a white buffalo calf. Lakota Chief Avrol Looking Horse of Rosebud, South Dakota, is keeper of the White Buffalo Calf Pipe. He has told the story of the White Buffalo Calf Woman on many occasions, including a conference on the Great Plains at the University of Nebraska. See Tom Hancock, "Bison as Plains Symbol and Sacrament," *Columns* (University of Nebraska–Lincoln), Spring–Summer 2000, 5, http://ascweb.unl.edu/alumni/columns. A version told by Joseph Chasing Horse

may be found at http://www.kstrom.net, accessed September 27, 2006. In 1994, when a white buffalo calf was born on the Wisconsin farm of a white family, she was immediately named Miracle, and the Sioux became her spiritual guardians. Miracle has her own website: http://www.homestead.com/WhiteBuffaloMiracle, accessed September 27, 2006.

29. The sacred hoop and its healing power cut across the traditions of many tribes. It is also sometimes known as the "medicine wheel."

30. Jim Banke, "Endeavour and Shuttle Crews Ready to Part Ways," December 1, 2002, http://www.space.com/missionlaunches.

31. Education generally has been at the top of the list of concerns for Indian parents, tribal officials, and activists. Margaret Connell-Szasz's work on education and self-determination is particularly relevant. The issues she covers—bilingualism, psychological trauma, poverty, parental involvement, designing curriculum, and the classroom environment for Indian children—seem intractable. See Margaret Connell-Szasz, *Education and the American Indian: The Road to Self-Determination since 1928* (1974; Albuquerque: University of New Mexico Press, 1999).

32. Andrea Schoellkopf, "Indians Lag in APS Testing," *Albuquerque Journal*, January 15, 2003, http://www.abqjournal.com.

33. New Mexico's Indians speak five major and distinct languages, each with several dialects. Given that more than one hundred tribes are represented in Albuquerque's public schools, the starting point for language problems is a major issue for students and the system. See John Mondragon, "What New Mexico Can Do for Its Struggling Indian Students," *Albuquerque Tribune*, December 18, 2002 (not online). The federal money for Indian children comes from Title IX of the Equal Opportunity in Education Act (1972) and the Johnson O'Malley Act (1934). That sum goes beyond the $8,000 the district spends per student generally. See U.S. Census Bureau, *Public Education Finances, 2007* (Governments Division, U.S. Census Bureau, 2009), Table 17: Per Pupil Amounts for Current Spending of Public Elementary-Secondary School Systems with Enrollments of 10,000 or More: 2006–07, p. 51. The district also receives about $1.2 million for other ethnicities for language acquisition. See http://www2.census.gov/govs/school/07f33pub.pdf, accessed October 16, 2009; Jennifer Lucero-Montoya, analyst, Albuquerque Public Schools, tele-

phone interview with the author, October 16, 2009.

34. Sitting Up had noted that sports, which drove him and his friends as teenagers, have lost their allure. In his marvelous book, Philip Deloria devotes an entire chapter to the culture of sports among Indians: "'I Am of the Body': My Grandfather, Culture and Sports," in *Indians in Unexpected Places* (Lawrence: University Press of Kansas, 2004), 109–35.

35. James E. Officer, "The American Indian and Federal Policy," in Waddell and Watson, *American Indian in Urban Society*, 9–65, 50.

36. Indian Health Service, "Facts on Indian Health Disparities," 2006, http://info.ihs.gov/files/disparitiesfacts-Jan2006. Although the 2000 census showed that 60 percent of American Indians live in urban areas, compared with about 38 percent in 1990, IHS urban health programs received just 1.1 percent of the total IHS budget authority and 1.3 percent of the amount spent on health services. These funding levels mean that IHS can serve about 16 percent of eligible urban Indians. See *A Quiet Crisis: Federal Funding and Unmet Needs in Indian Country* (Washington DC: U.S. Commission on Civil Rights, 2003), 46–47, accessed at http://www.usccr.gov/pubs/na0703/na0204.

37. The Albuquerque IHS unit serves the nineteen Pueblos of New Mexico, the Jicarilla and Mescalero Apaches, and the Alamo, Canoncito, and Ramah Chapters of the Navajo Nation. Also, in southern Colorado are the Southern Utes and the Ute Mountain Ute Reservation (extending into a small portion of southern Utah). In Texas the Ysleta del Sur Reservation is served. Additionally, numerous tribal members from throughout the United States who live, work, or go to school in the urban centers of the Albuquerque area are provided services in health facilities operated by the Indian Health Service. See http://www.ihs.gov/FacilitiesServices/AreaOffices/AreaOffices_index.asp, accessed March 8, 2005.

38. Leslie Linthicum, "Feds Ax Indian Clinic Bid for $5 Million," *Albuquerque Journal*, January 29, 2005, http://www.abqjournal.com; Cheri Lyon, chief executive officer, Indian Health Service Hospital (Albuquerque Service Unit, Albuquerque Indian Hospital), telephone interview with the author, July 14, 2002. The withdrawal of "shares" is also occurring nationally.

39. The Navajo Nation is divided into chapters or districts similar to

counties. The chapters are located in chapter houses, and each chapter has representation on the Navajo Nation's tribal council. George Hardeen, press officer, Office of the President and the Vice-President of the Navajo Nation, telephone interview with the author, September 26, 2006.

40. Jojola, *Urban Indians in Albuquerque*, n. 1.

41. Jojola, *Urban Indians in Albuquerque*, 47–57. These pages contain a number of responses to questions about quality of life and community values.

42. *American Indian Quarterly* 27, nos. 3–4 (2003). The entire issue is devoted to urban Indian women.

43. Robert Hamilton, "Tribe Invests Downtown in an Old Industrial City," *New York Times*, January 10, 2003, http://www.nytimes.com.

44. In the 2000s then governor George E. Pataki was encouraging the development of casinos across New York State and began to enter into agreements with tribes in Oklahoma and Wisconsin that had been pushed out of the state centuries before. His efforts did not always pay off. See Iver Peterson, "Midwest Tribes See Big Payoffs in the East," *New York Times*, March 24, 2003, http://www.nytimes .com; Kirk Semple, "2 More Tribes Drop Claims in Exchange for Casinos," *New York Times*, December 8, 2004, http://www.nytimes .com; Anahad O'Connor, "Interior Secretary Rejects Catskill Casinos Plans," *New York Times*, January 5, 2008, http://www.nytimes.com; Gail Courey Toenseng, "St. Regis Mohawks to Appeal Denied Land into Trust Application," *Indian Country Today*, January 14, 2008, http://www.indiancountry.com.

45. Grand Opening, Friendship House, San Francisco, April 22, 2005, author's notes.

46. Yet the number of Indians in the Bay Area remains minuscule—barely 93,000 among millions. California's Indian population exceeds 350,000, according to the 2000 census, http://quickfacts .census.gov/qfd/states/06000.html, accessed October 19, 2006.

47. Helen Waukazoo, interview with the author, November 14, 2002.

48. An excellent brief history of the Cherokee removal with related documents is Theda Perdue and Michael D. Green, *The Cherokee Removal* (New York: Bedford/St. Martin's, 1995).

49. Interview with the author, March 6, 2010.

4. The Way We Should

1. Peggy V. Beck, Anna Lee Walters, and Nia Francisco, *The Sacred: Ways of Knowledge, Sources of Life* (Tsaile AZ: Diné Community College Press, 1996), 272.

2. Catherine C. Robbins, "A Zoo in Peril Stirs a Debate about Navajo Tradition," *New York Times*, March 28, 1999, http://www.nytimes .com; author's notes. About 290,000 individuals are registered members of the Navajo Nation; more than 100,000 live away from the reservation.

3. Philip Deloria asserts that Indians achieved modernity because they enter the flow of history, not because of acculturation (*Indians in Unexpected Places* [Lawrence: University Press of Kansas, 2004], 231).

4. Beck, Walters, and Francisco, *The Sacred*, 103–6.

5. Navajo Nation Executive Branch, "State of the Nation Address and First Quarterly Report," presented to the Navajo Nation Council, winter session, January 1999, Kelsey A. Begaye, president, with accompanying statistical reports from the Office of Management and Budget, the Navajo Nation (author's collection); Trib Choudhary, interview with the author, February 25, 1999.

6. The Navajo Nation is not the only phone-poor reservation. About 68 percent of American Indian households have telephone service, compared with 83 percent of all households. See Federal Communications Commission, "Telephone Subscribership on American Indian Reservation and Off-Reservation Trust Lands, 2003," May 2003, tables 1, 3, http://www.fcc.gov/Bureaus/Common_Carrier/Reports/ FCC-State_Link/IAD/subsai03.pdf.

7. Leslie Linthicum, "Closing the Computer Gap," *Albuquerque Journal*, March 25, 2001, http://www.abqjournal.com.

8. Hardeen interview. Hewlett Packard helped finance the Tribal Digital Village linking southern California tribes.

9. See http://www.navajonationparks.org/zoo.htm, accessed September 27, 2006.

10. Nelson Luna, director/biologist, Zuni Fish and Wildlife Department, telephone interview with the author, October 19, 2009; Laurel Jones, "Birds for a Feather," *High Country News*, June 18, 2001, http://www.hcn.org/issues/205/10591; Harvard Project of American Indian Economic Development, "Honoring Nations: 2002," Zuni

Eagle Sanctuary, accessed October 5, 2007, http://www.ksg.harvard
.edu/hpaied/hn/hn_2002_eagle. Armstrong + Cohen Architecture,
Claude Armstrong and Donna Cohen designed the enclosure. The
design won the 2003/2004 President of the Jury Special Prize of the
Dedalo Minosse, an international prize for commissioning a building. See http://www.dedalominosse.org, accessed April 14, 2009.
For a story on the aviary's architecture, see http://www.dcp.ufl.edu/
arch, accessed April 1, 2009.

11. The death rate from alcoholism is 510 percent higher among Indians than other Americans; tuberculosis, 600 percent; diabetes, 189
percent; motor vehicle crashes, 229 percent; suicide, 62 percent; and
homicide, 61 percent. Finally, 12 percent of Indian homes lack a safe
and adequate water supply and waste facilities, compared to 1 percent for the general population. The infant mortality rate for American Indians and Alaska Natives is 8.5 (per one thousand live births)
versus 6.8 for the United States (all races). See Health Disparities
Trends, Indian Health Service, Facts on Indian Health Disparities,
January 2006, http://info.ihs.gov/Files/DisparitiesFacts-Jan2006.
pdf. American Indian mortality rates are at levels comparable to
those in Ukraine, Costa Rica, and Kuwait, which rank 158, 159,
and 160 among 225 countries surveyed, with the highest rate at 1,
Angola. The United States ranks 180, with a higher rate than Guam
(181) and Cuba (182). See http://www.cia.gov/library/publications/
the-world-factbook/rankorder/2091rank, updated April 9, 2009.

12. Information in this section is from *A Quiet Crisis: Federal Funding and
Unmet Needs in Indian Country* (Washington DC: U.S. Commission on
Civil Rights, 2003), accessed October 2, 2006, http://www.usccr
.gov/pubs/na0703/na0731.pdf#search.

13. For a brief history of the Indian Health Service, see Charles W. Grim,
"Reflections on the 50-Year History of the IHS," *IHS Primary Care Provider* 33, no. 12 (2008): 392, http://www.ihs.gov/provider/
documents/2000_2009/prov1208.pdf.

14. Grim, "Reflections," 49. Obama also exempted the IHS
from a government-wide "freeze" on funding. See National
Indian Health Board, summary sheet, February 2, 2010,
http://http://www.nihb.org/docs/02032010/
FY%2011%20Budget%20Summary%20Snapshot.pdf.

15. On average, per capita federal spending for Indian patients is about

$1,900 per person, compared with $5,000 for the general population. The U.S. government spends nearly $6,000 for each Medicare recipient and $3,803 for federal prisoners (*Quiet Crisis*, 44).

16. *Quiet Crisis*, 40.

17. Norman Ration, executive director, National Indian Youth Council, testimony before the U.S. Civil Rights Commission, Albuquerque, New Mexico, October 17, 2003, author's notes.

18. Matt Kelly, "In Critical Condition," Associated Press through the *Albuquerque Tribune*, March 21, 2002.

19. Lyle Jack, Sioux Nation councilman, testimony before the U.S. Civil Rights Commission, Albuquerque, New Mexico, October 17, 2003, author's notes.

20. Anne M. Marbella, Mickey C, Harris, Sabina Diehr, Gerald Ignace, and Georgianna Ignace, "Use of Native American Healers among Native American Patients in an Urban Native American Health Center," *Archives of Family Medicine* 7 (1998): 182, http://archfami.ama-assn.org/cgi/content/abstract.

21. *Quiet Crisis*, 40.

22. This section is based on Tieraona Low Dog's talk at the Twelfth International Congress of Traditional & Indigenous Medicine, August 17–22, 1998, at the University of New Mexico; interview with the author during those three days; and additional research. The conference was a joint effort between UNM and the Mexican Academy of Traditional Medicine (AMMTAC). It brings modern health care providers together with practitioners and researchers of indigenous traditional medicines to collaborate, report on the latest research, and examine what works, where, and why. See Catherine C. Robbins, "In Southwest, Doctor Meets Medicine Man," *New York Times*, September 14, 1998, http://www.nytimes.com; author's notes. Low Dog has been a keynote speaker on the same bill as Andrew Weil and other noteworthy health care professionals, for instance, the Sixth Annual Alternative Therapies Symposium & Exhibition, March 14–17, 2002, San Diego. In 2009 she was the director of the Fellowship at the Arizona Center for Integrative Medicine, headed by Andrew Weil.

23. Low Dog and a colleague attached a dissenting letter to the commission's final report, however. They stated that many of its recommendations would help maximize proven benefits of alternative methods, but it had not adequately addressed their limitations. They

wrote that they wanted "to give voice to the healthy skepticism" among Americans about alternative healing, despite their belief in its value. To see this letter, go to the website of the White House Commission on Complementary and Alternative Medicine Policy: http://www.whccamp.hhs.gov, accessed September 29, 2006.

24. Indians are not the only ones to take liberties with the symbol of medicine. While the American Medical Association, the Royal Army Medical Corps, and the Royal Canadian Medical Corps use the ancient symbol of the staff of Asclepius entwined with a single serpent, the U.S. Army adopted the caduceus, or the magic wand of Hermes or Mercury, a club with two entwined serpents topped by a set of wings.

25. Baines elaborated on his talk in Santa Fe with an e-mail to the author, March 26, 2010.

26. This section is based on the author's notes taken at the thirty-second annual meeting, Association of American Indian Physicians (AAIP), July 31–August 5, 2003, Santa Fe, and e-mail communication with Dr. Baines. A hero in the medical community, Baines has received the Henry J. Kaiser Family Foundation Merit Award. He also holds appointments to committees and boards at the Centers for Disease Control and Prevention, the Institute of Medicine, and the National Academy of Sciences. The Kaiser award is administered by the National Medical Fellowships, which presented it to Baines in 1982, his final year of medical school. National Medical Fellowships is the only private, nonprofit organization dedicated to improving the health of underserved communities by increasing the representation of minority physicians, educators, researchers, and policymakers in the United States; training minority medical students to address the special needs of their communities; and educating the public and policymakers to the public health problems and needs of underserved populations. See http://www.nmfonline.org, accessed October 2, 2006.

27. *AHS [Arizona Health Sciences] News* 16, no. 6 (2000), University of Arizona Health Sciences Center, http://www.ahsc.arizona.edu/opa/ahsnews.

28. Robbins, "In Southwest."

29. For thirty years the Pimas have allowed researchers from the National Institute of Diabetes and Digestive and Kidney Diseases (Na-

tional Institutes of Health) to study diabetes in their population. The center for the NIH study is the Hu Hu Kam clinic. For a summary of the Pima contribution to scientific study, see http://diabetes.niddk .nih.gov/dm/pubs, accessed April 13, 2009.

30. The creosote bush is ubiquitous in southwestern deserts. Growing in size from four to twelve feet, creosote produces small yellow flowers and tiny leaves, which Native people have used as emetics and antiseptics. See http://www.desertusa.com/creoste, accessed October 2, 2006.

31. For instance, in March 2006 the *American Heart Journal* published the results of a long-term study regarding the impact of prayer on patients undergoing heart surgery. The widely reported study asserted that prayer had no effect on the patient's recovery from heart surgery, although the group of patients who knew they were being prayed for was associated with a higher rate of complications. See Benedict Carey, "Long-Awaited Medical Study Questions the Power of Prayer," *New York Times*, March 31, 2006, http://www.nytimes. com; Herbert Benson, MD, et al., "Study of the Therapeutic Effects of Intercessory Prayer (STEP) in Cardiac Bypass Patients," *American Heart Journal* 151, no. 4 (2006): 934–42, http://www.ahjonline.com.

32. To my surprise, one of the thirty-something readers of this manuscript had no idea who Iron Eyes Cody was. For those of us who saw him on the "crying Indian" public service television commercials for the Keep America Beautiful campaign during the 1970s, Iron Eyes was a beloved figure. But he was not an Indian. A second-generation Italian American, Espera DeCorti nevertheless worked as a Hollywood performer and technical advisor on Indian lore and customs, owned a large collection of artifacts, acted as grand marshal for pow-wows, and served on the board of the Los Angeles Indian Center and the Southwest Museum. Iron Eyes Cody died in 1999 at the age of ninety-five. For a brief biography, see http://movies.nytimes.com/ person/13889/Iron-Eyes-Cody/biography, accessed November 1, 2009.

33. In his book *The Ecological Indian: Myth and History* (New York: W. W. Norton, 1999), anthropologist Shepard Krech III covers both the successes and the failures of the American Indian in managing resources. His work, though, has provoked controversy.

34. Evan T. Pritchard, *Native New Yorkers: The Legacy of the Algonquin*

People of New York (San Francisco: Council Oak Books, 2002), 76.

35. Jared Diamond's widely read book, *Collapse*, describes such "mistakes," including at Chaco Canyon (*Collapse: How Societies Choose to Fail or Succeed* [New York: Viking, 2005], 136–56). Thomas Alcoze, a professor in the School of Forestry at Northern Arizona University, Flagstaff, points out that the Chacoan decline coincided with the changes in the Toltec Empire of Mexico around the early thirteenth century (telephone interview with the author, August 4, 2009). Any instability would have affected the well-being of the Chacoans, who traded with peoples to the south. For a brief review of events in Mexico, including a description of the Turquoise Road, the ancient trading route between Mexico and New Mexico, see Michael D. Coe, *Mexico*, 3rd ed. (London: Thames and Hudson, 1984), 121–36; Robert J. Sharer, *The Ancient Maya*, 5th ed. (Stanford CA: Stanford University Press, 1994), 384–434.

36. The literature on the consequences of uranium mining on the Navajo Nation is extensive. Between 1996 and 1998 the University of New Mexico conducted the Navajo Uranium Miners Oral History and Photography Project, headed by Thomas Benally. For more information on this project, see http://elibrary.unm.edu/oanm, accessed October 2, 2006. Articles include Ben Daitz, MD, "Navajo Miners Battle a Deadly Legacy of Yellow Dust," *New York Times*, May 13, 2003, http://www.nytimes.com. Judy Pasternak produced an exhaustive four-part series on the Navajo mines in the *Los Angeles Times* in 2006: "A Peril that Dwelt among the Navajos," November 19; "Oases in Navajo Desert Contained 'A Witches' Brew,'" November 20; "Navajos' Desert Cleanup No More than a Mirage," November 21; "Mining Firms Again Eyeing Navajo Land," November 22; the series is available at http://www.latimes.com. For the story on the contaminated houses at Teec Nos Pos, Arizona, near the Four Corners, see Dan Frosch, "Uranium Contamination Haunts Navajo Country," *New York Times*, July 27, 2009, http://www.nytimes.com; Peter Iverson, *Diné: A History of the Navajos* (Albuquerque: University of New Mexico Press, 2002), 263.

37. Much of this section on California Indians' natural resources management is based on *Tending the Wild*, one of thirteen thirty-minute documentary programs produced by the California Indian Radio Project (CIRP) in 1998 and broadcast subsequently on public radio

stations (author's collection). For information, see http://
www.flickerfeather.org, accessed September 30, 2006. Also Rhoby
Cook, CIRP project director, interview with the author, November
2002.

38. Marion "Kat" Anderson and Thomas C. Blackburn, eds., *Before the
Wilderness*, Ballena Press Anthropological Papers, no. 40 (Banning
CA: Ballena Press, March 1993).

39. All text quotes by Frank Lobo, Katherine Saubel, and Lowell Bean
taken from *Tending the Wild*.

40. Alcoze interview.

41. John Larson quote taken from *Tending the Wild*.

42. Stephen Wolfram, *A New Kind of Science* (Champaign IL: Wolfram-
Media, 2002), from chap. 1, http://search.barnesandnoble.com/
A-New-Kind-of-Science/Stephen-Wolfram/e/9781579550080.

43. Petroglyphs at the Chaco Canyon complex include what archaeologists believe are symbols of the supernova of AD 1054 and the AD
1066 appearance of Halley's comet. See http://www.colorado.edu/
Conferences/chaco/tour/blanco, accessed October 2, 2006.

44. *The Mystery of Chaco Canyon: Unveiling the Ancient Astronomy of
Southwestern Pueblo Indians*, a film from the Solstice Project, directed
by Anna Sofaer, written by Anna Sofaer and Matt Dibble, 1999. This
film, which explicates the Solstice Project's findings, has aired on
Public Broadcasting Service stations. Other indigenous civilizations
in the Americas also used the heavens for purposes that combined
ceremony, mathematics, engineering, and/or agriculture. An example is the Machu Picchu–Llactapata complex. In a recent study,
a group of researchers has concluded that these astronomical relationships "show an extended ritual neighborhood of Machu Picchu,
containing geographical, astronomical, and cosmological meaning."
See J. McKim Malville, Hugh Thomson, and Gary Ziegler, "Machu
Picchu's Observatory: The Re-discovery of Llactapata and Its Sun-
Temple," 2004, http://www.thomson.clara.net/llactapa.html. This is
an English-language version of the original article first published in
the *Revista andina* 39 (2004).

45. Eleanor Babco, "The Status of American Indians in Science and Engineering," prepared by the Commission on Professionals in Science
and Technology for the National Academy of Engineering, 2005, 8,
http://www.cpst.org/NativeIV.pdf. Mainstream organizations like

the American Association for the Advancement of Science (AAAS) have expanded efforts to recruit Native Americans into the sciences within the framework of increasing minority participation through its Alliances for Graduate Education and the Professoriat. At the grassroots level, Native professionals founded American Indians in Science and Engineering (AISES) to offer financial and cultural support to students people from kindergarten to graduate work through its chapters across the United States.

46. Jennifer McKee, "Lab Bunkers No Longer Called 'Kivas,'" *Albuquerque Journal*, January 4, 2001, http://nl.newsbank.com/nl-search/ we/Archives.

47. *Bison* is the preferred term for the North American animal, although it is used interchangeably with *buffalo*. Both words have European origins. Still, *buffalo*, first recorded in 1635, is used more frequently than *bison*, first recorded in 1774. This book uses both terms. See http://dictionary.reference.com/search?q=buffalo, accessed October 16, 2006.

48. The army did not have an official policy of exterminating buffalo, but the military's role was ambiguous. Generals Philip H. Sheridan and William Sherman believed that killing the buffalo could weaken Indian resistance and their ability to wage war against the United States. Editors at the *Army and Navy Journal* contended that the Union had used similar tactics to deprive the Confederacy of supplies and food sources. Also, military forts sheltered professional hunters who destroyed the herds. But officers produced a "groundswell of military opposition." They complained to Henry Bergh, president of the American Society for the Prevention of Cruelty to Animals; he received a sympathetic ear from Sheridan. Also, individual officers intervened to stop the slaughter (Robert Wooster, *The Military and United States Indian Policy, 1865–1903* [New Haven CT: Yale University Press, 1988], 171).

49. In their restoration methods, the ITBC tribes generally view the bison as better than cattle for range health; cows thrive in wetland areas, not on arid plains. The tribes also don't like how the cattle industry treats its animals. Finally, the ITBC practices "nonintensive pastoralism," which means that humans rarely interfere with the bison's range habits. See Ken Zontek, *Buffalo Nation* (Lincoln: University of Nebraska Press, 2007), 91–92. Zontek surveyed thirty-five

ITBC member tribes: thirty tribes restore bison for spiritual and health reasons; the majority of tribes distribute bison products to their own communities and use bison for ceremonial purposes; most tribes receive support from tribal governments; and most are optimistic about the future of the program. Of the tribes he interviewed, twenty-seven use a "hands-off" strategy with the animals (173).

50. Fred Dubray, executive director, Inter Tribal Bison Cooperative, interview with the author, August 16, 2005. Also, Zontek reviews the history of the animal, its relationship to Native peoples and newcomers, and the efforts of various tribes to restore the animal (*Buffalo Nation*, 172–75). Matching their devotion to the buffalo, American Indians also developed strong horse cultures that lasted for about a century. NMAI's Heye Center exhibit, *A Song for the Horse Nation*, ran from November 2009 to July 2011. For a review, see Ken Johnson, "Brief, Productive Love Affair with 'Big Dog,'" *New York Times*, November 13, 2009, http://www.nytimes.com.

51. Kat Anderson quoted in *Tending the Wild*.

5. Where Hatred Was Born

1. Meeting between Indian leaders and Republican elected officials, January 14, 1998, San Felipe Pueblo, New Mexico, author's notes. I attended the meeting on assignment for Timothy Egan, *New York Times* correspondent who was developing a story on Indian sovereignty.

2. Brenda Norell, "Navajo President Forced to Resign," *High Country News*, March 2, 1998, http://www.hcn.org; Timothy Egan, "Another Leader of the Navajo Nation Resigns under a Cloud," *New York Times*, February 20, 1998, http://www.nytimes.com.

3. Lewis Kamb, "Bush's Comment on Tribal Sovereignty Creates a Buzz," *Seattle Post-Intelligencer*, August 13, 2004, http://www.seattlepi.nwsource.com.

4. The White House, "Memorandum for the Heads of Executive Departments and Their Agencies: Government-to-Government Relationship with Tribal Governments," September 23, 2004, http://www.whitehouse.gov.

5. Francis Paul Prucha, *American Indian Treaties: The History of a Political Anomaly* (Berkeley: University of California Press, 1994). A list

of the nearly four hundred ratified treaties appears in appendix B (446–502) of this standard work.

6. President Andrew Jackson signed the Indian Removal Act into law in 1830. See Theda Perdue and Michael D. Green, eds., *The Cherokee Removal: A Brief History with Documents* (Boston: St. Martin's, 1995). This slim volume is one of the best summaries of the Cherokee removal, and it includes many of the documents cited in this section. A vivid and powerful history of Indian removals between 1813 and 1855 is Gloria Jahoda, *The Trail of Tears* (New York: Random House/Wings Books, 1995).

7. Jamin B. Raskin, "Professor Richard J. Pierce's Reign of Error in the Administrative Law Review," *Administrative Law Review*, Winter 2005, http://www.indiantrust.com. This website dedicated to the Cobell suit is maintained by the Blackfeet Reservation Development Fund. See also Circe Sturm, *Blood Politics: Race Culture and Identity in the Cherokee Nation of Oklahoma* (Berkeley: University of California Press, 2002), 81. Chapters 3 and 4 tell the convoluted story of how the U.S. government used race to define peoples (52–107).

8. John Collier, memorandum, in *Hearings on H.R. 7902 before the House Committee on Indian Affairs*, 73rd Cong., 2nd sess., U.S. Department of the Interior, Washington DC, 1934, 16–18; Carl Waldman, *Atlas of the North American Indian* (New York: Facts on File, 2000), 197–202.

9. A convenient timeline of the history of California's Indians appears on the website of U.S. Senator Barbara Boxer, http://boxer.senate.gov, accessed February 8, 2006. See also Jake Page, *In the Hands of the Great Spirit* (New York: Free Press, 2003), 275. For the history of the Indians of San Diego under the authorities of Spain, Mexico, the United States, and white local governments and societies, Helen Hunt Jackson's *A Century of Dishonor* (1881; Mineola NY: Dover Publications, 2009) is still relevant. More recent sources include Delfina Cuero, *The Autobiography of Delfina, a Diegueño Indian*, as told to Florence C. Shipek (Morongo Indian Reservation: Malki Museum Press, 1970). Cuero is associated with the Jamul band, Jane Dumas's and Erica Pinto's people. In her biography, *Chief Marin: Leader, Rebel, and Legend* (Berkeley CA: Heyday Books, 2007), Betty Goerke draws on a number of sources for a moving narrative of Marin County's namesake and his people. See also Matthew F. Bokovoy, "Humanist Senti-

ment, Modern Spanish Heritage, and California Mission Commemoration, 1769–1915," *Journal of San Diego History* 48, no. 3 (2002), available online at http://www.sandiegohistory.org/journal; Jim Miller, "Just Another Day in Paradise," in *Under the Perfect Sun: The San Diego Tourists Never See*, by Mike Davis, Kelly Mayhew, and Jim Miller (New York: New Press, 2005), 162–64. Richard L. Carrico documents the theft of Indian lands in the San Diego area in *Strangers in a Stolen Land*, San Diego State University Publications in American Indian Studies, no. 2 (San Diego: San Diego State University, 1986). Today, California's Indian population is larger than that of any other state, up to 333,511, matching the earliest estimates. Los Angeles County has the largest number of Native Americans (76,155); in tribal areas, the top three are San Diego County (25,324); then San Bernardino (20,513); and Orange (19,924). See California Native American Heritage Commission, http://ceres.ca.gov, accessed May 14, 2009. These numbers are from the 2000 census. See also Robert F. Heizer and M. A. Whipple, *The California Indians: A Source Book* (Berkeley: University of California Press, 1971), 72.

10. Nora Livesay, "Understanding the History of Tribal Enrollment," newsletter of the American Indian Policy Center (St. Paul MN), Fall 1996, http://www.airpi.org. Also, this website includes a glossary of terms that the Bureau of Indian Affairs uses to define who is or is not Indian.

11. This review of termination and its consequences is from Charles Wilkinson, *Blood Struggle* (New York: W. W. Norton, 2005). In his reporting on the opposition to termination, Wilkinson lays out the policy and the struggle of tribes to regain their lands. Termination, however, provided a strong impetus for self-determination. See also Jack Utter, *American Indians: Answers to Today's Questions* (1993; Norman: University of Oklahoma Press, 2001), 398–401; and Veronica E. Velarde Tiller, *Tiller's Guide to Indian Country* (Albuquerque: BowArrow Publishing Company, 1996), 229, for a brief summary of termination in California. The guide also includes termination information for each ranchería.

12. Public Law 280, which Congress enacted in 1953, drastically changed the relationship between the federal government and Indians by shifting civil jurisdiction over selected tribes to certain states. Congress amended the act in 1968 by adding a tribal consent provision

and giving states the authority to return jurisdiction to the federal government. But these amendments were not retroactive, and not a single Indian nation has allowed state jurisdiction since 1968. For a long paper on Public Law 280, see the website of American Indian Development Associates, http://http://www.aidainc.net/Publications/pl280.htm, and the Department of Justice's National Institute of Justice, http://http://www.ojp.usdoj.gov/nij/pubs-sum/209839.htm, accessed June 1, 2010.

13. Dwight Dutschke, "American Indians in California," Santa Barbara Indian Center, Office of Historic Preservation, available online at http://www.cr.nps.gov/history/online_books/5views/5views1g .htm, accessed January 18, 2010. Ben Nighthorse Campbell, a member of the Northern Cheyenne Nation, also suggested this during his speech at the dedication of the NMAI in 2004. Campbell served as the Republican U.S. senator from Colorado from 1993 until 2005.

14. Philip Deloria, *Indians in Unexpected Places* (Lawrence: University Press of Kansas, 2004), 226.

15. Information about the federation is readily available on the University of California, Irvine's website: http://www.hnet.uci.edu, accessed October 19, 2006. The Gabrieleno band also has a useful website: http://click.nativeamericans.com/missionindianfederation .com, accessed October 16, 2006.

16. One-third of the eligible American Indian population had served in World War II, three times the national rate. See Wilkinson, *Blood Struggle*, 103.

17. Tex Hall, "The State of the Indian Nations Today: Mapping a Course for the Next Seven Generations," Washington DC, January 31, 2003. The text is available at http://www.manataka.org/page130.html, accessed January 3, 2011. Hall was also the chairman of the Mandan, Hidatsa, and Arikara Nations of North Dakota. More recent State of the Indian Nations addresses may be found on the site of the National Congress of American Indians, http://www.ncai.org, accessed October 16, 2006.

18. Troy Johnson, "The American Indian Occupation of Alcatraz Island," California State University, http://www.csulb.edu, October 16, 2006.

19. Page, *In the Hands*, 382–88. Also see the American Indian Movement's website: http://www.aimovement.org, accessed October 16, 2006.

20. Wilkinson, *Blood Struggle*, 206–40.

21. Joane Nagel, *American Indian Ethnic Renewal: Red Power and the Resurgence of Identity and Culture* (New York: Oxford University Press, 1996), 125–31. This is available online at http://books.google.com, accessed September 7, 2009.

22. Peter Iverson, *Diné: A History of the Navajos* (Albuquerque: University of New Mexico Press, 2002), 236–39, 192–93; Rudi Williams, "Former Sergeant Leads Destitute Tribe to Economic Prosperity, Self-Respect," *American Forces Press Service*, n.d., accessed October 16, 2006, http://www.pentagon.gov/specials/nativeam02/tribe.html.

23. Zah was chairman of the tribal council, the highest office at that time.

24. Author's notes, meeting at Albuquerque Indian Center, August 17, 2003.

25. Charlie Savage, "U.S. Agrees to $3.4 Billion Deal in Indian Trust Suit," *New York Times*, December 12, 2009, http://www.nytimes.com.

26. The website of the Native American Rights Fund (NARF) has a timeline and other information on the Cobell suit. See http://www.cobellsettlement.com.

27. While companies paid Navajos $25 to $40 per unit, they reimbursed others between $170 and $550. See Alan Balaran, "Site Visit Report of the Special Master to the Office of Appraisal Services in Gallup, New Mexico and the Bureau of Indian Affairs Navajo Realty Office in Window Rock, Arizona," U.S. District Court, District of Columbia, Civil Action no. 1:96CV01285 (RCL), August 20, 2003, 22–23, online at http://www.indiantrust.com.

28. Alan Balaran, "Site Visit Report of the Special Master to the Dallas, Texas Office of the Mineral Revenue Management Division of the Department of the Interior's Minerals Management Service," U.S. District Court, District of Columbia, Civil Action no. 1:96CV01285 (RCL), September 29, 2003, 5–6, online at http://www.indiantrust.com; John Files, "Indian Fund Officer Angrily Quits," *New York Times*, April 7, 2004, http://www.nytimes.com.

29. John Files, "One Banker's Fight for a Half-Million Indians," *New York Times*, April 20, 2004, http://www.nytimes.com.

30. Eric M. Weiss, "At U.S. Urging, Court Throws Lamberth off Indian

Case," *Washington Post*, July 12, 2006, A13.

31. This blistering attack from Judge Lamberth was widely reported when he made it. One source is Evelyn Nieves, "U.S. Berated over Indians' Treatment," *Washington Post*, July 13, 2005, http://www.washingtonpost.com.

32. The BIA provides services to 564 tribes within the government-to-government relationship. See http://www.bia.gov, accessed June 2, 2010. In the larger context of the entertainment industry, Indian gaming does not generate an extraordinary sum. In 2004 Time Warner alone brought in $42 billion in revenue, and the top four record companies brought in about $30 billion, representing 70 percent of the worldwide music market. See TWX, New York Stock Exchange profile, accessed December 16, 2005, http://www.marketwatch.nytimes.com; WMT, New York Stock Exchange profile, accessed December 15, 2005, http://www.marketwatch.nytimes.com; Who Owns What, "How Independent Is Your Favorite 'Indie' Label?" *Utne Reader (Wikipedia)*, November–December 2005, http://www.utne.com/2005-114/whoownswhat.aspx. Revenues from conventional gaming in Nevada brought in $11 billion and in New Jersey nearly $5 billion.

33. Center for California Native Nations, University of California, Riverside, "An Impact Analysis of Tribal Government Gaming in California," January 2006, http://www.newsroom.ucr.edu.

34. For a story on Asians' love of gambling, see Gary Rivlin, "Las Vegas Caters to Asia's High Rollers," *New York Times*, June 13, 2007, http://www.nytimes.com.

35. Jim Doyle, "Backlash on Betting; Californians Have Second Thoughts on Gambling," *San Francisco Chronicle*, October 24, 2004, http://sfgate.com.

36. For the survey, see Dan Morain, "Tribal Casinos Should Ante Up, Voters Say," *Los Angeles Times*, April 24, 2004, http://www.latimes.com. "Indian Gaming in California," from the Institute of Governmental Studies at the University of California, Berkeley, provides a précis of this history in that state. See http://www.igs.berkeley.edu, accessed October 11, 2006.

37. Wilkinson, *Blood Struggle*, 335–38. IGRA legislation has had mixed reviews from supporters and foes of gaming: it has been praised for turning over authority to the tribes but criticized for its loopholes.

For the text of IGRA and statistical material on Indian gaming, see the website of the National Indian Gaming Commission, http://www.nigc.gov. Additional information is available at the website of the National Indian Gaming Association, http://www.indiangaming.org, accessed October 16, 2006. See also NIGA, "The Economic Impact of Indian Gaming, 2006," accessed September 5, 2007, http://www.indiangaming.org; Jonathan Thompson, "The Ute Paradox," *High Country News*, July 19, 2010, http://www.hcn.org.

38. Lisa Petrillo, "Donation from Sycuan to Fund New Institute," *San Diego Union-Tribune*, July 25, 2005, http://www.signonsandiego.com/news/education.

39. Lori Weisberg, "The NIMBY Factor," *San Diego Union-Tribune*, February 19, 2006, http://www.signonsandiego.com.

40. Catherine C. Robbins, "Selling the White Man His Vice," http://www.voiceofsandiego.org, December 9, 2005; Onell R. Soto, "Casino Access in Dispute," December 27, 2008, http://www.signonsandiego.com.

41. For examples of such a dispute, see two op-ed columns written by Daniel Beltran, the chairman of the Lower Lake Rancheria Koi Nation, and Tony Daysog, a member of the Alameda City Council, *San Francisco Chronicle*, January 27, 2005, http://www.sfgate.com.

42. Danny Hakim, "U.S. Recognizes Long Island Tribe," *New York Times*, June 15, 2010; Ross Buettner, "Shinnecock Indians See Prosperity Ahead," *New York Times*, December 29, 2009, http://www.nytimes.com. As another story illustrates, the situation of the Shinnecocks is complex, with disagreements within the tribe as well as between tribal members and white residents of the Hamptons. Ariel Levy, "Reservations: A Tribe Plans a Casino in the Hamptons," *New Yorker*, December 13, 2010, 40–49, http://www.newyorker.com.

43. For information relating to Oneida lands, see http://www.oneidaindiannation.com, especially the sovereignty and land into trust links. For the 2008 and 2009 decisions and related documents, see Glenn Coin, "Feds: Give Oneidas 13,000 Acres in Trust," February 22, 2008; "Oneida County, Oneida Nation Reach Agreement on Land into Trust Issue," May 8, 2009; and Glenn Coin, "Judge Rules for Oneida Nation in Trust Case," September 29, 2009, all in *Syracuse Post-Standard*, at http://www.syracuse.com. For extensive documents on the Oneida claims, including state of New York sites, see

http://www.oneidanationtrust.com, accessed June 2, 2010.

44. "Casino Competition atop Recession Taking a Toll," *New London Day*, June 20, 2010, http://www.theday.com.

45. Erika Werner, "States Eye Indian Gaming Revenue," Associated Press, April 25, 2003. See also Rachel Myrow, "Indian Gaming Contract," National Public Radio, April 24, 2003, http://discover.npr .org; NIGA, "The Economic Impact of Indian Gaming, 2006"; Morain, "Tribal Casinos Should Ante Up"; Joel W. Martin, "Tribal Casino Money," letter, *New York Times*, January 24, 2006, http://www .nytimes.com. Ironically, Schwarzenegger's campaign slogan repeated almost verbatim a comment by Senator Arthur V. Watkins, who had led the termination movement. He said that Indians wanted benefits like roads and hospitals but were unwilling to "pay their share of it" (Wilkinson, *Blood Struggle*, 69).

46. John Hubbell, "Props. 68 and 70 Go down Big—Voters Like the Governor's Deals," *San Francisco Chronicle*, November 3, 2004, http:// www.sfgate.com; press release, Office of the Governor of California, "Governor Schwarzenegger Announces Indian Gaming Agreements," June 16, 2005, http://www.cgcc.ca.gov/compacts.

47. The Winnebago Tribe's media website maintains a long list of the stories written about the Abramoff cases since 2002; see http:// www.indianz.com, accessed October 17, 2006. For a history of Abramoff's dealings, see Susan Schmidt and James V. Grimaldi, "The Fast Rise and Steep Fall of Jack Abramoff," December 29, 2005, and Susan Schmidt, "Abramoff Is to Begin Sentence Today," November 15, 2006, both in *Washington Post*, http://www.washingtonpost .com. See also Deborah Solomon, "Lobbying Reservations," *New York Times Magazine*, February 26, 2006, http://www.nytimes.com; John J. Miller, "The Projects on the Prairie," *Wall Street Journal*, January 27, 2006, W11, http://www.wsj.com.

48. The most-cited version of this myth was provided by Washington Matthews and published in the *Journal of American Folklore* 2, no. 5 (1889). It is available widely, for instance, http://webroots.org/ library, accessed January 11, 2005.

49. Dennis Wagner, "Navajos Bet First Casino Is a Winner," *Arizona Republic*, November 17, 2008, http://www.azcentral.com; Kathy Helms, "It's Open! Fire Rock Casino 'Dream Come True' for Navajo," *Gallup Independent*, November 20, 2008, http://www

.gallupindependent.com; Michelle Torado, "Apache Stronghold Golf Course Reopens after Recession Shutdown," Arizona Indian Gaming Association, April 21, 2009, http://www.azindiangaming. org; George Hardeen, press officer, Office of the President and Vice-President, Navajo Nation, telephone interview with the author, September 26, 2006.

50. Hall's column was published in several venues. See Tex Hall, "American Indians and the Abramoff Scandal; You Don't Know Jack," *San Francisco Chronicle*, January 27, 2006, http://www.sfgate.com.

51. Joel Martin, principal investigator, "An Impact Analysis of Tribal Government Gaming in California," Center for California Nations, University of California, Riverside, January 2006, http://www.ccnn .ucr.edu; Mindy Marks and Kate Spilde Contreras, "Lands of Opportunity: Social and Economic Effects of Tribal Gaming on Localities," *Policy Matters* (University of California, Riverside) 1, no. 4 (2007), http://www.cniga.com/UCRiversideStudyVol2.pdf.

52. Mike Spector, "Casino's Debt Talks Are Test of Tribal Bets," *Wall Street Journal*, July 2, 2010, C1, http://www.wsj.com.

53. A record of gaming revenues is available at Gaming Revenue Reports, National Indian Gaming Commission, accessed April 23, 2009, http://www.nigc.gov. The fastest growth in 2007 (20 percent) occurred in the region that includes Kansas, Texas, and Oklahoma. The slowest (1.6 percent) was in the region comprising California and northern Nevada. The region that includes Connecticut and New York, home to some of the nation's largest casinos, registered less than 3 percent growth. See Eric Gershon, "A Weaker Hand," *Hartford Courant*, October 5, 2008, http://www.courant.com; Mike Gallagher, "Gaming Tribes Fear End to Good Times," *Albuquerque Journal*, January 9, 2005, http://www.abqjournal.com; Peter Sanders and John R. Emshwiller, "At Indian Casinos, Odds Grow Longer for Some Tribes," *Wall Street Journal*, September 27, 2005, http://www.wsj.com.

54. Robbins, "Selling the White Man."

55. National Museum of the American Indian, film for visitors; Michael Coleman, "N.M. Played Large Role in Creating Nat'l Museum of the American Indian," *Albuquerque Journal*, September 16, 2004, http:// www.abqjournal.com.

56. Philip S. "Sam" Deloria, director, American Indian Law Center, University of New Mexico, interview with the author, February 5, 2006.

In 1994 Deloria estimated the number of Indian lawyers exceeded 1,500; about 250 Indians were law students at that time. See *New Mexico Law Review* 24 (1994): 291; "A Report of the Multicultural Women Attorneys Network," prepared by the Federal Bar Association and the Native American Bar Association, August 1998, http://www.abanet.org.

57. Before his appointment as head of NMAI, Richard West practiced law in Albuquerque with Kevin Gover, who would become West's successor at the museum. Gover had also headed the BIA.

58. National Tribal Justice Resource Center, preface to *Tribal Justice Systems, Directory Listing* (Boulder CO: National Tribal Justice Resource Center, 2002). See also http://www.tribalresourcecenter.org, accessed November 25, 2009.

59. Author's notes, Federal Bar Association, Twenty-Seventh Annual Indian Law Conference, "Reaffirming Tribal Sovereignty in an Era of Judicial Activism," April 4–5, 2002, Albuquerque, New Mexico.

60. Author's notes, Federal Bar Association. See also an interview in the conference papers: John P. LaVelle, "Strengthening Tribal Sovereignty through Indian Participation in American Politics: A Reply to Professor Porter," in *Reaffirming Tribal Sovereignty in an Era of Judicial Activism* (Washington DC: Federal Bar Association, 2002), 70–80. The interview was excerpted from *Kansas Journal of Law and Public Policy* 10 (2001): 533. At the time, LaMere was a member of the Democratic National Committee and became the chairman of the DNC's Native American Caucus.

61. See note 60. See also the paper presented by David Getches, "The Supreme Court's Recent Jurisprudence and Indian Jurisdiction," in *Reaffirming Tribal Sovereignty*, 1–9. Getches was the founding executive director of NARF. In an appendix to the conference papers, Getches provides an exhaustive review of Supreme Court cases from 1958 to 2000. See also N. Bruce Duthu, "Broken Justice in Indian Country," *New York Times*, August 11, 2008, http://www.nytimes.com. Duthu, a lawyer, is a professor of law at the Vermont Law School and holds an adjunct appointment in Native American studies at Dartmouth. He is also the author of *American Indians and the Law* (New York: Penguin, 2009). At the time, William C. Canby Jr. was the senior judge for the U.S. Court of Appeals for the Ninth Circuit (author's notes). He is the author of the textbook *American Indian Law in a Nutshell* (1988; Ea-

gan MN: Thomson West, 2009). In 2006 NCAI adopted a sovereignty initiative that kicked off with Indians embarking on a cross-country, coast-to-coast relay run. It began on Washington's Quinault Reservation and ended on the steps of the Supreme Court Building. Documents and stories relating to the sovereignty initiative are available on NCAI's website: http://www.ncai.org, accessed October 13, 2006.

62. The Tribal Law and Order Act is Title II of H.R. 725, accessed August 4, 2010, http://frwebgate.access.gpo.gov/cgi-bin/getdoc .cgi?dbname=111_cong_bills&docid=f:h725enr.txt.pdf. Also, John Dossett, phone interview with the author, August 9, 2010. In addition, Michael W. Savage, "Obama to Sign Bill Targeting Violent Crime on Indian Reservations," *Washington Post*, July 29, 2010, http://www.washingtonpost.com.

63. LaVelle, "Strengthening Tribal Sovereignty," 71–73.

64. Philip S. "Sam" Deloria, director, American Indian Law Center, University of New Mexico, interview with the author, October 25, 2005. Established in 1967, the American Indian Law Center is funded by the Bureau of Indian Affairs and by contracts for services it provides; UNM provides office space. See http://lawschool.unm.edu/ailc, accessed October 17, 2006. Deloria has headed the AILC since 1972 from a small office, a tiny staff, and funding through contracts with federal, state, and tribal governments and nonprofit organizations. The AILC has taken on a number of projects while also preparing Indians for law school: training newly appointed tribal judges; reviewing and enhancing tribal children's codes; and revising Felix Cohen's *Handbook of Federal Indian Law*, the classic treatise on Indian law.

65. Spector, "Casino's Debt Talks."

66. Emma Brown, "Tribe Brings On the Tourists," *High Country News*, February 20, 2006, http://www.hcn.org; "The Hualapai Nation Unveils All-New Destination Experience at Grand Canyon West," August 22, 2005, at the Hualapai tribe's public relations website, http://www.prnewswire.com.

67. After the Civil War, the federal government demanded that the Five Nations in Indian territory abolish slavery. The Cherokee Nation had already abolished slavery in 1863. In July 1866 the Five Nations and the government negotiated a series of treaties through which the tribes allowed adoption of the freedmen residing in their territories. The measures were highly controversial from the beginning, espe-

cially for the Cherokees, whose population became increasingly diverse. The Cherokee Nation resisted federal requests that the freedmen be given tribal citizenship. The government stepped in with a suit, *Whitmore v. Cherokee Nation and United States*, to settle the matter in 1895. Not only did the government impose the citizenship requirement on the Cherokees, but it also ruled that the freedmen were entitled to more than $900,000 of the $7.2 million owed the Cherokee Nation for a property settlement. See Sturm, *Blood Politics*, 76–78.

68. See H.R. 2824, accessed April 20, 2009, http://thomas.loc.gov.

69. Wyatt Buchanan, "Celebration, Setbacks for Gay Indigenous People; They'll Mark Parade Grand Marshal, Loss on Marriage Front," *San Francisco Chronicle*, June 25, 2005, http://sfgate.com.

70. Thomas E. Sheridan and Nancy J. Parezo, *Paths of Life: American Indians of the Southwest and Northern Mexico* (Tucson: University of Arizona Press, 1996), 248.

71. Catherine C. Robbins, "Expanding Power for Indian Women," *New York Times*, May 28, 1987, http://www.nytimes.com; Yvonne Shinhoster Lamb, "Navajo Chief Justice Claudeen B. Arthur, 62," *Washington Post*, December 3, 2004, B09, http://www.washingtonpost.com; Monica Davey, "As Tribal Leaders, Women Fight Old Views," *New York Times*, February 4, 2006, http://www.nytimes.com. A chronicle for the Fire Thunder controversy is available in the archives of *Indian Country Today* at http://www.indiancountry.com, keyword: cecelia firethunder, accessed October 9, 2007.

72. Matt Franklin quote from author's notes, Conference for Tribal Leaders, September 20–22, 2005, Sacramento, California; Cathy Robbins, "Indian Tribes Ready to Respond to Disasters," October 22, 2005, http://www.voiceofsandiego.org; Connie Reitman, interview with the author, September 21, 2005. Homeland security increasingly intrudes on tribes along border areas. By 2010 Mexican drug cartels had invaded the Tohono O'odham Nation in Arizona. Federal agents swarmed over the reservation, where tribal members felt so unsafe that they could no longer gather traditional foods. Also, the cartel threatened to kill tribal members unless they helped transport marijuana through the reservation. See Erik Eckholm, "In Drug War, Tribe Feels Invaded by Both Sides," *New York Times*, January 25, 2010, http://www.nytimes.com.

73. Lorie Sturgeon-Sandoval, "Q & A with Anna Sandoval," program, Traditional Gathering and Seventeenth Annual Pow-Wow, Sycuan band of the Kumeyaay Nation, September 8–10, 2006, 24.

74. Donald Bartlett et al., "Wheel of Misfortune," *Time*, December 16 and 23, 2002; John Emshwiller and Christina Binkley, "As Indian Casinos Grow, Regulation Raises Concern," *Wall Street Journal*, August 23, 2004, A1, http://www.wsj.com.

75. The conflict between the Agua Caliente band of Palm Springs and the Quechan band of California and Arizona is particularly revealing. See James P. Sweeney, "2 Tribes' Casino Deals Say a Lot about Clout in Legislature," *San Diego Union-Tribune* (Copley News Service), August 19, 2006, http://www.signonsandiego.com.

76. Jeff Benedict, *Without Reservation: How a Controversial Indian Tribe Rose to Power and Built the World's Largest Casino* (New York: Harper Collins, 2000). Among other "exposés" of Indian gaming are numerous articles in the *Wall Street Journal* and *Time*'s two-part series, "Wheel of Misfortune," December 16 and 23, 2002.

77. Anthony Gulig, a specialist in U.S. and Canadian Indian policy at the University of Wisconsin–Whitewater; Dirk Olin, "Crash Course: Tribal Recognition," *New York Times Magazine*, November 24, 2002, http://www.nytimes.com. At the time he wrote this article, Olin was national editor of *American Lawyer*.

78. Sheridan and Parezo, *Paths of Life*, xxiv–xxv.

79. Iverson, *Diné*, 51–57; Peter Nabokov, ed., *Native American Testimony* (1978; New York: Penguin, 1991), 157. This excellent book presents Indian recollections of the stories of white-Indian encounters from 1492 to the present. One of the selections is a narrative of the Navajo removal by Chester Arthur, a relative of the famous twentieth-century Navajo statesman Henry Chee Dodge. Numbers of deaths during the Long Walk and during internment are hard to pin down. A steady population of 7,500 lived at Bosque Redondo between 1864 and 1868. The leading demographer of Indian populations says simply that deaths exceeded births during those years and that the Long Walks itself had a "high mortality rate." See Nancy Shoemaker, *American Indian Population Recovery in the Twentieth Century* (Albuquerque: University of New Mexico Press, 1999), 32–33. For a brief account of the natural and human history of Canyon de Chelly, Northern Arizona University has a web narrative within its site

titled "Colorado Plateau, Land Use History of North America," accessed February 5, 2008, http://www.cpluhna.nau.edu.

80. Bosque de Redondo dedication, Fort Sumner, New Mexico, June 4, 2005, author's notes. Thanks to Gordon Bronitsky for giving us a ride to the event and for his illuminating comments. He is the founder and president of Bronitsky and Associates, LLC, which specializes in international cultural marketing. See also http://www.nmmonuments.org, accessed January 18, 2006.

81. Nabokov, *Native American Testimony*, 193–96; and this Yankton Sioux website: http://www.yanktonsiouxtourism.com, accessed November 13, 2005.

82. Gregg Bourland as told to Susan Burton, "A Pox on Our House," *New York Times Magazine*, September 22, 2002, 100.

83. Joseph P. Kalt, director of the Harvard Project on American Indian Economic Development: "Tribes no longer have to hope for or rely upon the efforts of outside environmental groups or pro bono law firms." Nelson D. Schwartz, "Far from the Reservation, but Still Sacred?" *New York Times*, August 12, 2007, http://www.nytimes.com; Wilkinson, *Blood Struggle*, 329–51.

84. See http://www.ftsumnerchamber.com, accessed January 19, 2006.

85. For a beautifully written and photographed account of a white woman living in the canyon for a summer, see Jeanne M. Simonelli and Charles D. Winters, *Crossing between Worlds* (Santa Fe: School of American Research, 1997).

86. Bonnie Tsui, "Blazing New Trails in Native American Lands," *New York Times*, August 23, 2009, http://www.nytimes.com.

6. *The Drum*

1. Catherine C. Robbins, "The Distinctive Life and Dances of the Pueblo Indians," *New York Times*, September 7, 1980, http://www.nytimes.com.

2. Remarkably, of nearly 2,900 of the pueblo's residents over the age of five, 88 percent speak English and Keres, according to the 1990 census, p. 2, accessed October 24, 2006, http://censtats.census.gov/data/NM/280353400.pdf.

3. Joe Sando, *Pueblo Profiles: Cultural Identity through Centuries of Change* (Santa Fe NM: Clear Light Publishers, 1998), 151. Mr. Sando,

a member of Jemez Pueblo, has written several books and is the foremost Pueblo historian.

4. The term *costume* is highly inappropriate. One would not use the term to describe clerical vestments, and Pueblo dances are religious occasions. Many other Indian social events are rooted in ceremonial occasions, so *attire* might be the proper term for those occasions, while *regalia* works for powwows.

5. Catherine C. Robbins, "The Heartbeat across Cultures," *Albuquerque Tribune*, November 26, 1999 (unavailable online); Maria Williams, interview with the author, October 15, 1999. Williams teaches in the Native American Studies and Music Departments at the University of New Mexico.

6. Balance is a goal in Puebloan cultures, and that includes ceremonies. Governance is in the hands of the cacique and other religious officials, while the *koshari* are sacred clowns who entertain the people and who also have a serious purpose as connectors between people and the spirit world. Although the basic structure of ceremonial life is consistent across Pueblo life, variations are common. For a brief description of precontact Pueblo Indian ceremonial organization, which is visible today, see Ramón Gutierrez, *When Jesus Came, the Corn Mothers Went Away: Marriage, Sexuality and Power in New Mexico, 1500–1846* (Stanford CA: Stanford University Press, 1991), 8–36. In this section, Gutierrez describes the social and cultural characteristics of Puebloan society that the Spanish arrival disrupted. For instance, the friars forced the Natives to kneel before them and kiss their hands and feet. For the Pueblos, this was an act of humiliation because they had never knelt before their gods or leaders (49). Also, two slim volumes are handy guides to Pueblo life: Bertha Dutton, *Indians of the American Southwest: The Pueblos* (New York: Prentice-Hall, 1975); and Daniel Gibson, *Pueblos of the Rio Grande* (Tucson AZ: Rio Nuevo Publishers, 2001). Chapter 2 in Joe S. Sando's *Pueblo Nations: Eight Centuries of Pueblo Indian History* (Santa Fe NM: Clear Light Publishers, 1998) is also useful.

7. This section is based on the author's notes taken during activities at the Bird Song Festival, December 17, 2005, Agua Caliente Museum, Palm Springs, California, including author interviews with Michael Mirelez and O'Jay Vanegas, as well as O'Jay Vanegas, telephone interview with the author, April 12, 2006.

8. A useful compilation of powwows is available from the Book Publishing Company of Summertown, Tennessee. It is available in bookstores. On the web, see http://www.powwows.com, http://www.gatheringofnations.com, groups.msn.com/THEPOWWOWSITE/home, accessed October 23, 2006. These sources also explain dance styles, the competition, and powwow etiquette.

9. This definition is from the exhibition narrative for a show at the MacKenzie Gallery, Regina, Saskatchewan, Canada, http://www.civilization.ca/media/docs/fspow01e, accessed October 24, 2006. See also Susan Braine, *Drumbeat . . . Heartbeat: A Celebration of the Powwow (We Are Still Here: Native Americans Today)* (Minneapolis: Lerner Publishing Group, 1995), 10. See also http://www.powwow-power.com/powwowhistory, accessed October 23, 2006.

10. Indians frequently have local homecomings and reunions for families and tribes that are not strictly speaking powwows. The Sioux call their events *wacipi*, and northern California Indians use "big time."

11. The reversal of fortune for the Baronas, like that of other Kumeyaay-Diegueño groups in Southern California, has been startling. When the city of San Diego bought reservation lands from the Capitan band for a reservoir in 1931, the band used the money to buy the 5,800-acre Barona Ranch. It became the Barona Reservation. The Baronas' recovery accelerated when they opened a casino in 1994 that has grown into one of the largest in the state. The Barona band of 536 lives on the reservation. See http://censtats.census.gov/data/US/2500155.pdf, http://www.baronatribe.org/history/history, accessed May 14, 2009.

12. This section is based on the author's attendance at several Gatherings. See also Catherine C. Robbins, "Gathering of Nations," *Crosswinds Weekly*, April 24, 2003, 10 (unavailable online).

13. The Gathering's management and financial matters have raised some questions about its integrity. See Robbins, "Gathering of Nations."

14. Tara Browner, *Heartbeat of the People: Music and Dance of the Northern Pow-Wow* (Urbana: University of Illinois Press, 2002), 2.

15. Brent Michael Davids, interview with the author, December 4, 1999, and telephone interview, May 2, 2006; David Lockington, telephone interview with the author, May 25, 2006; Catherine C. Robbins, "Classical Powwow," *Albuquerque Tribune*, December 10, 1999 (unavailable online); Molly Sheridan, "Composer Brent Michael Davids

Brings a Native American Pow Wow into the Concert Hall," *Symphony Magazine*, May–June 2000. The *Powwow Symphony* premiered at Popejoy Hall at the University of New Mexico on December 10 and 11, 1999.

16. This section is based on the author's notes from an interview with Tate, Avery, and other Native composers, with samples of their works, heard on *Native America Calling*, October 2, 2006. The interview is available in the archives of *Native America Calling*, http://www .nativeamericacalling.com. Tate's site is http://www.taloaproductions .com/home, and Avery's is http://www.dawnavery.com. More information about Raven Chacon is at http://www.music.calarts .edu/~rchacon/source, accessed October 26, 2006. The First Nations Composer Initiative (FNCI) is at http://www.fnci.org, accessed October 23, 2006. Native American composers and musicians also produce lively and complex popular music. This book does not cover them chiefly because of space limitation, but the reader can see and hear them on the web. A starting point is Koahnic Broadcasting's list of artists and record labels: http://www.knba.org/kbc/music_links.shtml, accessed January 4, 2011.

17. In 1936 F. Scott Fitzgerald wrote, "The test of a first-rate intelligence is the ability to hold two opposed ideas in the mind at the same time, and still retain the ability to function." *The Crack-Up* (New York: New Directions, 1962), 69.

18. "Washington Tribes in Action," Tribal Economic Development Summit, August 21–24, 2005, Quinault Beach Resort, Ocean Shore, Washington; author's notes.

19. This section is drawn from the author's notes taken at the Tribal Economic Development Summit, August 21–24, 2005. Also Veronica Tiller, interview with the author, August 22, 2005.

20. Veronica E. Velarde Tiller, *Tiller's Guide to Indian Country* (Albuquerque: BowArrow Publishing Company, 1996).

21. "A Free Press; a Free People," annual meeting, Native American Journalists Association, August 11–14, 2005, Lincoln, Nebraska, author's notes; Dan Lewerenz, interview with the author, August 12, 2005; Frank King, interview with the author, August 13, 2005. NAJA, which is currently based at the University of Oklahoma, celebrated its twenty-fifth anniversary in 2009.

22. Founded in 1828, the *Phoenix* is the oldest Indian newspaper in the

United States, with a circulation of about sixty thousand. To see a copy of the act, go to http://www.cherokee.org/Phoenix/CherokeeFreePressAct71500da.pdf, accessed October 17, 2006.

23. This report, which was compiled in 2002 and updated in 2003 with a discussion of Indian names for mascots in several newspapers, is available on NAJA's website: http://www.naja.com/news/releases/030619_mascot/, accessed October 17, 2006.

24. Patricia Loew, e-mail to author, September 27, 2005.

25. Panel discussion, annual meeting, Native American Journalists Association, August 12, 2005.

26. Harlan McKosato, "Gaming Changes Native American Tribes," *All Things Considered*, National Public Radio, May 20, 2005.

27. Newsroom Employee Census, American Society of Newspaper Editors, 1999, updated April 25, 2006. The census for several years is available on the ASNE website: http://www.asne.org/index.cfm?id=1138, accessed October 19, 2006.

28. The following section is based on several sources: Catherine C. Robbins, "Indian Country Sends a Stronger Signal," *New York Times*, February 4, 2001, http://www.nytimes.com, as well as the author's notes for the story, including interviews. For additional information about the Hopi Foundation, see http://www.hopifoundation.org, and for the Hopi Nation, http://www.hopi-nsn.gov. Listen to KUYI 88.1 FM streaming at http://www.kuyi.net, Hopi sites accessed January 16, 2011.

29. Robbins, "Indian Country." For information and live streaming, 11:00 a.m. Mountain Time, see http://www.nativeamericacalling.com and video streaming at http://www.mytribetv.com, accessed July 7, 2010. Also Harlan McKosato, interview with the author, December 29, 2000; Richard Towne, general manager, KUNM, interview with the author, January 3, 2001, Albuquerque, New Mexico.

30. Hartwig Isernhagen, *Momaday, Vizenor, Armstrong* (Norman: University of Oklahoma Press, 1999), 85. In an interview in this book, Vizenor said, "'Indians' are the most simulated universal victims. Victims have no humor; they offer the world nothing but their victimization, and that makes people who invest in them feel better" (85).

31. Many of NAC's programs are available in its online archive: http://www.nativeamericacalling.com, accessed October 19, 2006.

32. For a list of programs produced by Koahnic with CPB funding, see http://www.cpb.org/programs/grantee, accessed October 18, 2006. Additional support comes from the Ford Foundation, the John D. and Catherine T. MacArthur Foundation, various universities, and Nebraska's state humanities council.

33. In 2005, for instance, the Viejas band of Kumeyaay Indians purchased a 50 percent interest in the Broadcast Company of the Americas, a San Diego–based media organization with five stations.

34. Frank Blythe, interviews with the author on December 4, 2000, and August 15, 2005; Shirley K. Sneve, interview with the author, August 15, 2005. Sneve is currently the NAPT's executive director. For additional information about NAPT, see http://www.nativetelecom .org, accessed January 16, 2011.

35. See http://www.fcc.gov/indians, accessed October 16, 2006.

36. Evan T. Pritchard, *Native New Yorkers: The Legacy of the Algonquin People of New York* (San Francisco: Council Oaks Books, 2002), 122–24. Verrazano's letter to King Francis I of France in 1524 is in appendix 3 (394–404).

37. Linda Cordell, quoted in Jim Erickson, "Unearthing Canyon's Clues: Mysteries of Anasazi Revealed in Chaco's Centuries-Old Corn," *Rocky Mountain News*, May 15, 2004. The *Rocky Mountain News* has ceased publication. The article is available at https://verify1.newsbank. com/cgi-bin/ncom/RM/ec_signin, September 24, 2009. See also Robert F. Heizer and Albert B. Elsasser, *The Natural World of the California Indians* (Berkeley: University of California Press, 1980), 52. The authors, among the most prominent anthropologists of the California Indians, note that to ascribe the success of precontact societies to their simplicity, as opposed to our own world's technological complexity, is misleading. No matter the level of complexity, Indian societies "were successful in that they were organized in ways that assured the participants that the even flow of life and events would continue" (52).

38. Alexis de Tocqueville, *Letters from America*, trans. Frederick Brown, *Hudson Review* 62, no. 3 (2009), November 16, 2009, http://www .hudsonreview.com. See also Gloria Jahoda, *The Trail of Tears* (New York: Random House/Wings Books, 1995), 85.

39. Photographing Pueblo dancers is usually forbidden, but Kennedy worked out a set of protocols with tribal leaders who allowed him to

complete a portfolio of ten dancers from several New Mexico pueblos. Digital versions of the Pueblo photos and a Lakota portfolio, along with an explanation of Kennedy's process, are available on the web at http://davidmichaelkennedy.com/dancers/, accessed October 26, 2006.

7. Buckskin Boxes, Galactic Explosion

1. Luna first performed *The Artifact Piece* in 1987 at San Diego's Museum of Man.
2. Jesse Cooday, interview with the author, April 6, 2006.
3. Feder quoted in Joyce Herold, "Norman Feder's Double Standard: Case Studies in Critical Examination of Objects," in *Studies in American Indian Art: A Memorial Tribute to Norman Feder*, ed. Christian Feest, *European Review of Native American Studies*, July 2001, 4–15, 14.
4. Feder used the term *primitive*, which is generally avoided today.
5. Norman Feder, *American Indian Art* (New York: Harry N. Abrams, 1965), 21.
6. Hill and Harjo were quoted in Ken Shulman, "The Buckskin Ceiling and Its Discontents," *New York Times*, December 24, 2000, http://www.nytimes.com. The story covered a discussion of the "buckskin ceiling" during a conference at the NMAI's Heye Center in conjunction with the exhibit *Who Stole the Teepee?* Hill was the curator for the show, and Harjo is the president of the Morning Star Institute, an American Indian legislative group based in Washington.
7. The French government, however, had already recognized Allan Houser with a Palmes académiques (a decoration for services to education) in 1954, and he had had shows in San Francisco, Washington, and Chicago. For a biography and other information about Allan Houser, see http://www.allanhouser.com, accessed December 2, 2009.
8. Joyce Szabo is a specialist in American Indian art at the University of New Mexico. Interview with the author, May 4, 2006.
9. W. Richard West, interview with the author, November 28, 2005.
10. For an overview of the layers of the Indian arts market, see Nancy Parezo, "A Multitude of Markets." This is one of several articles in a special issue of the *Journal of the Southwest* 32, no. 4 (1990), ed.

Joseph Carleton Wilder, titled "Inventing the Southwest," accessed June 6, 2010, http://digital.library.arizona.edu/jsw/3204/markets .html.

11. The *Sunset* image, from its February 1903 issue, is available online: http://www.sunset.com/posters. *Sunset* sells this poster today for $50. A Californian by birth, Maynard Dixon (1875–1946) was a prolific and talented artist of western landscapes and people. For more about the artist, see http://www.maynarddixon.net, accessed June 5, 2009; Erika Marie Bsumek, *Indian-Made: Navajo Culture in the Marketplace, 1868–1940* (Lawrence: University Press of Kansas, 2008), 4 (for the reference to the Navajo Indian League, see 189; for the statistic on income, see 205n). Also Frances Pohl, lecture, San Diego Museum of Art, January 5, 2007.

12. Robert W. Rydell, *World of Fairs* (Chicago: University of Chicago Press, 1993), 73–77, 88–90, 104–5; Matthew Bokovoy, *The San Diego World's Fairs and Southwestern Memory, 1880–1940* (Albuquerque: University of New Mexico Press, 2005), 115–17, 117.

13. Author's notes, Annual Indian Fair, Museum of Man, San Diego, June 10–11, 2006. Bedard (Cree/Inupiat) starred in Chris Eyres's film *Smoke Signals* (1998) and provided the title voice for the animated Disney film *Pocahontas* (1995).

14. Maureen Littlejohn, "Indian Art Markets: A How-To Guide," *American Indian* (NMAI), Summer 2009, 18–25. This article includes a list of two dozen markets across the United States. Available online at http://www.nmai.si.edu, accessed June 1, 2009. Some events are dedicated entirely to arts and crafts, although others, like Gallup's Intertribal Ceremonial, are multipurpose.

15. For basic information about the Santa Fe Indian Market, including its history, see http://swaia.org/index.html, accessed June 4, 2010. Molly H. Mullin, *Culture in the Marketplace* (Durham NC: Duke University Press, 2001), 128–72, is particularly relevant. See also the SWAIA website, http://www.swaia.org; Bruce Bernstein, "A Story of Creation: Tradition and Authenticity at Santa Fe's Indian Market," in *Changing Hands: Art without Reservation 1: Contemporary Native American Art from the Southwest*, ed. David Revere McFadden and Ellen Napiura Taubman (London: Merrell Publishers, 2002), 103–8. Chris Wilson explores the roots of Santa Fe's cultural history in *The Myth of Santa Fe: Creating a Modern Regional Tradition* (Albuquerque:

University of New Mexico Press, 1997), 72–73, 169–80. Following chapter 5, Wilson inserts "Interlude: Coyote Consciousness," which shows the various ethnic manifestations of the coyote in Santa Fe's arts markets, from paintings to T-shirts. He includes a reproduction of one of a series of posters by Jerome L. Milord that first appeared in 1989 and took off like wildfire into postcards and souvenirs. It showed a woman in Native dress lying on a Hispanic rug and surrounded by accoutrements of the Southwest, such as a pink howling coyote statue, a corner beehive oven, a ceiling with vigas, a large Indian drum, and carved furniture. The caption for the card: "Another Victim of Santa Fe Style." Note that Indians have sold their wares on the street, so to speak, for decades, for instance, under the portal of the Palace of the Governors in Santa Fe and at La Placita Restaurant in Albuquerque.

16. Kate McGraw, "Indian Arts Director Moves Ahead," *Albuquerque Journal*, March 1, 2008, http://www.abqjournal.com.

17. Boston philanthropist and ethnographic avocationalist Mary Cabot Wheelwright collected songs with Navajo singer and medicine man Hastin Klah, while Frances Newcomb reproduced sand paintings. To house their collection, the Wheelwright Museum opened in 1937, just fifteen years after the first Indian market, with a focus on traditional arts; today it also exhibits contemporary works. See http://www.wheelwright.org, accessed July 8, 2010.

18. "Ugh! Ugh! How!" *Time*, December 7, 1931, http://http://www.time.com.

19. For this section, see W. Jackson Rushing III, "Marketing the Affinity of the Primitive and the Modern: Rene d'Harnoncourt and 'Indian Art of the United States,'" in *The Early Years of Native American Art History: The Politics of Scholarship and Collecting*, ed. Catherine Berlo (Seattle: University of Washington Press; Vancouver: University of British Columbia Press, 1992), 191–236. This book is available online for subscribers at http://ets.umdl.umich.edu, accessed October 27, 2006.

20. Established in 1935, the board was a Depression-era program to promote financial independence among tribes by increasing the marketability of their crafts. Through the Indian Arts and Crafts Act of 1990, the IACB also reinforces definitions of Indian work and sets out penalties for selling items as Indian art that are not Indian made.

Scott S. Smith, "The Scandal of Fake Indian Crafts," *Cowboys and Indians*, September 1998, http://www.cowboysindians.com/articles/ archives. Feder also discussed the process of change and commercialization, especially after 1850, in *American Indian Art*, 46, 52.

21. Rushing, "Marketing the Affinity," 195, 198, 203.

22. Harnoncourt organized a similar show for the Golden Gate International Exposition of 1939. See *Dictionary of Art Historians*, http://www.dictionaryofarthistorians.org. Norman Feder recognized this exhibition as one of the efforts to popularize Indian arts (*American Indian Art*, 22).

23. For instance, the Whitney Museum in New York, the Walker Art Center in Minneapolis, and the Nelson-Atkins Museum in Kansas City. In 1989 the Eiteljorg Museum of American Indians and Western Art opened in Indianapolis to display the collection of Indiana businessman and philanthropist Harrison Eiteljorg, who, like Heye, encountered American Indians and their art while working in mining ventures in the West. In addition, museums like the Heard in Phoenix, founded in 1929, expanded significantly. See Bruce Bernstein, "Contexts for the Growth and Development of the Indian Art World in the 1960s and 1970s," in *Native American Art in the Twentieth Century*, ed. W. Jackson Rushing III (London: Routledge, 1999), 60–61.

24. The project cost a million dollars, a huge sum in the early twentieth century. Catherine C. Robbins, "Collecting Indians," http://www .voiceofsandiego.org/articles, November 11, 2006; A. D. Coleman, "Curtis: His Work," introduction to *Portraits from North American Indian Life* (New York: Outerbridge and Lazard/E. P. Dutton, 1972), v–vii. Curtis, of course, was not the only photographer of Indians. Laura Gilpin worked in the Southwest for six decades. Joseph Kossuth Dixon was a photographer for the Wanamaker Department Store's Expedition to the American Indian of 1908, which produced an early motion picture, *The Song of Hiawatha*. See the website of Indiana University's Mather Museum of World Cultures, accessed June 4, 2010, http://www.indiana.edu/~mathers.

25. Ross Frank, associate professor, Department of Ethnic Studies, University of California, San Diego, lecture, San Diego Public Library, September 17, 2006.

26. The photo of the Snake Dance that includes non-Indian observers,

taken by John Wallack in 1890, is available at http://www
.old-picture.com/united-states-history-1900s-1930s/
Indians-Moqui-Snake-dance.htm, accessed September 26, 2007.
An image of *A Hopi Man* and the caption are available at http://
curtis.library.northwestern.edu/curtis/info.cgi?id=nai.12.
port00000022.p, accessed December 30, 2010.

27. Christopher Cardozo, Louise Erdrich, and Anne Makepeace, *Edward Curtis: The Women* (London: Little, Brown, 2005), 3; Margarett Loke, "Images That Are Glorious and Gloriously Unreal," *New York Times*, January 6, 2002, http://www.nytimes.com; George Birdeau, in *Coming to Light*, a documentary by Anne Makepeace, Bullfrog Films, 2000.

28. This section for the Heye Center comes from my notes on viewing *First American Art* and *New Tribe New York* in 2006 and *Who Stole the Teepee?* online at various times; also cited sources. The dates for the three shows were as follows: *Who Stole the Teepee?*, October 1, 2000–January 21, 2001; *First American Art*, April 24, 2004–May 29, 2006; *New Tribe New York*, January 29, 2005–April 9, 2006.

29. *Who Stole the Teepee?* was produced by NMAI and Atlatl, a nonprofit Native arts organization, and is available in digital format on NMAI's website: http://www.nmai.si.edu/exhibitions/ who_stole_the_teepee, accessed October 27, 2006.

30. Joanna Bigfeather, interview with the author, April 27, 2006. Bigfeather is an artist and independent curator.

31. The items in *First American Art* were from the collection of Charles and Valerie Diker, cochairs of the Heye Center.

32. Dress, belt, and awl, ca. 1879, artist unknown, Wasco; child's moccasins, ca. 1900, artist unknown, Lakota; olla, ca. 1900, artist unknown, Acoma. Images are available at http://www.nmai.si.edu/ exhibitions/first_american_art, accessed June 7, 2009.

33. Gerald McMaster, "The New Tribe Artists," in *New Tribe New York: The Urban Vision Quest*, exhibition catalog (Washington DC: NMAI Editions, Smithsonian Museum of the American Indian, 2005), 20–45.

34. This section also draws on the author's notes on viewing the MAD shows in 2002 and 2006 and cited sources. At the time of the first show, 2002, MAD's name was the American Crafts Museum, which changed in the interim. The exhibits also received wider distribution when they traveled across the United States to communities including Indianapolis, Anchorage, Tulsa, Minneapolis, Tucson, and Lub-

bock, cities that are usually not on the New York exhibition circuit. The catalogs for the first two shows: David Revere McFadden and Ellen Napiura Taubman, general editors for both catalogs, *Changing Hands: Art without Reservation 1: Contemporary Native American Art from the Southwest* (London: Merrell Publishers, 2002); *Changing Hands: Art without Reservation 2: Contemporary Native American Art from the West, Northwest and Pacific* (New York: Museum of Arts and Design, 2005).

35. Judith H. Dobrzynski, "Honoring Art, Honoring Artists," *New York Times*, February 6, 2011, http://www.nytimes.com.

36. Wilson, *The Myth of Santa Fe*, 331. As a rough comparison, http://www.YellowPages.com enumerates 1,025 galleries, dealers, and consultants in the New York area (accessed July 11, 2006).

37. Pamela Michaelis, e-mail to the author, June 20, 2006.

38. "Native Shirt Fetches Record Price," *BBC News*, May 12, 2006, http://news.bbc.co.uk/2/hi/uk_news/scotland. See Sotheby's for a brief history of American Indian auctions and for catalogs with prices: http://www.sothebys.com, accessed June 16, 2010.

39. For a photo of New and others in the Kiva Craft Center in Scottsdale, see *Arizona Memory Project, Scottsdale Remembers: Recollections of Our Past* (Arizona State Library), accessed June 6, 2010, http://azmemory.lib.az.us.

40. Bigfeather interview. For a review of twentieth-century Indian art, including the Santa Fe Indian School and the IAIA, see Bruce Bernstein, "Contexts for the Growth and Development of the Indian Art World in the 1960s and 1970s," in Rushing, *Native American Art*, 57–71, esp. 67–68. For more about the Santa Fe Indian School and Navajos, see "Beneath a Turquoise Sky: Navajo Painters and Their World," Traditional Fine Arts Organization, Inc., commentary on an exhibit of this name at the National Cowboy and Western Heritage Museum, Oklahoma City, 2005, http://www.tfaoi.com/aa/4aa/4aa452.htm. See also Guy Cross, "Straight Talk with Bob Haozous," *THE Magazine*, August 2003, http://www.themagazineonline.com/AUG03/interview2.

41. Richard West has noted that tribes can exercise greater control over museum holdings; NAGPRA gives them the political and moral authority to do so. In addition, control is absolute when tribes and even artists own their own facilities. In Santa Fe several Native artists and their families operate their own galleries: Niman Fine Arts

for the Naminigha family and the Allan Houser Gallery and Allan Houser Compound. West is a trustee of the Ford Foundation, which in 2009 pledged $10 million to establish the Native Arts and Culture Foundation, the first of its kind in history. Additional contributions come from the Rumsey band of Wintun Indians and other sources. Based in Portland, Oregon, the organization will support the work of American Indian and Alaska Native and Hawaiian Native artists. Four advisors from different tribes have formed a leadership circle headed by Walter Echo Hawk (Pawnee). Robin Pogebrin, "New Group Is Formed to Sponsor Native Arts," *New York Times*, April 22, 2009, http://www.nytimes.com.

42. Ramona Sakiestewa, artist's statement, in McFadden and Taubman, *Changing Hands: Art without Reservation 1*, 94.

43. Quick-to-See Smith, interview with the author, June 6, 2005. Visitors to the Navajo Reservation can spot hogans regularly. Pueblos occupy their ancestral villages, and while some have built modern ranch-style houses, others remain in traditional dwellings. The longhouse is having a revival in Washington State, at least for ceremonial purposes. Washington State's Squamish Tribe completed its first longhouse since 1870 on the banks of Squamish's downtown in 2009. The nearby Port Gamble S'Klallam tribe uses a longhouse for its community center.

44. Images of Joseph Carignano's paintings can be seen at http://lakeshorecountryjournal.com, accessed October 27, 2006.

45. Quick-to-See Smith interview. The artist is an enrolled member of the Confederated Salish and Kootenai Indian Nation, with Shoshone and Métis (French Cree) heritage.

46. Author's notes while viewing *Made in America*, University of New Mexico Museum, February and May 2005. Until April 2007, the show toured the nation as a program of the Museum of New Mexico.

47. Indians forced off their Native lands lost their traditional game and wild foods, so women concocted fried bread out of rations of lard, salt, and flour to sustain their families. Today, however, health care providers in Indian Country contend that it has contributed to obesity, diabetes, and hypertension. Suzan Shawn Harjo, "My New Year's Resolution: No More Fat 'Indian' Food," *Indian Country Today*, January 20, 2005, http://www.indiancountry.com/content.cfm?id=1096410209.

48. An image is available at the Electronic Educational Village of Long Island University, accessed October 25, 2006, http://eev.liu.edu/eevillage/HeckscherMM.

49. An image is available on the website of the Mildred Lane Kemper Museum of Washington University, Women Artists in the Washington University Collections, accessed October 27, 2006, http://www.artsci.wustl.edu/~artarch/womenartists/Contemporary/Quick-to-See_Smith.

50. The sources for this section include James Luna, interview with the author, Palomar Community College, November 11, 2006; Lisbeth Haas, "Pablo Tac: Memory, Identity, History," in *James Luna: Emendatio*, published in conjunction with the exhibit at the Venice Biennale, June 9–November 6, 2005 (Washington DC: National Museum of the American Indian, 2005), 49–53. That catalog includes the following essays: Paul Chaat Smith, "Luna Remembers," 17–22, 34–35, 44; Truman T. Lowe, "The Art of the Unexpected," 13, 22. Author's notes for the artist's lecture and slide show at the University of California, Riverside, January 27, 2006; "Venice Biennale Presented Great Challenges and Rewards for NMAI Staff," *Insight*, the newsletter of NMAI, Fall 2005, 1; Gerald McMaster, "James Luna," *Indian*, the magazine of NMAI, Fall 2005, 35; a DVD of the performance rehearsal at NMAI included with *James Luna: Emendatio*; the artist's website, http://www.jamesluna.com/jamesLUNA1, accessed October 27, 2006; viewing the installation portions only at NMAI's Heye Center, New York City, April 2008; Lisbeth Haas, e-mail message to the author, June 21, 2006; John R. Johnson and Dinah Crawford, "Contributions to Luiseño Ethnohistory Based on Mission Register Research," *Pacific Coast Archaeological Society Quarterly* 35, no. 4 (1999): 79–102. Tac's manuscript, written about 1835, has been published as *Indian Life at Mission San Luis Rey: A Record of California Mission Life by Pablo Tac, an Indian Neophyte*, ed. M. Hewes and G. Hewes (Old Mission San Luis Rey, California, 1958), 11–29. See also Blake Gopnik, "Indian Artists in Venice: Off the Traditional Path," *Washington Post*, July 24, 2005, http://www.washingtonpost.com.

51. Luna had several partners for *Emendatio*. Rick Pelasara, NMAI's supervisor of exhibit production, built the installations, with additional work from Karen Fort, the museum's deputy assistant director of exhibits and public spaces. After meeting in Venice to see

the space and talk, Luna and Pelasara began work, with Luna planning and conceiving the project in California and Pelasara building it in Washington. The project was daunting. The pieces had to float; nothing could be nailed into a wall, so everything had to be raised on tripods; this was both a creative and construction challenge. Also, the exhibit had to travel to Italy in cases that could be collapsed and transported flat. Luna saw the results in May, and the exhibit was shipped to arrive in Venice in time for the Biennale's June 9, 2005, opening. Jorge Arévalo Mateus wrote the music for *Emendatio*. He never saw the visual elements of *Emendatio*, but he knew Luna's vision and even arranged an eagle song for organ. Luna, clearly moved by Mateus's originality, had a single word for the composer: "Damn!" The curators for *Emendatio* were artists Truman Lowe (Winnebago) and Paul Chaat Smith (Comanche).

52. Founded in 1859, the Cooper Union for the Advancement of Science and Art is both a school with academic programs in architecture, art, and engineering and a meeting house for speakers and public events. See http://cooper.edu, accessed June 7, 2010.

53. Associated Press, "Ariz. Petroglyph May Have Recorded Supernova," *Albuquerque Journal*, June 6, 2006, http://www.abqjournal.com. The researcher is John Barentine, an astronomer at the Apache Point Observatory in Sunspot, Arizona. The petroglyph is in White Tank Mountain Regional Park, a Maricopa County park near Phoenix.

54. Dan Namingha, artist's statement, in McFadden and Taubman, *Changing Hands: Art without Reservation 1*, 82.

55. Steven Deo, artist's statement, in McFadden and Taubman, *Changing Hands: Art without Reservation 2*, 65; e-mail message to the author, March 27, 2007.

56. An image is available at http://http://www.boisestate.edu/firstnations/Cooday/index.htm, accessed October 27, 2006.

57. *American Indian Art Magazine*, Summer 2006, 107 (unavailable online).

58. Chaat Smith, "Luna Remembers," 25.

59. Paul Chaat Smith, *Everything You Know about Indians Is Wrong* (Minneapolis: University of Minnesota Press, 2009), 25.

60. Holland Cotter, "Postcards from Canada's New North," *New York Times*, July 23, 2009, http://www.nytimes.com.

61. Kathleen E. Ash-Milby, "Contemporary Native American Art in the

Twenty-First Century; Overcoming the Legacy," *European Review of Native American Studies* 19, no. 1 (2005): 49–54; Ash-Milby, interview with the author, April 3, 2006.

62. James Luna, interview with the author, November 11, 2005.
63. Shulman, "The Buckskin Ceiling."
64. Thomas Krens, interview, *The Charlie Rose Show*, Public Broadcasting Service, January 3, 2006. One of my own frustrations in a class I took in Native American literature was that the discussion rarely ventured beyond the works in their social context (struggle, oppression, etc.) to literary qualities (e.g., metaphor and language). I found that a young Pueblo writer in the class shared my frustration.
65. Scott Garen and Joy Harjo (Muskogee/Creek), *A Thousand Roads*, directed by Chris Eyres (Cheyenne/Arapaho). Available for viewing at NMAI, the Heye Center, and on tour around the country.

Disclosures

1. Ben McGrath, "Strangers on the Mountain," *New Yorker*, March 1, 2010, 50–55. A book about Indians in what is now New York City, Long Island, and the lower Hudson Valley is Evan T. Pritchard, *Native New Yorkers: The Legacy of the Algonquin People of New York* (San Francisco: Council Oak Books, 2002). Pritchard debunks many myths—including another refutation of the legendary twenty-four-dollar transaction for Manhattan—although some critics have found his research uneven. Also, *American Indian*, the magazine of the National Museum of the American Indian, devoted most of its fall 2006 issue to Native New York.
2. In 2002 the Heye Center of the National Museum of the American Indian in New York mounted a photo exhibit—*Booming Out*—about the Mohawk steelworkers who first "walked iron" in 1886, when they built a bridge over the Saint Lawrence River. Author's viewing of the show; Sarah Bayliss, "An Image Wedded to the Skyline," *New York Times*, July 7, 2002, http://www.nytimes.com.
3. Pueblo dogs live outdoors, like other reservation dogs. "Rez dogs" are legendary, although they are sometimes starved, abused, or without inoculations; tribes across the country are trying to address these issues.
4. I have the same disturbing thoughts about my Jewish friends who

lost family in the Holocaust or African American friends whose ancestors suffered and might have died during the passage or in slavery.

5. The ad appeared in *Spirit*, the magazine of Southwest Airlines, June 2004, 52.

6. Michael Kimmelman, "In Germany, Wild for Winnetou," *New York Times*, September 12, 2007, http://www.nytimes.com. A sampling of Tex comics is in the author's collection.

7. The ads ran widely from 2001 to 2006 in publications like *Harper's*, the *New Yorker*, and the *New York Times*.

8. Larry McMurtry, *Oh What a Slaughter: Massacres in the American West, 1846–1890* (New York: Simon and Schuster, 2005), 2.

9. Author's talk at University High School, San Francisco, October 9, 2003.

10. Robert H. Fuson, ed., *The Log of Christopher Columbus* (Blue Ridge Summit PA: Tab Books, 1992), International Marine Publishing, log entry of October 12, 1492, 75–76. In this entry, Columbus relates a conversation in which the men of San Salvador describe how people from nearby islands capture them. He concludes, "I believe that people from the mainland come here to take them as slaves."

11. As Alexis de Tocqueville coolly wrote of American Indian removals, "it having been demonstrated that one square mile could nourish ten times more civilized men than savages, it followed logically that wherever civilized men settled, savages had to make way for them. What a splendid thing is logic!" (*Letters from America*, trans. Frederick Brown, *Hudson Review* 62, no. 3 [2009], November 16, 2009, http://www.hudsonreview.com).

12. A census map shows where Indians live by counties. It is not a thing of beauty, but it shows how close Indian Country is for many Americans: http://www.census.gov/population/http://www/cen2000/atlas/pdf/censr01-107.pdf.

13. Jojola, *Urban Indians in Albuquerque*, 76.

14. Landscape or place is not merely a "sacred place" or even just "home"; it is everything. See Thomas E. Sheridan and Nancy J. Parezo, *Paths of Life: American Indians of the Southwest and Northern Mexico* (Tucson: University of Arizona Press, 1996). As the introduction to this collection of essays states: "Each group has a unique relationship with a particular landscape" (xxii). The authors explore that relationship as it shapes religion, the arts, language, and social

and economic life among ten groups, for instance, the Diné within the boundaries of the four sacred mountains (3–93) and the Hopis on their mesas (237–66).

15. *Mannahatta/Manhattan: A Natural History of New York*, an exhibition based on *The Mannahatta Project* at the Museum of the City of New York, May 20–October 12, 2009. Author's notes, October 7, 2009, and http://www.mcny.org/images/content/1/1/11600.pdf. Landscape ecologist Eric Sanderson was the lead scientist for *The Mannahatta Project*, a collaboration between the museum and the Wildlife Conservation Society. The project's website is http://themannahattaproject.org. Also see Eric Sanderson, *Mannahatta: A Natural History of New York* (New York: Abrams Books, 2009).

16. Steven Newcomb, "Perspectives: Healing, Restoration, and Rematriation," *News & Notes*, Spring–Summer 1995, 3, http://ili.nativeweb.org. Newcomb is a columnist for *Indian Country Today* and the cofounder and codirector of the Indigenous Law Institute (ILI). Also, e-mail messages to the author, September 11, 2006.

BIBLIOGRAPHIC ESSAY

The primary sources for this book are people interviewed for previously published stories and my notebooks for the stories. To those I added research, travel, university classes, and readings that are cited in the notes. Over a period of thirty years living in New Mexico, I also absorbed much through observation, conversations, and reading that might not be, strictly speaking, "sources." I have learned to treat both Indian and white sources with the same degree of analysis, ascertaining their particular perspectives and how they illuminate the shape and details of a situation.

The following essay highlights some of the sources I used most frequently and with the most pleasure. Most appear in the notes, but a few were simply part of my reading over the years.

American Indians have kept their stories and their history alive within their communities for centuries. Increasingly, they have written it down for the rest of us. Tribal websites are important sources for creation stories, history, information about living communities, and even language lessons. Veronica Tiller's *Tiller's Guide to Indian Country* is nearly indispensable for basic information. With mostly wonderful writing, the Deloria family accompanies us along the rocky road between Indian and mainstream life. Vine Deloria Jr.'s classic *Custer Died for Your Sins* remains fresh and relevant. Philip Deloria illuminates white America's long-standing and strange obsession with Indian life in *Playing Indian*. In *Indians in Unexpected Places*, he offers a new perspective on assimilation and survivance. Joe Sando's useful works about Pueblo Indians include *Pueblo Nations: Eight Centuries of Pueblo Indian History*. Paul Chaat Smith writes with a winning style in *Everything You Know about Indians Is Wrong*, a collection of his essays that appeared in 2009, after I had written most of this book. I came late to the outstanding contributions of Gerald Vizenor. While some commentators describe him as one of our most important Native thinkers or some variant, he is an original and challenging thinker and stylist in any category. The list of works by American Indian fiction writers and poets is so long that to choose among them is difficult. Ojibwe writer and critic David Treuer correctly says that the work of Indian artists is too often read as ethnography rather than literature. Indeed, I urge friends to pick up these works because they are wonderful to read. Sherman Alexie, Leslie Marmon Silko, Joy Harjo (Muskogee), and Simon Ortiz come immediately to mind as authors to whom I turn.

I have relied on several works from both academic and nonacademic non-Indians. Peter Nabokov consistently offers penetrating works about American Indian history, thought, and ordinary life. I turned frequently to *Native American Testimony*, a compendium of Indian voices he edited; I have given *Running*, about running among Indians, to my daughter, a marathoner. Jake Page's *In the Hands of the Great Spirit* and

Charles Wilkinson's *Blood Struggle* are informed surveys of American Indian history, including recent events. The National Park Service's online book *Five Views: An Ethnic Historic Site Survey for California* was produced by scholars from the state's universities and is a useful first stop for California Indian history. In *Diné, a History of the Navajos*, Peter Iverson brings together a lifetime of knowledge. John Kessell's *Kiva, Cross and Crown* is a rich vein for the early Pueblo world, even though it is primarily about Pecos. Sherry Robinson's *Apache Voices* recovered Apache oral histories that add up to eloquent individual portraits. For muted but eloquent testimony to the European American betrayal of Native America, *The Cherokee Removal*, a slim volume by Theda Perdue and Michael D. Green, is dispassionate and devastating. Similarly, Francis Paul Prucha's *American Indian Treaties: The History of a Political Anomaly* recites the details of treaties and ends with a useful list of all the agreements.

Smaller presses, including those that are tribally owned, have published a veritable flood of books. For California, Heyday Books is indispensable, while university presses at Nebraska, New Mexico, Arizona, Oklahoma, and others produce treasures. Tribal and other museum shops often feature collections of Native stories on their shelves. For a compendium of sacred and secular stories from many tribes, *American Indian Myths and Legends* by Richard Erdoes and Alfonso Ortiz (San Juan Pueblo), although published in 1984, remains valuable. A shorter and more general work is *The Mythology of Native North America* by David Leeming and Jake Page.

In no way could I physically follow up thirty years of stories and observations. Thanks to colleagues in journalism I have been able to leverage my own stories and direct readers to additional material about events I have witnessed and written about. Although news organizations have increased their coverage of Indian Country, unfortunately, too much of that coverage has focused on gaming. In the 1990s some newspapers developed Indian beats, covering a range of issues, although such progress has been cut short because of the crisis in the journalism business. In writing this book, I found myself turning regularly to a group of reporters and publications. From the *New York Times* and *High Country News* are Tim Egan, national correspondent in the Northwest; Jim Robbins (no relation); Monica Davey; and James Brooke and Iver Peterson, former Denver bureau chiefs who have since left the paper. *High Country News*, a distinguished monthly from Colorado, regularly covers substantive Indian issues in environmental and cultural contexts. At other newspapers I have followed the reporting of Leslie Linthicum (*Albuquerque Journal*), Chet Barfield (*San Diego Union-Tribune*), Jodi Rave (*Lincoln Journal-Star* and Lee Newspapers), and writers at the *New Yorker*. Mark Trahant (Shoshone-Bannock) is a distinguished reporter and editor. He was at *Indian Country Today* and later on the editorial board at the now-defunct *Seattle Post-Intelligencer*. A Kaiser Media Fellow, he reports on his blog, http://www.marktrahant.com. I have relied on the weekly *Indian Country Today* (http://www .indiancountry.com), the *Navajo Times* (http://www.navajotimes .com), and a number of Native newspapers. *Native America Calling* is required listening, and the Winnebagos' http://www .indianz.com collects articles from both mainstream and Indian publications. In the broadcast press, Daniel Kraker, KNAU Radio (NPR), Flagstaff; Harlan McKosato of *Native America Calling*; and reports from *National Native News* have been most useful. Aaron Huey's work on Pine Ridge is both devastating and inspiring.

The endnotes reflect my desire to direct readers to a wide range of sources, including scholarly and popular or mainstream venues such as libraries; different media, including printed books and other publications as well as electronic; and the

Internet, which reflects that diversity. The Internet can be both a valuable starting point as well as a place to explore more deeply. The History News Network (http://hnn.us) consistently delivers well-researched articles about the world, including Indian Country. The number of websites in and about Indian Country has exploded. Readers can use these sites to do their "homework" for visiting reservations or just to sample tribal news, thinking, and culture. Most search engines will locate a tribe's site, but here are a few URLs that will lead to the tribes as well as for tribal networks and organizations.

> http://www.ncai.org: This is the site for the National Congress of American Indians, with links to hundreds of tribal sites.
> http://www.500nations.com: This site has basic information about more than five hundred tribes by state and links to those tribes.

Links to councils or networks of tribes by region:

> http://www.itcaonline.com/index.html: Inter-Tribal Council of Arizona.
> http://www.itccinc.org: Inter-Tribal Council of California.
> http://www.colvilletribes.com: Links to Washington State tribes.

Links to professional, arts, and other organizations:

> http://www.indiangaming.org: National Indian Gaming Association, representing Indian gaming interests, with updates on the Indian Gaming Regulatory Act; state gaming groups also have their own sites.
> http://www.nigc.gov: National Indian Gaming Commission, the federal gaming regulatory and information agency.

http://www.nmai.si.edu: National Museum of the American Indian/Smithsonian Institution.

http://www.nativeamericacalling.com: *Native America Calling.*

http://www.narf.org: Native American Rights Fund/ *Cobell v. Norton* and other lawsuits.

INDEX

Page numbers in italic refer to illustrations.

Abramoff, Jack, 177, 178
Acoma Pueblo NM, 54, 63, 65–66
Acowitz (Ute Indian), 39–40
activism, 57, 73, 83, 164–69, 307n12
Agent, Dan, 219
agriculture, 3, 4, 27, 145–47; and field rotation, 51, 87–88, 144
Alaska Natives, xvi, 166
Albuquerque NM, 60, 249–50, 278; author's move to, 269–70, 271; and education, 98–102, 105–6, 313n13, 314n21, 316n33; Gathering of Nations in, 207–8, *213*; health care in, 104–5; household incomes in, 313n15;

petroglyphs near, 47–48, 150; population of American Indians in, 89, 90–91, 98–99, 311n5, 314n18; and suburbanization, 109–10, 113–15; support services in, 94–98, 101–8, 315n25; Trumbull neighborhood, 92–93, 107. *See also* urban Indian communities
Albuquerque Astronomical Society, 150
Albuquerque Indian Center, 92, 93, 94–96, *102*, 108, 196
Albuquerque Public Schools (APS), 98–102, 313n13, 316n33
Alcatraz Island CA, 165, 307n12
alcoholism, 136, 309n24, 320n11; on reservations, 79–80, 82, 89, 92–93, 315n25. *See also*

alcoholism (*cont.*)
 substance abuse
Alcoze, Thomas, 147–48, 154,
 324n35
Alexie, Sherman, xiv; *The Lone
 Ranger and Tonto Fistfight in
 Heaven*, 12
Allen, Beulah, 81
Allen, W. Ron, 158
Alvarado, Hernando de, 28–29
Alvord, Lori Arviso, 278
Ambrose, Andy, 256
American Anthropological
 Association, 41, 46
American Crafts Museum. *See*
 Museum of Arts and Design
 (MAD)
American Ethnological Society, 41
The American Indian (Scholder),
 264
American Indian Art (Feder), 236,
 239
American Indian College Fund,
 154, 278
American Indian Community
 House, 236, 266
American Indian Law Center
 (AILC), 183, 337n64
American Indian Movement (AIM),
 57, 83, 165
*American Indian Reservations and
 Indian Trust Areas* (Department
 of Commerce), 216
American Indians, xvi; and ac-
 tivism, 57, 73, 83, 164–69,
 307n12; and alcoholism,
 79–80, 136, 309n24, 315n25,
 320n11; in anthropology, 44,

49; in archaeology, 50, 51–52,
 53–54; and assimilation, 74,
 99, 101, 163, 278–79, 307n13;
 belief systems of, 140; and
 blood quantum, 75, 160–61,
 162, 185–86, 308n16; courtesy
 toward, 280–81; diet of, 142,
 352n47; and elder respect, 127;
 and identity, 75–76, 84, 88,
 113–14, 228, 290n8, 308n16;
 in journalism, 218–23; and languages, 20, 25, 26, 27, 30, 69,
 70, 75, 99, 114, 218, 307n11,
 316n33, 340n2; in law, 179–81,
 183, 335n56, 337n64; life ex-
 pectancy of, 133, 320n11; and
 mentoring, 106–7; and military
 service, 164, 330n16; and
 names, 61, 63–65, 96–97, 98;
 and "Pan-Indianism," xvi, 91,
 108, 314n22; and pop culture,
 xii, xiv, 67, 278; population of,
 xiv, 89, 90–91, 161, 289n6,
 291n1, 305n1, 311n5, 314n18,
 318n46, 328n9; and poverty
 rates, 91, 99, 124, 178, 313n15;
 preservation policies of, 53–55;
 as "primitives," 38, 43, 345n37;
 in science, 119–20, 135, 136,
 147–54, 325n45; and stereotypes, xi, xv, 8, 12, 60, 122, 133,
 172, 184, 185, 270, 277–78,
 293n11; and telephone service,
 128, 319n6; and time as process, 12, 293n11; "vanishing"
 of, xiii, 43–44, 236, 239–40,
 244–45. *See also* Navajo Nation;
 sovereignty; urban Indian com-

munities; *and individual pueblo and tribal names*

American Revolution, 159, 173

America's Child (Deo), 252, 262–63

AMTRAK Southwest Chief. *See* Southwest Chief

"Anasazi," 43, 300n41. *See also* Ancestral Puebloans

Ancestral Puebloans, 44, 51, 88, 223, 232; architecture of, 43, 300n43; and petroglyphs, 47–48, 150, 325n43, 354n53. *See also* Chaco Canyon; Mesa Verde

Anderson, Marion ("Kat"), 145, 154

animals: eagles, 125, 127, 131–33; and the Navajo Nation Zoo and Botanical Park, 117–20, 121–22, 123, 124–27, 129–31, 133, 135; and Zuni Eagle Aviary Sanctuary, 131–33

Anschuetz, Kurt, 50, 51, 237

anthropology, xii, 34, 37–42; American Indians in field of, 44, 49; and education programs, 41; and ethics, 46, 49–50; and technology, 44; and tourism, 38; women in field of, 46, 299n33. *See also* archaeology

Anza, Juan Bautista de, 146

Apaches, 90, 97, 104, 218, 271, 289n6, 317n37; and history, 28, 190, 295n16

Archaeological Conservancy, 48

archaeology, 15–16, 239, 294n9; American Indians in field of, 50, 51–52, 53–54; and collaborative work, 50–53; compliance-driven, 44–45, 48, 52–53; development of, 40–41, 43, 44–45, 47–50; and expedition sites, 38–40, 41, 42–43, 48, 298n29, 299n33; perception of, as grave robbing, 17, 25, 37, 294n10; and petroglyphs, 47–48, 150, 325n43, 354n53; and preservation policies of American Indians, 53–55; and technology, 48; women in field of, 299n33. *See also* anthropology

art, 94, 102, 266–67; and the "buckskin box," 237, 238–41, 244, 250; in casinos, 170; and collectors, 249–50, 253; contemporary, 254–66; and definition of "authentic Native work," 236–38, 239–40, 242, 255–56, 265–67, 348n20; and education, 81, 253–54; and "Indian markets," 240, 241–42, 251, 253; and museum exhibits, 235–36, 243, 244, 245–49, 254–55, 256–62, 265–66, 349n23, 350n28, 350n34, 353n51; Navajo, 80–82, 128, 239, 243; and tourism, 239–40, 241

Arthur, Claudeen Bates, 186–87

The Artifact Piece (Luna), 235–36

Arviso, Tom, 219

Ashiwi. *See* Zunis (Ashiwi)

Ash-Milby, Kathleen, 266

assimilation, 163, 278–79, 307n13; and education, 74, 99, 101. *See also* termination and relocation

Auger, Rose, 141, 142, 143
"Aunt Jane." *See* Dumas, Jane
("Aunt Jane")
Avery, Dawn Kawenno:ta'as:
Tripartita, 210–11
Avila, Elena, 141, 142

Babbitt, Bruce, 168
Bahkyula (Bahkyush people), 34,
297n26
Baines, David Ray, 139–41,
322n26
Balaran, Alan, 168
Bandelier, Adolph, 39
Bandelier National Monument, 31
Banks, Dennis, 57
Barboncito, 191
Barentine, John, 354n53
Barona powwow, 205–6, 342n11.
See also Kumeyaay people; pow-
wows
Barona Ranch Casino, 170
Bean, Lowell, 146
Bedard, Irene, 241
Begay, Fred, 81, 230
Begay, Notah, 69
Begay, Robert, 54
Begaye, Kelsey, 118, 120, 123, 124
Bender, Scott, 118, 124–25, 246
Benedict, Ruth, 42, 46, 50
Bergh, Henry, 326n48
BIA. *See* Bureau of Indian Affairs
(BIA)
Bigfeather, Joanna, 246, 253, 255,
350n30
Birdeau, George, 245
Bird Song and Dance Festival,
202–3

bison, 151–54, 326nn47–49,
327n50
Black Eagle (drum group), 56,
305n73
Blackfeet Nation, 167–68
Blomberg, Nancy, 248
blood quantum, 160–61, 162,
185–86, 222; and identity, 75,
228, 308n16. *See also* identity,
American Indian
Bluehouse, Milton, 118, 120
Blythe, Frank, 229, 230
Boas, Franz, 41, 42, 50
Bokovoy, Matthew, 240–41
Bosque Redondo, *175*, 189–91,
192, 281, 339n79. *See also* sovereignty
Bourland, Gregg, 192
Braine, Susan, *214*, 224, 226–27
Brown, Willie, 111, 112
Browne, John, 151
Browner, Tara, 208
Bsumek, Erika, 239–40
"buckskin box," 237, 238–39, 240,
244, 250. *See also* art
"buckskin ceiling." *See* "buckskin
box"
buffalo. *See* bison
Buffalo Dance, 197, 200–201. *See
also* ceremonials
Bureau of (American) Ethnology,
41
Bureau of Indian Affairs (BIA),
31, 152, 162, 253, 332n32,
336n57; and land manage-
ment, 166, 167–68, 173; and
termination and relocation,
163

Burger, Warren, 181
Bush, George H. W., 16
Bush, George W., 70, 158, 183
Byrd, Joe, 219

Cabrilho, João Rodrigues, 3
Cabrillo. *See* Cabrilho, João
   Rodrigues
Cabrillo Festival, 5–6, 9, 10–11,
   292n6, 293n10
Cabrillo National Monument, 1,
   2–3, 5–6, 9, 10, 196
California Indian Radio Project,
   145, 146
Campo, Dwain, 56
Canby, William C., Jr., 181,
   336n61
Cannon, T. C., 238, 264
Canyon de Chelly AZ, 122, 129,
   190–91, 192–93. *See also*
   Navajo Nation
Canyon de Chelly (Curtis), 244
Capone, Patricia, 21, 32
Cardinal, Douglas, 55
Carleton, James T., 190
Carson, Christopher ("Kit"), 190
"casino Indians," 172. *See also* ste-
   reotypes
casinos. *See* gaming
*Celebrate 40,000 Years of American
   Art* (Quick-to-See Smith), 258
ceremonials, 12, 115, 232; and
   animals, 127, 129, 131–32;
   and attire, 199, 200–201, 206,
   341n4; Bird Song and Dance
   Festival, 202–3; and cornmeal
   use, 20, 33, 64, 201, 276;
   and dancing, 26, 197–201,

204, 205–7, 276; and drums,
   196–97, 199, 206–7; naming
   ceremonies, 64, 96–97, 98;
   and the National Museum of
   the American Indian (NMAI),
   55–57; powwows, 203–8,
   213, 342nn10–11; and Pueblo
   Indians, 197–202, 203, 274,
   276, 341n6; and religion,
   199–200, 208, 276, 341n6;
   and repatriation of remains at
   Pecos, 20, 24–25, 33–34, 36;
   and tobacco use, 95–96; and
   tourism, 78, 201–3, 204
Certificate of Degree of Indian
   Blood (CDIB), 162. *See also*
   blood quantum
Chaat Smith, Paul, 260, 265,
   353n51
Chaco Canyon, 27, 28, 65, 88, 150,
   325nn43–44; as archaeological
   site, 39, 43, 299n33; and the
   Chaco Synthesis Project, 45,
   49, 301n50; decline of civilization in, 144, 324n35; population estimates, 295n13
Chacon, Raven: *Lightning*, 211
Changing Hands (exhibit), 248, 262
Chase, Landis, 20–21
Cherokees, 59, 219, 289n6, 305n1;
   and the Cherokee Free and
   Independent Press Act, 219;
   and the Cherokee Removal,
   113, 157, 160, 328n6; freedmen, 185–86, 337n67; and
   tribal membership, 185–86,
   337n67
"the Chief." *See* Southwest Chief

Choudhary, Trib, 123–24
Church, Casey, 115
Church, Lora, 115, 196
Cicuye people, 28, 29
Circle of Light (Kahn), 80–82
Circle of Light Navajo Educational Project (CLNEP), 81–82
Clark, William, 4, 38
Clayton, Lorenzo, 248, 252, 261–62
Cliff Palace, 39–40, 43. *See also* Mesa Verde
Clinton, William J., 48, 138
Cloud Image (Namingha), 262
Cobell, Elouise, 167–69
Coby, Alonzo, xv
code talkers (Navajo), 69, 70, 307n11. *See also* Navajo Nation
colonization, European, 159, 217–18, 231–32, 295n12. *See also* explorers
Columbus, Christopher, 279, 356n10
Colville Cultural Resources Protection Act, 53, 303n66
compacts (gaming revenue-sharing agreements), xv, 109, 173, 174, 179, 184, 290n7, 334n45. *See also* gaming
compliance-driven archaeology, 44–45, 48, 52–53. *See also* archaeology
Connell-Szasz, Margaret, 316n31
Cooday, Jesse, 236, 243, 264
Cook, Holly, 222
Cordell, Linda, 45, 50, 231–32
Cordova, Judith, 48
Corn Dance, 197, 198, 200. *See also* ceremonials

cornmeal, 20, 33, 64, 201, 276. *See also* ceremonials
Cortés, Hernán, 5
Cotter, Holland, 265
Coulter, Mary, 239
Council of Energy Resource Tribes (CERT), 216
Coyhis, Don, 96, 97–98
Cripps, John T., 186
Cuero, Delfina, 161
cultural resource management (CRM), 45, 48. *See also* archaeology
Curtis, Edward, 243–45, 246, 264, 349n24
Cushing, Emily, 298n29
Cushing, Frank Hamilton, 39, 41, 298n29
Custer Died for Your Sins (Deloria), 49
Cyndee (Pecos descendant), 19

Dalton, Doran, 223, 227
dancing, 26, 197–201, 204, 205–7, 341n4. *See also* ceremonials
Dancing with Photons (videos), 230
Davids, Brent Michael, 229; *Powwow Symphony*, 208–10
Davis, Gray, 174
Dawes Act of 1887, 160–61, 162, 185, 308n16. *See also* blood quantum
DeCorti, Espera (Iron Eyes Cody), 144, 323n32
Deloria, Philip ("Sam"), 119, 183–84, 185, 319n3, 337n64
Deloria, Vine, 49, 50

Denver Art Museum, 236, 242–43, 248–49

Deo, Steven: *America's Child*, 252, 262–63; *Perpetual Stream*, 265–66

Desert Archaeology, Inc., 52–53. *See also* compliance-driven archaeology

d'Harnoncourt, René, 243

diabetes, 105, 136, 138, 142, 322n29, 352n47; death rate from, 320n11. *See also* health care

diaspora, Indian, 88–89, 97, 204. *See also* urban Indian communities

DiMattio, Terry, 10, 11

Diné (the People). *See* Navajo Nation

Diné Bikéyah. *See* Navajo Nation

Diné Community College, 120–21, 166

Dixon, Joseph Kossuth, 349n24

Dixon, Maynard, 239, 347n11

Dolchok, Lisa, 141, 142

Domenici, Pete, 48

Doot'izhii Dziil (Turquoise Mountain of Strength). *See* Mount Taylor

Dorgan, Byron L., 183

Dossett, John, 182–83

Douglas, Frederic H., 243

drums, 56, 97, 112, 115, 195–97, 198, 199, 206–7, 305n73. *See also* music

Dubray, Fred, 151–54

Dumas, Jane ("Aunt Jane"), 1, 2–3, 6, 7, 8–11, 14, 269; honors received by, 10

Dunn, Dorothy, 250, 253

Durham, Jimmie, 238

Duthu, N. Bruce, 181

Eagle Aviary Sanctuary, 131–33

eagles, 125, 127, 131–33. *See also* animals

Eakins, Thomas, 39

economic development, 83–84, 124, 178, 217; in the Navajo Nation, 77, 83, 123–24, 130, 166. *See also* gaming

education, 69, 89, 94, 313n13, 314n21, 316n31; and art, 253–54; and assimilation, 74, 99, 101; boarding schools, 61, 73–75, 307n13; and casino revenue, 109; and languages, 69, 99, 316n33; and parental involvement, 100–102; and urban migration, 98–102, 105–6, 109

Edward S. Curtis: The Women (Erdrich), 245

Eiteljorg, Harrison, 349n23

Ellis Tanner Trading Company, 80–82

Elson, Mark, 53

Embassy of Tribal Nations, 164, 176

Emendatio (Luna), 251, 258–61, 353n51

Erdrich, Louise: *Edward S. Curtis: The Women*, 245

ethnography: and art, 245, 248. *See also* anthropology

expatriation, 11–12, 88–92,

expatriation (*cont.*)
　311n3. *See also* repatriation;
　urban Indian communities
explorers, 6, 217–18, 279–80; and
　agriculture, 3, 4, 144, 146; and
　anthropology, 38; and coloni-
　zation, 159, 217–18, 231–32,
　295n12; and place names, 63,
　64, 295n15; and population
　of pre-contact North America,
　291n1; from Spain, 3–4, 27,
　28–29, 47, 231, 295nn15–16,
　296n17, 341n6
Exposition of Indian Tribal Arts
　(1931), 243

Feder, Norman, 236–38, 242, 248,
　255–56, 349n22; *American
　Indian Art*, 236, 239. *See also* art
Federal Bar Association: Indian
　law division, 180–81, 183
Federation of Mission Indians, 164
Fewkes, Jesse Walter, 39, 40, 50
Fire Rock Casino, 177–78
Fire Thunder, Cecelia, 187
First American Art (exhibit), 245,
　246–47, 257, 266, 350n28,
　350n31
Fitzgerald, F. Scott, 211, 343n17
flags (Native American), 1, 2–3, 6,
　7, 9–11, 196, 269, 293n10
Flathead Salish (people), xi–xii
Fonseca, Harry, 253
Fort, Karen, 353n51
Fort Rosecrans Military
　Reservation, 4–5
Fort Sumner. *See* Bosque Redondo
1491 (Mann), 231, 291n1

Foxwoods Casino, 170, 178, 188
Frank, Ross, 244–45
Franklin, Benjamin, 159
Franklin, Keith, 113, 196
Franklin, Matt, 187
freedmen (Cherokee), 185–86,
　337n67. *See also* Cherokees
Friendship House, 110–12
From Folsom to Fogelson (National
　Park Service), 35

Gachupin, Raymond, 23–24
Gallup NM, 60, 78–80, 129,
　310n31
gaming, 134, 318n44; benefits
　of, 312n11; and casino archi-
　tecture, 170; and economic
　development, 83–84, 124, 178,
　217; history of, 169–71; and
　media reporting, 188, 221–22;
　opposition to, 172–73, 177,
　188; rejection of, by Native
　Americans, 31, 77, 124, 177–
　78; and revenue, 65–66, 169,
　171–72, 178, 222, 332n32,
　335n53; and revenue-sharing
　compacts, xv, 109, 173, 174,
　179, 184, 290n7, 334n45; and
　sovereignty, 109–10, 156, 169,
　178–79, 184–85, 187–89; sup-
　port for, 170–71
gangs, 72, 75–76, 99
Garcia, Lorissa, 114
Gates, Henry Louis, Jr., 265
Gathering of Nations, 207–8, 213.
　See also powwows
General Allotment Act. *See* Dawes
　Act of 1887

Getches, David, 181, 336n61

Gilpin, Laura, 349n24

Gingrich, Newt, 155, 156–58

Gonzales, Alberto, 183

Gordon, Gerry, 225

Gorman, Carl (Nelson Carl), 61, 70, 72, 73, 74, 81

Gorman, Mary, 69–70

Gorman, R. C., 72

Gorman, Zonnie, xi, 71, 83, 86, 87, 166, 305n4; as AMTRAK guide, 60, 61, 62, 63, 65–68, 85; and family life, 69–70, 72–74, 83, 85, 86; name of, 61; and reservation problems, 75–76; and tourism job, 78, 80–82. See also Navajo Nation

Gover, Kevin, 336n57

Grant, Saginaw, 204

Gray, Harold, 95, 102

Great Sioux Nation. See Sioux

Guassac, Louis, 9–10

Hale, Albert, 156–58, 165, 219

Hall, Tex, 165, 178, 330n17

Hancock, John, 300n43

Haozous, Robert (Bob), 253, 254, 266

Harjo, Susan Shown, 237, 346n6

Harrison, David, 216

Harrison, Merry, 51–52

Harvard University, Peabody Museum. See Peabody Museum of Archaeology and Ethnology (Harvard University)

Harvey Indian Tour ("Indian Detour"), 239

Hatam, Manuel, 8

Hathaway, Loline, 118, 124–26

Haudenosaunee, People of the Long House (Iroquois League), 64, 88, 159, 306n9

health care: and environmental issues, 143–44; herbalism, 8, 9, 137–39, 142–43, 293n9, 323n30; and the Indian Health Service, 79, 90, 103–5, 133–34, 136–37, 166, 317nn36–37; and spirituality, 143, 323n31; traditional medicine, 8–9, 133, 136, 137–44, 321nn22–23

Hefflefinger, Tom, 183

Hemenway, Mary, 39

Hemenway Southwestern Archaeological Expedition, 39, 40

herbalism, 8, 9, 137–39, 142–43, 293n9, 323n30. See also health care

Herrington, John Bennett, 136, 150

Hewett, Edgar Lee, 39, 41, 42, 241, 243

Heye, George Gustav, 54, 246, 304n71

Heye Center, 235–36, 245–48, 265, 266, 304n71, 355n2. See also National Museum of the American Indian (NMAI)

Hill, Richard, 237, 346n6

Hodge, Frederick, 298n29

hogans, xi, 62, 77, 305n5, 352n43. See also teepees

Hollow, Walt, 140–41

Hollywood Casino, 272, 274

Holy People, 118, 121, 126–28.

Holy People (*cont.*)
 See also religion
Hopi Foundation, 225, 226
Hopis, 56, 65, 245; and compli-
 ance-driven archaeology, 52–
 53; and preservation policies,
 54; radio station (KUYI), *214*,
 223–28, 229
Hoskie, Anderson, 126–27, 141,
 142–43
House, Donna, 55
A House Made of Dawn (Momaday),
 34, 297n26
Houser, Allan, 238, 254, 263–64,
 346n7
Hua-na-tota, 28. *See also* Jemez
 Pueblo NM
Hubbard, Clyde, 207
Huey, Aaron, 92–93
Hweeldi. *See* Bosque Redondo
Hyde, Frederick, 39
Hyde Exploring Expedition, 39.
 See also Chaco Canyon

identity, American Indian, 84; ap-
 propriation of, by European
 Americans, 290n8; and blood
 quantum, 75, 228, 308n16; and
 reservations, 75–76; and urban
 American Indians, 88, 113–14.
 See also American Indians
Indian Art of the United States (mu-
 seum exhibit), 243
Indian Arts and Crafts Board
 (IACB), 243, 348n20
Indian Country, definition of, xvi,
 109. *See also* American Indians
Indian Detour. *See* Harvey Indian
Tour ("Indian Detour")
Indian Fair. *See* "Indian markets"
Indian Gaming Regulatory Act
 (IGRA), 169, 332n37. *See also*
 gaming
Indian Health Service, 79, 90, 133,
 317n37; funding of, 103–5,
 134, 136–37, 166, 317n36; and
 trust responsibility, 134, 136.
 See also health care
"Indian markets," 240, 241–42,
 251, 253, 347n15. *See also* art
Indian Removal Act (1830), 160,
 328n6
Indian Reorganization Act (IRA),
 161–62
Indians. *See* American Indians
Indian Self-Determination and
 Education Act, 84–85, 163,
 166, 169
"Indian time," 12, 293n11. *See also*
 stereotypes
Indian wars, 159, 160, 161
indigenous people. *See* American
 Indians
Institute for American Indian Arts
 (IAIA), 250, 253–54
Inter Tribal Bison Cooperative
 (ITBC), 151–54, 326n49
Inter-Tribal Indian Ceremonial, 78
*An Introduction to the Study of
 Southwestern Archaeology*
 (Kidder), 42–43
"Iron Eyes Cody," 144, 323n32
Iroquois League (Haudenosaunee,
 People of the Long House), 64,
 88, 159, 306n9
"Ishi" (Yahi/Yana man), 46

Isleta del Sur, 65, 104

Jack, Lyle, 134, 136

Jackson, Andrew, 113, 160, 328n6

"Jackson Whites" (Ramapough Lenapes), 270. *See also* Lenapes

Jacob, Dianne, 179

James (Pecos descendant), 19

Jamul Reservation, 8, 172

Jefferson, Thomas, 38

Jemez Pueblo NM, 31, 104, 296n20; and assimilation, 30–31; burial mound at, 15–17; history of, 26–27, 28–30, 295n14; population of, 28, 30; and repatriation of Pecos Pueblo remains, 2, 16, 17–25, 30, 31–34, 36, 37, 281–82, 293n2, 294n4; runners, 30–31, 296n21; virtual museum of, 54, 304n69

Johns, Jasper: *Map*, 257

Johnson, Lyndon B., 30, 81, 163

Johnson, Samuel, 254

Jojola, Theodore, 107, 109

Jones, Johnpaul, 55

Jourdain, Floyd, 222

Kahn, Chester: *Circle of Light* (mural), 80–82

Kaweshtima (Place of Snow). *See* Mount Taylor

Kennedy, David Michael, 345n39; *Tesuque Buffalo Dancer*, 232–33

Kennedy, John, 163

Kidder, Alfred Vincent ("Ted"), 50; *An Introduction to the Study of Southwestern Archaeology*, 42–43; and Pecos Pueblo burial mound, 15–17, 18, 42

King, Frank, 220

Kirtland Air Force Base, 93–94

Kisko, Gerard, 141, 142

Klah, Hastin, 348n17

Koahnic Broadcasting Corporation (KBC), 226–27, 229. *See also* media; radio station (KUYI)

Krens, Thomas, 267

Kroeber, Alfred, 41, 42, 46

Kumeyaay-Diegueño Nation. *See* Kumeyaay people

Kumeyaay people, 8, 83–84, 110, 161, 205; flag of the, 1, 2–3, 6, 7, 9–11, 196, 269; and Kumeyaay-Diegueño Unity, 9; language of the, 10; and powwows, 205–6, 342n11

KUYI (radio station), 214, 223–28, 229

Lamberth, Royce C., 168–69

LaMere, Frank, 181, 183, 336n60

land reclamation, xv, 166, 173

languages, 75, 114, 218, 340n2; and the Acoma Language Nest, 114; and code talkers, 69, 70, 307n11; and educational policy, 69, 99, 316n33; and "kiva" meaning, 150–51; Towa, 20, 25, 26, 27, 30

Larson, John, 149

Lawrence, D. H., 296n21

LeBeau, Bennie E., 51–52

LeBow, Fred, 30–31

Lekson, Stephen, 49–50, 295n13

Lenapes, 144, 270, 282

Lewerenz, Dan, 220, 223

Lewis, Meriwether, 4, 38

Liebling, A. J., 220
Lightning (Chacon), 211
Lincoln, Abraham, 20
Link, Martin, 129–30
Littlechild, George, 246
Lobo, Frank, 145
Lockington, David, 208–10
Locust, Carol, 141, 143
Loew, Patricia, 221–22
Lomaomvaya, Michah, 52–53
The Lone Ranger and Tonto Fistfight in Heaven (Alexie), 12
Long Walk (Navajo), 189–91, 339n79. *See also* Bosque Redondo; Navajo Nation
Looking Horse, Avrol, 315n28
Lord, Erica, 235–36
Los Alamos National Laboratory (LANL), 31, 81, 149, 150–51
Low Dog, Tieraona, 137–39, 143–44, 321nn22–23
Lowe, Truman, 353n51
Lucero, Jimmy, 223–24
Lucky Bear Casino, 170
Luna, James, 262, 266; *The Artifact Piece*, 235–36; *Emendatio*, 251, 258–61, 353n51
Luna, Nelson, 132
Lyon, Cheri, 104

MacDonald, Peter, 77
Madalena, Joshua, 19, 25
Made in America (Quick-to-See Smith), 256–57
Magill, Margaret, 298n29
Mahle, Harlan, 224, 225
Malevich, Kasimir, 267
Manifest Destiny, 44, 280

Mankiller, Wilma, 186
Mann, Charles, 291n1; *1491*, 231, 291n1
The Mannahatta Project (exhibit), 282, 357n15
Map (Johns), 257
"Marie," 269, 271–77; and family relationships, 277; and religious life, 276
Marshall, John, 160
Martine-Alonzo, Nancy, 98, 99, 100, 101–3
Martinez, Mario, 247
Martinez, Paddy, 62
Mashantucket Pequots, 54, 109–10
Mason, Charlie, 39
Mateus, Jorge Arévalo, 353n51
May, Karl, 278
Mayo, Lisa, 247
McGrath, Ben, 270
McKenzie, Taylor, 81
McKerchie, Burt, 226
McKerchie, Marshall, 226
McKosato, Harlan, 214, 222, 227–29
McMurtry, Larry, 279
Mead, Margaret, 42, 46
media, 230, 345n33; and newspapers, 219–23; radio station KUYI, 214, 223–28, 229
medicine, traditional. *See* health care
Meriam Report, 307n13. *See also* assimilation
Mesa Verde, 42, 44, 88; Cliff Palace at, 39–40, 43
Mexican-American War, 4, 39,

296n17, 308n8
Mexico, 3–4
Michaelis, Don, 249
Michaelis, Pamela, 249, 250
Michelson, Alan, 247–48
Miguel, Gloria, 247
Miguel, Muriel, 247
Miller, John J., 177
Milord, Jerome L., 347n15
mining, 62–63, 65, 77, 144–45, 324n36. *See also* natural resource management
Minuit, Peter, 270
Mirelez, Michael, 203
Miss Indian World Contest, 207–8
Mohegan Sun Casino, 178
Momaday, N. Scott, 34, 37, 296n21; *A House Made of Dawn*, 34, 297n26
Monroe, Dan L., 249
Morgan, Lawrence, 189–90
Morgan, Lewis Henry, 41
Morgan, Michelle, 33
Morris, Irvin, 77
Morrison, Georg, 238
Mount Taylor, 65, 306n8; names of, 63
Murphy, Dennis, 225
Murphy family, *101*, 114–15
Museum of Arts and Design (MAD), 248, 262, 265–66, 350n34
Museum of Mankind, 256
Museum of Modern Art (MOMA), 243, 256
Museum of New Mexico, 41, 241, 242
Museum of the American Indian

(MAI), 54–55, 270, 304n71
music, 195–96, 199–200, 208–11; and drums, 56, 97, 112, 115, 195–97, 198, 199, 206–7
Mussorgsky, Modest, 254
Myer, Dillon S., 163
Myre, Nadia, xii
Mythistoryquest (Clayton), 252, 261–62

Nabokov, Peter, 293n11, 303n62, 339n79
NAGPRA. *See* Native American Graves Protection and Repatriation Act (NAGPRA)
Namingha, Dan: *Cloud Image*, 262
Napolitano, Janet, 64–65
National American Indian Court Judges Association, 180
National Congress of American Indians (NCAI), 164–65, 183, 336n61
National Eagle Repository, 131, 162
National Historic Preservation Act (1966), 49
National Indian Council on Aging (NICOA), 95
National Indian Gaming Association, 174
National Indian Health Board, 134
National Indian Youth Council, 103, 105
National Museum of the American Indian (NMAI), 2, 54–57, 155, 267, 304n71, 336n57; Heye Center, 235–36, 245–48, 265, 266, 304n71, 355n2. *See also* art

National Native American Law
Students Association (NNALSA),
176, 180
National Park Service (NPS), 5–6,
192; *From Folsom to Fogelson*,
35; and the Pecos Pueblo repatriation, 19, 20, 23, 24, 33. *See
also* Chaco Canyon
National Tribal Justice Resource
Center, 180
Native America Calling (radio pro-
gram), 214, 227–29, 230
Native American Community
Academy, 94, 100
Native American Design
Collaborative, 55
Native American Graves
Protection and Repatriation
Act (NAGPRA), 2, 13, 47, 48,
49–50, 85; and art, 238, 254,
351n41; and number of re-
mains returned to tribes, 18,
297n24; and the Pecos Pueblo
remains, 16, 17–18, 21, 22–23,
31–33, 34; signing of the, 16.
See also repatriation
Native American Journalists
Association (NAJA), 218–23
Native American Music Awards
(Nammys), 68–69
Native American Public
Telecommunications (NAPT),
229–30
Native American Rights Fund
(NARF), 168, 336n61
Native Americans. *See* American
Indians
Native Arts and Culture

Foundation, 351n41
Native people. *See* American
Indians
natural resource management,
166–67, 324n37; agriculture
and forestry, 51, 87–88, 144,
145–49; and bison, 151–54;
mining, 62–63, 65, 77, 144–45,
324n36
Navajo Museum, 126, 127–28, 129
Navajo Nation, 82, 107, 331n27;
and alcoholism, 79–80, 82; and
art, 80–82, 128, 239, 243; and
Bosque Redondo, 175, 189–91,
192, 281, 339n79; chapter
divisions in the, 317n39; and
code talkers, 69, 70, 307n11;
Department of Archaeology,
54; digital network of the, 128;
and Diné name, 306n9; and
economic development, 77, 83,
123–24, 130, 166; and gaming,
77, 124, 177–78; and gangs,
72, 75–76; and hogans, xi, 62,
77, 305n5, 352n43; homeland
of the, 59–60, 63, 85–86,
90–91, 117–18, 122–23,
190–91, 192–93; and the Long
Walk, 189–91; marching band,
74–75; and mining, 62–63, 77,
144–45, 324n36; population
of the, 59, 289n6, 305n1; and
preservation policies, 53–54;
and religion, 118, 120, 121,
126–28; and sovereignty, 156–
58, 166–67, 168–69, 186, 215;
and storytelling, 63, 76–77,
125; and suicide, 82, 89–90;

and tourism, 77, 124, 130, 192–93; tribal government, 77, 120, 156, 157, 186–87. *See also* American Indians

Navajo Nation Cultural Resources Protection Act, 303n66

Navajo Nation Zoo and Botanical Park, 117–20, 121–22, 123, 124–27, 129–31, 133, 135. *See also* Navajo Nation

New, Lloyd Kiva, 253

Newcomb, Frances, 348n17

Newcomb, Steven, 283

A New Kind of Science (Wolfram), 149–50

New Mexico Symphony Orchestra, 109

Newsom, Gavin, 111

newspapers, 219–23, 343n22. *See also* media

New Tribe New York (exhibit), 245, 247–48, 261–62, 350n28

New York Roadrunners Club, 30–31

New York Times, xvi, 21–22, 192–93, 244, 257, 265, 294n4, 314n20, 315n25

Nixon, Richard M., 84, 163

Nordenskjold, Gustav, 40

The North American Indian (Curtis), 244

Norton, Gale, 168

Obama, Barack, 134, 168, 182

Office of Navajo Economic Opportunity (ONEO), 166

Oglala Sioux. *See* Sioux

Oklahoma Land Run (1889), 47

Oktibihah (Tate), 210

Oneidas, 87, 170, 173, 219, 333n43

Ortiz, Simon, xiv, 48

Osage with van Gogh (Cannon), 264

Oystercatcher Rattle (Singletary), 263

Padilla, Randy, 23, 24, 37

Panama-California Exposition, 240–41

"Pan-Indianism," xvi, 91, 108, 314n22. *See also* American Indians

Passamaquoddy Tribe, 166

Pataki, George E., 318n44

"Patterson bundle," 51–52

Peabody Museum of Archaeology and Ethnology (Harvard University), 16, 18, 21–22, 23, 31–34, 46; and medical studies of Pecos remains, 33, 297n25; and number of remains, 32, 297n24

Pecos, Regis, 24

Pecos Conference, 43, 45, 51–52

Pecos Ethnographic Project, 23

Pecos National Historical Park, 19. *See also* Pecos Pueblo NM

Pecos Pueblo NM, 26, 28, 30, 88; burial mound at, 15–17, 42; history of, 26–27, 28–30, 294n11, 295n12; map of, 35; population of, 29–30; and repatriation of ancestral remains, 2, 16, 17–25, 30, 31–34, 36, 37, 281–82, 293n2, 294n4; ruins of, 27. *See also* Jemez Pueblo NM

Pelasara, Rick, 353n51
the People (Diné). *See* Navajo
    Nation
Pepper, George H., 39
Perez, Jon, 137
Perpetual Stream (Deo), 265–66
Petroglyph National Monument,
    48
petroglyphs, 47–48, 150, 325n43,
    354n53. *See also* archaeology
Philip III (Spain), 20
Phillips, Tom, 112
Phillips Academy, Andover, 16,
    20–21, 42. *See also* Peabody
    Museum of Archaeology and
    Ethnology (Harvard University)
Pico, Anthony, 83–84
Pictures at an Exhibition
    (Mussorgsky), 254
Piestewa Peak, 64–65, 306n10
Piestewa, Lori, 64–65
Pine Ridge Reservation, 83, 89,
    92–93, 230, 314n19. *See also*
    reservations; Sioux
place names, 63, 65, 66, 295n15,
    306n8, 306n10
Plummer, Cathlena, 127–28
Point, Susan, 263
Point Loma. *See* Cabrillo National
    Monument
Polk, James K., 306n8
Pootoogook, Annie, 265
Popé, 29
Portolá, Gaspar de, 4
Posu Gai Hoo-oo (Where Water
    Slides down Arroyo). *See* Sandia
    Mountains
Powell, John Wesley, 40–41

Powell, Ron, 112
powwows, 203–7; Barona
    powwow, 205–6, 342n11;
    Gathering of Nations, 207–8,
    213; and homecomings,
    342n10; sponsorship of, 207.
    See also ceremonials
Powwow Symphony (Davids),
    208–10
Preservation of American
    Antiquities Act (1906), 40
"primitive" art, 236, 240. *See also*
    art
Pueblo Bonito NM, 39, 43, 88. *See*
    also Chaco Canyon
Pueblo Revolt of 1680, 29, 161,
    273, 295n16
pueblos. *See* Ancestral Puebloans;
    and individual pueblo names
Putnam, Frederic W., 41, 46,
    303n61

Quick-to-See Smith, Jaune, xi–xii,
    238, 255–58, 262
Quinault Casino and Resort, 170,
    212

radio station (KUYI), 214,
    223–28, 229. *See also* Koahnic
    Broadcasting Corporation
    (KBC); media
railroad. *See* Southwest Chief
Ramapough Lenapes ("Jackson
    Whites"), 270. *See also* Lenapes
Ramos, Marisa, 94
Randolph, Hans, 40
Ration, Norman, 103–4, 105–7,
    108

Red Lake Chippewa Reservation, 196, 222, 312n10
Redmond, Bill, 155, 156
Rehnquist, William, 181
Reitman, Connie, 187–88
religion, 115, 120, 276, 341n6; Holy People (Navajo), 118, 121, 126–28; and missionaries, 4
rematriation, 282–83. *See also* repatriation
Reno, Janet, 168
repatriation, xii, 13–14, 132–33, 282–83; and activism, 83, 269; and art, 255; and the Cabrillo Festival flag ceremony, 10–11; and media coverage, 294n4; of Pecos Pueblo ancestral remains, 2, 16, 17–25, 30, 31–34, 36, 37, 281–82, 293n2, 294n4; and sacred objects, 293n3, 297n24; and sovereignty, 2, 185. *See also* expatriation; Native American Graves Protection and Repatriation Act (NAGPRA)
reservations, 86, 277–78, 312n9; alcoholism on, 79–80, 82, 89, 92–93, 315n25; and education, 89, 99; employment rates on, 91; and gangs, 72, 75–76; and Indian identity, 75–76; Jamul, 8, 172; and jurisdiction, 181–83, 336n61; Pine Ridge, 83, 89, 92–93, 230, 314n19; and population, 305n1; and poverty, 124, 178, 313n15; Red Lake Chippewa, 196, 222, 312n10; and "rez dogs," 273, 355n3; Sioux, 83,

89, 92–93, 230, 314n19; and suicide rates, 82, 89–90, 92; termination and relocation, 88, 162–65, 236, 237–38, 311n3, 329nn11–12; urban migration from, 88–92. *See also* gaming; Navajo Nation; urban Indian communities
Return (Point), 263
Rhodd, Ben K., 37
River Rock Casino, 170
Roche, David M., 250
Rockefeller, John D., Mrs., 243
Roosevelt, Franklin D., 161–62
Roosevelt, Theodore, 40
Route 66 Revisited: It Was Only an Indian (Teters), 264

Sakiestewa, Ramona, 55, 255
Sanderson, Eric, 357n15
Sandia Mountains, 66, 173; American Indian names for, 66
Sandia National Laboratories, 93–94, 314n21
Sandia Pueblo NM, 109, 173
San Didacus. *See* San Diego CA
San Diego CA: and the Cabrillo National Monument, 1, 2–3, 5–6, 9, 10, 196; and the Fort Rosecrans Military Reservation, 4–5; Indian Health Center in, 8–9
Sandlin, Stephanie, 183
Sando, Ruben, 20
San Felipe Pueblo NM, 155, 197, 201–2, 272–75; and education, 277; and religion, 276
San Francisco CA, 110–12,

San Francisco CA (*cont.*)
318n46. *See also* urban Indian
communities
San Mateo. *See* Mount Taylor
San Miguel. *See* San Diego CA
Santa Fe NM, 278; art galler-
ies in, 249, 351n41; Indian
Market, 240, 241–42, 251, 253,
347n15; School of American
Research, 41
Santa Fe Indian School, 61, 114
"Santa Fe style," 239, 347n15
Saubel, Katherine, 145, 146
Scares Hawk, Duane, 94, 102
Scholder, Fritz, 238, 253, 264
Schoolcraft, Henry Rowe, 38
School for Advanced Research, 41,
242, 299n37
School of American Research. *See*
School for Advanced Research
Schwarzenegger, Arnold, xv, 174,
290n7, 334n45
Self-Determination Act. *See*
Indian Self-Determination and
Education Act
Serra, Junípero, 4, 161
Shendo, Bennie, 20
Sheridan, Philip H., 326n48
Sherman, William Tecumseh,
190–91, 326n48
Shinnecock Indian Nation, 173,
333n42
Shirley, Joe, Jr., 86, 186, 189
Sickey, David, 177
Singletary, Preston, 263
Sioux, 59, 96–97, 153, 187, 289n6,
315n28; and burial practices,
191–92; and health care, 134–

35; reservations of the, 83, 89,
92–93, 230, 314n19. *See also*
American Indians
Sitting Up, Norman, 92–93, 98,
317n34
"Sky City." *See* Acoma Pueblo NM
Skywalk, 185
Sloan, David N., 191
Sloan, John, 243
smallpox, 88, 192
Smith, Chadwick, 219
Smith, Jaune Quick-to-See. *See*
Quick-to-See Smith, Jaune
Smith, Neal Ambrose, 258
Smithsonian Institution, 32, 41,
256; and the National Museum
of the American Indian (NMAI),
2, 54–57
Sneve, Shirley K., 229, 230
Society of American Indians, 164
Sofaer, Anna, 150
Solstice Project, 150, 325n44
Soto, Hernando de, 3
Southwest Association of American Indian Arts (SWAIA), 242
Southwest Chief: Navajo guides on
the, 60, 61, 62, 65–68, 310n31;
ridership of the, 305n2; route
of the, 59, 60, 61–63, 65–68
Southwest Indian Foundation, 79,
309n21
sovereignty, 109–10, 155–56, 175,
176, 179, 192–93, 223; and
activism, 164–69; and blood
quantum, 162, 185–86; and
casinos, 156, 169, 179, 184–85,
187–89, 192; definition of,
156–58, 183–84; history of,

158–62, 189–92; and home-
land security, 187, 338n72; and
the Indian Self-Determination
and Education Act, 84–85; and
jurisdiction on reservations,
181–83, 336n61; and leadership, 187–88; legal defense of,
179–82, 186–87; and repatriation, 2, 185; and termination
and relocation, 162–65; and
treaties, 159–61; and tribal
governments, 183–85, 186–88;
and tribal records, 215
Spain, 3, 4, 28–29, 295nn15–17
Squaw Peak (Piestewa Peak),
64–65, 306n10
Stanford Pow Wow, 204. See also
powwows
stereotypes, xv, 8, 122, 133,
277–78; and art, 239, 240–41,
247, 264; "casino Indians,"
172; and Edward Curtis, 245;
"Indian time," 12, 293n11; and
"Jackson Whites" as derogatory
term 270; and sovereignty, 184,
185; and the teepee, xi, 60
storytelling, 26, 49, 76–77; and
Coyote tales, 125; and creation
myths, 63, 97, 151; and gambling, 177; and White Buffalo
(Calf) Woman, 96–97, 315n28
Struck By the Ree (chief), 191–92
substance abuse, 82, 89, 95–96,
111, 137, 182, 315n25. See also
alcoholism
suicide, 82, 89–90, 312n10
Sunrise, Beulah, 207
"survivance," xiii, 281

Swentzell, Roxanne: Vulnerable,
262
Szabo, Joyce, 238, 248

Tafoya, Juan Ray, 19–20, 22, 25
Talbot, B., 39
Tanner, Ellis, 80–82
Taos Pueblo NM, 50, 166
Tapahonso, Lucy, 77
Tate, Jerod Impichchaachaaha':
Oktibihah, 210
Taylor, Loris, 225
Taylor, Zachary, 63, 306n8
teepees, xi–xii; and stereotypes, xi,
60; symbolism of the, xi, 255.
See also hogans
Tending the Wild (documentary),
324n37
termination and relocation,
162–65, 236, 237–38, 311n3,
329nn11–12; and settlement
patterns, 88. See also reserva-
tions
Tesuque Buffalo Dancer (Kennedy),
232–33
Teters, Charlene, 264
Thompson, Daisy, 98, 99–101,
102, 103
Thorne, William, 278
Tiller, Veronica Velarde, 212, 213,
215–18
Tiller's Guide to Indian Country
(Tiller), 215, 216–18
Tocqueville, Alexis de, 232,
356n11
Tohe, Laura, 77
Tosa, Paul, 16–17, 18, 25–26, 126
tourism, 5–6, 79, 278; anthropo-

tourism (*cont.*)
logical, 38; and art, 239–40, 241–42; and ceremonials, 78, 201–3; and Hispanic heritage (Cabrillo Festival), 5–6; and Jemez Pueblo, 31; and the Navajo Nation, 77, 124, 130, 192–93; and powwows, 204; and rail adventures, 239
trading posts, 82, 309n25
"trail of tears." *See* Cherokees
treaties, 159–61, 163, 191, 337n67. *See also* sovereignty
Treaty of 1868, 191
Tribal Law and Order Act (TLOA), 182–83, 337n62
Tribal Map 2001 #2 (Quick-to-See Smith), 257
Tripartita (Avery), 210–11
Truman, Harry S., 163
Tsoodzi (Turquoise Mountain of Strength). *See* Mount Taylor
Turning Stone Resort Casino, 170

University of New Mexico, 87, 132, 215, 256, 269, 277; anthropology department, 41; Gallup branch campus of, 68; and Gathering of Nations, 207–8; and health care training, 137, 138; Hospital, 105; Law School, 179–80; Nammys at, 68–69; Press, 217; and study of Albuquerque's Indian community, 107–8
uranium mining, 62–63, 65, 144–45, 324n36
urban Indian communities, 93,

271, 311n6; and art, 247–48; and culture, 107–9, 113–15; and education, 98–102, 105–6; and health care, 8–9, 103–5, 133–34, 136–37, 317nn36–37; and household income, 91, 313n15; and leadership, 110–12; and mentoring, 106–7; migration to, 88–94, 311n3; populations of, 89, 90–91, 98–99, 311n3, 311n5, 314n18, 328n9; and religion, 115; and sovereignty, 109–10; and suburbanization, 109–10, 113–15; support services in, 94–98, 101–8, 110–13, 314n22, 315n25; and the trust relationship, 103–5, 108. *See also* American Indians
urban migration. *See* urban Indian communities

Vanegas, O'Jay, 202–3
Vásquez de Coronado, Francisco, 3–4
Vaughn, Charlie, 185
Venice Biennale, 236, 251, 258–61. *See also* art
Verrazano, Giovanni da, 47, 231
Vizcaino, Sebastián, 4
Vizenor, Gerald, xiii, 228, 344n30
Vulnerable (Swentzell), 262

Waique, Al, 30–31
Walatowa NM, 30, 34. *See also* Jemez Pueblo NM
Walters, Harry, 120–22, 128–29, 130, 143
Wannabe Nation (Cooday), 264

Warrior for the 21st Century
(Quick-to-See Smith and
Smith), 258
Waters, Frank, 296n21
Watkins, Arthur V., 162, 334n45
Watson, Rubie, 33, 34
Watson, Susan, 186
Waukazoo, Helen, 110–12
Waukazoo, Marty, 112
Wauneka, Annie, 81
Weixelman, Joseph, 39–40, 44,
299n32
Weller, Lou, 55
We Shall Remain (TV program), 230
West, W. Richard (Rick), 2, 55, 56,
57, 69, 155, 238, 254, 336n57,
351n41
Wetherill, Marietta, 39–40
Wetherill, Richard, 39–40
Whatley, William, 22–23, 32
Wheelwright, Mary Cabot, 348n17
Wheelwright Museum, 242,
348n17
White, Sammy Tone-Kei, 209
White Bison Native American
Alliance for Wellbriety, 96–98
"white cards" (Certificate of
Degree of Indian Blood), 162.
See also blood quantum
Whitney Museum of American

Art, 256, 349n23
Who Stole the Teepee? (exhibit),
245–46, 255, 346n6, 350n28
Wilcox, David, 295n14
Wilkinson, Charles, 171
Williams, Maria, 199–200
Wilson, Woodrow, 5
Window Rock AZ: Navajo Nation
Zoo and Botanical Park in,
117–20, 121–22, 123, 124–27,
129–31, 133, 135
Wingspread Collector's Guide,
249–50
Winter Dance, 197. *See also* cer-
emonials
Wolfram, Stephen: *A New Kind of
Science*, 149–50

Yawakia, Gordon, 95–96, 102
Yazzie, Alfred, 126, 127

Zah, Peterson, 166–67, 331n23
Zoo and Botanical Park (Navajo
Nation), 117–20, 121–22, 123,
124–27, 129–31, 133, 135. *See
also* Navajo Nation
Zuni Eagle Aviary Sanctuary,
131–33
Zunis (Ashiwi), 39, 131–33